Hannah Knows Best

PEARLS OF WISDOM FOR MOMS

WHO ARE SERIOUS ABOUT RAISING

CHILDREN WHO LOVE GOD!

Brenda McClure

This book is lovingly dedicated to my mother,

Carol Noel Perlman,

and my mother-in-law,

Jean Marguerite McClure

—both moms who have passed down a legacy of faith,
as Hannah did, through their passion and love for God and His Word.
God's Word, and faith in Him,
is the most treasured jewel they could ever have bequeathed to me!

Table of Contents

A Collaboration of Love

Commit your works to the LORD,
and your thoughts will be established.

Proverbs 16:3

In the fall of 2017, I was humbled and honored to share little bits of wisdom on parenting with a group of pastors' wives. My personal testimony is full of many lessons God has shown me throughout my years of teaching, ministering to families, and raising seven children. These truths are discovered through the example of Hannah and her son, Samuel, in the Bible. Little did I realize that those pieces of wisdom, put together, could become very transformative!

After listening to my workshop, my sweet mother-in-law, Jean, encouraged me to write down all that God had shown me over the years—thinking that practical insights might encourage, inspire, and help other moms raise their children according to God's pattern of parenting. Unsure about the timing with so many little ones at home, I took the matter to prayer. God, then, gave me a heavy burden for moms, who are raising children in today's culture. With an outline in hand and a burning passion within my heart, God gave me the grace to write *Hannah Knows Best: Pearls of Wisdom for Moms Who Are Serious about Raising Children Who Love God.*

This book will take you on the journey that the Lord has brought me through, as I sought to raise children for His glory, as well as the lessons I learned regarding parenting along the way.

Many Thanks

If anyone is blessed by anything in this book, the thanks and glory can only be given to God. It is His word, His wisdom, His insight, and His understanding that have instructed me in my own life and throughout this project. My constant prayer as I have committed this work to Him, has been, "establish my thoughts." So, thank you so much, Lord for the grace to complete this book—may You, and You alone, be glorified through it! Thank you for allowing me to be Your voice! May You use it to raise up modern-day Samuels to accomplish Your will!

Jean McClure, my mother-in-law, who encouraged me to write this book in the first place. I so appreciate your encouragement and prayers.

John Rosemond, author of *Parenting By the Book.* Thank you for opening my eyes, removing my guilt, and sending me on a quest to understand God's role for me as "Mother."

To so many others who have graciously prayed for, encouraged, and challenged me as I have written this book—especially, Sarah Venable, Susi Lim, Andrew and Jenny Vandever, Marilyn Schuler, Angelica Gomez, Mari Hernandez, Jessica Jolly, Betty Ochoa, Eliza Perez, Laura Munguia, and Stephanie Minick. Thank you! I so appreciate your prayers, feedback, collaborative thoughts, and edits!

C.H. Spurgeon, Amy Carmichael, F.B. Meyer, Matthew Henry, Elizabeth Elliot, Oswald Chambers, Mrs. C.H. Cowman, A.B. Simpson, and many more—the "cloud of witnesses" and "heroes of the faith" who have given me insights into His Word, where my feeble mind could never have taken me! It has been an honor to have "conversations" with these great men and women of the faith, who have gone before me and become "friends!" Each of them have given me glimpses of God's glory, for which I am eternally grateful.

Our moms' group at Calvary. I appreciate your grace in allowing me to share my book with you! Thank you for your feedback, suggestions, and questions, which have enabled me to make this book more helpful to readers.

All my past students and their families. It has been a joy and delight to serve you. Thank you for teaching me so much about parenting, and for your graciousness as I was, and still am, learning to be a mom and teacher—they really do go hand and hand!

Our precious congregation. I have been so blessed and humbled by your love, grace, and friendship. Thank you for making it a joy and honor to serve the Lord in San Jose. I love you all so much!

My loving children: Daniel, Micah, Joshua, Samuel, Hannah, Abigail, and Ruth. Thank you for being so gracious with your crazy mom and encouraging me to write this book—much of which is about you! Thank you for allowing me to share your stories, our precious memories, with others. I could not be more honored or proud of such wonderful children, who bring constant delight to my soul.

Of course, Michael! You are the best husband and father a woman could ask for. Without your leadership, I would have ruined our lives, and our children's lives, over and over again. Thank you for your daily laying down of life and your godly example for each of us to follow. I love you so much!

Introduction

Do not conform to the pattern of this world, but be transformed by the renewing of your mind. Then you will be able to test and approve what God's will is—his good, pleasing and perfect will.

Romans 12:2

The moment the nurse laid my firstborn son, Daniel, in my arms, my life was turned upside down, literally! I thought, "How can love like this exist?" I determined then to do my best to be the best mom ever for my son! This is probably just about every mother's dream as she holds her new, precious baby for the first time—and when she arrives at home, it becomes her lifelong quest!

Our culture defines the "best mom ever" as the one who does the most for her children. She's the mom who has the best dressed children, the most elaborate parties, and weekly playdates. She packs the best lunches, helps her children with their projects and homework, and enrolls her children in whatever sport or hobby they are interested in. Her children do not lack any good thing—and it is all because of mom! In fact, the dining room is her children's play room—filled with imaginative toys for creative play. She makes sure her children have every opportunity possible, so they can walk through whatever door they choose. The more involved she is in her children's lives, the better mom she becomes.

This new expectation for women is leaving moms stressed, pressured, and weighed down with endless guilt. This idea that women have to over-identify themselves with their children and their children's success—while giving them a dream life—is a new cultural standard driven by our progressive society, and even embraced in the church. Moms don't realize that, in doing more for their children, they are not necessarily leaving them better off.

If we go back one hundred years, or even fifty years, the cultural standard for the "best mom ever" would be completely different. The family and home looked very different than they do today. The center of a home used to be the family, rather than the individual child. And everyone worked together, each contributing as a valuable member, in order for the family to survive. Today, children have become the center of the family, and their happiness has become the chief end. As Hosea 4:6 attests, "Our children are being destroyed for a lack of knowledge." If we study the scriptures, we can see a biblical pattern for raising godly children that has been proven effective—for thousands of years!

In my early years as a mother, I bought into this lie of the culture—hook, line, and sinker. Yet God, through the power of His Word and His Holy Spirit, intervened and saved my family. As I spent daily time with

Him and obeyed His voice, He utterly transformed my parenting style. When I say, "transform", I really mean a complete transformation in our philosophy regarding how my husband and I were raising our children. Rather than aligning our parenting philosophy to the patterns of the world, we began aligning it to the pattern found in God's Word. God revealed the context for this pattern through the life of Hannah as she raised her son, Samuel.

As I have studied the life of Hannah, I have gleaned so many pearls of wisdom that Michael and I have implemented in our home, which has produced children who love God and desire to glorify Him with their lives. Our children are not perfect, but they do have a biblical worldview and a strong desire to please God. Michael and I are not perfect parents, and we have made, and will continue to make, our share of mistakes. However, we are determined to learn and grow from them. We are so grateful that we know a perfect parent: God—who, in His word, has given us everything we need to know about raising godly children. We are still growing and learning how to apply these truths to our lives—as God's wisdom is infinite! As parents, we must continue to be faithful to search out His wisdom as we raise children in today's progressive world.

A Word of Encouragement

Please note, I am going to share with you much of our family's story and the way we have applied truths found in Hannah's story to our lives. When reading a book like this one, it is easy to become overwhelmed and decide to set it aside. If you find yourself feeling this way, I want to encourage you to press on and see what God wants to teach you through the life of Hannah. Take just a chapter at a time to pray over and digest. I am convinced that no matter what season you are in—whether single or married, with toddlers or teenagers—as a mom, you can glean practical ideas from this book to implement in your home, which will transform the destiny of your children.

Remember, this book is meant to encourage and inspire you—not condemn you! As 2 Corinthians 7:10 tells us, godly sorrow changes our minds and leads to salvation, not regret. Right now, you might be doing things very differently in your home, and you may realize that you need to make changes—and that is okay. That's what this book is all about. We must remember, children are adaptable, and they will love and respect us for making parenting changes that line up with God's Word. They may not like the changes at first, but they will thank us later.

As we explore Hannah's life together, may you look to the Lord for guidance, allowing His Holy Spirit to show you how to implement each of these principles. How you do so may be very different than the way Michael and I have—and that's okay. God will give you the wisdom you need for your family. If you are married, pray, asking the Lord to give you and your husband wisdom in making decisions for your family— especially if you and your husband are not on the same page. If you are a single mom, and God is asking you to do something different in how your are raising your children, take the lead and do it. Always look to God's Word as your guide, as it leads to truth and blessing. Don't look back; just move forward in what God is calling you to do. Remember, your children's lives are at stake!

Hannah's Influence

Trust in the Lord will all your heart, and lean not on your own understanding, in all your ways acknowledge Him, and He will direct your paths.

Proverbs 3:5-6

I love to bake! And, parenting is like baking a cake. Michael, my husband, likes to say that when it comes to parenting, "What you bake is what you will eat for the rest of your lives!" If you want to make a lemon cake, there are specific ingredients you will need to mix together to end up with a lemon cake. You cannot forget any ingredients—especially lemons—if you want the cake to turn out.

In our culture and churches today, there are parents who desire to raise their children to be godly, hard-working, loving, and others-centered — honest children of character who are focused on building God's kingdom. Yet, they are not putting in the proper parenting "ingredients" to create such a young man or woman.

On top of that, putting in the right ingredients is not enough; you also need to mix them in the right way. You can't be all discipline and no love—too much mixing—or too much love and not enough discipline—too little mixing. Hannah knew the right way to mix the right ingredients to raise a godly son who would bring glory and honor to God all the days of his life. I have come to realize, that when it comes to raising godly children, *Hannah Knows Best*!

Our Story

Ever since I was young, I longed to get married and have children, all so that I could be a mom. I didn't just want to be any mom; I wanted to be the best mom, ever! My childhood was spent with endless hours of training—playing with dolls (specifically, Cabbage Patch Kids). As a mom, I was going to give my children a fairytale childhood, one that I had always dreamed of having myself. This dream life consisted of a Victorian house with a white picket fence and lots of children. In my picture-perfect life, I was going to can food from our garden, make gourmet meals every night, give my children Pinterest birthday parties (before Pinterest even existed), be the team mom for their games, take my girls to ballet lessons (where they would perform in the Nutcracker), and the list goes on! In short, I would give my children everything I never had as a child, and they would love me for it. I didn't realize it then, but my philosophy of raising children didn't line up with God's Word. Instead, it lined up with the culture.

When I started dating Michael at the age of eighteen, I was delighted to find out that he wanted a lot of children, as well. Not only did he want many children, but he also liked the idea of living in a Victorian house with a white picket fence in the country. Our dreams collided. It was a perfect match!

Two years later, we were married. Five years after that, we started having children. Twenty-three years since, we are living the life of our dreams—minus the country, the Victorian house, and the white picket fence. However, we have all the truly important things: a loving marriage, lots of children, a Spirit-filled home, and the knowledge that our lives are pleasing to God! We didn't get where we are by following our own plans, but by laying them down in obedience to the Lord.

Obedience in small things is the foundation for obedience in big things, but a few of our decisions have had big long-term effects. The first big decision Michael and I made—after five years of marriage—was answering God's call to go into ministry. (Well, He had actually called us a few years earlier, but it took a couple of years for me to agree to surrender to His plan!) When we were first married, I knew that God had a special call on my husband—I think that is why I was attracted to him. But, as time went on, I began to understand what that call required, and I wasn't sure that I wanted to answer it.

What it really boils down to is that, as my eyes were opened up to the hardships and sacrifices of ministry, I knew that my husband would no longer be mine, but God's. However, He reminded me that my husband was already His, and I would be held accountable if I kept him from serving God. I had so many fears—I thought my children would be rebellious, I would never be able to afford a house, my husband would forsake me and our children for the church, and the list goes on. These fears were not valid, of course, and they were the opposite of the faith that God calls each of us to live out daily. God reminded me that He was worth everything, and that blessing comes through obedience. I knew my life was no longer my own—and my husband no longer belonged to me, but to the Lord. So, I obeyed.

Then, God asked me to "lend Him my body." By this time, I had four children, all boys. I had had two c-sections, I was determined not to have another, and I did not want to have any more boys. At this point, I found myself praying for wisdom from God about whether Michael or I should have more children. I knew that children are a blessing from the Lord, and I didn't want to miss out on any blessing. One day, I read a devotional from *Streams in the Desert*, and J. Gregory Mantle wrote: "In that body I bore the world's sin upon the tree, and through its offering once for all My followers are sanctified. *But I need a body still: wilt thou not lend Me thine?*"[1] After reading these words, I knew that God was asking me to lend Him my body—to bring forth life that would bring Him glory and honor. So, I obeyed.

Next, God asked me to start a school. At the time, I was homeschooling our children. However, our church had a huge facility that could easily house a school—kindergarten through high school—and we had tons of children in our church. Michael loved the curriculum we were using at home, and he wanted to start a school for our church using the same materials. And, he wanted me to do it! I enjoyed being at home with my six children (at that time), and I knew the amount of work it would take to start a school. For two years, I said, "No!" Finally, Michael told me that he would find someone else to start the school if I would not—and our children would have to go. So, I said, "Yes!" in obedience to Michael and the Lord.

In between these big decisions were all the little surrenders and daily "picking up of my cross" to follow God: giving up of my rights, dying to my desires and dreams, forgiving people who hurt me, choosing not to flee from the hardships we endured, learning and growing into the leaders God has called us to be. In short, these were the little decisions to seek God daily, to lean on Him for direction.

In the midst of my busy life, I constantly asked God for wisdom and guidance on how to be the best mom ever. I wanted godly children more than anything, so I searched for wisdom from God's Word, books, and others who had gone before me. Every birthday, when I blew out my candles, I would pray that my children would love God with everything within them. Every Christmas, my children would ask me what I wanted, and I would always say, "For you to love God with all your heart, soul, and mind—all the days of your life." Whenever I would meet an adult who had walked with God all their life, I would ask them, "So, what did your parents do? Why did you never fall away from the Lord?" I wanted God to lead, to guide, and to show me what I needed to do to raise children who loved Him more than anything. And, God answered my prayer and heart's desire, but not in the way I was expecting!

Unraveling the Lies
Seven years ago, I had a husband to support in ministry; six children to raise and train up in the Lord; and a school, home, and women's ministry to run. I had no room in my life for any of the things I thought I would be doing as a mom. I couldn't take my children to music lessons, ballet, soccer, or anything like it. Not only did I have no money, I had no time! My children were not coming home from school to fresh, homemade cookies, gourmet meals, a clean house, or their beds made. Instead, they were coming home from school and doing all the chores: folding and putting away laundry, helping with dinner, washing dishes, and more. I didn't have time to do their homework with them or go to the store to buy the best supplies for their projects.

And, do you know what the crazy thing was? My kids were sweet, responsible, independent, others-centered, thankful, and hard-working. I kept asking Michael, "Why are our children turning out so well, when I am such a horrible mother?" You see, I believed the culture's lie that the more I did for my children, the better a mom I was. I thought that the more I served my children, and the more opportunities I gave my them, the better they would turn out. That was a rotten lie! In fact, when moms build their lives to revolve around their kids, the children become entitled. And, isn't that exactly the crisis we are facing with children in this generation?

Not only did I feel like a horrible mother, I also labored under a huge amount of guilt. I felt immense pressure from others, and from what I believed the best moms should do. My children's teachers were upset because I wasn't helping my children with their homework, or because my children did not perfectly match the dress code. I wasn't able to reciprocate play dates because of lack of time. My children could not play sports because I needed to clean my house on Saturdays, I didn't have time to run them to practices, and I couldn't afford the fees. I could not keep up with the demands of the culture. I carried this guilt on my shoulders, and lived in a constant state of defeat. I knew I was obeying God's perfect will for my life, but I wondered why I felt so conflicted inside. My cues were coming from the culture, and I was a captive of its lies!

God took me further and further away from the life I had once dreamed of. As I continued to read and obey His Word, He led me to a place where my children could grow into the godly men and women I longed for them to be. As I daily trusted in God, He literally directed my path in a direction I would never have taken on my own. In choosing not to follow my own understanding—and daily saying yes to the little and big things He asked of me—God saved me from going in a direction that would have destroyed my children's lives. Proverbs 3:5-6 really works!

Over a course of a few years, God began to unravel the lies I had believed, and to reprogram my mind based on the patterns of parenting found in His Word. The result: a heavy weight was lifted! I have felt abundant freedom in raising my children according to the patterns found in God's Word rather than those of the culture we are living in. I have come to realize that the "best mom ever:"

1. **Finds her identity in Christ**, not in the role of mom, or in the performance of her children!

   If then you were raised with Christ, seek those things which are above, where Christ is, sitting at the right hand of God. Set your mind on things above, not on things on the earth. ***For you died, and your life is hidden with Christ in God.*** *When Christ who is our life appears, then you also will appear with Him in glory.*

   — Colossians 3:1-4 (emphasis added)

2. **Seeks first the kingdom of God.** She receives direction from God's Word, follows God with all her heart, and desires to please and obey God no matter what others may think or say!

Trust in the Lord with all your heart, and lean not on your own understanding; in all your ways acknowledge Him, and He will direct your paths.

—*Proverbs 3:5-6*

3. ***Makes necessary sacrifices*** to raise her children according to the patterns of parenting found in God's Word, not allowing anything to prevent her from fulfilling God's call!

Do not conform to the pattern of this world, but be transformed by the renewing of your mind. Then you will be able to test and approve what God's will is—his good, pleasing and perfect will.

— *Romans 12:2*

Hannah's Influence

There is a classic poem I love, written in 1865, titled, "The Hand that Rocks the Cradle is the Hand that Rules the World." We can see the truth of this saying in the life of Hannah and her son, Samuel. Hannah's story can be found in the first two chapters of the first book that bears her son's name, 1 Samuel. Hannah lived during the time of Israel's Judges, when everyone did which was right in their own eyes, and the Word of the Lord was rare!

Hannah's life stands out as quite an exception when compared to the people of her day. Her amazing faith is a wonderful example for every woman and mother. She is best remembered for giving birth to Samuel, and then giving him to God. Samuel was the last judge in Israel, the first prophet, and a priest who interceded with God on behalf of the people. It was Samuel's faith that brought revival to Israel. God used Samuel mightily, appointing him to anoint the first kings of Israel, Saul and David, and to serve as their counselor. Samuel was a man of prayer who constantly brought the people's needs and condition to God. However, Samuel would never have been such an amazing man of God if Hannah had not made the sacrifices necessary to raise such a man!

It was Hannah's life, and her sacrifice of Samuel, that allowed God to be glorified once again amongst His people! It was her "hand that rocked the cradle" that literally "ruled the world" for the glory of God! As Henry Halley, author of the *Halley's Bible Handbook*, states, "All honor to Hannah. A noble Example of Motherhood."[2]

Years ago, I taught a Bible study on the life of Hannah. Through this study, God gave me several insights into parenting that profoundly affected the way Michael and I have chosen to raise our children. I was struck by the great similarities between the days of the Judges and the culture we live in today. Yet, Hannah was able to raise a man of God, who became God's voice to the people and led a divided nation back to God! When I read this, my heart exclaimed: "This is exactly what I want for my children!"

However, as I continued to study Hannah and her relationship with Samuel, I realized that she raised her son very differently from many others in her culture—where everyone did what was right in their own eyes, worshiping pagan idols, and hiding God's Word from their children. Hannah's identity was found in God, and she was willing to make the needed sacrifices to raise her child according to the patterns of parenting found in God's Word. This bible study led me on a quest to discover how to be a mom like Hannah—and not like a mom from our culture. Hannah was the example I needed of a woman who did everything required to raise a mighty man for God!

My love and appreciation for Hannah began well before this Bible study. Three years after Michael and I were married, I experienced my second miscarriage at the age of twenty-three. My whole life's dream was to be a wife and mom! Michael and I married young after promising our parents we would both finish college. So, we rushed through college, taking eighteen to twenty-one units each semester. Then, when the time was right to start our family, I miscarried twice—I was devastated!

I poured out my heart to the Lord, and He gave me a promise found in Psalm 113:9, "He settles the childless woman in her home, as a happy mother of children." (NIV) This verse was for me! I knew it, and I claimed it! Not only did God promise I would have children, but He also promised I would be happy and at home with them. In my Bible, the cross reference for this verse was the life of Hannah. So, I read her story. Hannah was barren, and she desperately wanted a child. In her moment of despair, she cried out to God at the Tabernacle, promising to give her child as an offering to Him, if He would only give her a child. And God blessed Hannah, giving her a son, Samuel. In that moment, I realized what God was asking of me: He wanted me to give Him my children—before they were even born!

A year later, I had my first son, Daniel. And, then, God gave me, Micah, Joshua, and Samuel. When I was finally expecting a girl, Michael and I prayed and asked God what He wanted us to name our first and—as we thought—only daughter. He said, "Hannah," to remind me of the promise He had given me and fulfilled abundantly.

When we were expecting our sixth child, Abigail, I found myself praying earnestly, asking God to show me whether or not He wanted me to get my tubes tied after this pregnancy. I truly believe that children are a gift from the Lord—and while I did not want to miss out on any gift from God, I was also about to have my fourth c-section!

One day, I was lying sick in bed, listening to the *KIDS Bible* with one of my sick children. The story of Hannah came on. As I listened, the narrator said, "Hannah was blessed and her life was full and she had six children, four boys and two girls." All of the sudden, the Lord spoke to my heart, "That's you, Brenda. I have fulfilled My promise to you!"

Wow! I looked back, and saw how He fulfilled it—completely! I was a happy mother at home with six children, just like Hannah. I even had the same amount of children with the exact same genders. God had heard the cry of my heart, and He answered it!

The story of my children continued two years ago when I gave birth to my seventh child, Ruth. It started with Michael and I in Hawaii, watching older couples walk by as we ate dinner together. We were talking about being married for twenty years, and the way time had passed, when I looked at Michael and said, "Let's live life backwards. If you were sixty, what is one thing you would wish you had done different —and let's do it!" Mike replied, "I wish we would have had more children." Six weeks later, we found ourselves driving down the I-5 to get my tubes untied. I told Michael, "This is crazy! Are we doing the right thing? I just need God to give me a sign." Five minutes later, on the side of the road, we saw a sign: "Choose Life." God is so faithful! He literally gave us a sign that day. We knew we were making the right choice to bring another life into the world to love and serve God!

Best Mom Ever

Through the years, Hannah has become a very special woman to me, and she has taught me so much about being the "best mom ever". She was not a mom who idolized her children, or who wrapped her life around them. Instead, she was a mom who kept God at the center of her life, and made all the necessary sacrifices to have godly children! She lived a life of faith, gave her children to God, saturated them with God's Word, and taught them how to pray. She fought to enable her children to grow before God's presence, enabled them to build their character, and helped them to discern God's voice. She was willing to let her children live without luxuries her culture thought were necessities. She was a mom brave enough to discipline her children, who feared what God thinks rather than what her children think. Hannah's example is an inspiration, and her wisdom is what moms need today.

As you read this book on the relationship between Hannah and her son, Samuel, my prayer is that you might be inspired to raise godly children according to the pattern found in God's Word. May Hannah's story and her "twelve pearls of wisdom" encourage you, as they have me, to make the needed sacrifices to raise children, who will bring God glory and honor!

Questions to Consider

1. Have you bought into the lie of the culture: "The more you do for your children, the better mom you are?" If so, how?

2. Are you burdened with guilt over the demands our culture places on the role of mom? What is causing you to feel guilty? What are you doing for your children out of cultural pressure that can be cut out of your life?

3. Some moms over-identify themselves in their role as mom, while others find their identity in Christ. If the former is true for you, how can you begin to shift your perspective and find your identity in Christ?

4. Are you spending time in God's Word daily, so He can lead and direct you in the raising of your children? If not, what change(s) can you make in your life so time with God becomes a greater priority?

5. What dreams do you have that are patterned after the culture rather than God's Word?

6. What are the three marks of the "best mom ever," according to the patterns found in God's Word? Are you fulfilling this description? Which one do you need to work on the most?

7. Is there something that God has asked of you that you have not obeyed? Are your children reaping the consequences for that omission? How can you remedy your situation?

Notes

[1] Gregory Mantle, quoted in Mrs. Charles E. Cowman, *Streams in the Desert* (Grand Rapids, Michigan: Zondervan Publishing House, 1925), 294.

[2] Henry Halley, *Halley's Bible Handbook* (Grand Rapids, Michigan: Zondervan Publishing House, 2000), 219.

Hannah's Getting

In those days there was no king in Israel:
everyone did what was right in his own eyes.

Judges 21:25

And the word of the LORD was rare in those days;
there was no widespread revelation.

1 Samuel 3:1b

Hannah's story takes place in ancient Israel during the time of the Judges. During this time in history, Joshua and the wilderness-bred generation of Israelites died off, and a new generation found themselves settled in Canaan, a land of plenty. There, they lapsed into the easy-going ways of their idolatrous neighbors. It was a time when "everyone did what was right in their own eyes" (Judges 21:25).

During this time, God's people continuously fell into a cycle of prosperity, idolatry, captivity, and repentance. When the Israelites worshipped God, they prospered. In their prosperity, they became complacent, and began worshiping idols and false gods, which would lead them into suffering under foreign oppressors. Eventually, God would have pity on His people and raise up a Judge to deliver them from their enemies. However, when the Judge would die, the people would turn away from God and worship idols - again! This cycle went on and on for about four hundred years.

The beginning of the first book of Samuel gives us a little more insight into this time of Israel's history: "And the word of the LORD was rare in those days; there was no widespread revelation" (1 Samuel 3:1b). During this time theirs was a "demoralized priesthood, an alienated people, a silent God."[1] The voice of God became a legend of the past, rather than an experience of the present. His earthly representation was seen as corrupt and powerless—just a tradition of days gone by. How true is is that throughout the history of the world, whenever the Word of the Lord is rare in a culture, everyone does what is right in their own eyes!

Our Foundation in Ruins
Our culture looks very similar to the one we find in the book of Judges. The Word of the Lord is rare, and everyone does what is right in their own eyes.   Like the Israelites, in our prosperity, we have become idolaters, and have been taken captive by progressive thought.   As

Dwight L. Moody once asserted, "We can stand affliction better than we can prosperity, for in prosperity we forget God."[2] Our neglect of God, His word, and His ways can be seen in every area of our society.

Our culture has changed so much over the past one hundred, fifty, twenty, and even the last ten years. My ninety-two year old grandmother tells me all the time that she could never have imagined the state of the world today! She was born into a culture where everyone had a common identity, the country was united, and people held the same values and ideals. In today's culture, everyone is isolated, and there are no common values. Everyone is, literally, doing whatever is right in their own eyes. Our culture has completely thrown out its Christian heritage and replaced it with new, liberal ideas.

In 1920, J. Gresham Machen predicted the demoralization of our society in his book, *Christianity and Liberalism*. He warned readers of the dangers of a new religion, known as "liberalism," which was undermining true Christianity. Liberalism stemmed from advances in scientific thought. With an increased focus on the scientific method, Christianity has suffered greatly, as every area of culture has endured a "modern lust of scientific conquest." Machen explains the contrast between Christianity and liberalism so clearly:

> *It is no wonder, then, that liberalism is totally different from Christianity, for the foundation is different. Christianity is founded upon the Bible. It bases upon the Bible both its thinking and its life. Liberalism on the other hand is founded upon the shifting emotions of sinful man.*

Today, our culture is based upon the "shifting emotions of sinful man." We live in an age of relativism, where everyone does what is right in their own eyes. Feelings trump facts, absolute truths do not exist, individual rights matter most, and man is believed to be innately good. These beliefs, clothed in the supposed science of evolution, lead to the modern-day lie that man is constantly progressing and becoming more advanced in his thinking.

John Rosemond, author of *Parenting By the Book*, defines this progressive mindset. He says that it:

> *...holds that just as most new technologies (such as computers) are better than old technologies (typewriters), new ideas are better than old ideas. For the most part the progressive mind-set rejects tradition.*

The progressive mindset rejects tradition, but no institution experiences stronger hostility than Christianity, as Christianity is based upon the authority of a by-gone age found in the Bible. It is no wonder that our culture has done away with the truths that have been held for thousands of years, replacing them with progressive lies!

Modern technology is aiding in the spread of relativism and progressive lies. Technology, in and of itself, is neutral: it has the power to do both good and evil! During the Middle Ages, the invention of the printing press launched Europe out of the Middle Ages and into the Reformation—what an amazing use of technology! In fact, Martin Luther called the invention of the printing press the "supreme act of grace by which the gospel can be driven forward." He was right! With the help of the printing press, the Bible was able to get into the hands of many people, who could now read God's Word in their own native language. This ushered in the Protestant Reformation.

What technologies do we have today? Communication technology made a major leap with radio and television in the 1920's. The computer was invented in the 1980's. Today, smartphones, tablets, the internet, movies, and social media advance the "whims of man" at an unprecedented rate. The progressive mindset has crept into every area of life. It is being taught to our children in the public schools, and has even crept into the church! We can see this shift in thought within the church, specifically, as Christians look to the world—modern medicine, drugs, psychology and philosophy—for answers, rather than the wisdom and insight that comes from the Word of God!

Technology not only advances progressive ideas, but it also isolates people within marriages, families, neighborhoods, and communities. If technology is not molding and shaping us with its worldly values, it is numbing us with its entertainment. As a culture, we are so distracted that we don't have time for God's Word, which is the only place we can find truth! The Word of God is vanishing, and so is the truth that sets men free. The result: Without the Christian foundation that our country was built upon, our moral framework has crumbled and is being washed away. We are standing in a heap of cultural ruins!

The Destruction of Families

No matter which area of society you look at today, you can see our culture breaking apart at the seams. Suicide rates, rebellion against parents and authority, identity issues, depression, anxiety, divorce rates, teen pregnancy and abortions, cutting, violence, and school test scores all scream that something is wrong! The world, with all its new, progressive programs and philosophies, is not getting better; rather, it is falling apart. Today, we have more resources, more information, more opportunities, more affluence, more cutting-edge science, updated statistics, and more varied study methods than ever! These progressive programs and ideas are widely thought to improve our wellbeing, yet families and children's lives are falling apart like never before.

Families used to be on the same page as each other when it came to the raising of children. There was consistency in moral values, and that produced consistent results. Parents instilled positive character in their children because they were all in it together, and committed to raising good citizens. In fact, neighbors and schools were thanked when they disciplined someone else's child because it was their way of caring for the child.

Today, everyone is on a different page when it comes to parenting, even within the church. Every family follows a different parenting philosophy, and no one agrees with one another. Parenting one or two children seems to be an overwhelming task, whereas our grandmothers managed ten just fine. In today's culture, we are shocked when a child raised in the church stays set apart for the Lord and walks with God as an adult. In years past, we would have been shocked if a child did *not* turn out!

In his book, *Already Gone*, Ken Ham explains that two-thirds of the children raised in the church will walk away from the Christian faith by the time they finish college![3] It has been said that "freedom is never more than one generation away from extinction,"[4] and at the rate our children are falling away from the faith—we are in trouble! Noah Webster explains how our freedom depends upon children being trained in righteousness:

> *In my view, the Christian religion is the most important and one of the first things in which all children, under a free government, ought to be instructed...No truth is more evident to my mind than that the Christian religion must be the basis of any government intended to secure the rights and privileges of a free people. The opinion that human reason, left without the constant control of divine laws and commands, will preserve a just administration, secure freedom and other rights, restrain men from violations of laws and constitutions, and give duration to a popular government, is as chimerical as the most extravagant ideas that enter the head of a maniac. The history of the whole world refutes the opinion; the Bible refutes it; our own melancholy experience refutes it."*[5]

As a culture, we are destroying ourselves from the inside out. In Hosea 4:6 God declares that, "My people are destroyed for lack of knowledge." Our lack of understanding of what God's Word says, with the failure to obey it, is destroying our families and children!

Captivated by Lies
We can glean additional insight into what is happening in our culture today through Paul's description of people in the last days. It is a great mirror into our culture:

> *But know this, that in the last days perilous times will come. For men will be lovers of themselves, lovers of money, boasters, proud, blasphemers, disobedient to parents, unthankful, unholy, unloving, unforgiving, slanderers, without self-control, brutal, despiser of good, traitors, headstrong, haughty, lovers of*

pleasure rather than lovers of God, having a form of godliness but denying its power. And from such people turn away.

— *2 Timothy 3:1-5*

It is shocking to see how our culture fits this description so perfectly. What Paul continues to write is even more alarming:

For of this sort [people listed above] *are those who creep into households and make captives of gullible women loaded down with sins, led away by various lusts, always learning and never able to come to the knowledge of the truth.*

— *2 Timothy 3:6-7*

These verses surprisingly reflect what is happening to women in our culture. The enemy has crept into the homes of precious women through modern technology, loaded them down with sin and guilt, and drawn them away by their own lusts. Women think they are learning from the streams of information, yet they never come to the knowledge of the Truth. Instead, they are being held mentally captive within their own homes.

When Paul says the captives are "gullible woman," he means women who are easily influenced. It is critical that we, as women, practice discernment in regards to what we allow into our hearts and minds via technology. We can easily be deceived when we allow the enemy to speak lies to us and take us captive—as he did with Eve in the Garden of Eden. The result: death and destruction in our lives! James 1:14-15 warns us of this very thing:

Each person is tempted when he is lured and enticed by his own desire. Then desire when it has conceived give birth to sin, and sin when it is full grown brings forth death.

— *James 1:14-15*

All of us can be easily influenced when the lies are packaged in the right way. The lies are coming at us faster than we can imagine and in greater number than ever before. In fact, the average person checks their phone every twelve minutes, and spends approximately nine hours and twenty-two minutes behind screens every day.[6] We are bombarded with information all day long! With so much data coming our way, it is difficult to filter out what is true and what is a lie. Progressive, modern lies are molding and shaping us whether we realize it or not—especially in regard to how we raise our children. Paul warned us against this in Colossians 2:8:

Beware lest anyone cheat you through philosophy and empty deceit, according to the tradition of men, according to the basic principals of the world, and not according to Christ.

As a culture, we are throwing out God's Word and standards to embrace new philosophies and empty ideas, which take us captive and cost us greatly! And, as Paul exhorted us in 2 Timothy 3:5, "from such...turn away."

Do Not Conform to This World
Instagram, Pinterest, Facebook, newsfeeds, movies, advertisements, YouTube, magazines and books on modern psychology all want to mold and shape us— and our children—after the patterns of the world. But, what does God's Word have to say about this?

Do not conform to the pattern of this world, but be transformed by the renewing of your mind. Then you will be able to test and approve what God's will is—His good, pleasing and perfect will.

— Romans 12:2

If we want to raise godly children in today's culture, the only place we should get our wisdom is from God's Word! We should not adjust our parenting skills to adapt to the culture. As we spend time in God's Word, He will renew our minds, and give us the ability to discern what is His good, pleasing and perfect will. Not only does God's Word renew our minds, but by meditating in His Word, our thoughts, wisdom and truth will become the influence that enables us to make wise decisions. John 8:31-32 states: If you abide in My word, you are My disciples indeed. And you shall know the truth, and the truth shall make you free."

God's Word has all the wisdom we need to raise children today! Paul reminds Timothy:

But as for you, continue in what you have learned and have become convinced of, because you know those from whom you learned it, and how from infancy you have known the Holy Scriptures, which are able to make you wise for salvation through faith in Christ Jesus. All Scripture is God-breathed and is useful for teaching, rebuking, correcting and training in righteousness, so that the servant of God may be thoroughly equipped for every good work.

— 2 Timothy 3:14-17

Not only does God's Word make us wise for salvation, it is also useful in the teaching, rebuking, correcting, and training of our children in righteousness. Only God's Word thoroughly equips our children "for every good work" that God has prepared for them to do!

Our Hope: Modern Day Samuels

We see these principles in action in the life of Samuel. Matthew Henry writes, "Samuel is the pattern of child religion and service, to which teachers (and parents) should aim that their children may be conformed."[7] Samuel was raised in the days of the Judges—days just like ours—yet he was untouched by the culture, set-apart! Our culture needs modern-day prophets, now more than ever, who hear God's voice and will be used by Him to call His people to repentance!

The English Methodist preacher William Sangster declared, "The church is painfully in need of leaders. I wait to hear a voice and no voice comes...I would rather listen than speak—but there is no clarion voice to listen to."[8]

Give me a man of God—one man,
One mighty prophet of the Lord,
And I will give you peace on earth,
Bought with a prayer and not a sword.[9]

We, too, can raise modern-day Samuels, prophets who are God's ambassadors in today's culture, where everyone is doing what is right in their own eyes, and where the Word of the Lord is rare! As parents, it may seem like we are walking in uncharted territory as we raise our children in the modern, progressive world. However, when the world around us changes, we can still hold on to God's Word as our guide, especially when it comes to raising our children—because God's Word never changes! So, how do we raise Samuels in our dark days? We do not raise Samuels by chance or accident, nor do we get them without great cost. Our answer will come as we study the life of Hannah!

Questions to Consider

1. In what way is our culture like the days of the Judges?

2. In what ways has technology isolated and divided marriages, families, and communities?

3. How do you see Hosea 4:6 being fulfilled by parents in our culture?

    > *My children are being destroyed for lack of knowledge of God's Word.*
    >
    > *— Hosea 4:6*

4. How is your home set apart from other homes in your community?

5. When it comes to raising your children, can you think of a way you have conformed to the culture rather than the patterns found in God's Word?

6. Are you willing to make the necessary sacrifices to raise a modern-day Samuel? What sacrifices do you feel God might be asking of you to enable this to happen?

7. How much time do you spend gleaning knowledge from God's Word versus the empty philosophies of the world?

Notes

[1] Alexander MacLaren, *MacLaren's Expositions of Holy Scripture, Volume 1* (Grand Rapids, Michigan: WM. B. Eerdmans Publishing Co., 1959), 269.

[2] D.L. Moody, "Good Reads," accessed August 1, 2019, https://www.goodreads.com/quotes/232387-we-can-stand-affliction-better-than-we-can-prosperity-for

[3] Ken Ham and Britt Beemer, *Already Gone* (Arkansas: Master Books, 2009), *21*.

[4] Ronald Regan, "*Good Reads*," accessed July 19, 2019, https://www.goodreads.com/quotes/13915-freedom-is-never-more-than-one-generation-away-from-extinction

[5] Noah Webster, in "Reply to a Letter of David McClure, ESQ., on the Subject of the Proper Course of Study in the Girard College, Philadelphia," A Collection of Papers on Political, Literary, and Moral Subjects, October 25, 1836, 291.

[6] Common Sense Media, "New Report: Parents Spend More Than Nine Hours a Day with Screen Media, December 6, 2016, accessed July 20, 2019, https://www.commonsensemedia.org/about-us/news/press-releases/new-report-parents-spend-more-than-nine-hours-a-day-with-screen-media

[7] Matthew Henry, *Matthew Henry's Commentary of the Bible, Volume II* (New York: Fleming H. Revell Company, 1708), 282.

[8] William Sangster, quoted in Oswald Sanders, *Spiritual Leadership* (Chicago: Moody Press, 1976), 18.

[9] Ibid., 2.

Hannah's Sorrow

And she was in bitterness of soul,
and prayed to the LORD and wept in anguish.

1 Samuel 1:10

In Hannah's culture, being a mom was everything! From the ancient Israelites' perspective, children were a blessing and gift from God—and the more children you had, the more blessed you were. Not only did children help contribute towards a family's survival, they were a source of protection and provision. Having children also meant that the husband's name would survive. When a woman was barren, it was absolutely devastating. It was not uncommon for a husband to take another wife in order ensure the survival of his family or tribe.

In 1 Samuel, we are introduced to Hannah, who "was in bitterness of soul" (1:10) because she was barren. Not only was she childless, but her husband's other wife, Peninnah, was extremely jealous of Hannah. Peninnah was jealous because, despite Hannah's barrenness, Elkanah loved Hannah more than Peninnah, the mother of his children.

Every year, Elkanah's family would travel from the mountains of Ephraim to the Tabernacle at Shiloh to offer their sacrifices unto the Lord. Elkanah would offer sacrifices, giving a portion to Peninnah and each of her children. Then, he would give a double portion to Hannah because he loved her more. This partiality drove Peninnah to jealously, so she sorely provoked Hannah.

Now, Hannah had two heartaches: the first from her barrenness, and the second from the cruelty of Peninnah's jealousy. Year after year, Hannah would pray for a child, but to no avail, for God had closed her womb.

It can be very hard to understand the depth of sadness a woman experiences as a result of barrenness, especially in the culture of Hannah's times. However, Scripture gives us a glimpse at this sorrow:

There are three things that are never satisfied,
Four never say,"Enough!":
The grave,
The barren womb,
The earth that is not satisfied with water—
And the fire never says, "Enough!

— Proverbs 30:15-16

In these verses, the barren womb is compared to death, drought and famine, and a raging fire—a complete scorching and destruction of one's family, land, and home! This is barrenness to a woman.

What is even more heart-wrenching is that "the LORD had closed Hannah's womb" (1 Samuel 1:5). It was God's decision to allow her to be barren. In ancient Israel, a women's identity was wrapped up in having children. All of Hannah's hopes and dreams would have been dependent on having children. And, as if not having a child wasn't hard enough, Hannah had Peninnah constantly rubbing it in.

Hannah was so devastated that she wept and could not eat or drink the yearly peace offering. She was so distraught that she could not participate in what was supposed to be a time of rejoicing. From Hannah's perspective, her life was in complete ruins. She was childless, and her husband had another wife, who was treating her cruelly. Her home was not a refuge; instead, it was a place of misery.

Hannah's Vow

Seeing her distress, Elkanah attempted to console Hannah. He gently reproved her, saying, "Hannah, why do you weep? Why do you not eat? And why is your heart grieved? Am I not better to you than ten sons?" (1 Samuel 1:8).

We see Hannah respond to her husband. She came to the table and ate in celebration of the peace offerings they gave to the Lord. Then, after they finished feasting, Hannah arose and went to the Tabernacle, where God promises to meet His people, His house of prayer. Hannah came as close as she could to the presence of God, and there, she poured out her heart to Him. 1 Samuel says that "she was in bitterness of soul, and prayed to the Lord and she wept in anguish!" (1:10) In desperation, she made this vow:

> O LORD of hosts, if You will indeed look on the affliction of Your maidservant and remember me, and not forget Your maidservant, but will give Your maidservant a male child, then I will give him to the LORD all the days of his life, and no razor shall come upon his head.
>
> — 1 Samuel 1:11

In her prayer, Hannah made a vow to the Lord. She told Him that if He would remember her and grant her request for a male child, then she would "give him to the LORD all the days of his life, and no razor [should] come upon his head" (1 Samuel 1:11). Hannah's child would have already been in God's service as a Levite; but through Hannah's vow, he would also be a Nazarite, meaning he would not cut his hair or drink wine. He would be completely set apart for the work of God.

Hannah's vow to give her child to God was a choice she made before Samuel was even conceived! We too can choose to devote our children to God's service before they are born or conceived. As I shared previously,

God asked this of me for my children. Is He asking you to do the same? C.H. Spurgeon writes: "...parents have a right to dedicate their children to God, as living sacrifices and spiritual priests; and an obligation is thereby laid upon them to serve God faithfully all the days of their life."[1]

Hannah's vow was just what God was waiting for. Jon Courson puts it this way, "Previously, Hannah wanted a son to give her husband. God, however, wanted a prophet to give to a nation."[2] God's ways are always so much greater than ours! God had something much bigger and bolder, greater and grander in mind for Hannah and her son. He just needed to get her to the place of desperation, where her prayers would line up with what He desired.

Hannah laid her greatest desire on God's altar, through prayer, at the Tabernacle. Thankfully, we do not have to go to the Tabernacle to pour out of our hearts to the Lord. We can call out to God at any time and in any place, and He hears us! In Jeremiah 33:3, God pleads with us and says, "Call to Me, and I will answer you, and show you great and mighty things, which you do not know." Remember, as Psalm 34:18 (NIV) states, "The Lord is close to the brokenhearted and saves those who are crushed in spirit."

Believing God's Promises

After Hannah made her vow to the Lord, she continued to pour out her heart to Him. Though Hannah's lips moved, she prayed inwardly. We see that Eli, the High Priest, was watching Hannah as she prayed. He confronted her and accused her of being drunk. Notice that Hannah didn't lash out at Eli, as she was in the presence of the Lord. Instead, she responded to Eli's accusation saying, "I am a woman of sorrowful spirit. I have drunk neither wine nor intoxicating drink, but I have poured out my soul before the LORD. Do not consider your maidservant a wicked woman, for out of the abundance of my complaint and grief I have spoken until now." (I Samuel 1:15-16) Eli then responded, "Go in peace, and the God of Israel grant your petition which you have asked of Him" (1 Samuel 1:17). This blessing was a word from the Lord. As the High Priest, Eli had the ability to speak on behalf of God.

By faith, Hannah believed the word of Eli. She trusted that God had heard and would answer her prayer. We know that Hannah believed this because the scripture says she "went her way and ate, and her face was no longer sad" (1 Samuel 1:18) What faith! After laying down her desire before Him, God gave Hannah a promise. She chose to believe God would answer her request—and went forth with joy.

Second Corinthians 1:20 states: "For all the promises of God in [Christ] are Yes, and in Him Amen, to the glory of God through us." We can believe in God's promises, found in His Word, and claim them as truth! Samuel Rutherford exhorts us: "Believe in God's Word and power more than you believe your own feelings and experiences. Your Rock is Christ, and it is not the Rock which ebbs and flows, but your sea."[3]

When God gives us a promise, we can either choose to believe in His Word or to continue to live in fear, doubt, and sorrow. Hannah chose to trust God, and was filled with joy as a result. We, too, can hold on to God's promises for our lives as we walk through our sorrows with joy!

Free From Offense

When we go through times of sorrow, it is very important that our hearts are right before God. During these times, we can easily become offended at God or others because of the trials we endure. When we don't deal with offense in our hearts properly, we allow the enemy to get a foothold in our lives. Ephesians 4:26b (NIV) states, "Do not let the sun go down while you are still angry, and do not give the devil a foothold."

Hannah had every reason to be offended—consider the cruelty of Peninnah, the lack of compassion and subsequent reproof from Elkanah, and the misunderstanding of Eli. However, rather than holding on to these offenses, she poured out her heart to the Lord in faith, allowing God to do the work He desired in her life.

God needed Hannah to be free from the injustices of others in order to have her heart in the right place to raise a godly son, and give her dearest treasure to Him. When we come into the presence of God, pour our hearts out to Him, and believe in His promises like Hannah, we leave a changed person.

Today, the enemy still uses offenses in our lives—caused by other women, our husbands, or even the church—to keep us from being the mom that God has called us to be. The status of our hearts directly impacts how we raise our children! When we hold on to the offenses of others, they impair and cripple us, affecting the decisions we make as we raise our children.

Take a moment to consider this: If Hannah had held onto an offense against Eli, would she have been able to bring her son, Samuel, to the Tabernacle to be raised by him? So often, the enemy uses offenses to keep us in bondage and hold us and our children captive.

I have seen firsthand how the enemy has used offenses in a woman's life to take out her children over and over again. What can this look like?

- A woman becomes upset and embittered with her husband. Satan uses her anger as a foothold, and—rather than discipling and training her children—she constantly tears down her home as she "punishes" her spouse.

- A friend, neighbor, or family member says or does something hurtful; so the woman chooses to grab ahold of the offense, meditate on it, and allow the devil to dictate how she responds. Her children learn that it is alright to respond bitterly to offense.

- A woman becomes upset because the church is not meeting her needs or doing what she expects it to do. Or, perhaps, she has an issue with a person within the church, which leads to an offense. The woman pulls away from, spreads discontent about, or leaves the church with her children.

Consider how this last example affects the woman's children. When the mom pulls away from serving at and regularly attending church, her children follow. As a result, they are no longer plugged into the church, no longer hearing the word of God, and no longer maintaining the godly friendships they have developed there—all of which are necessary for a strong relationship with Christ.

Similarly, what happens when a mom speaks negatively about the church in front of her children? Whether she realizes it or not, she communicates to her children that the church is not something to love, to build up, to protect, to learn from. Rather, it is a place to criticize, complain about, and judge. The unfortunate result is that her children will not grow up thinking the church is a valuable place to learn and grow; instead, they will see it as a place full of hypocrites, and want nothing to do with it. And, in this battle, the devil has won.

As mothers, we set forth an example of love and grace towards others when we forgive their offenses. When we are faithful to follows Christ's example in this way, we are demonstrating to our children the power of the Gospel!

Another way the enemy captivates us is through childhood offenses. Many times, women have endured verbal, physical or sexual abuse as children. When women suffer from such abuses, it can be a long journey towards healing. Many women struggle with healing in this area all of their lives. One result is that they have determined in their heart to make sure their child never receives this same treatment. That is a blessing. However, when their resolution impairs them from obeying God's word when raising their children, this can become a huge problem. I have seen this over and over again in the church - women not yet free from their childhood abuses, choosing fear to guide them as they raise their children- rather than the Word of God. However, to be the mom that God has called you to be, you must make the effort to be free of the past, and to forgive those who have hurt you. Without receiving the help you need, you cannot be the mom that your children need. Praise God for the forgiveness and healing that comes through Jesus Christ! A wonderful resource for moms who desire healing can be found in Tammy Brown's book, *Healed and Set Free*.

We live in a sinful, fallen world, and every relationship we have will fail us and provide many opportunities for offense. Some of the things God will call us to endure are going to be really hard—like Hannah's barrenness and the pain that came with it. However, we must ensure that we do not grab on to offenses, or allow the enemy to use them to take us captive. Satan wants our children; and if he has to take us down to get to them, he will!

As I reflect upon my life, I can see how the enemy has tried to take me captive over and over again—and a couple of times, he almost took me out for good. One incident, I remember quite vividly. Years ago, I had something happen that I was convinced I could not get over. Someone I love dearly said and did something extremely hurtful. It wasn't just the event that hurt me; I kept meditating upon it, and the enemy spoke lies to me about the situation. Before I knew it, the incident became so much bigger than I could ever have imagined! In the midst of all this turmoil, I felt the Spirit of God tugging at my heart, trying to break through. But, the thoughts in my mind were so strong, I felt like I did not have the power to escape! I had been taken captive.

One day, while I was still battling this situation, I was in my garage organizing a bookshelf and talking to God. As I was sorting books, God began to speak to me. I saw a book titled *Forgiveness*. And, God said, "Brenda, forgive her." I said, "Lord, I can't! It hurts too much." Then, a few minutes later, I came across another book, *The Calvary Road*. Again, God spoke to my heart: "Because of Calvary, you can forgive!" I said, "Lord I *really* can't forgive her." A few minutes later, I read the title *Let Go* by De Fenelon. God clearly said to me, "Brenda, let go of this." I finally agreed, "I will forgive her—but You have to do it through me, as I cannot do it in my own strength!" And when I made this choice, God gave me the power to forgive her.

Forgiveness did not come through my own strength, but rather as a result of a decision I made based on the Cross and the forgiveness that God had given me. And when the enemy or my flesh continued to bring the situation to mind, I had to declare, "I forgave her for that!"—taking the thought captive!

You see, the enemy wants to take you captive. He not only wants to destroy you, but also your children. He doesn't want you to think you have any choice in the matter; but, you do! You are in control of your destiny—not another person or situation—no matter how heart-breaking an offense was. Where do we get the power to forgive? At the Cross. As we gaze upon it and receive God's forgiveness, He gives us the grace to forgive others in turn.

When our hearts are free from offense—as we pour out our hearts to the Lord and allow His Spirit to wash and cleanse us—we will be free to do whatever God asks of us on behalf of our children.

The Blessing of Sorrow

Sorrow is God's gift to those whom He loves and desires to use to further His kingdom. Many of God's "greats" experienced very hard things so that God could use them to accomplish His will among His people. Warren Wiersbe put it this way in his book, *On Being a Servant of God*:

The God of creation and redemption is also the God of history who is at work in the affairs of nations. He sent Joseph to Egypt to get things ready for Jacob and his family so that He might build a mighty nation. He had Moses born at just the right time to deliver Israel from bondage. He prepared Joshua to lead the people victoriously into the promised land. He gave barren Hannah her long-prayed-for son and then used him to bring the wayward nation back to His covenant. Those things were not accidents; they were appointments.[4]

God used Hannah's sorrow to get her to the place where she would be willing to give Him her son, Samuel! Hannah wanted a son for herself, but God wanted a man to be His voice accomplishing His will.

Ecclesiastes 7:3 states, "Sorrow is better than laughter; for by the sadness of the countenance the heart is made better." It is better for us to experience sorrow; for through sorrow, God enables our heart to be in the place He needs it to be. God allows us to suffer for a specific purpose. When we surrender to and seek Him in the midst of suffering, He uses it to accomplish His will through us. In *Streams In the Desert*, Cowman writes:

When sorrow comes under the power of divine grace, it works out a manifold ministry in our lives. Sorrow reveals unknown depths in the soul, and unknown capabilities of experience and service....It is sorrow that opens up within us the capacities of the heavily life, and it is sorrow that makes us willing to launch our capacities on a boundless sea of service of God and our fellows.[5]

Without her sorrow—the barrenness of her womb and all the heartaches that came with it—Hannah would not have been prepared to be the mother the nation of Israel needed to raise a prophet of God. As C.H. Spurgeon writes:

I do not think that Hannah would have been a suitable mother for Samuel if she had not first of all been of a sorrowful spirit. It is not everyone who can be trusted to educate a young prophet. Many a fool of a woman has made a fool of her child. He was so much her "duck" that he grew up to be a goose. It needs a wise woman to train up a wise son, and therefore I regard Samuel's eminent character and career as largely the fruit of his mother's sorrow, and as a reward for her griefs.[6]

What a service Hannah rendered to the Lord and His people by vowing to give up her dream for God's purpose! When we pour out our souls to the Lord, cast our dreams and desires upon His the altar, and give Him everything as Hannah did, God will line up our wills with His.

God's ways are so much higher than ours, and His dreams for our life far surpass our own! Hannah could never have imagined the blessing that would come through her sorrow.

Questions to Consider

1. How does our culture today value children compared to how children were valued in ancient Israel?

2. What promise has God made to you—that you have forgotten—that you need to claim and hold onto today?

3. Is there a sorrow you are experiencing that you need to give to God so He can accomplish His will in and through your life?

4. What unfulfilled desire do you have that God is asking you to lay upon His altar? Are you willing to give it to Him?

5. What offenses are you hanging on to that you need to pour out before the Lord, so you can be the mom that God has called you to be?

6. Have you dedicated your children to God? If so, when? Have you shared this decision with your children? — If not, you can dedicate your children to God even now!

Notes

---

[1] Matthew Henry, *Matthew Henry's Commentary of the Bible, Volume II* (New York: Fleming H. Revell Company, 1708), 279.

[2] Jon Courson, "1 Samuel 1 Sermon," Searchlight with Pastor Jon Courson, accessed August 9, 2019, https://www.joncourson.com/playteaching/W3161

[3] Samuel Rutherford, quoted in Mrs. C.H. Cowman, *Streams in the Desert,* (Grand Rapids, Michigan: Zondervan Publishing House, 1925), 87.

[4] Warren Wiersbe, *On Being a Servant of God* (Grand Rapids, Michigan: Baker Books, 1993), 139.

[5] Cowman, *Streams in the Desert,* 46-47.

[6] C.H. Spurgeon. "A Woman of A Sorrowful Spirit," in *The Metropolitan Tabernacle Pulpit Sermons Preached and Revised by C.H. Spurgeon During the Year 1880,* Volume 26 (Pasadena, Texas: Pilgrim Publications: 1980), 46.

Hannah's Season

Train up a child in the way he should go,
and when he is old he will not depart from it.

Proverbs 22:6

To everything there is a season,
a time for every purpose under heaven:

Ecclesiastes 3:1

Hannah returned home from Shiloh, God remembered her, and she conceived a baby boy. When he was born, she named him Samuel, which means "heard of God," because God had heard her prayer. And, Hannah remembered her vow to the Lord.

When it came time for the yearly sacrifice, Hannah did not go up to Shiloh because she wanted to wait until her son was weaned. Then, she would take Samuel to the house of the LORD, and he would remain there forever. In those days, women would nurse their children for about three to four years—and those years must have been so precious to Hannah! God had fulfilled her heart's desire. As Psalm 113:9 declares, *"He settles the childless woman in her home as a happy mother of children, Praise the LORD."*

What a reminder this is for us: our time with our children is short. We should cherish the time we have, and be intentional about the training of our sons and daughters during that time, just as Hannah was with Samuel. She was not even willing to take a trip to the Tabernacle until the time was right.

While scripture does not tell us about these years, we know that Hannah was a thoughtful, diligent, and intentional mother because, when she delivered her son to the Tabernacle around the age of three, he worshiped the Lord! Samuel didn't cling to his mother's leg and throw a fit. Rather, he followed his mother's example, and worshiped the living God. What training! Hannah had such a short window in which to educate her son, but her work was effectively done in that time. Matthew Henry writes: "...[Samuel's] mother designing him for the sanctuary, took particular care to train him up to that which was to be his work in the sanctuary."[1]

When parents receive the blessing of a child from God, they receive a life that they are called to mold and shape with the goal of "[giving] a saint to God,"[2] as we see with Hannah.

Our Role as Mom

Motherhood is such a precious time in a woman's life. Many people say that the days of motherhood are long, but the years are short—and they are so right. I remember when my oldest son, Daniel, was born. People would tell me, "Watch out! You will blink, and his childhood will be over!" Well, I blinked, and he is turning eighteen!

Our time of influence in the lives of our children is very short. We have no idea where the Lord will direct our children, or what He will call them to do. So, our time with them must be a time of intentional and calculated training for the kingdom of God—through every season of life.

Ruth Bell Graham, wife of evangelist Billy Graham, considered herself a career woman. She said, "My career is being a wife and mother. Bill has the earth for his parish. I have a home and five children for mine." Ruth Graham was so right! As mothers, our home should be a little church, where the work of the ministry is done daily in our children's lives. This ministry within our home can be summed up with one word: discipleship.

After the resurrection and before His ascension into heaven, Jesus gave the disciples one last command, recorded in Matthew 28:19-20:

> Go, therefore and make disciples of all the nations, baptizing them in the name of the Father and of the Son and of the Holy Spirit, teaching them to observe all things that I have commanded you; and lo, I am with you always, even to the end of the age.

This passage is the Great Commission—and for a mom, this commission is her biggest mission! It is not only the salvation of her children's souls, it is also the discipleship of her children. Webster's 1828 Dictionary defines the verb, "disciple" (what you do to someone who is your disciple): "to teach; to train, or bring up."

As a mother, it is our primary duty to train, teach, and bring up our children in the ways of the Lord. Where can we get the wisdom we need to train up our children in the way they should go? God's Word! This is not a task we should take lightly. As Elisabeth Elliot wrote:

> ...the mother who is fashioning the souls of the men and women of tomorrow, [must] learn at the highest of all schools and from the Master-Sculptor Himself, God. To attempt this task [of motherhood], unprepared and untrained is tragic, and its results affect generations to come.[3]

We only get one chance to raise our children, and God has given us all the wisdom we could possibly need in His Word. Not only that, He's given us the strength as well - through the power of His Holy Spirit.

The life of Timothy is a wonderful example of a child raised in the ways of the Lord from childhood. Timothy was taught the Scriptures from a very young age by his mother, Eunice, and his grandmother, Lois (2 Timothy 1:5). Not only did the Word of God bring Timothy to salvation in Christ, but it was also used to teach, train, and instruct him throughout his life. In 2 Timothy 3:14-17, Paul encourages Timothy:

> *But you must continue in the things which you have learned and been assured of, knowing from whom you have learned them, and that from childhood you have known the Holy Scriptures, which are able to make you wise for salvation through faith which is in Christ Jesus. All Scripture is given by inspiration of God, and is profitable for doctrine, for reproof, for correction, for instruction in righteousness, that the man of God may be complete, thoroughly equipped for every good work.*

When we use God's Word to teach, correct, exhort, and instruct our children, they become "complete", and "thoroughly equipped" to do the work God has called them to do.

Seasons of Parenting

As moms, our influence in our children's lives can be divided into four seasons: service, training, mentorship, and friendship. Within each season, we are given specific responsibilities or roles as parents, in order to produce children who are trained and equipped for life. As Proverbs 22:6 promises, "Train up a child in the way he should go, and when he is old he will not depart from it."

In *Parenting: From Surviving to Thriving*, Charles Swindoll expounds upon this verse, expounding from the Hebrew text:

> *Cultivate a thirst, initiate a hunger, create an appetite for spiritual things in the lives of children of any age, as long as they are living under your roof, and do it in keeping with the way they are bent—disciplining the disobedience and the evil while affirming and encouraging the good, the artistic, the beautiful. As children begin to grow into adults, their paths will be aimed directly towards the Savior, and they will continue to walk in His sovereignty.[4]*

As we take the time to cultivate the hearts of our children regardless of their age, we will reap the blessing of children who are set apart, walking with God, and following His ways! However, if we do not take the time to train up our children, there is no promise for us. I meet so many parents who cling onto this verse, but have not taken the time to disciple their children in the ways of the Lord. Oh, they might have taken them to church on Sundays, but that it not enough. Our mission is great, and it is going to take tremendous sacrifice to fulfill our call!

These seasons of parenting might sound revolutionary to you, as they are not marketed in modern parenting books. However, they are not new. Parents for thousands of years have successfully implemented these "seasons" to help their children grow into independent adults. I, personally, owe a special thanks to John Rosemond, author of *Parenting by the Book,* for opening my eyes in this area—and for opening the eyes of many other parents as well!

Seasons of Parenting: An Overview

Please note that some of duties in each season of parenting overlap as noted below.

Season	Age	Parent's Role	Parents Responsibility
1	0-3	Servant/ Trainer	Love, nurture, provide basic needs, schedule, and impart faith. **15-month Transition:** Train, discipline, teach manners and self-discipline.
2	3-12	Trainer	Love, discipline, train, provide for basic needs, teach service, and help children discover God-given gifts.
3	12-18	Mentor	Love, discipline, instruct, teach technology manners, continue service, cultivate God-given gifts, hold the line, and get children ready to launch.
4	18+	Friend	Love and mentor. Transition into friendship.

Season #1: Servant to Child (0-3)

But You are He who took Me out of the womb;
You made Me trust while on My mother's breasts.
I was cast upon You from birth.
From My mother's womb You have been My God.

Psalm 22:9-10

This season was Hannah's season with Samuel—and how precious those three to four years must of been! I am sure she savored every second.

During this season, we are servants to our children. It is our duty as mothers to love, comfort, feed, protect, and care for our children. We need to take care of their basic needs. For most moms, this season comes naturally, since God has created women to be nurturers. During the servant season, we love on our babies by kissing them, singing to them, praying for them—bringing love and security to their lives.

If you are a mom who has to work outside the home, it is so important that you ensure those watching your children during this season share the same biblical values you do. That way, you can be sure your children will be disciplined and trained in a way that compliments your parenting.

Schedule

Today, there is a lot talk about keeping things "unstructured," especially when it comes to children. However, this is a very progressive way of thinking. I believe a lack of scheduling is one of the main reasons mothers are so worn out and exhausted.

Putting my children on a schedule—even in the hospital—really helped me. I was so blessed to have a friend give me the book *Baby Wise* as a pregnancy gift. It saved my life! As a result, I had a three hour break in the afternoon while my babies napped, and my husband and I had a date every night after they went to bed at 7:30 p.m.

By creating a schedule for your baby, your life will not revolve around your little one. You don't want your life to be managed by the whims and desires of your child. It may seem harmless when your baby is little, but some parents are still living lives managed by the whims and desires of their teenage and adult children.

In times past, babies were put on schedules, and homes were structured. Today, our homes should be places of order. As 1 Corinthians 14:40 states, "Let everything be done decently and in order."

Impart the Faith

Our children are never too young for you to start cultivating a love for God and His Word in their hearts! Matthew 19:14 states "Let the children come to Me, and do not forbid them; for of such is the kingdom of heaven."

We can accomplish this by praying for and with your children (even while they are in your womb and, later, as you nurse them). When we put our precious children to bed, we can read them a Bible story and sing worship songs—or put on recordings of God's Word and worship music. One of the very first things, Michael and I taught our children were praise songs. My younger boys loved the "B-I-B-L-E" song. Every night, they would grab their Bible and declare, "I stand alone on the Word of God, the B-I-B-L-E, Bible!" That is such an important doctrine for our little ones to know! Our sweet Ruth's favorite song is "I Love You, Lord." Matthew 12:16b states "Out of the mouth of babes and nursing infants you have perfect praise." Each of these things mold and shape your children into little disciples of Jesus!

Discipline

Obedience is one of the very first disciplines parents are responsible to teach their children. Obedience starts with a rebuke. Then, when a rebuke is not heeded, it is time for discipline.

Discipline starts very early for a child. When a toddler puts their hand near the stove, in the toilet, or on an electrical outlet, it is time to give them a swat on the hand and say, "No, no!" When a child runs into the street, bites their brother, or hits their sister, it is time for a spank on the bottom or thigh. These types of behavior are not acceptable.

Remember, a baby or toddler cannot reason with you, so a dirty look or time out isn't going to work. The purpose of discipline is to save your child from harm; and a swat on the hand, bottom, or thigh is painful enough to teach them they should not do something again. During this season, your discipline should be prompt. Your children are young, so they won't necessarily remember why they are being disciplined if you wait an hour or two.

We all want our children to be be safe and obedient. Discipline will be covered more in-depth in later in the book; but please note, that it must start at a young age.

Teach Manners

Manners refer to the behavior and conduct of a child. As a mom, it is our job to teach our children basic manners—as our culture is not teaching it. Why should we teach manners? Because they show that we care for and respect others, an attribute that God desires to see in all of His children.

Several basic manners we should teach our children include saying "Thank you," "Please," and "You're welcome." When grandparents come to visit, we need to teach our children to say hello, give their grandparents a kiss, and say thank you for gifts or their grandparents leave. Teach your children to say hello to someone when they come over, looking them in the eyes. Whenever you are talking to an adult, don't let your children interrupt. If you children scream for something, don't give it to them. Teach your children to ask for it nicely. It doesn't look so pleasant when children are still throwing tantrums as teenagers if they don't get their way.

These are all very basic manners, yet they are becoming increasingly uncommon in our culture today.

What They See

Growing up, I used to sing a song, titled, "O Be Careful Little Eyes What You See." The song reminds us that "[our] Father up above is looking down with love, oh be careful little eyes what you see!"

As a culture, we have done a poor job discerning what our little ones see on a regular basis. However, this sheltering is so important! Books, images, words, and activities occurring in our environment literally mold and shape our children.

Don't Grow Weary

This first season of parenting can be very tiring! Some days as mothers, we experience bliss; and on others, we don't know how we can possibly go on. Some days, it feels as if all you do is change diapers, wipe noses, and fill endless cups of water! How exhausting, right? Matthew 10:42 has a word of encouragement for weary moms: "And whoever gives one of these little ones only a cup of cold water in the name of a disciple, assuredly, I say to you, he shall by no means lose his reward."

God sees your labor of love towards your children, and He will reward you—in this life and in the one to come! Despite our feelings, we must not grow weary, for blessing comes to those who have been faithful. Galatians 6:9 offers this exhortation: "And let us not grow weary while doing good, for in due season we shall reap if we do not lose heart."

My season at home with little ones lasted a very long time, as I had six babies in eight years. However, as I look back on my "years of bliss," I see how all the energy and hard work has paid off.

This first season with our children is so important. It was the only one Hannah had with her son—yet, Samuel received enough training to prepare him for a life time of service unto the Lord. Don't underestimate this first season or miss out on the blessings that come with it!

Season #2: Train Your Child (3-12)

Train up a child in the way he should go,
and when he is old he will not depart from it.

Proverbs 22:6

In the second season of parenting, our goal is to train our children with love, through reproof, and with discipline. We must teach them how to behave, have manners, treat their siblings well, honor authority, work hard, be diligent, and so much more. This is a working season for parents—not a serving season—as we teach their children how to serve. These years are for molding and shaping our children's lives, as we teach them what you value and what they should value, too. If we are faithful during these years, we will reap the blessings when we enter the mentoring years.

A Thirst For Christ

During the second season, we need to share the gospel often with our children, giving them many opportunities to receive Christ! As soon as our little ones can sit still, do a family Bible study. Pray before meals, thanking the Lord for the food He has provided. Praying with our children every night before bed should be a habit. Encourage them to pray for the things they need and want. As soon as our children can read, we need to encourage them to read the Bible. As mothers, we need to help our children develop a personal relationship with Jesus Christ, by talking about God, His goodness, His Word, and His creation all day long. Allow the presence of God to reign supreme in your home!

Michael and I have spent countless hours with our children during the second season, praying, teaching Bible stories, talking about and reading God's Word. Michael would use finger puppets and stuffed animals to teach Bible stories to the children as they lay in their beds each night. I can't tell you how many times Buzz Lightyear received the Lord during those precious evenings! The time we invest into teaching our children about God and His Word are foundational to a godly life—don't miss out!

Teaching Service

These are the years to teach our children to serve in the home, at church, and within the community. While we will discuss service more later, we must start allowing our children to become independent—as young as the age of three!

Purchase a stool and teach your three year old to get their own cup of water, put their clothes away, and pick up their toys. As our little ones get older, have them make their own breakfast, prepare their lunches, clean the bathrooms, and do their own laundry. Our children will gradually learn to do more until they are old enough to do all the chores in the house.

One of the greatest gifts a mom can give her children is the realization that their home, church, and school were not created for their enjoyment, but rather for their training and service—as they work to build the kingdom of God. As soon as our children are capable, have them begin to serve in the church nursery or another Sunday school class. Our children can stock pews, set up for VBS, do whatever the is needed. As soon as your children realize that they were created to serve rather than to be served, their life will be revolutionized—and so will yours!

Discipline

Children, especially in their younger years, respond well to firm, yet loving discipline. This discipline comes can be a verbal reproof, a spanking, the taking away of something, and occasionally, a time-out. If you spank a child in the early years within the second season, they will be happy and full of joy five minutes later, as if nothing had happened.

The purpose of discipline is to teach your children how to self-govern. They cannot learn to do so on their own. Discipline takes a lot of work. But remember, the sins of a three, four, or five year old left unchecked looks very ugly in a thirteen, fourteen, or fifteen year old! Sin grows bigger and becomes harder to root out the older a child grows. For more information on discipline, refer to Chapter 18.

Train

Your goal, during the second season, is to train your children in your values. This is the time when "quality time" does not overshadow "quantity time." Your time with your children is time spent demonstrating how to live and what to value. This includes teaching valuable life skills—cooking, cleaning, organization, how to treat others, and most importantly, how to run and operate a Christian home.

Discovering Their Gifts

Your children each have their own special talents and abilities—and it is up to you, as their parents, to discover them. Encourage your children to find ways to use them their God-given talents and abilities to build God's kingdom. You might have a gifted painter, writer, or preacher on your hands—and you just need to take the time to discover it.

Be Diligent

The temptation during this season is to start taking it easy as your children grow older and more capable. If you "loosen the reins" too early, you will loose your vision for your child. You must remain diligent —as everything is at stake.

The second season of parenting is for the molding and shaping of your children. These are not the years when you put your children in front of the television, distract them with video games, or throw an iPad at them. You can't expect your children to have Christ-like character if you do not train and instruct them in the Scriptures. Everything you do during these years of training must be intentional.

Season #3: Mentor Your Child (13-18)

But as for me and my house,
we will serve the Lord.

Joshua 24:15

During the third season, your children's character is pretty much formed, and they are who they are. Your new role is to mentor your children, guiding them through decisions and teaching them to learn from their mistakes. You must start to let your children go—so they are completely independent of you by the age of eighteen. However, please remember that they are still under your roof. You must hold your children to the standard found in God's Word. As Joshua 24:15 states, "But as for me and my house, we will serve the Lord."

Develop Their Relationship with Christ

It is the parents' responsibility during the third season of parenting to ensure that their children are in a place where they can grow in their relationship with Christ. This is the age where many children start to fall away from Christ! While we cannot force our children to have a relationship with God, we are responsible for making sure our children hear the Word of God and have opportunities to grow as God's Word captures their heart. During this age, it is so important that our children attend youth group and church camps, so they can develop relationships that will encourage them in their relationship with God.

As a family, spend time in God's Word and in prayer. It has been said that a family who prays together, stays together—and it is so true! Go on mission trips with your children and serve together at church. Not only will this enable you to bond with your children, but it will also demonstrate that the kingdom of God is a priority in your life. Make sure your children establish a habit of spending time in God's Word. Develop a Bible reading plan with your children so they are reading God's Word daily. This will ensure that they are learning about God and His ways.

When our boys were first entering this season of parenting, Michael offered them money to read the entire Bible in a year. This was one of the best investments we could have made! Just last week, my thirteen year old son, Joshua, told me that he is "hoping to tell his grandchildren one day that he has read his Bible hundreds of times." What a goal!

Mentorship

One of the parents' main roles during this season is mentorship. As mentors, mothers and fathers guide their children through decision-making, friendships, relationships, school, work, and life. Mentorship cannot be accomplished unless parents spend time with their children.

At the McClure home, we often find our children sitting on our bed at night, wanting to talk. Don't miss out on any opportunity to talk with your children during this season, as they need your wisdom! If your children shut down all of the sudden, you must realize that something has happened. As parents, we need to get "dirty." Pray and ask God for wisdom, discernment, and the ability to do whatever it takes to get to the bottom of things. Don't forget that your child's life is at stake! You may need to take your children to coffee, go through a devotional with them, or simply make them more of a priority if you want to unravel what is going on in their life.

Before your children go through puberty, it is so important that you spend time with them- explaining what is going to be happening with their body, talk to them regarding peer pressure, dating, purity and so forth. The world has all sorts of ideas regarding sexuality, and we need to make sure we are sharing with our children our values, especially, what God's word says regarding these issues, as they will determine their future. We have been so blessed to have taken our children through the resource: *Passports to Purity* by Family Life. Our boys, who have gone through this book, have all committed to wait until they are eighteen to date. They have also agreed that they will make sure that they get mom and dads approval before pursuing a spouse.

Your job, as parents, is to make sure you and your husband are the number one influence in your children's life. Don't let friendships, social media, or the latest online game take your rightful place. Fight for your relationship with your children. And how do you keep this relationship or get it back once it is gone? Spend time with your children, be interested in their interests, talk to them, do whatever it takes.

Service
By the third season, our children should really be pulling their weight. Not only should they be running the household chores, but they should also be a serious help to our churches and communities.

Discipline
Discipline looks different in the third season of parenting, but it is still necessary! We can no longer spank them and expect them to come out of their rooms a changed person—rather, these things will provoke their anger, especially if we lose our temper, too.

During this season, we need to be cautious and discerning as we decide when and how to bring things up and talk to our children. Yet, we must deal with issues in their lives. One day soon, they they will be gone, and we will no longer have this opportunity. It is so important that we show our children that we respect them as individuals and that we love them too much to allow sin to continue unchecked in their life.

When your teenagers need discipline, take away something precious, charge them money, or send them to their room. Talk them through their sin and make sure they learn from it. We must be sure that we take our children to God's Word so they can see what God says about their sin. Whatever punishment you decide on, you must make sure it is painful— so they won't ever want to do it again! Please see the chapter on discipline for further reference.

Technology Manners
As your children reach their teenage years, you should gradually introduce your children to technology and teach them how to use it

responsibly. Some simple manners and rules might include: no technology at the dinner table, looking at people rather than your phone when they are talking to you, putting your phone away when Grandma and Grandpa come for a visit, and so forth.

Whenever teenagers come over to the McClure house, we ask that they put their phones away or in a basket by the front door. This practice ensures that everyone gives their friends the attention they deserve, and no one is looking at things that might not follow "house rules."

I know many other families who require all phones to be turned in at night, so their children cannot text in their rooms or go on the Internet in the evenings. Remember, your house is *your* house—and "as for me and my house, we will serve the Lord" (Joshua 24:15) means everyone!

Cultivate Their Gifts
By this season, we have most likely discovered your children's gifts and interests. Now, it is time to help them cultivate their gifts, so they can be used for the glory of God.

Prepare to Launch
Don't forget that, during the teenage years, you are helping to mentor and coach your children as they prepare to launch into life. Our goal is to help guide our children towards a career that will enable them to use their gifts for the benefit of others and the glory of God. It is not our job to make things happen for them; rather, we should encourage and guide them as they come up with a plan for their life.

Before we launch your children into adulthood, they need to have had a job. We will talk further about this in the chapter on service, but we cannot expect our children to have the practical working and money managing skills they need in life without practice.

Stand Firm
During this season, it is important for us to realize that we are not our child's friend yet. We are still in charge! It is our responsibility to make our children go to church, work, and hold them accountable with their chores. We must continue to hold a standard in our home. This standard includes what our children are able to do, what they can watch, and what friends they can hang out with.

Remember, Joshua 24:15 states, "But as for me and my house, we will serve the Lord." We need to remind our teenagers that we are accountable to God for everyone who lives in our house—and they must obey what we ask of them as long as they are living in our home. In doing so, we are pleasing God.

Don't Give Up
Michael and I have met so many people who give up on parenting when their children reach this season. Even if your child is walking in sin, they are not dead, and you can still make all the difference in their life! You

might need to find support, spend a lot of time in prayer and fasting, and restructure your entire home—but it is worth it!

Season #4: Lifelong Friend (18+)

Happy is the man who has his quiver full of [children];
They shall not be ashamed,
But shall speak with their enemies in the gate.

Psalm 127:5

Once our children have reached the fourth season of parenting, we are now our children's friend. And if we have done a good job in the first three seasons, we will not only be blessed with a wonderful, life-long friend, but we will also continue to be their mentor. We will be happy and unashamed, as our children bring us honor throughout our life.

If your child is still living at home, don't forget that they need to abide by all of your "house rules"—especially when it comes to attending church, serving in the home, and contributing to the family. Remember, Joshua 24:15, "But as for me and my house, we will serve the Lord."

Common Mistakes

Many parents get into a lot of trouble when they try to switch up or play the the wrong role in certain seasons. Below, you will find seven common parenting mistakes.

Mistake #1: Being a Friend Too Early
One of the biggest parenting problems today is parents trying to be their child's friend rather than their parent. I hear moms of school age children say, "My daughter is my best friend." Nowhere in Scripture are we told that our role as mother is to be a friend to our children! Instead, we are called to love our children and train them up in the ways of the Lord!

If you are trying to be a friend to your child during the first three seasons of parenting, your children will not respect you. The goal of parenting is not for our children to like us; instead, our goal is to raise children to be men and woman of character. By cultivating your children's heart through discipline and training- gaining their respect, you will receive a good friend—one who is a blessing to you once they reach adulthood, not sooner!

Mistake #2: Not Leaving the Servant Season
Parents today struggle with leaving the servant season of parenting. It is not uncommon to see parents cooking, cleaning, and picking up after

their children well into their teenage years. But, we do our children a huge disservice by continuing to serve them until they leave our homes.

Many moms today continue to serve their children after the age of three because they believe it is the best way to demonstrate their love for their children. This is what I thought, too. However, serving your children throughout their life leads to a sense of entitlement—they believe the the world needs to continue to serve them once they reach adulthood. Scripture has a lot to say about teaching children the importance of serving. And we don't want our children to miss out on this blessing!

Another problem we find in our culture today is jobless children who live with their parents into their late twenties and thirties. Recently, I spoke with a man who never was disciplined as a child. He told me, at the age of thirty-six, that he is never is going to work for anyone ever again. He hates bosses and does not want anyone telling him what to do. I see this sense of entitlement in young adults today—and it's root is continual service in place of discipline during the appropriate seasons of parenting.

Mistake #3: Lack of Engagement

One vital mistake parents are making is the failure to engage. We arrive home after a busy day, exhausted—and, we either want a break or the opportunity to just do what we need to do without interruptions. So, we allow our children to occupy themselves with movies, video games, or surfing the internet.

None of these things enable us to accomplish our greatest mission, though. Instead, they allow the enemy to win, as he uses this precious time to mold and shape our children according to the pattern of the world. If we want godly children, we must spend time discipling our children!

In his book *Spiritual Leadership*, Oswald Sanders writes: "Disciples are not manufactured wholesale. They are produced one by one, because someone has taken the pains to discipline, to instruct and enlighten, to nurture and train one that is younger."[5] We have been called by God to instruct, enlighten, nurture, and train our precious children in the ways of the Lord! Yes, discipleship requires pain and sacrifice. However, if we do not do it, we will miss out on the blessing of godly children. I know a pastor's wife, who has raised children in the ministry, whose biggest regret was being so busy in the ministry that she neglected the discipleship of her children. We do not want to look back on the seasons of parenting full of regret.

As mothers, we need to take time and allow our children to be part of our life. We can do this by having them help in the kitchen, eating dinner as a family, reading a book full of godly values together, enjoying a tea party, playing a game, etc. The time we have with our children is precious!

On another note, attending church every Sunday or sending your children to a private, Christian school should and must not take the place of you discipling your children at home. For a child to be properly discipled, they must be trained at home first—and at church and school, second.

Mistake #4: Making Excuses

Throughout our years in ministry, Michael and I have heard many excuses for parents not training their children. Some say their children don't respond to discipline because they are strong-willed or rebellious. Others say discipline doesn't work. These are lies that parents believe and use as excuses to not engage in the training of their children.

The age of your child does not matter—if they are in your home, they are worth the time and effort to train! We should never, ever give up on our children! The Bible says that if we do not do put forth the effort to train, discipline, and teach our children, then we do not love them (Proverbs 13:24).

Mistake #5: Giving Children Too Many Choices

Another common mistake the parents of today make is allowing their children to lead their home. This transfer of authority from parent to child happens when children are given too many choices. Parents innocently ask their little ones what they would like to eat for lunch, what they want to do with their free time, and who they want to have come over and play. Over time, however, these children become conditioned to getting what they want, and they become decision makers in their home before they are mature enough to make major life decisions. Their parents end up having no say in their lives, as the children choose their own school, what church the family attends, and their level of involvement in various activities—all to the detriment of themselves and their family.

When you give your children too many choices, they think that every decision you make is up for negotiation. Parents struggle with fussing and arguments anytime their children don't want to do something. Their children are used to making their own choices; and they think that if they can pressure their parents long enough and argue loud enough, they will eventually get what they want.

Additionally, family psychologist John Rosemond explains that the result of too many choices is entitled children who believe their parents exist to please them.[6] Remember, as the parent, you are called to train your children. Your job is not to make your children happy, but holy! When your children realize that they were not placed on earth to fulfill their every whim and desire, but rather to glorify God, everything changes! Our every decision and action as parents needs to promote this truth.

Mistakes #6 Being Too Busy

It is possible to keep your children so busy with activities, schooling, and other achievements that you, as parents, have no time to spend with them. Yet, it is important that you do not neglect the training of your children! Without time, you cannot train your children in the virtues they will need to live godly lives that glorify God.

Today, our culture places so much pressure on families to enroll their children in sports, foreign language classes, and other extra-curricular activities. While these are not bad in and of themselves, they can get out of hand fast—especially if you have more than one child with multiple activities apiece. Remember, your home and family should be the highest priority in your life. As parents of seven children, Michael and I came upon this problem early on. We were so encouraged when we came upon this advice from Warren Weirsbe:

> *The problems get more complicated when the children get older and start getting involved in piano lessons, sports, slumber parties, baby-sitting, part-time jobs, and all the other rites of passage that belong to modern life. That's when we all have to start practicing the give-and-take of managing the family circus, the first rule of which is, nobody is always in the center ring. Once we agree on that, things become easier.*[7]

Being in the ministry, we have had to simplify even more than most families. However, it has enabled our family to become very close as we spend so much time together- especially serving. We need to make sure that we do not allow the culture to pressure us into choosing our children's achievements and activities over their character.

Mistake #7: Forsaking The Family Meal

The family meal is one of the most important ways you can impart your values to your children. In fact, family meals have been a foundational tradition within the homes of Western civilization for thousands of years. From the ancient table we read about in the Old Testament through recent American history, the family meal has been an important part of the family. It served as a time the family could gather together throughout the day to reconnect and pass on their values from one generation to the next. Today, families find it harder than ever to gather together and fellowship over a meal because of the many activities and busy schedules of each family member. The abundance of restaurants and inexpensive fast foods hasn't helped, either.

Secular studies confirm that eating meals together as a family has many benefits. It improves a child's academic achievement, strengthens family bonds, encourages healthy eating, curbs risky behavior, and the list goes on. From a Christian perspective, the family meal is a time to enjoy one another's company, reconnect after a busy day, and discover what dad thinks about different situations arising in his children's lives.

The family meal is a time when families can discuss what is going on in the community and world through the lens of God's Word. The love that comes from a homemade meal—along with the awe and wonder of children as a truth is discovered, the bond that is created through the sharing an anecdote in a good book, the joy and delight of a good laugh over the day's events—all produce fond memories that children will carry with them throughout their lives!

Recently, at our dinner table, my son, Micah, informed me that while reading *Pride and Prejudice*, I reminded him of Mrs. Bennet- without being annoying! That gave us a good laugh! What memories we make when we take time to gather together at the family meal. Truly, the blessings of a family meal can not be overstated!

Drastic Intervention

If you find yourself making one or more of these common parenting mistakes, don't worry! Children are very resilient and trainable. However, I encourage you to do everything you can—even if it is drastic—to get your relationship with your child right.

Proverbs 29:25 states, "The fear of man brings a snare, but whoever trusts in the LORD shall be safe." As a mom, you cannot fear what your children will think if you take away their phone, computer, or iPad; pull them out of all their activities; or ask them to start doing chores. They may not like it at first, but they will love and respect you in the end! And remember, respect turns into friendship and love when your children are older.

Years ago, I read a fascinating story about Kenjon Barner, a candidate for the Heisman Trophy Award. In the article, the college football player described how his father had saved his life.

Kenjon Barner was at his eighth grade graduation when his dad overheard his plans for the following weekend. Realizing that his son was up to no good and mixing with the wrong group of friends, he decided to pull his son out of public high school and place him in a tiny, private, Calvary Chapel Christian school.

At the time, Kenjon thought this decision was the end of his life; but in fact, it was his salvation—literally! Not only did Kenjon start hanging around godly friends, but he started walking with God. Since the school was so small, it didn't have a typical football team. All the students on the team had to play eight on eight. The result: everyone quickly discovered their strengths, as well as the areas they needed additional practice to become really good.

Barner's football career advanced through college until he was nominated for the Heisman Award in 2012.[8] The most fascinating aspect of this article was where Kenjon's friends ended up: jail. By pulling him out of public school and away from ungodly friends, his father literally rescued him. Kenjon Barner didn't realize it at the time, but his father had saved his life!

From this story, you learn that you must be willing to do whatever it takes to win your children to Christ. As parents, you are accountable before the Lord for the discipleship of your children. Your job is not to ensure your children's happiness. When your children are holy before the Lord and walking in the way of truth, they will receive the blessing of a right relationship with God—and they will be happy!

What if your children are grown? That's okay! Ask the Holy Spirit to lead and guide you as you establish the relationship you should have with your children. Your faith matters, today—not what mistakes you have made in the past. God, in us, can make a huge difference in lives of our children and grandchildren today.

Embracing Your Season

For those of you who have been mothers for some time, you know how quickly these seasons pass. Katrina Kenison provides additional insight:

> *Just when I figure out how to mother a kindergartener, it seems, I have a first-grader standing before me instead. I have just learned how to love and live with a nine-year-old when the nine-year-old vanishes, leaving preadolescent in his place. They don't stay still long enough for me to have my fill of them ever, at any stage. "Stop!" I want to shout. "Let's just do it this way for a a while, let's stay right here." But the movement is inexorable—up and out, away, into the future.*[9]

Sometimes it is hard to embrace new seasons with our children, especially when we are constantly looking back with nostalgia and wanting previous seasons back again. However, God has blessings in store for us in every season of parenting. And, He wants us to be looking forward to the next season with faith, rather than fear!

We need to be ready to embrace each season that God has for us. Constantly looking back or living in fear of the future keeps us from fulfilling the roles that God has called us to fill, causing us to miss out on receiving the blessings He has prepared for us.

Truly, there are blessings in every season of your child's life. And, I have been told—by many who have gone before me—that, if we are faithful, the fruit of grandchildren surpasses any season we have already experienced with our own children. As Proverbs 17:6 (NIV) declares, "Children's children are a crown to the aged." So, whatever season you are in, embrace it. And if you are faithful, the best is yet to come!

Questions to Consider

1. Are you taking the necessary time to disciple your children? What change(s) are necessary to enable you to spend more time implementing your values?

2. What seasons are you currently in with your children? How are you fulfilling your role within this season?

3. What mistakes are you making within your parenting season(s)? What might you do to remedy these mistakes?

4. Can you name any activities that your child is involved in that might be keeping you from imparting your values?

5. Is there a drastic measure you need to take to rescue your children and begin implementing your values? How might you accomplish this?

6. Have you allowed your children to make choices that were not the best ones for them or your family? How might you remedy the situation?

Notes

[1] Matthew Henry, *Matthew Henry's Commentary of the Bible, Volume II* (New York: Fleming H. Revell Company, 1708), 283.

[2] Elisabeth Elliot, *The Shaping of a Christian Family* (Grand Rapids, Michigan: Fleming H. Revell, 1992), 99.

[3] Ibid., 95-96.

[4] Charles R. Swindoll, *Parenting: From Surviving to Thriving* (Nashville, Tennessee: Thomas Nelson, 2006), 15.

[5] Oswald Sanders, *Spiritual Leadership* (Chicago: Moody Press, 1976), 150.

[6] John Rosemond, "Parenting Habits That Lead To Child Tyrants," Hartford Courant, October 28, 2015.

[7] Wiersbe, *On Being a Servant of God* (Grand Rapids, Michigan: Baker Books, 1993), 98.

[8] Eric Adelson, "Kenjon Barner, Heisman candidate, had his life changed by a tiny school." Yahoo! Sports, November 9, 2012.

[9] Carolyn Mahaney, *Feminine Appeal* (Wheaton, Illinois: Crossway, 2003), 60.

Hannah's Submission

Wives, summit to your own husbands, as to the Lord.
For the husband is head of the wife, as also Christ is the head
of the church; and He is the Savior of the body.
Therefore, just as the church is subject to Christ,
so let the wives be to their own husbands in everything.

Ephesians 5:22-24

Hannah's faith, sacrifice, and dedication in training Samuel in the ways of the Lord would have been null and void if she had failed to respect and submit to her husband, because the marriage union, defined in God's Word, is one of the most powerful forces in raising a godly child. Nothing demonstrates a mother's faith in God more than her ability to love, respect, and submit to her husband. For, in doing so, she proclaims the power of the gospel to her children and the world.

When we consider Hannah's story, it is evident that Elkanah was the spiritual leader of his home: every year, he traveled to the Tabernacle to offer sacrifices on behalf of himself and his family (1 Samuel 1:3). Hannah's submission to her husband can be seen through her willingness to journey to the Tabernacle with him (1 Samuel 1:7) and take part in the feast at the prompting of her husband (1 Samuel 1:8-9)—even though she was upset and not hungry.

Our husband's leadership and our submission to this leadership are key in raising up children who are secure in the faith, grounded in God's Word, and ready to take on the world for His glory!

God's Design for Marriage

After God created man, He stated that it was not good for man to be alone. So, He created woman to be a suitable helper (Genesis 2:18). God took a portion of man, Adam's rib, and used it to create the first woman, Eve (Genesis 2:21). Together, a husband and wife are made complete— reflecting the image of God, and representing His glory.

As women, we must realize that we were created to be a wife first and foremost, before we were created to be a mother. Our love and care for our children should come out of our marriage. So often, in today's culture, a woman falls in love with the man of her dreams, but he quickly becomes her second priority once they have children together. But, this should not be the case. A wife is not called to be her husband's helper *until* they have children, but to be his helper as the two raise children together, and after their children are grown.

Godly marriages are a picture of God's love for His church. God is glorified when the world sees a properly ordered home, yet these types of homes are becoming more and more rare—even within the church. As the culture's definition of marriage changes, God's Word must remain our guide and source of truth.

Years ago, my children came across a wooden sign that read, "Good moms have sticky floors, dirty ovens, and happy kids." They loved this saying, so a friend bought the sign for me one Mother's Day. When I joyfully hung it in my kitchen, Michael wanted to change the sign to read, "Good moms have happy husbands." How true! When we make our marriages our priority—by loving and respecting our husbands—our homes are in order, and our children's lives are balanced. Therefore, our husbands—and children—are happy!

There is nothing more powerful in the lives of children than a father who leads his home, and a mother who respects and follows the leadership of her husband. Children blossom under this kind of unity. A godly family is a picture to our children and the world of God's design for marriage and the basic family unit. It should be an inspiration for the culture to follow.

A Home Rightly Ordered

In creating male and female, God created two equal beings in His image. Genesis 1:27 states: "So God created man in His own image, in the image of God He created him; male and female He created them." Neither male nor female is better than the other, but both are designed distinctly different in order to represent various attributes of God. Both are equal in worth—man is not greater than woman, nor is woman more valuable than man. Both are joint heirs together in Christ (1 Peter 3:7). Understanding these truths is essential when it comes to understanding submission.

In Ephesians 5:22-28, Paul describes the roles that God has assigned man and woman within the marriage union:

Wives, submit to your own husbands, as to the Lord. For the husband is the head of the wife, as also Christ is the head of the church; and He is the Savior of the body. Therefore, just as the church is subject to Christ, so let the wives be to their own husbands in everything.

Husbands, love your wives, just as Christ also loved the church and gave Himself for her, that He might sanctify and cleanse her with the washing of water by the word, that He might present her to Himself a glorious church, not having spot or wrinkle or any such thing, but that she should be holy and without blemish. So husbands ought to love their own wives as their own bodies, he who loves his wife loves himself.

Wives are commanded to submit to their husbands in the same way they submit to the Lord. Then, husbands are commanded to love their wives with a perfect love, which washes and cleanses, making their wives glorious!

We are called to submit to our husbands. So, what is submission? Webster's 1828 Dictionary describes submission as "the act of yielding to power or authority; surrender of the person and power to the control or government of another." As wives, we are commanded to surrender authority to our husbands by God, our Creator. Just as the church is subject to Christ, so too are wives subject to their husbands. What a beautiful picture of God's love for His church!

When a man and woman first get married, a husband must learn to lead, and a wife must learn to follow. For this to happen, the wife must get out of the way, and allow her husband to learn—and that often means he must fail. This process is not about who is right and who is wrong. There is blessing in store for a wife who submits to her husband even when her husband makes a huge mistake. It is okay for a wife to share her heart with her husband, and to influence his decision, yet he must be the one responsible to make the final decision. Our God is a God of order, and He desires our homes to be rightly ordered.

Our Culture and Submission

One of the consequences of sin entering the world was that marriages lost their balance. In Genesis 3:16, God told Eve, "Your desire shall be for your husband, and he shall rule over you." In other words, wives would no longer joyfully submit to their husbands; rather, they would desire to usurp their husband's authority. Submitting to our husbands no longer comes easily. For a woman to fulfill her role as a wife, she must daily submit her heart to God and constantly check her heart for sin. It takes more faith than ever for a wife to trust God enough to allow her husband to take the leadership role in marriage.

And, in case our sin nature was not enough of a struggle, our culture loudly proclaims that no woman should submit to any man—after all, women have spent hundreds of years fighting to receive equal rights with man. Nowhere in our culture—and rarely in the church—are woman encouraged or taught the blessings that come through biblical submission. Since the beginning of time, families have been ordered in this God-ordained fashion, and with our modern thinking, we have done away with the wisdom of the ages!

Concerning submission in marriage, Elisabeth Elliot writes:

When people decide to "wing it" and arrange things according to personal whim or comfort, they make a terrible mess, as Adam and Eve demonstrated when she took the initiative and Adam failed to protect her, as he made to do, from that wrong choice. In recent years, with much discussion and protests about rights and equality, people have tried to rearrange just about everything, the word traditional has become a pejorative, and we have lost a great deal.[1]

I agree with Elisabeth Elliot, whole-heartedly! As women, we have lost a great deal to our progressive thinking. In demanding an equal role with man, we have given up our protection, our honor, our value, and so much more. Not to mention the joy and peace that comes through having a marriage that is pleasing to God!

Excuses for Not Submitting

Often, women try to justify their lack of respect or refusal to submit to their husband based upon past decisions their husband has made. Perhaps their husband made a huge mistake, and they can't forgive them for it. Or, perhaps the wife doesn't feel like her husband is spiritual enough to make godly decisions regarding the family or children.

Some women might be tempted to think, "Certainly, the Lord didn't mean I have to submit in this area!" Yet, Scripture is clear, wives are to submit to their husbands in everything (Ephesians 5:22-24). There are no clauses, exceptions, addendum, or footnotes! Wives are to be subject to their husbands in small things (e.g., what he enjoys eating, what to do on Saturday) and the big things (e.g., finances, where to live, where to attend church, how to raise children)—everything!

As women of faith, we cannot allow excuses to stop us from obeying God. Our husbands are not and will never be perfect. They are sinners—just like us. God knew our husbands would fail when He commanded us to submit to them, yet He still asked it of us. We are called to honor and respect our husbands with obedience and submission, whether they are worthy of it or not. Submitting to our husbands becomes easier when we remember that God commands us to submit to them. In submitting to our husbands, we are submitting to the Lord—who is perfect. We can trust that He will take care of the results.

Consider Elkanah and Hannah's marriage. Elkanah had two wives, and he allowed Hannah to suffer under Peninnah's mistreatment (1 Samuel 1:6-7). Hannah could have thought, "Elkanah doesn't know what he is doing, and he is not protecting me against this other woman. I cannot submit to that type of leadership." Instead, she submitted to her husband as to the Lord!

Christian life, in general, is one of surrender. God calls each of us to surrender to Him and His will for our life. Jesus, our wonderful example, submitted His life to His father. He came to the earth, lived a perfect life, and gave Himself up to be crucified for the sins of humanity. Through Christ's submission to His Father, we have been given the wonderful gift of salvation! In the same way that Jesus submitted to His Father, we are to submit to our husbands, knowing in reality- we are submitting to Christ.

In Titus 2:5, wives are admonished to submit to their husbands so "the word of God may not be blasphemed." When we fail to submit to our husband, the gospel has no power in our life. The respect we give to our husband declares God's amazing love to our children and the world. It draws our children to Christ, and encourages our children to desire marriage.

(When speaking about submission, I am not referring to wives, who are in an abusive situation or if your husband is asking you do to something illegal or immoral. If your husband is abusive, I encourage you to go to your pastor and get help.)

Submission in Action
What does godly submission look like? John Piper defines it as a wife's "divine calling to honor and affirm her husband's leadership and help carry it through according to her gifts."[2] As women, we are called by God to use the gifts He has given us to help our husband as he leads our family. These gifts can be practical, like cleaning, cooking, decorating, running errands, and so on. They also include: ideas, suggestions, encouragement, prayer, insight, wisdom, and correction with humility when needed. The type of help we give our husbands looks different in each home, and may change from season to season of marriage, as every husband has different gifts and different needs from his wife. One thing is for certain: when we use our gifts, we must use them to bless our husbands—and when we do, we are being a true helper, indeed.

So often, women go into marriage not understanding their God-given role to bless, help, and support their husband. Instead, they desire their husbands to serve them. Yet, this desire is not aligned with how God designed marriage to operate. Yes, out of sacrificial love, our husbands should serve us, but they were not created to fulfill our every whim. This type of attitude and expectation can be really destructive, as it breeds discontent, and indirectly pulls our home down rather than building it up. Proverbs 14:1 offers this exhortation: "The wise woman builds her house, but the foolish pulls it down with her hands." What influence we have in our home and on our husband. When we remember that God has called husbands to lead, and wives to submit through loving service—everything is put in focus.

The Beauty of Submission
God's Word is full of examples of women who exemplified submission in action. In so honoring their husbands, they became more attractive, and God was glorified. Abraham's wife Sarah is a great example. First Peter 3:3-6 tells us that she adorned herself with submission:

> *Do not let your adornment be merely outward—arranging the hair, wearing gold, or putting on fine apparel—rather let it be the hidden person of the heart, with the incorruptible beauty of a gentle and quiet spirit, which is very precious in the sight of God. For in this manner, in former times, the holy women who*

trusted in God also adorned themselves, being submissive to their own husbands, as Sarah obeyed Abraham, calling him lord, whose daughters you are if you do good and are not afraid with any terror.

As women, our greatest adornment should be an inner beauty—"the hidden person of the heart"—rather than designer clothes, stylish hair, or expensive jewelry. In fact, a woman's character defines who she is more than her outward beauty. Remember, "Charm is deceitful and beauty is passing, but a woman who fears the Lord, she shall be praised" (Proverbs 31:30). In other words, outward beauty fades as years pass, but the inner person grows more beautiful with every passing day. One of the the most beautiful attributes a women can possess is a gentle and quiet spirit, which leads her to submit to her husband. A woman, who adorns herself with submission, displays her faith and trust in God—and Proverbs declares she shall be praised.

During the Civil War, someone once said, "A man's prospect of domestic felicity [i.e., happiness in marriage] does not depend upon the face, the fortune, or the accomplishments of his wife, but upon her character."[3] Our husbands are indeed blessed when we are women of character! And one of the most beautiful character traits we can possess is submission!

Consider Hannah. She had every right to be bitter and hard-hearted because of her life circumstances—her barrenness, her husband's second wife, Peninnah's constant provocation, and her husband's lack of protection and discernment regarding the things she experienced. Yet, Hannah's faith, displayed in her submission to God and her husband, enabled her to become loved and cherished by her husband. Scripture states that Elkanah loved and adored Hannah, so much so that he gave her a double portion when he offered sacrifices at the Tabernacle (1 Samuel 1:5).

Hannah's submission enabled her to move her husband's heart—and, ultimately, God's heart. God gave her her heart's desire, children! Her submission prepared Hannah to be the mom she needed to be, to raise a son who would transform a nation for God's glory.

Respect and Expectations

Many women refuse to submit to their husbands out of a lack of respect. Often, this lack of respect is due to unmet expectations and offense. As wives, we expect our husband to be or act in a certain way, and when he does not meet our expectations, we become offended, and lose our respect for him. In our offense, we punish our husbands, often by refusing to submit, or acting disrespectfully, rudely, selfishly, unthankfully—bringing division into our marriage and home.

When it comes to marriage, wives must realize that, "We can't have it all!" Meaning, there is no perfect husband who has every quality we dream of in a man. Too often, wives focus on the 10% they don't like about their husband, forgetting about the 90% they do love, and the reason why they married them in the first place. Our husbands are not perfect, and we shouldn't expect them to be. If we do, we are setting ourselves up for disappointment. When we have a hard time respecting or being thankful for our husband, it is so important that we remember the qualities that attracted us to him in the first place. We should also ask God to reveal attributes we can value in our husband. As we begin meditating on the blessings and gifts our husband has, we will find our whole perspective changed.

As wives, we must remember that there is only one perfect man, Jesus Christ. We cannot expect our husbands to be perfect, or even close to it. They are human, and their hearts are rooted in sin—as are ours. In her book *It's My Turn*, Ruth Bell Graham writes:

> *I pity the married couple who expect too much from one another. It is a foolish woman who expects her husband to be to her what only Jesus can be: always ready to forgive, totally understanding, unendingly patient, invariably tender and loving, unfailing in every area, anticipating every need, and making more than adequate provision. Such expectations put a man under an impossible strain.[4]*

When we release our husbands from our unrealistic expectations, and look to God to fulfill our needs, they will be blessed indeed! And we will find that our whole attitude towards them will be transformed.

When Husbands Don't Believe

What if your husband is not a Christian? First Peter 3:1-2 describes our responsibility: "Wives, likewise, be submissive to your own husbands, that even if some do not obey the word, they, without a word, may be won by the conduct of their wives, when they observe your chase conduct accompanied by fear." Even if a woman's husband is not saved, she is still called to submit to him. God may use the wife's submission, gracious words, and loving actions to draw the husband to Him.

Throughout my years in ministry, I have met many precious women who have won over their husband to the Lord through their submission. Their faithful devotion to God, displayed through their gracious words and loving actions towards their husband, won them to the gospel.

I have a dear friend who has five children and an unsaved husband. Like many women, she was raised in the church, but walked away from the Lord, and married a non-believer. Since then, she has fallen in love with the Lord, and wants to be the wife and mom God has called her to be. She is doing her best to raise her children in the ways of the Lord, but she often found herself growing frustrated at her husband for doing the opposite of what God's Word says parents should do. She and her husband were constantly challenging each other, so I suggested she do some reading on her role as a wife.

After reading Carolyn Mahaney's book, *Feminine Appeal*, she sat in my living room, and told me of her revelation: "If I am the best mom ever, yet am not a wife pleasing to God, nothing I do on my kids' behalf matters." My friend realized that her faith—displayed in her love for and submission toward her husband—was the biggest influence in her children's lives.

The Power of Submission

Often women think, "I'll submit to my husband when he starts loving me as Christ loved the church." However, we are not responsible for our husband's obedience. We are only responsible for our obedience. We must do the right thing before God! If we want our husbands to love us, we must submit to and respect them—just see what will happen! Godly submission is the key to our husbands becoming the men we desire them to be, and to us receiving the love for which we so desperately long. If submission can draw an unsaved husband to faith, imagine what it can do within a Christian marriage. The blessings are endless!

We can see the power of submission in Hannah's example. As a result of her submission, Elkanah loved Hannah dearly, even though she had no children. His heart was overwhelmed with gratitude for his wife, who brought him so much delight that he made sure his he thanked God for his blessing by giving Hannah a double portion of his yearly offering.

Do you want your husband to love and cherish you deeply? Then try loving God enough to submit to your husband. In her book *Creative Counterpart*, Linda Dillow writes about the power of submission:

> *Submission is your only hope of changing your husband. Your husband will change as you allow him to be the head of his home and as you are submissive to him. He will not change by your nagging, belittling, suggesting, reminding, or mothering.*[5]

In frustration, wives often start nagging their husband, reminding them of the things they should and should not be doing. However, nagging only drives your husband away, and discourages him from becoming the man you desire. Proverbs 19:13b says "the contentions of a wife are a continual dripping"—and it is is better to dwell on the rooftop than with such a wife (Proverbs 21:9)! When we choose to love, respect, honor, and submit to our husband—whether he deserves it or not—our marriage will be transformed through our obedience to God.

For more serious issues within marriage, I would recommend Gary Thomas's book *Sacred Influence* as a resource. This book gives a wife practical ideas on how to minister to her husband, and how to inspire him to be the man that God wants him to be.

Submission and Raising Children

Parenting As One Flesh

When God designed man and woman to become one flesh, he purposed that their love would bear children and build the human race.

> *For this reason a man shall leave his father and mother and be joined to his wife, and the two shall become one flesh." This is a great mystery, but I speak concerning Christ and the church. Nevertheless let each one of you in particular so love his own wife as himself, and let the wife see that she respects her husband.*
> — Ephesians 5:31-33

This idea of one flesh does not stop with bringing children into the world. God wasn't just thinking of conception and birth. Rather, he designed a husband and wife to raise their children as one flesh, as well. A husband and wife, as one flesh, are equally important when it comes to making decisions and training children.

Today, it is not uncommon for a man and woman to get married, become one flesh, and produce children, who become the focus of the woman's life (rather than her relationship with her husband). Scripture is clear: children are to be raised by and honor both parents. Ephesians 6:1-3 states: "Children, obey your parents in the Lord, for this is right. 'Honor your father and mother,' which is the first commandment with promise: 'that it may be well with you and you may live long on the earth.'" Yet today, in many homes, mom is the parenting expert, and dad is the assistant, which turns a man and woman's God-ordained roles on their head within the home.

A husband and wife each bring wisdom and insight into the training of children. Both are needed in parenting, as the devastating effects of uninvolved or absentee fathers in our world attests. A husband brings leadership, protection, logic, security, safety, provision, and wisdom. A wife brings influence, nurture, insight, discernment, and a heart filled with emotions. Each of these qualities are needed to raise children, who are loved, secure, and valued.

As we have raised of our children, Michael and I have needed both of our gifts and personalities. I remember when we had our second son, Micah. I sat in the hospital bed, feeling a bit sad for my son, Daniel. Up to that point, he had received all our love and attention—and now he was going to have less of us! When Michael brought Daniel to visit us in the hospital, I shared my feelings with Michael. His response: "What are you talking about? This is the best thing for Daniel. We just gave him a best friend for life! His life is going to be so much better off because of Micah." These words were exactly what I needed to hear to gain a fresh perspective and snap out of my emotions.

Michael has always been an instrumental part in the of raising our children. With his logic, he has the ability to sift through all the emotions and get to the heart of the matter—whereas, I often get so lost in the emotions that I sometimes miss the point. In return, I have helped Michael by giving him insight into our children's lives. Often, Michael gives direction for the children, then delegates me to carry it out. When I feel tired and overwhelmed by the children, he easily steps in, and gets everything under control. When the children don't listen, he steps in, gives orders, and the children obey. Together, Michael and I reflect the character of God to our children as we balance each other out.

A House Divided

In many cases, parents desire to parent as one flesh, but they are on completely different pages when it comes to how to raise their children.

In some instances, the husband and wife come from completely different backgrounds, and they are each trying to implement a different set of values with their children. This discord is one reason God calls us not to be "unequally yoked" in marriage—it affects how we raise our children! God desires a husband and wife to be equally yoked, so they raise godly offspring (Malachi 2:15).

Even spouses who were raised with similar values will have issues with parenting when they are not on the same page. Sometimes, a wife parents based on her emotions, and a husband on his logic. Other times, a husband does not lead, and a wife does not submit—or they are not under the Holy Spirit's control. It is so important that a husband and wife are on the same page when it comes to raising children. As the Bible says, "if a house is divided against itself, that house cannot stand" (Mark 3:25).

Parents who are on the same page bring security to a child's life. John Rosemond gives us insight into the blessings of a united marriage in relation to child-rearing:

> For the marriage to raise the children means husband and wife are of one flesh, one mind where there children are concerned. They see their children through one set of eyes, adhere to one child-rearing plan (God's), aim at one set of goals, share one set of values, and act as one body when it comes to loving, teaching, and discipling their children.[6]

How do we accomplish having "one mind" where our children are concerned, when we start off on different pages? First, we must seek God in prayer. Ask for wisdom and oneness. If our husband is not saved, we must pray for our husband's salvation. Second, we should make sure we are both in the word, received wisdom and leading from God. Another good idea to consider is attending a parenting class at church or reading through a Christian parenting book with our spouse once a week. I would suggest Ray Comfort's book, *How To Bring Your Children to*

Christ and Keep them There, or John Rosemond's *Parenting by The Book*. Read a chapter together, discuss what it says, and find ways of implementing it. (I do not recommend secular parenting classes or books, as the information will most likely be contrary to God's Word.)

Often, wives struggle to get on the same page as their husband when it comes to implementing God's Word into parenting. The best advice I have is for the wife to go to her husband and tell him, "I have been praying about implementing this parenting idea, and I was wondering if you would pray about it, as well. Do you think God might be leading us in this direction?" Doing so allows her husband to be a part of the decision.

Being on the same page within marriage takes a lot of prayer, communication, compromise (on both sides), openness, and humility. It requires a teachable spirit and a desire to learn and grow together. Unity and oneness requires effort! Sometimes, a couple may even need to go their pastor or Christian counselor to sort out issues. However, it is worth it for the sake of their marriage and their children!

Submission in Parenting

When we don't agree with a decision our husband is making—and he decides to make it anyways—what do we do? Submit. The enemy wants Christian spouses to be divided, and he will do whatever it takes to cause division in homes. He wants wives to usurp their husband's authority, and encourages them disobey God and their husband—like he did with Eve in the Garden!

As a Christian wife, you must understand that God will not allow your husband to make decisions that will destroy your family or your life. God blesses your obedience and submission. Sometimes choosing submission is a huge test of faith, but it is not your duty to make the final decision. While you can stand up for what is right and encourage your husband, you must submit to your husband, and trust God with the decision, allowing Him to work.

Submission is where the rubber meets the road. Our depth of faith is displayed in our obedience to God and toward our husband. A woman who submits to her husband is not weak. Instead, she is a woman who displays her amazing faith in God. Through God's grace, she has conquered her desire to usurp her husband's authority and demand her own way. She has allowed the Spirit to rule in her life, rather than the natural inclination of her flesh.

Sometimes, a husband will make the wrong decision as he leads his family—but God will never let it ruin our life. Consider Pontius Pilate. When Jesus stood trial before Pilate, his wife sent a message to her husband, "Have nothing to do with that just Man, for I have suffered many things today in a dream because of Him" (Matthew 27:19). Pilate's wife had dreamt of Jesus's innocence, and she urged her husband to set him free. However, persuaded by the crowds, he did not listen to the counsel of his wife. Jesus was sentenced to be crucified. While Pilate did not make the right decision, God used it to accomplish His will: the death and resurrection of His Son and the salvation of humanity. What a beautiful picture! When we choose to submit to our husband's decision—even when it is wrong—God will bless our submission. His will is still going to be accomplished in our marriages, our children's lives, and His kingdom. We can trust God with our lives as we, in faith, submit to our husbands.

Throughout our marriage, my husband has made many decisions that I have not agreed with, but none of them have destroyed our life. In fact, many of them have saved it! When I allow Michael to lead (even when I don't agree with him), God blesses the decision, and it always turns out in the end. It may not turn out the way I would have liked it to, but it always turns out for good. Not only is God glorified, but my children and the world see God's Word in action.

Looking back, I remember a specific time that Michael made a decision that I did not like. We argued about it constantly, which only resulted in my complete frustration. After spending time in prayer, God assured me that He would not let my husband make a decision that would ruin our lives. From that point on, I stopped bringing up the subject, as Michael already knew where I stood. Instead, I brought it to God. In the end, God ended up closing the door, so Michael couldn't walk through it. Only God could have brought peace to our home, and enabled this to happen.

However, this hasn't always been the case. I remember when I wanted to send Daniel to a private, Christian high school in town. We applied, went to the family interview, and had Daniel take the tests required for registration. Upon acceptance, Michael confidently said that Daniel would not be attending that high school; instead, I would home school him. After questioning Michael several times, I realized he was not going to budge. As a result, I had to let my plans go, and submit by faith. Once I obeyed, God assured me that this was God's will for Daniel's life. Many times, I have had to step out in faith, through submission to my husband, before God assures my heart that He is in the decision. Looking back, I realize that sending Daniel to that high school would have been a financial hardship on our family, and the worldly influences he would have been exposed to would have lured him away from us.

A rightly ordered home reflects Christ and His church to the world, and God is glorified as a result. Today, the world needs to see godly marriages and families more than ever before—and where do we find these modeled if not in the church and within Christian homes?

Playing Interference
Often, women want their husband to lead, but when he tries to do so, they jump in and intervene. For example, dad steps up to discipline the children or deal with a problem, and mom jumps in and gets upset at him for not handling the situation they way she would. She starts to defend

the children: "Oh, he didn't mean it." "She had a hard day." Rather than submitting to the Holy Spirit's control, she allows emotions to rule her. Perhaps she thinks that her husband will be too hard on the children, or cause them some sort of emotional damage.

In these types of situations, we must remember that a healthy fear—reverence and respect—for our husband is good. We and our children should fear him in the same way they fear God. Hebrews 12:9-10 reminds us:

> Furthermore, we have had human fathers who corrected us, and we paid them respect. Shall we not much more readily be in subjection to the Father of spirits and live? For they indeed for a few days chastened us as seemed best to them, but He for our profit, that we may be partakers of His holiness.

Our husbands correct our children in the way that seems best to them, and our children should pay them respect, as a result.

It is important that our husbands have a strong presence in our home. God made men leaders for a reason; their gifts are necessary in the raising of children—especially sons. While our husbands will not always get it right, God will bless their leadership in our homes.

When we intervene, we undermine our husbands' authority, as we choose not to support their leadership in our homes. As wives, we need to allow our husbands to be a leader in our children's lives, so they will respect and support him.

What if your husband does something blatantly wrong? In the moment, you must support him as the leader of your home. Don't let your children know you don't agree. Your husband wants your support in the same way you desire his support. You must keep your emotions in check, and remember that he is not perfect. Sometimes, he will overreact, and get angry. What if you see an unhealthy pattern in how your husband handles things? First, pray for him, Second, when you have a chance to bring up what you see, do it in humility and love. He will appreciate your love and care! However, if you husband is abusive or blatantly out of line on a regular basis, I would encourage you to talk to your pastor, and get help.

When asked why some children turn out and others do not, Michael's grandmother, Carol McClure, used to answer, "When mothers don't respect their husbands, the children usually don't turn out." She would follow this up with a story about a family her children knew as they grew up. The couple had three boys, just like Michael's grandparents. The mom was a really strong woman, who did not respect her husband at all. One time, the dad asked one of his sons to mow the lawn. The son's response: "Mow it yourself!" before walking away. None of the boys turned out.

When wives do not respect their husband, children do not respect their father. And, if they do not respect their earthly father, they will not transfer that respect to God, their Heavenly Father. The way our children respond to God and the Gospel stems directly from the way we respect and submit to our husband's leadership in the home.

Supporting a Husband's Leadership

What about a husband who does not lead, or does not want to be involved in the discipline and leadership of his home? This problem is much more common than you think! There are many reasons for his apathy: he may be too tired to lead, he may not have an example of a father who led, or he may not be allowed to lead.

If you are struggling with your husband's lack of leadership, I want to encourage you to use your godly influence to inspire your husband to lead. Set up your home in a way that encourages him to make decisions for the family. Carolyn Mahaney describes the godly pressure exerted by turning to your husband for leadership in this way:

> ...have you ever had someone lean on you with his or her full body weight? What happened? Of course, your natural reaction was to exert the counter-pressure necessary to hold that person (and yourself) up. This is a picture of the effect of submission on our husbands. It places godly pressure on them. It allows them to feel the full weight of their responsibility. More often than not, they rise to the challenge.[7]

When we submit to our husbands, and look to them for leadership, they grow as leaders!

What does this godly pressure look like practically? Here are a few ways you can encourage your husband to lead:

1. *Keep your husband in the loop.* — Let him know what is going on with your children. He probably will have some good ideas and insight on how to deal with your children.

2. *Include your husband in your decision making.* — The next time your children ask you if they can do something, tell them you will have to ask dad what he thinks before you make a decision. Doing so will train your children to honor and respect their father, and look to him for leadership.

3. *Ask your husband's opinion.* — When your children ask you a question, tell them to ask daddy later. Prep him for the question in advance, then encourage your child to bring it up again.

4. *Listen to your husband.* — When your husband has an opinion, listen to and value it. Don't act like his input is not valuable or valid.

5. *Support your husband's decisions.* — Remember, your husband makes decisions logically, as opposed to emotionally. When you are speaking with your children, ask them, "What did dad say?" before telling them, "Then, that's what I say. Daddy is the one in charge. You need to listen to him." Even when you don't agree, support your husband!

6. *Support him at home.* — Don't talk badly about your husband. Make sure your children know that dad's word is the final authority in your home. Make it clear that you and daddy are on the same page—even if you aren't. And, if you aren't, figure out how to get there.

7. *Structure your home to provide leadership opportunities.* — Ask your husband to pray before meals. Have him lead a family Bible study. It might not be his idea, but you can make sure the kids are in their pajamas, alert and on the couch ready to hear from their father. Ask him if you can order a devotional for him to read through with the children. Watch him lead!

8. *Share with him the things you are learning.* — As you grow in your relationship with the Lord, reveal to your husband the things that God has shown you. Ask him what he thinks and how you can implement what you are learning into both of your lives and your family.

9. *Allow him to be part of the finances.* — Some men do not have time to manage the family's finances on top of their job and commitments outside the home. If you help your husband in this area, make sure you include him as you make financial decisions for the family. Ask him where he wants to put the money, and let him know what things cost before he makes a decision on vacations, children's activities, giving, etcetera.

Navigating our relationship with Christ, our husband, and children along with all of our other responsibilities is a full-time job. Martin Luther asserts: "One learns more of Christ in being married and rearing children than in several lifetimes spent in study in a monastery." I couldn't agree more!

Being the Spiritual Leader
When I was young, my dad was not saved, so my mother took my siblings and me to church, and said our prayers with us. Every night, we would pray that Dad would come to know God. My mom cleaned houses so she could pay to send her three children to a private Christian school. Her sacrifice spoke volumes to us as children—we knew that God was the most important person in the world, worth every sacrifice!

Although my dad was not a Christian, my mother's love and respect for him enabled us to love and respect our father, as well. We knew who was in charge of our home—dad. His word was the final authority. Yet, we also knew that when it came to the Kingdom of God, we were to look to our mom and our church for direction, and for answers to our spiritual questions. All three of us children are walking with God today, and raising our children to walk with God, too.

When men do not lead spiritually, sometimes women are called to take up the role of spiritual leader. Consider Deborah in the days of the judges. There was no man to lead Israel, so God raised up a woman to do His work. A father's role as the leader of his home is vital to the spiritual well-being of his children. But, what if he is not saved, or is uninterested in growing his faith and leading his family spiritually? Then his wife has to take on the role of spiritual leader in their home. Doing so does not negate her calling to respect and submit to her husband, however. (Remember, Ephesians 5:33 states: "...let the wife see that she respects her husband.")

As wives, we must not be discouraged if our husband is not fulfilling his role as spiritual leader. Instead, we must remember that our faith has influence over our children. Think about all the men and women since the time of Christ who can trace their faith back to the example of their mother. A mother's faith is powerful! Rather than growing dismayed with the state of our husband's relationship with God, we must focus on our own relationship with Him. As we grow in faith, God's love, filling us, will spill over into our husband and our children's lives, encouraging them to thirst for the Living Water that will satisfy their soul. And, when your husband starts to grow in his faith, make sure you allow him to take over the role of spiritual leader in your family.

The Miracle of Submission

I want to make one last plea for submission. If you desire a rich and meaningful marriage, submit. God cares about your marriage, and we can fully trust that He has perfectly ordained the role that you and your husband have within it. He wants to give you a blessed and fulfilling marriage. You might think that it will take a miracle for God to transform your marriage—yet our God is a God of miracles. In fact, His first miracle was at a wedding.

The wedding was in Cana, and there was a shortage of wine. When Mary, Jesus's mother, found out about the lack of wine, she immediately ran to Jesus. She told the servants at the wedding, "Whatever He says to you, do it."(John 2:5). Jesus told them to fill water jars and take some of the water to the master of the feast. When the servants did what Jesus said, they discovered that Jesus had turned the water into the most rich and delicious wine. As a result, Jesus' glory was manifested throughout all of Galilee. If you are looking to turn water into wine in your marriage, follow Mary's advice: "Do what Jesus says." What does Jesus say? He tells wives to "submit unto their husband as unto the Lord" (Ephesians

5:22). Are you willing to submit and watch God perform a miracle in your marriage?

Carol May McClure

Carol May McClure, Michael's grandmother, was one of the most beautiful women I—and everyone who had the privilege to know her—have ever known. She was nominated as USC's Homecoming Queen in 1942, and, soon after, won the heart of her husband, John McClure. Carol radiated beauty from the inside out. Anyone who spent time with her felt loved and special. At Calvary Chapel Costa Mesa, she ran the prayer ministry for thirty years. Carol loved God, His people, and His kingdom.

It was not just Carol's love for God that made her beautiful, however. She was devoted to her husband, John, and adorned herself with submission. John ruled over their home as the leader, and Carol joyfully submitted to his leadership. Their marriage was a beautiful picture of a well-ordered home, and their four children all grew up to become mighty men and women of God. It was also a wonderful picture to the world of God's love for the church. However, their marriage wasn't always that way!

Though she grew up attending church, Carol did not become a Christian until her children were teenagers. Soon after, her husband also received the Lord. At first, Carol grew frustrated and upset at John—his faith was slow to grow, and he wasn't demonstrating it in the way she expected. She began to nag him constantly.

In time, God revealed to Carol that her role wasn't to nag John into becoming the man God had called him to be. Rather, her role was to grow into the woman God had called her to be. She was simply to love and respect John, then move aside, and let God work in him. Over time, Grandpa John grew to be a mighty man of God. He did not become the man Carol expected him to be, a man who taught Bible studies, or led some type of ministry. Instead, he became the man God desired and designed him to be.

John and Carol attended home fellowships. John served on the church board for over twenty-five years. and became a spiritual pillar for his children and grandchildren. On a few occasions, Pastor Chuck Smith said, "If I was going to start a church and could only take one couple with me, it would be John and Carol McClure." Those who knew them would all agree that Carol was "the crown of her husband" (Proverbs 12:4). She not only influenced her husband's faith, but she also inspired all of the McClure children and grandchildren through her example of a godly wife and mother.

Like Hannah, Carol's submission to her husband displayed the power of the Gospel to the world. If we want to transform the lives of those around us, we, too, must demonstrate our faith in God through our submission to our husband. In so proving our faith, our hearts become willing to make any sacrifice necessary for Him—even if He requires our dearest treasure.

Questions to Consider

1. Do you put your husband's needs before your children? Is your identity in being your husband's helper, or in being a mother? If your answer as "in being a mother," what can you do to make your husband more of a priority?

2. In what areas have you not submitted to your husband?

3. Do your children respect your husband? If they do not, what can you do to encourage them to respect him?

4. Are there any areas where you struggle to respect your husband? — Create a list of the things that you are thankful for about your husband and start praising him for those things.

5. How can you use your influence to encourage your husband in his leadership role?

6. Is your husband the leader of your home? If not, how can you restructure your home so he is in his rightful place?

7. Are there any areas that you and your husband not on the same page? How can you work towards getting on the same page (e.g., reading a book together, praying together, making a compromise, going to counseling, etc.)?

Notes

[1] Elisabeth Elliot, *The Shaping of a Christian Family* (Grand Rapids, Michigan: Fleming H. Revell, 1992), 75.

[2] John Piper, "A Vision of Biblical Complementarity: Manhood and Womanhood Defined According to the Bible," *Recovering Biblical Manhood and Womanhood*, John Piper and Wayned Grudem, eds. (Wheaton, Ill.: Crossway Books, 1991), 53.

[3] Wayne Erbsen, *Manners and Morals of Victorian America* (Asheville, North Carolina: Native Ground Books & Music, 2009), 69.

[4] Ruth Bell Graham, *It's My Turn* (Old Tappan, N.J.: Revell, 1982), 74.

[5] Linda Dillow, *Creative Counterpart* (Nashville: Nelson, 2003), *138*.

[6] John Rosemond, *Parenting by the Book* (New York, New York: Howard Books, 2007), 120.

[7] Carolyn Mahaney, *Feminine Appeal* (Wheaton, Illinois: Crossway, 2003), 147.

Hannah's Sacrifice

I prayed for this child, and the LORD has granted me what I asked of him. So now I give him to the LORD. For his whole life he will be given over to the LORD. And she worshiped the LORD there.

1 Samuel 1:27-28

After Samuel was weaned and his training was complete, Hannah prepared for her annual trip to the Tabernacle to celebrate the peace offering. To fulfill this offering, the offerer was required to bring a perfect animal, without blemish, to sacrifice on the altar as a "sweet-smelling aroma" unto the Lord. Both the offerer and the attending priests were given a portion of the offering. The peace offering was meant to be a picture of God and the sinner at peace with each other with all issues between them perfectly settled. Many times, the peace offering was also celebrated as a fulfillment of a vow, as we see in the case of Hannah.

For believers today, the peace offering is a picture of reconciliation, foreshadowing Jesus Christ's death on the cross. It is a picture of "God in the Christ, reconciling the world unto himself, not imputing their trespasses unto them" (2 Corinthians 5:19).

At the Tabernacle, Hannah brought her very best as a sacrifice to the Lord: three bulls, one ephah of flour, a skin of wine—but the dearest sacrifice she brought was Samuel! After slaughtering the bull and burning it upon the altar, Hannah brought Samuel before Eli. She reminded him who she was and the vow she had made to the Lord. Hannah said:

> *Pardon me, my lord. As surely as you live, I am the woman who stood here beside you praying to the LORD. I prayed for this child, and the LORD has granted me what I asked of him. So now I give him to the LORD. For his whole life he will be given over to the LORD.*
>
> —1 Samuel 1:27-28

Can you imagine? Hannah stood before Eli, the High Priest, offering up the dream of her life—Samuel, a young boy of three—as a gift to the Lord. This must have been quite a scene! As she sacrificed her dearest treasure to the Lord, fulfilling the vow she had made, Hannah was not weeping. Rather, she and Samuel were worshiping God!

What a difference from Hannah's last visit to the Tabernacle. Then, she had wept and prayed; now, she brought her offering, the very thing she had prayed for, to the Lord with praise and thanksgiving. Psalm 126:6 declares, "He who continually goes forth weeping, bearing seed for sowing, shall doubtless come again with rejoicing, bringing his sheaves with him." What a beautiful picture of answered prayer!

Hannah worshiped and showed her love for God by giving Samuel to Him. When we do the same thing—as we give our children to God through our words and actions—our sacrifice, too, is a "pleasing aroma" and a demonstration of our love for Him.

Dedicate Your Children

When Hannah said, "I give him to the LORD," she meant that she was dedicating Samuel to a life of service to God. In dedicating her only son to God, Hannah dedicated her entire life and future to God. In reality, Hannah was simply returning her son to the Lord because Samuel was already His! Any gift we give to God is lent from the Lord, as it was His gift in the first place. Matthew Henry, an English preacher, writes: "Whatever we have given to God, it is what we have first asked and then been given by him in the first place. All our gifts to him were first his gifts to us. He will certainly repay it, with interest, to our advantage."[1]

When we consider our own children, we should look at Hannah's example and dedicate them to God as an outward sign of our willingness to "give our children to the Lord." For centuries, Christians have done so, "giving their children back to God," through a dedication ceremony in their home or at their church.

Hannah's Choice

Notice that Samuel was not given a choice. His mom did not ask him if he wanted to live at the Tabernacle and serve God—Hannah knew it was his mission: to serve and glorify God. And, she made every necessary sacrifice to ensure that her son was the Lord's.

Our children, today, should not be given a choice of whether or not they want to be "given to God"—this choice is yours. It is the very reason they were created! As mothers, our job is to ensure that our children know that we have dedicated them to a life of service to God. And it is their destiny to fulfill it.

A Sacrifice of Praise

As Hannah gave her son to God, she did not do it with tears; rather, she gave Samuel to God with thanksgiving in her heart—not only for her son, but also for God allowing her to partake in His plan for humanity. Hannah declares: "My heart rejoices in the LORD; My horn is exalted in the LORD. I smile at my enemies, because I rejoice in Your salvation. (1 Samuel 2:1)

Notice how Hannah magnified God with her song of praise. She did not say, "Isn't my son so cute? Can you believe that God gave me an adorable child, who is so smart and sweet and obedient?" No. She simply gave glory to God! As Matthew Henry notes, Hannah does not...

> commend Samuel for [being] the prettiest child, the most toward and sensible for his age that she ever saw, as fond parents are too apt to do. No, she overlooks the gift, and praises the giver; whereas most forget the giver and fasten only on the gift. Every stream should lead us to the fountain; and the favors were given from God should raise our admiration of the infinite perfections there are in God. There may be other Samuels, but no other Jehovah.[2]

Isn't this convicting? As mothers, I am sure we have all boasted of our children rather than God, who has given us our precious gifts and is doing the work in their lives. Jeremiah reminds us that it is God who deserves all the glory—and if we are going to boast, it should only be in Him!

> Let not the wise man glory in his wisdom, Let not the mighty man glory in his might, Nor let the rich man glory in his riches; but let him who glories glory in this, That he understands and knows Me, That I am the LORD, exercising lovingkindness, judgment, and righteousness in the earth. For in these I delight," says the LORD.
>
> — Jeremiah 9:23-24

Hannah's song (1 Samuel 2:1-10) continues and is full of praises to God for His wonderful attributes: His unspotted purity, His almighty power, His unsearchable wisdom, and His unerring justice. Hannah is a wonderful example, for each of us women, of where to place our affections. When we see God for who He is, there is no sacrifice we are unwilling to make for Him.

Beware of Idolatry

A precious friend received this advice at her baby shower: "A baby is a wonderful addition to a family; not the center of the universe." Often, when God blesses us with children, they easily become the center of our universe—especially for mothers who received a child through a struggle. It would have been easy for Hannah to make an idol out of Samuel due to an excessive love for her son—after all, he was the answer to the longing of her heart.

It would have been easy for her to say, "Lord, I know I committed to give you Samuel, but I think my plan is going to be much better for his life. He needs to grow up at home, where he can live in comfort and be with his family. I will love him and teach him all about You and Your word! After all, the whole country knows about Eli's two wicked sons.

Eli does not know how to raise a godly son. I will raise Samuel for You. Who else will love and take care of him better than his mother?"

Yet, Hannah did not take the easy path! She knew that God needed to be the center of her life, not Samuel. She had faith that God's plan for her son were so much better than any plan she could make. This knowledge and trust was developed through Hannah's years of suffering —as she chose to press into God and make Him the center of her life. C.H. Spurgeon writes about Hannah's song:

> First, she now knew that the heart's truest joy is not in children, nor even in mercies given in answer to prayer, for she began to sing, "My heart rejoices in the Lord" — not "in Samuel," but her chief delight was found in Jehovah. "My horn is exalted in the Lord" — not "in that little one whom I have so gladly brought up to the sanctuary." No. She says in the first verse, "I rejoice in your salvation," and it was even so. God was her great joy, and His salvation her delight. Oh! it is a great thing to be taught to put earthly things in their proper places, and when they make you glad to still feel, "My gladness is in God; not in grain and wine and oil, but in the Lord himself; all my fresh springs are in him.[3]

Too easily, the blessings of this life can become an idol in our life— almost without our knowing it. Often, the only way we become aware that this has happened is our lack of peace. As defined in Websters 1828 dictionary, an idol can be "anything on which we set our affections; that to which we indulge an excessive and sinful attachment." It is anything that usurps the place of God in the our hearts.

As mothers, we can so easily "indulge an excessive and sinful attachment" towards our children, allowing our children to usurp the place of God in our hearts. Our children are made in our image—it can be so easy to take an excessive delight in them and make sacrifices for their pleasure, rather than for God. How do you know when your children have become your idols?

- When their happiness take priority over being obedient to God!

- When you are serving your children with your time, energy, and money—rather than God.

- When your children's friendships, activities, and achievements become more of a priority than God's kingdom!

The problem is that our modern culture pressures moms into making idols of their children. If a mom is not overly involved with the inner workings of her children's life, then she is not considered to be a mother who measures up.

As a young mom, I had to make a decision: to obey God or to choose my children over Him. I had dreams for my life and how I was going to raise my children. These dreams included being completely available for my children. I planned to spend all of my time and energy ensuring their lives were full of joy and complete as they participated in activities, sports, music, and art lessons—you name it! I honestly thought that, in doing these things, my children would have all the characteristics they needed to become the godly children I desired. What a lie foisted upon our culture!

Praise God His wisdom never fails! In daily seeking God and obeying His voice, I found myself in a completely different place than I ever imagined with godly children—not perfect children, as we are definitely a family of sinners, but children who desire to please God.

In retrospect, God revealed to me that my dreams were to build my children's kingdom. However, God wanted my children and me to build His kingdom. He wanted me to make sacrifices for Him, not for my children!

This does not mean that I don't make sacrifices for my children—I cook, clean, wash laundry, sew buttons, wipe noses, clean throw-up, and so much more. However, instead of driving around and watching my children play sports, arranging play-dates with friends, and pouring money into activities for my children to enjoy, I spend my time and energy building God's kingdom with my children.

Our family babysits church children, bakes cookies for our neighbors or a church bake sale, makes centerpieces out of wood for our annual Christmas Coffee, hands out flyers for upcoming church events, attends Bible studies and prayer meetings, practices for mime presentations to share God's love in our church and community, takes music lessons to lead in worship, and helps with whatever the current need is within our church. You see, God wants my children and I to live a life of sacrifice for Him. He does not want me to live a life of sacrifice for my children. What a complete paradigm shift!

As mothers, we must each come to a "Moriah moment" with each of our children. Remember how God asked Abraham to offer up his one and only son, Isaac, his dearest treasure, upon Mount Moriah (Genesis 22:1-18)? God needed to know that He meant more to Abraham than his son, Isaac. Abraham obeyed immediately. Just before he sacrificed his son on the altar at Moriah, God stopped him, providing a ram for the sacrifice. God then knew there was nothing that Abraham would hold back from Him. He knew He could use Abraham to raise up a nation for His glory.

When we give up our children for God—like Abraham and Hannah—God is faithful to give them back to us. When we dedicate and devote them to Him, our children become a greater blessing in our life than we could have ever imagined.

God is a jealous God, and He will not let anything or anyone take His place in our life. If we continually choose our children over Him, we will reap the consequences. Unless we sacrifice our children to Him, God will rip them from our hands in some type of judgement. This judgement may include a broken relationship or a really selfish child, who thinks the world revolves around them. Spurgeon states, "That which we have idolized shall either be broken from us, or we shall be broken off from it."[4] However, if we give our children to God—as a sacrifice of praise—we will receive them back again, as God's children, along with more blessing than we could have ever imagined! The choice is ours.

My mother-in-law, Jean McClure, was born into a lovely, upper class Christian family in Pasadena, California. Her father was a well-renowned surgeon, and she lived a picture perfect life—until she was sent across the country to Florida to attend a private Christian boarding school, Hampden Dubose Academy, in high school. It was so hard for Jean to be away from her parents' love and the comforts of home at such a young age. In fact, since Florida was so far away, she couldn't even make it home for the holidays.

Years later, Jean asked her mother why she was sent away at such a young age. Her mother explained that God had told her to do so—through the life of Hannah. God told her that if she gave up Jean for Him, as Hannah gave up Samuel, then she would receive Jean back again. And, she was right! God did an incredible work in my mother-in-law's life through her schooling. Not only did she learn alongside some of the most precious young ladies from well-known Christian families all over the world, she also met many other friends through the wonderful curriculum she was taught. She fell in love with "greats" like Amy Carmichael—and received a vision for her life: to spend it serving God in full-time Christian service! Jean's boarding school experience was the perfect training ground for her. She has spent years traveling and living out of a suitcase, as she shares the love of Jesus throughout the world.

Is God Enough?
When we make our children our idols, we are basically telling God that He is not enough. Is God enough? He was enough for Hannah! Does your heart exclaim as David's did, "Whom have I in heaven but you? And there is nothing on earth that I desire besides you" (Psalm 73:25). In *You and Me Forever*, Lisa Chan writes, "That giant, all encompassing love we feel for our children should be lost and swallowed up in our love for Jesus."[5]

Jesus is enough to satisfy every longing of our hearts! We do not need to grasp onto the blessings of this life to satisfy our deepest longings. Christ, His life, His cross, His glory is what we need—daily. Samuel Rutherford writes, "I am most joyously content that Christ would break all my idols to bits. It renews my love for Christ to see that he is jealous of my love, and will have all to Himself."[6]

Does the love of Christ satisfy the longings of your heart? If not, consider His sacrifice, and see the love that He demonstrated toward you. Dwell upon His glory and majesty, and praise Him for His attributes! You will soon realize how awesome and worthy He is of all our praise—and of all our sacrifices.

Sacrificing Our Children to Pagan Gods

If God is not enough, and you don't sacrifice your children to Him, they will still end up on an altar, as a sacrifice to a pagan god. The gods of this world constantly pursue us, and desire our worship—and we as humans are created to be worshipers. It is said that every heart has a God-shaped hole that can only be satisfied by God. As mothers, we so often run to the gods of this world in hopes that they can satisfy. And we end up sacrificing our children on their altars as a result.

In the pagan cultures of Old Testament times, babies were literally sacrificed on a fiery altar to the god of Molech. Sacrifices were also made to the gods of Baal, Asheroth, Dagon, and others. Today, our gods are many, and we worship them by sacrificing our precious children on their altars. These gods include: money, pleasure, technology, sex, self, fame, materialism, beauty, and the list goes on. The gods are endless in our culture as modern technology breeds pagan worship.

How do we sacrifice our children to these gods? One obvious way is through abortion. Our culture literally kills babies to worship the gods of sex, beauty, money, and self.

Yet, the other ways we sacrifice our children to these gods are not so obvious. It can happen as a result of our seemingly harmless desire for comfort and ease, wealth and pleasure. We are too busy or too tired to engage our children, and we let technology entertain them; we let movies that are not pleasing to God babysit them. We do not want to disappoint our children, or we do not want to get messy and deal with their tantrums, so we give them everything they ask for.

Michael and I have a heavy burden for children in public schools and would like to make a plea for parents to consider sending their children to Christian school or homeschooling. Children spend more awake hours at school than with us at home. When they go to schools that do not teach our Lord's values, they spend time being trained in the carnal and pagan ways of the world that goes against the Lord's values we are trying to instill in them. Ray Comfort pleads with Christian parents by stating, "If you are sending your children to a secular school, do you realize that you are handing them over to the world? You are saying to the ungodly, "Train up my child."[7] In sending our children to public school, we inadvertently put our children on the altar of the pagan god. I know this is hard, but it must be recognized. Today's generation of Christian children are being sacrificed to the gods of this world and they are being swallowed up by it.

When we worship the gods of this world—and sacrifice our children in the process—we miss out on the blessing of godly children! The big lie of our culture is that it is no big deal.   It is not that bad.   This lie, however, is merely justification of our actions.   Many believe their children are going to be a Christian influence to their non-Christian families. However, "Many Christian children in government schools are converted to an anti-Christian worldview rather than evangelizing their school mates."[8] If we allow our children to be sacrificed to pagan gods, we cannot be surprised when they grow up, wanting nothing to do with the "living God"—and end up sacrificing their children to false gods as well.

Bind the Sacrifice

Hannah told Eli, "as long as he lives he shall be lent to the LORD!" (1 Samuel 1:28). She meant that, after she gave Samuel as an offering, that was it. She wasn't coming to take him back.

Like, Hannah we need to give our children to God and not take them back. So often, we give our children to God—only to take them off of the altar and interfere with what God wants to do in their life! Our sacrifice of our children to God is not a one time offering, where we give them to God and then take them home to do whatever we please. No. It is a continual offering made unto the Lord. How do we do this? We bind our children to the altar.

When an animal sacrifice was brought to the altar, it was a living sacrifice. The priests were commanded to "Bind the sacrifice with cords, even unto the horns of the altar" (Psalm 118:27). Then, they would kill the sacrifice and burn it, offering a "sweet-smelling aroma" unto the Lord.

As moms, we must realize that our children are "living sacrifices." We, too, need to tie our children to the horns of the altar and not let them escape from the fire! Their very life depends upon it.

In Homer's epic, *The Odyssey*, we read the story of Odysseus' ten-year journey home to Greece after the Trojan War.   During his long journey at sea, he encounters all sorts of creatures and gods, who try to capture him and keep him from returning home to his wife, Penelope.

At one point, Odysseus's ship sails by the place where the Sirens dwelt.   These monsters lured men away through beautiful music and promises to make the men wise.   Once the Sirens captured a man, however, their wives and children would never see them again—all that was left were their bones with flesh still rotting out of them thrown into a heap.

Knowing the danger he was about to encounter, Odysseus ordered his men to put wax in their ears. Desiring to hear Sirens' beautiful music for himself, Odysseus had his men tie him up to the mast of his ship, so he could hear their captivating voices but not be ensnared by them. As the ship sailed past the island, Odysseus heard the beautiful music and longed to go to the Sirens. He begged his men to untie him from the mast; instead, his determined and homesick men bound him all the tighter!

In the same way, we must tie our children to the "mast," so they will not be enticed away by foreign gods from the "living God" to whom their life is committed. The gods of this world constantly call for us to turn aside and worship them; their lusts war against our soul. Our hearts are idol magnets, and the only way we can enable our children to stand against the pressure of the gods of this culture is to bind them to the altar.

We can do so when we refuse to allow our children to partake in things that are not pleasing to God. Our children are a "living sacrifice" unto God, and as such, they must live a life of self-sacrifice, pleasing to God to whom they have been given! They are to be set-apart and holy.

Another way we can bind our children to the altar is by allowing God to have His perfect way in the lives of our children! We might need to allow our children to walk through something really hard—like Hannah did, in allowing Samuel to be raised at the Tabernacle. However, if we truly desire to raise children who belong to God, we must allow God's will to rule in our children's lives.

We can also continually bind our children to God's altar through prayer. It is only in daily surrendering our children to the Lord through prayer that we are able to allow Him to accomplish His will in our child's life. Matthew Henry writes: "Note, those that have in sincerity devoted their children to God (with a vow) may with comfort pray for them, that God will establish the word sealed to them at the same time that they were sealed for him."[9]

As mothers who have given our children to God, we ought to pray for God's will to be done in our children's lives. We should ask Him to make them godly young men and women, who love the Lord with all their heart. We need to pray for the strength to daily bind our children upon the altar. Then, when we watch our children suffer or endure hard things, we need to ask God to help us not jump onto the altar and untie their cords or set them free.

We must not meddle with the work God is doing in our children's lives. They have been called to "present their bodies a living sacrifice, holy, acceptable to God, which is their reasonable service" (Romans 12:1). Our job, as mothers, is to train them, teach them, coach them, love them, pray for them—not meddle! In binding our children to the altar, we show them the blessings of partaking in the sufferings of Christ, and our children will come to see sacrifice as a vital part of their Christian life.

Binding your child to the altar may sound a bit morbid, but it is truly a beautiful picture when we look at it through the lens of the cross. Our precious Lord, Jesus Christ, became the ultimate sacrifice when He willingly gave up His life on the cross of Calvary for the sins of the world. He was the "living sacrifice" tied to the horns of the altar. It was His hands and feet that were nailed to the cross—and He bears the marks of His sacrifice unto this day! Christ must be our example, as He calls each and every one of His followers to be a "living sacrifice."

As mothers, it is difficult to see our children bear the marks of the cords that tie their hands and feet to the altar. Yet, all of Jesus' disciples will bear the marks of the cross if they are truly following Him. It is much better for our children to bear the marks of living for Christ, than to bear scars from being chewed up and spit out by the world—because we untied them from the altar.

For me, dedicating my children to God is easy. They are His, and I want God to be glorified in their lives. However, watching God work in them is so much harder! I want to go to the altar, untie my children, and meddle in the things God wants to do in their lives. Yet, God calls me to, daily, put my children on the altar and allow Him to do with my children as He chooses! He does not want me to pray for my children's comfort, ease, or happiness. Instead, I am to pray for Him to accomplish His will in their lives, for their character to grow through hardship, so they might be used to serve God to the fullest. Amy Carmichael writes: "If I refuse to allow one who is dear to me to suffer for the sake of Christ, if I do not see such suffering as the greatest honor that can be offered to any follower of the Crucified, then I know nothing of Calvary love."[10] This is very counter-cultural, but, it is the message of the cross! Jesus says, in Luke 14:26-27: "If anyone comes to me and does not hate his own father and and wife and children and brothers and sisters, yes, and even his own life, he cannot be my disciple. Whoever does not bear his own cross and come after me cannot be my disciple."

Remember, our greatest mission as moms is to train our children to become disciples of Jesus. Jesus says, "If you cannot bear your own cross and come after Me, you cannot be My disciple." As we bind our children to the altar, they will create habits of denying themselves, enduring hard things, and making sacrifices for God.

You might be thinking, "I can't do that! My children will rebel!" However, if you are raising your children in a loving home, where Christ presence reigns supreme- your children can not help but to surrender to such a great love!

As our children grow, we should slowly start loosening the cords that bind them to the altar. By the time we untie them fully, they should be so trained that they do not think it strange or burdensome when they must pick up their cross and follow Jesus—because they have had a lifetime of training towards this end. When we remember our mission, it becomes easy to bind our children to the altar and keep them there.

My Sacrifice: Daniel John McClure

In raising my own children, I have had to daily bind them to the altar and refuse to make them my idols. I, too, feel the pressure of the culture, and it is only through the power of the Holy Spirit that I am able to sacrifice them on the altar. I have to spend time with God, daily, to get the perspective and grace I need to be the mom God has called me to be.

As I mentioned before, I gave my children to God before they were conceived, especially my first son, Daniel. When he was born, he was the fulfillment of my hearts desire. While I knew that he belonged to God, Daniel became my idol, as can so easily happen with a first child. Unlike Hannah, I did not worship the Giver, but rather the gift. Thankfully, as more children came—along with a lot of responsibility—I was forced to turn to God and worship Him rather than my children. Praise God for His faithfulness in my life!

Michael and I dedicated Daniel, as a baby, before our precious congregation as an outward declaration that he belongs to God. His name means "God is my gracious judge," and we have reminded him of his name many times. Daniel knows that his life has been dedicated to God for His service, and our prayer is that God will continue to reveal His perfect will to our son—and that he will walk in it.

Every year, on Daniel's birthday, we re-dedicate him to God. We anoint him with oil and, as a family, lay hands on him and pray for him. We ask God to accomplish His will through Daniel's life, and we remind Him that his purpose and destiny is to glorify God in all that he does.

As parents, we have had to give Daniel to God over and over again. Our first big test was when Daniel was two. I had just delivered Micah a week prior, when my brother-in-law, Mike, came over to tell me that Daniel had had a terrible wagon accident. He had split open his head and had a concussion! We took Daniel to the emergency. He needed stitches and a brain scan. I remember crying out to God in the car, "We prayed that you would protect Daniel only a few minutes ago while having dinner, why didn't You answer?" God spoke to my heart, "Brenda, I did." In that moment, I realized that something far worse could have happened, but God was watching over my firstborn son. In that moment, I had to give Daniel back to God, trusting that His ways were much higher than mine.

About six months later, we realized there was something wrong when Daniel was still not talking. Shortly thereafter, he was diagnosed with Apraxia. I wondered, "Is he going to be able to talk normally? Will this affect how he thinks?" and so on. I was heart-broken, and very fearful for his future. My dreams for Daniel's life seemed to all be crashing down, but that was when I had to place Daniel back onto the altar. I had to realize that God was in control, and He was going to accomplish His perfect will in Daniel's life.

When I took Daniel to the Lord, He spoke the most amazing word to me through a devotional by C.H. Spurgeon. In Exodus 4:12, the Lord said to Moses, "Now therefore go, and I will be with thy mouth, and teach thee what thou shalt say." Spurgeon expounded upon this verse:

> *Many a true servant of the Lord is slow of speech... In such a case it is well to remember that the Lord made the tongue which is so slow, and we must take care that we do not blame our Maker. It may be that a slow tongue is not so great an evil as a fast one... Pharaoh had more reason to be afraid of stammering Moses than of the most fluent talker in Egypt: for what he said*

had power in it: he spoke plagues and deaths. If the Lord be with us in our natural weakness we shall be girt with supernatural power. Therefore, let us speak for Jesus boldly, as we ought to speak.[11]

Basically, God reminded me that He had made Daniel's tongue, and He was going to use my son's weakness for His glory! Daniel would speak, but it will be through His power. Daniel is now eighteen, and he has become God's mouthpiece as he teaches children's ministry, leads worship, and performs in plays. Because we laid him on the altar, God's will - not mine - has directed Daniel's life.

Then came the middle school years. Daniel is a very eccentric child, and he had nothing in common with the boys in his middle school classes. The boys would tease him for fun, and he did not feel like he had any friends. Daniel was an emotional wreck, crying all the time. As his mom, it was really hard to watch.

One day, I decided I was going to pull Daniel out of our school—the one we started at our church. I told Michael, and he very quickly set my heart straight, telling me, "We are not pulling Daniel out of school. This is the best thing for Daniel. He needs to learn this lesson now if he is going to be a leader. Why would we send him to a school that is not teaching the curriculum he needs just so he can have different friends? Friends are not the most important thing—it is how God is growing him through this situation. His friends are his brothers. God is doing a work."

Praise God for a husband who kept me from meddling in Daniel's life! Michael and I made a commitment to take this situation to God in prayer, allowing Him to accomplish His will through Daniel. We prayed that he would grow through the situation and learn how to be a good friend, and God answered our prayer. Today, we look back at those middle school years as a precious gift from God in Daniel's life.

Throughout the years, we have had so many little battles with Daniel, as he pressured us to untie the cords that bound him to the altar. We have had battles over his obsession over the spider-man costume, the Nintendo DS we would not let him buy with his birthday money, the fact that he was the only student at school without a cell phone, the shows he couldn't watch, the clothes he wore, the events he couldn't attend, the people he couldn't hang out with! We constantly told him, "Daniel, go read your Bible!" Our desire was not to please Daniel, but was to keep him on the altar, allowing him to become the man God wanted him to be.

Daniel's sinful nature wanted to run to the gods of this world, but we had to teach Him to dwell on the altar of the living God. Today, Daniel looks back on the past eighteen years and thanks us. I must tell you—it took a lot of resolve to not give in to the pressure of our son, the gods of this world, and the culture!

This past year, God had called Daniel to attend a year-long missions program for his senior year of high school. It was the completion of his training in our home before he turned eighteen and become an adult.

Being a Samuel, Daniel obeyed God's call. Two weeks into the program, away from home for the first time, he called home crying. Daniel missed us; it was so hard for him. My heart broke! I wanted to jump on a plane and go pick him up! As I was praying for Daniel and working on this book, the Lord spoke to my heart, saying, "Brenda, I didn't ask you to drop off Daniel at the age of three. I am asking you to drop him off at seventeen." What a wonderful reminder, that if God could ask Hannah to physically give up her one and only son to the Lord at the age of three, I could obey as well.

Are You Willing?

My question for you, today, is this: do you love God enough to give your children to Him? Is your heart so full of gratitude that you are willing to give up the gift for the Giver?

In a sense, Hannah's son foreshadows Jesus. Samuel was the perfect, longed for son, who was sacrificed by his mother to save a nation. Similarly, our loving God gave up His one and only Son to die on the cross of Calvary as the ultimate sacrifice for the sins of humanity. He gave us His Son so that we can willingly give up ours for Him! Are you willing to give up your son or daughter to be used by God to accomplish His plan for the world?

God will never ask something of us, that He has not already done for us. In the words of C.T. Studd, the famous Indian and African missionary: "If Jesus Christ is God and died for me, then no sacrifice can be too great for me to make for Him." Knowing what Christ suffered and gave up on our behalf should enable us to willingly lay down our precious children as a sacrifice to Him.

Hannah's delight was in God, and she willingly gave her precious, longed-for son to Him as her very best offering. The result: She received him back again—not just as a son, but a man whom God used to transform a nation. We can trust our children to God. In fact, our legacy depends upon it!

Questions to Consider

1. When have you given your children to God?

2. Are you willing to give your children to God? If so, say a prayer now, committing to do so.

3. How are you and your children building God's kingdom together?

4. Are you sacrificing your children to false gods? If so, how?

5. In what area of your children's life do you continually meddle?

6. In what areas do you struggle with making your children your idol(s):

   • When their happiness take priority over being obedient to God?

   • When you are serving your children with your time, energy, and money—rather than God?

   • When your children's friendships, activities, and achievements become more of a priority than His kingdom?

7. Is God enough for you? If your answer is no, how can you daily allow God to satisfy the desires of your heart?

Notes

[1] Matthew Henry, *Matthew Henry's Commentary of the Bible, Volume II* (New York: Fleming H. Revell Company, 1708), 283.

[2] Ibid., 284.

[3] C.H. Spurgeon. "A Woman of A Sorrowful Spirit," in *The Metropolitan Tabernacle Pulpit Sermons Preached and Revised by C.H. Spurgeon During the Year 1880*, Volume 26 (Pasadena, Texas: Pilgrim Publications: 1980), 44-45.

[4] C.H. Spurgeon, *Cheque Book of the Bank of Faith* (Great Britain:Christian Focus Publications, 1996), 304.

[5] Francis Chan & Lisa Chan, *You and Me Forever; Marriage In Light Of Eternity* (San Francisco, California: Claire Love Publishing, 2014), 176.

[6] Nick Harrison, Editor, *His Victorious Indwelling; Daily Devotions for a Deeper Christian Life* (Grand Rapids, Michigan: Zondervan, 1998), 23.

[7] Ray Comfort, *How To Bring Your Children to Christ and Keep Them There* (Bartlesville, Oklahoma: Genesis Publishing Group), 150.

[8] Ibid.

[9] Henry, *Matthew Henry's Commentary of the Bible*, 282.

[10] Amy Carmichael, *If* (Fort Washington, Pennsylvania: Christian Literature Crusade, 1938), 66.

[11] Spurgeon, *Cheque Book of the Bank of Faith,* 215.

Hannah's Pearls of Wisdom

My son, hear the instruction of your father,
And do not forsake the law of your mother;
For they will be a graceful ornament on your head,
And chains about your neck.

Proverbs 1:8-9

My daughter Hannah loves pearls. In fact, she has worn them nearly all her life. Someone gave her a set up bubblegum pearls when she was three, and she never took them off. She wore them when she went to bed, took a bath, and even when she went swimming. Eventually, after a few years, they broke. We keep having to buy her new ones. At any rate, Hannah looks stunning in pearls; they are a graceful chain around her neck.

When we follow the wisdom gleaned from the life of Hannah, our spiritual mother, we too can look stunning, graced with a ring of pearls around our neck. How do we look stunning? We glorify God, and reap the blessings of raising children who bring glory and honor to God. There is no greater compliment or honor someone could possibly give me than to tell me that one of my children blessed them in some way!

As I have studied the life of Hannah, God has revealed several insights into parenting that Michael and I have implemented in our home. Our desire, more than anything else, is for our children to be God's voice—modern day prophets to this lost and dying world. We want them to be men and women set apart for the work of God. If you, like Michael and I, long for your children to bring repentance to our nation—to be men and women, who are willing to decrease so He might increase—then you, too, must make necessary sacrifices like Hannah!

In this next section, I have listed twelve pearls of wisdom I have gleaned from studying the life of Hannah. Please note that these parenting insights are not all-inclusive or absolute. The truths found within this book are meant to be implemented with the leading of God's Spirit. As you do, God will work in and through your family, impacting your children in ways you could not even imagine!

These pearls are also meant to be understood as a comprehensive whole, not out of context, just as the message and wisdom from Hannah is only understood if we recognize the big picture. For example, binding our children to the altar will only work if we are allowing them to grow before God's presence. Otherwise, our children will rebel. We are to discipline our children and have them live without, but with, God's amazing sacrificial love through it all! If we do not have love, only rules and regulations, our children will only resent us!

Michael and I are still finding new ways to more fully implement these truths in our family, and we are always discovering new wisdom as we continue to study the way Hannah raised Samuel. We pray that Hannah's "pearls," and the examples of how we have applied them to our family, will be a blessing to you as you seek to raise godly children for His glory!

Pearl of Wisdom #1

Live a Life of Faith

Charm is deceitful and beauty is passing,
But a woman who fears the Lord, she shall be praised.

Proverbs 31:30

Hannah's faith in God was the most important influence in Samuel's life. Without her faith, she would not have been the mother the people of Israel needed to raise a man who would transform their nation. Hannah's faith was not just a set of beliefs; it was a way of life. She demonstrated her great faith when she poured out her heart to God in prayer at the Tabernacle; when she vowed to give her son to God; when she remembered her vow, and gave Him her most treasured possession, Samuel; and when she trusted God enough to leave Samuel at the Tabernacle year after year.

Hannah's faith was a huge part of Samuel's life—he must have known how much his mother longed for him, yet she still gave him to God. Every day, Samuel lived with the realization that his mom loved God more than him. Her faith transformed his life! In fact, the faith of Hannah directly influenced Samuel throughout his entire life—even though he only spent a few, short years with his mother.

A Mother's Faith

When we consider all the characteristics and accomplishments we might possess as women today, the only thing that really matters is our faith in God. Proverbs 30:31, states: "Charm is deceitful and beauty is passing, but a woman who fears the Lord, she shall be praised." A mother who fears God more than anything is a most powerful force to be reckoned with. It has been said that "there is no higher height to which humanity can attain than that occupied by a converted, heaven-inspired, praying mother."[1]

Throughout history, there are thousands of examples of how a mother's faith transformed her child's life. Consider the Old Testament: The faith of Moses's mother, Jocobed, enabled her to trust her son to God. Recognizing that Moses was an extraordinary child, she hid him for a time before placing him in a floating basket on the Nile River, where he was found by Pharaoh's daughter. By God's grace, Jocobed was able to continue nursing her son, training him during his first few years in Pharaoh's palace—launching his life on a mission to save the nation of Israel.

In the New Testament, Elizabeth, the mother of John the Baptist, raised a son whose mission was to prepare the way for the Lord. Elizabeth's faith helped shape John, so that his soul's desire was for God to increase as he decreased (John 3:30).

The faith and fervent prayers of Monica, the mother of St. Augustine of Hippo, were instrumental in bringing her son to the Lord. Mary Ball Washington, the mother of George Washington, raised her children alone after her husband died. She read Bible stories to them every evening as they sat on the tiles in front of the fireplace. Charles Spurgeon's mother, Eliza, read the Bible to her children every Sunday evening and pled with them to give their lives to Christ. Her faithfulness and many prayers were instrumental in shaping the "Prince of Preachers."

In my own life, Michael and I have both been blessed with godly mothers—and on Michael's side, two grandmothers—who rose daily at five a.m. to spend time in God's Word and prayer. What a legacy of faith we have been given! And, what a grave example for us to set and follow!

What Is Faith?

Once we confess our sins and receive Jesus Christ as Lord over our life (1 John 1:9), we become women of faith. Romans 10:9 says "that if you confess with your mouth the Lord Jesus and believe in your heart that God has raised Him from the dead, you will be saved." As Christians, we are called to live a life of faith—no longer living to satisfy our flesh, but now living to please the Lord (Hebrews 11:6). "But without faith it is impossible to please Him, for he who comes to God must believe that He is, and that He is a rewarder of those who diligently seek Him."

My favorite definition of faith is "complete trust in God", no matter what happens. Faith is belief that God is in control and will accomplish all that He has promised in His word. "Faith is not a sense, nor sight, nor reason, but taking God at His word."[2] F.B. Meyer writes, "There is no kind of need, trial, persecution, experience, for which faith is not the sufficient answer! It is the master key for every lock of difficulty."[3]

Our faith demands action. Faith without works is no faith at all. There is a famous old saying that, "When faith goes to market, it always takes a basket."[4] Meaning, we have to trust God to work in our life and live in a way of expectancy - always confident in our God, who is faithful to His word.

When we lack faith, what are we supposed to do? Ask God for more faith, and go straight to His Word! When we read God's Word, our faith is strengthened. As we continue to live our lives in faith, we grow, and so does our faith. Faith is like a muscle: the more we exercise it, the stronger it becomes. I love what C.H. Spurgeon writes regarding faith: "Little faith will bring your souls to heaven, but great faith will bring heaven to your souls."[5]

Faith In Action

What is the opposite of faith? Fear, doubt, anxiety, frustration, shrinking back, and giving up. Consider for a moment the amount of faith it must have taken for Hannah to drop Samuel off to be raised in the Tabernacle, where wickedness was rampant. She could have easily kept Samuel at home out of fear—who knew what would happen at the Tabernacle with Eli and his sons in charge! However, Hannah didn't allow her fear to overcome her faith. She trusted God with her dearest possession despite the circumstances. What faith!

As mothers, we need to make decisions for our children out of faith, not fear, as Hannah did. If we find ourselves full of fear, we are not trusting Christ. Hebrews 10:37-39 reads:

> For in just a little while, and He who is coming will come and will not tarry. Now the just shall live by faith; but if anyone draws back, My soul has no pleasure in him. But we are not of those who draw back to perdition, but of those who believe to the saving of the soul.

Fear and faith cannot coexist! We cannot be women of faith while living in fear. The Bible declares that "perfect love casts out fear" (1 John 4:18).

As mothers, we must be women of faith if we want to impart our faith to our children. If we live in fear, our children will recognize that our faith is not real—and they will not want anything to do with it! We must remember that our faith directly impacts our children. Faith is caught, not taught. We cannot expect our children to be amazing Christians, totally set apart for God, passionate for His word, loving with the things He loves and hating the things He hates, if we do not lead by example. Children learn, not just through the things we say, but also by what we do. Our faith should be producing fruit that spills over into our children's lives.

Remember, as mothers, our goal is to disciple our children and teach them how to live a life of faith. Jesus said, "A disciple is not above his teacher, but everyone who is perfectly trained will be like his teacher" (Luke 6:40). Our children cannot escape our example—it is their teacher, whether we recognize it or not!

My sweet Ruth, who is two, constantly pushes the kitchen chair to the counter so she can open the cupboard and grab my spices. She, then, takes spoons out of my drawer, opens the spices, and pours them into cups and bowls, making a complete mess. Yet, I know what she is doing! She wants to cook, just like mommy. What a constant reminder Ruth is to me: my children watch my every step and follow my example. What they do is a mirror of what they see in my life—for good and bad.

Building Faith

Too Busy for God?

Often, I hear mothers of young children say, "I am too busy to read my Bible, go to Bible Study, or faithfully attend church." Years ago, at a conference, I sat in a small group session, where we talked about what our devotional life looks like. I remember hearing a pastor's wife with four little children say she did not have time to read God's Word. I wondered, "How does she do it? She is raising four children in the ministry, and she doesn't need to read God's Word?" Well, years have passed, and sadly her children's lives are a shipwreck; they are in and out of prison, have children out of wedlock, addicted to drugs and alcohol.

As mothers, we often so busy ourselves in the seasons of parenting that we end up not having time for God. We think, "Oh well, I'll have time for Him when the children are older." However, it is when we are raising our children that we need God the most. We make decisions every day that affect our children's eternal destiny. Our children watch us with precious, little eyes, seeing where our true priorities lie. Everything is at stake when they are young—everything!

When we have children, we do not have the time or luxury to *not* be in God's Word or in His presence. This is the time that we need His wisdom the most. It does not take long to figure out that children do not come with a manual; we need God's Spirit to give us wisdom and guidance to raise the precious children He has given us.

When we think that we are busy, we must remember how busy our Lord Jesus was during His ministry on earth. In the midst of His busy life, He made time for His Father. In John, after Jesus spent the whole day ministering, He woke up early the next morning to spend time with God. If Jesus, God in flesh, needed to spend time in in His Father's presence, how much more do we?

Growing Faith

We are commanded to pursue faith. Second Timothy 2:22 states, "Flee also youthful lusts; but pursue righteousness, faith, love, peace with those who call on the Lord out of a pure heart." The word *pursue* means "to run after." We are commanded to run after and diligently seek faith. As mothers today, it is easy to occupy our time with "youthful lusts" through the escape that technology brings into our homes. We must be careful to not put these things that come easily—"youthful lusts"—before the things that are most important—pursuing faith in our Lord Jesus Christ.

As Christian women, it is imperative that we continue to grow in our faith in God. We will never have perfect faith until we are with our Savior in glory; but until then, we must remain teachable, willing to learn new things and grow in our relationship with Him. Greg Laurie, pastor of Harvest Ministries, states: "The Christian life is one of progression, growth, and constant change. The simple fact is that you are either moving forward as a believer or you are moving backward."[6] As women of faith, we should be looking forward to opportunities to grow our faith! We should be faithful at church, in reading God's Word and prayer. As our churches hold events, as much as possible, be eager to attend so we might grow our faith! Retreats, coffees, teas, Bible studies and the sort should be something we look forward to, rather than avoiding.

As I train my children, one thing that is really impactful is the understanding that I can never take my children further than I have gone myself. If I want my children to live lives of faith, then I must first live a life of faith myself. With that said, I am so grateful for the lessons I have learned and my past failures, for they have allowed me to grow in my relationship with God. Now, I can pass these lesson down to my children and the other young people I teach. If I want them to be teachable and grow in their relationship with God, they must first see an example of a life of faith that is growing in Christ in me.

How do we grow our faith? We grow in faith as we receive instruction at church and fellowship with others, as we seek God through prayer and the reading and obeying of His word.

Making Church a Priority

If we desire to grow our faith—and build up the faith of our children—it is important that we make church a priority in our life. In Hebrews 10:34-35, we are commanded to: "...consider one another in order to stir up love and good works, not forsaking the assembling of ourselves together, as is the manner of some, but exhorting one another, and so much the more as you see the Day approaching." God has created the institution of the church as a place where we gather together as believers and worship Him. While assembling together, we are called to fellowship in Christ as we glean from His Word, worship Him, and encourage one another in Christ. It should be the most precious time throughout our week and a day we look forward to with anticipation.

It is amazing to me how much the attitude of our culture has changed in regards to church attendance, even among Christians. In Elisabeth Elliot's book, *The Shaping of a Christian Family*, she paints a picture of what life was like on a Sunday when she was growing up. She explains that on the Lord's Day:

> *We always went to Sunday School, and we always went to church. Of course. These are public means of grace, and there was never any discussion about our going, any more than about family prayers or any of the regular habits our parents kept. Wherever the Lord's people were gathered together, there we were supposed to be.*[7]

What a contrast with the attitude of believers today! Today, people don't feel a need to be in church on a regular basis for a number reasons.

Rather than a commandment to obey, many people believe that going to church is a "good idea"—if the weather doesn't call for a day at the park or the beach, if our children are not playing a sports game, if we don't have any projects going on at the house, or if we have had enough "me" time already during the weekend.

Whenever we skip church, we not only miss out on an opportunity for God to minister to us, but we are also teaching our children that church is optional—only a good idea.

I remember walking to church in the rain with my mother as a little girl because our car had broken down. My mother's dedication in attending church impacted me greatly and instilled in me an understanding of the importance of going to church each week. To this day, I cannot skip church even when I am on vacation!

God commands us to have regular fellowship with other believers. I can't tell you how many times I have gone to church, and had my whole perspective change by the time I walk out the doors. Whether it is the worship, the message from the Word, or the encouragement we receive from others in the fellowship, church is transformative in our lives!

However, there are times when we cannot be in fellowship because of illness. I remember a time when my children were little and not being able to go to church for weeks because of sick children. It was really hard to be the one who stayed home—as Michael was the pastor—week after week, caring for our sick little ones. What I really needed during those weeks was fellowship with believers, as well as God's Word and perspective in my life! Matthew Henry encourages women, who have to stay home with children during this early season, by stating:

> *Those that are detained from public ordinances by the nursing and tending of little children may take comfort from this instance, and believe that, if they do that with an eye to God, he will graciously accept them therein, and though they tarry at home they shall divide the spoil.*[8]

How encouraging that there are blessings in store for mothers who have to stay home and take care of their little ones! And, praise God for modern technology and the ability to live stream a church service or listen to a podcast at a later time, so we don't have to miss out on being fed the Word of God. But, we should be careful to not let these things replace regular church attendance. Fellowship with believers only takes place when we attend the service.

Today, there are many precious parents whose children no longer attend church. Perhaps they were saved later in life, or their children decided, after moving out of their house, to no longer attend church. How heartbreaking! We must remember that we only have our children for a short time—and we must use that time wisely. By choosing to attend church regularly and make it a priority, we are not only forming our children's character, we are also instilling in them a habit for life. A habit that they will need all the more as our world becomes increasingly dark.

In our home, we have this saying, "When you feel like not going to church the most; that is when you need it the most." And isn't that so true? The crazy thing is that, when we obey God and go to church when we don't feel like it, we are always blessed more than we could have imagined!

If we don't make church a priority in our lives, our children will not think that God is the most important person in our life. So, be excited about church. Tell your children that it is a privilege to go to church, as so many people around the world do not have the same freedom and blessing.

Read God's Word

One way we can increase our faith is to spend time in God's Word daily. Romans 10:17 tells us that "faith comes by hearing and hearing by the word of God." The more time we spend in God's Word, the greater our faith grows—and the bigger impact it can have in our children's lives. As we read God's Word, He speaks to us. He convicts us of our sin; He gives us wisdom and insight into different situations; He encourages our heart, gives us perspective, and leads and directs us—especially as we make decisions that pertain to our children. When we read God's Word and obey it, we will grow in faith.

Too often I hear moms say, "I am so busy being a mom that I don't have any time to spend in His Word!" Often, these same moms can find the time for Facebook or surfing the internet. I have found that whenever I have neglected God's Word and run from one thing to the next, my longings are never satisfied. It is not until I open up God's Word and allow Him to speak to me that my soul is satisfied and my perspective changed. At times like these, I always think, "Why didn't I just go to God's Word in the first place?" What we all need to remember is that our hearts are idol magnets, and only God and His Word will satisfy the deepest longings of our heart!

It is easy for Christian women to run to the internet, rather than their Bible, for spiritual food. They look up their spiritual horoscope, the verse of the day, popular Christian books and blogs, entertaining speakers and devotional podcasts—and think they have spent quality time with God. While turning to technology might be the norm for our culture, it is not going to enable us to be the moms our children need us to be; it will not enable us to raise modern-day Samuels. We need to have a solid time of daily Bible reading to accomplish our God-given mission as moms!

It is important that we realize that our faith will not grow unless we spend time reading God's Word. Moreover, our children will not spend time in God's Word if we do not! We cannot expect ourselves or our children to have faith in God, a biblical worldview, or the wisdom needed to live this life for His glory, if we do not read God's Word. Going to church is not enough, we must also be in God's Word. If reading God's

Word has not been a regular habit, I would suggest that you start reading the Gospels: Matthew, Mark, Luke, and John. These books will help you experience Jesus firsthand, as you read about His life and teachings. If you read one chapter a day, you will finish each book in about a month. They say it only takes thirty days to form a habit. From there, I would finish reading the New Testament before moving back to Genesis.

Sometimes, I find it hard to get through certain sections of scriptures —like Leviticus. When I find myself reading the same paragraphs over and over again, I use a Bible app and follow along in my Bible as it reads it aloud to me. You will be amazed at how many chapters you can read when you are following along as someone reads to you! One day, I was shocked to realize I had read through fifteen chapters in 2 Kings! The chapters were so juicy that it seemed like mere minutes had passed!

Another suggestion I have is to choose a Bible translation that is easy to understand, like a New King James Bible. In the past, I have also used the *Life Application Bible*. This translation has maps and notes at the bottom of each page, so I can more easily understand what I am reading. I have found that taking the time to get into God's word every day is the fight of my life! Our flesh wants what is comfortable and easy, yet in order to spend time in God's word we need to be disciplined.

When my children were little, especially during the years when I wasn't sleeping at night and still nursing babies, I would leave Bibles and devotional books all around the house. Then, whenever I had a spare moment, I would take a little break to read my Bible or a short devotional to get a little "fix." I would also listen to praise music throughout the day. Sometimes, Michael and I would turn on a Bible movie for our children at strategic times so that I could have personal time with God. I also made sure I attended Bible studies, so I would be forced to dig deep into God's Word throughout the week—and there was free babysitting! Many times, when Michael would come home from work, he would watch the kids and allow me to spend some time in the bedroom or at a local coffee shop, where I would work on my Bible study or just spend time in the Word. Today, I have made a deal with myself, that I am not allowed to look at my email or the news without first spending time in God's Word. I also make sure that I don't keep my phone in my room at night when I sleep, so when I wake up I am forced to spend time in God's Word rather than enabling technology to be a priority in my life. There is really no excuse for moms not to be in God's Word—it is just a matter of managing our priorities.

This past spring, I woke up early one morning to spend time reading the Bible. I walked into the living room to find three of my children, cuddled in blankets on the couch and on the floor heaters, reading their Bibles. As I made coffee, I asked God in absolute awe, "What did I do to deserve this?" And, He so clearly spoke to my heart, "Faith is not taught; it is caught."

Take Time to Pray

Taking time to pray is another way we demonstrate and build our faith. Many women think, "I don't have time to pray." However, it has been said that "No praying man or woman accomplishes so much with so little expenditure of time as when he or she is praying."[9] By making a daily habit of prayer, we demonstrate that we believe and trust in God. In doing so, we can change the course of eternity. James 5:16 says, "The prayer of a righteous man is powerful and effective." As moms, we must realize that a prayer-less life is a powerless life. Prayer is a vital part of a Christian's life. It not only allows us to have fellowship with God, it also gives us a fresh vision of our Father, renews our strength, and changes the destiny of people's lives, especially our children's!

Years ago I read a book by Jill Briscoe titled *Prayer that Works*. In it, she explains that "prayer that works takes work!" Isn't that the truth! However, over time it becomes easier. C.H. Spurgeon writes:

> *No doubt by praying we learn to pray, and the more we pray the oftener we can pray, and the better we can pray. He who prays in fits and starts is never likely to attain to that effectual, fervent prayer that availeth much. Great power in prayer is within our reach, but we must go to work to obtain it. Let us never imagine that Abraham could have interceded so successfully for Sodom if he had not been all his lifetime in the practice of communion with God.[10]*

I know many women get overwhelmed at the idea of praying. They think that, unless they pray a certain way, their prayer will not not be effective or good enough. However, that is not the case. God desires us to come to Him as we are and give Him what we can. We can start simply: praying with our children as they go to bed and at meals times. Then, we can build prayer into our weekly, family devotional times. We can create a prayer list that we pray through during our personal Bible time; we can take a few minutes to pray about what the things we are learning and about our current needs.

Prayer is simply talking to God the way you would talk to your husband, a friend, or your children. I have known many Christians who have their prayer time in the car, in the shower, or as they take walks. God does not care when or where you pray, as long as you take the time to talk with Him.

Jesus' life demonstrates the importance of prayer. He would often get up early to spend time with His father. In *Streams in the Desert*, Lettie Cowman writes:

> *If Jesus, the strong Son of God, felt it necessary to rise before the breaking of the day to pour out His heart to God in prayer, how much more ought you to pray unto Him who is the Giver of*

every good and perfect gift, and who has promised all things necessary for our good.[11]

If it was necessary for Jesus, the Son of God, to pray, how much more important is it for us to pray?

As mothers, our prayers can greatly impact our children's lives. There is no one better to pray for our children than mothers! Who knows our children better than us? Who understands their deep struggles and needs better than us? Our children should know that we are praying for them and seeking God on their behalf. They should see us praying daily and hear us pray for them, specifically. Our prayers play such an important role in imparting our faith to our children. Spurgeon writes of the importance of prayer in the upbringing of Reverend John Angell James:

> *Like most men who have been eminent and honored in the Church of Christ, he had a godly mother, who was wont to take her children to her chamber, and with each separately to pray for the salvation of their souls. This exercise, which fulfilled her own responsibility, was moulding the character of her children, and most, if not all of them, rose up to call her blessed. When did such means ever fail?[12]*

The importance of a mother's prayers in her children's life cannot be overestimated.

Obedience

If we read God's Word, go to church, and pray daily, yet are not obeying what He is asking us to do—watch out! Obedience is the key to faith. When God convicts our hearts, as we read His Word or listen to our pastor preach, we must obey. If we do not, we need to be careful that our hearts do not become hardened. By continually ignoring the pricking of God's Spirit in our lives, out hearts can become hardened and no longer responsive to Him. This is a terrible place for us to be—especially as mothers. If you have not heard from God in a long time, then run back to Him today. When you find yourself in this place, you have moved, not Him—but the good news is that He is only one step away!

Many times, it hurts to obey God. We often have to humble ourselves, do something we don't want to do, or make a decision that hurts. However, our faith requires sacrifice. We must be willing to give up our life just as our Lord obediently sacrificed His life on the cross of Calvary. We may not do what we desire, but obedience makes our lives pleasing to Him. Remember, we are a living sacrifice and if we are training our children to be living sacrifices, we must be one as well.

Is there a show or movie you should not be watching? Are you participating in activities, maintaining friendships, or spending your money on things that are not pleasing to God? If so, surrender them in obedience.

The Christian life is a continual surrendering of our rights for the right of Jesus Christ to be Lord over our life. If our family, children, neighbors, and co-workers cannot see that Christ has made a difference in our life, then our faith is fruitless. It will not impact anyone, let alone our children. They need to see a faith that is real.

Find a Mentor

Finding a mentor is a very important way to grow in faith. A mentor is a relationship with someone who is further along the journey of faith that can help guide you in your own Christian walk.

I have been so blessed to have a mom and mother-in-law who have given me so much godly wisdom. I have also been blessed to learn and glean from godly women in my church. Years ago, I had one precious mentor and friend who had raised three godly children, who I would constantly ask questions of. I wanted to glean all that I could from her about being a Christian wife and mother in today's world.

Many of my mentors have been a part of our church's Women's Bible Study. Over the years, I have gleaned so much wisdom as I have listened to these ladies teach God's Word or lead table groups—and I have grown powerfully in my faith. If your church doesn't have a Women's Bible Study, you might want to ask your pastor or pastor's wife if you could help start one. It would be an enormous blessing to your church! There are so many wonderful resources today to aid churches as they start studies for their congregants—just make sure they are biblically-based.

If you do not have a mentor in your church, might I suggest you find one in a good, godly book? When I was young in the ministry, I was blessed to have been given various classic, Christian books, which fed my soul and enabled me to grow in my relationship with God.

One book, which I would recommend to every women, is *Feminine Appeal* by Carolyn Mahaney. This book is based upon Titus 2 and was specifically created to mentor younger women in the faith. I have read it over and over, as I always have areas in which I need to grow.

There are also many great missionary biographies, as well as Christian living books and devotionals, that can help you grow in your faith in Christ. (You will find a list of my favorites at the end of this book.) Two of Amy Carmichael's books, *Edges of His Ways* and *Whispers of His Power*, have been wonderful mentors to me through the years. My mother-in-law introduced me to these books years ago, and they have been a huge part of my growth as a Christian. I am sure they would be a blessing in your life, too.

Imparting Faith

Faith in Our Home

In the medieval world, European towns would place a cross in their marketplaces as a reminder that every transaction occurs under the shadow of the Cross. As women of faith who daily walk in the grace and forgiveness of Christ, we must ensure that the Cross is the center of every transaction in our life—especially within our homes. What does the cross represent? Death to self, humility, forgiveness, love, repentance, and sacrifice!

As mothers, we need to demonstrate our faith, as we live our lives day in and out. Our homes should be filled with love, repentance, and forgiveness—all symbols of faith embodied in the cross. What does this look like? Our faith should be active. Our children should see our lives being transformed day in and out by the Gospel of Jesus Christ. They should see our faith growing. Our children should be able to tell how God's Word, a sermon, or a devotional is changing us and aiding us in our decision making.

We must also recognize that we sin every day. You might not realize it, but your children do! When you fail—by yelling, complaining, falsely accusing your children—it is so important that you admit your sin and confess it. "If we say that we have no sin, we deceive ourselves, and the truth is not in us. If we confess our sins, He is faithful and just to forgive us our sins and to cleanse us from all unrighteousness." (1 John 1:8-9)

Because of Jesus's work at Calvary, we must be willing to put things right with others, especially our children. I have often had to tell my children that I am sorry for yelling at them, being short with them, or acting indifferently towards something that was important to them. Children forgive so easily, and they learn how to deal with conflict when we model it for them. They know that we are not always right, and they appreciate it when we humbly come to them and ask for forgivenesses.

Roy Hession, author of *The Calvary Road*, talks about how we can bring revival to our homes. He states:

> *Brokenness is the opposite of hardness. Hardness says, "It's your fault!" Brokenness, however, says, "It's my fault." What a different atmosphere will begin to prevail in our homes when they hear us say that. Let us remember that at the Cross there is only room for one at a time...You must go alone, saying, "I'm wrong."* [13]

When we demonstrate conviction of sin and our need for forgiveness, we show our children that the Gospel is real. This is huge! Our children are not going to to be drawn to a faith that is not real. "Fake" faith makes them sour towards the things of the Lord rather than thirsty for the living God.

As mothers, we don't want to be hypocrites—always correcting our children and asking them to repent without ever recognizing our need for forgiveness, as well. This hypocritical attitude will cause our children to flee from the Gospel as fast as they can.

I cannot tell you how many people I have met who want nothing to do with Christ because of the examples of the authorities in their life. Perhaps they had a really hard father, who was all about rules and regulations. Or, maybe they attended a Catholic school, where the nuns were mean and legalistic—not loving. I know one precious, young man who doesn't want anything to do with the Gospel because His father, who was a pastor, lived a life completely opposite of the Gospel. He believes that Christ didn't "work" for his father, so He must not be real.

Our job as mothers is to cultivate a thirst for the living God in our children—and nowhere is this done more effectively than in our homes. We will talk about accomplish this task later in the book; however, your heart, being right before God and your children, is the place to start!

Sharing the Gospel

As mothers of the faith, our primary duty is to share our faith with our children throughout the day. How can we do this? We need to talk about God in every conversation, read books that focus our children's thoughts on God, play music that worships God, pray at our mealtimes, disciple our children as we discipline them, and so on.

When our children were little, Michael and I spent every evening in their bedrooms, reading to them, and telling them Bible stories. We answered questions about God and spent time in prayer together. During this time, each our children were convicted of their sin and decided to accept Jesus into their hearts. Some have received Jesus many times because Jesus has touched their hearts often!

The daily prayer of our six older children is, currently, that sweet, two-year old Ruth would get saved as soon as possible. We have her praying, singing worship songs, and reading Bible stories—but she is still too young to comprehend the Gospel. Around the age of three, most children have the ability to realize they are sinners. Usually, a Gospel story or a time of discipline causes them to mourn over their sin, realize they need forgiveness from God, and decide to receive Christ as their Savior.

As I write this chapter, Christmas is approaching, and our family has a special Nativity tradition. The little ones get to set up the Nativity scene in a place where they can touch and play with it throughout the season. This tradition helps them understand an amazing truth: at Christmas, we celebrate the coming of our Savior, Jesus Christ, into the world to save us from our sins. The Nativity scene helps this truth become tangible in their precious little hearts. As women of faith, our mission needs to be to find ways to share the Gospel in every season.

Whether or not our little ones have decided to receive Jesus, the Word of God should be continuously pricking at their hearts. We need to do all we can to help our children be sensitive towards the things of God from a young age. The reality of sin and our need for a Savior should be an everyday topic of conversation within our homes, especially since we fail each other on a daily basis. We need to constantly remind our children of our continual need for Christ's washing and cleansing throughout the day. Remember, our children follow our example. When they see that we fail daily and ask for forgiveness, they see the Gospel demonstrated before their very eyes—and see their need for the forgiveness of sins, as well.

Many times, parents have come to Michael and asked him to talk with their children about salvation. While he is always happy to meet and share the Gospel with their children, their salvation is really the responsibility of the parents. Spurgeon writes: "Let us never be guilty, as parents, of forgetting the religious training of our children; for if we do we may be guilty of the blood of their souls."[14] *How to Bring Your Children to Christ* is a great resource to help you share the Gospel with your children. In this book, Ray Comfort explains how important it is for your child to recognize they are a sinner and realize their need for salvation. He also explains how to lead them into the sinner's prayer and a relationship with Christ. He warns parents about false conversions, which many children have unfortunately experienced.

When my daughter, Hannah, turned eight, she received a diary for Christmas. She had wanted it very badly, and set out to write in it as soon as possible. "What would an eight year old find to write in a diary?" I wondered. Well, I set out to find out. When I opened the diary and read her precious words, I was blessed beyond measure. She said, "Last night I asked Jesus in my heart. This time, it was for real." My heart was so overjoyed! When we share the gospel with our children throughout their childhood years, don't be surprised to find that Jesus is constantly touching their hearts and convicting them of their sin- so they may declare, time and time again, "This time was for real!"

Last Christmas, one of my sons asked me, "Mom, what do you want for Christmas?" I answered, "For you to love the Lord with all your heart, soul, and mind all the days of your life." He replied, "Mom you already have that. So, what do you want for Christmas?" There is no better gift than to see your children walking with God! However, it is a gift we reap only if we are faithful to sow the seeds of faith from the time they are young, as we live out our faith and share the Gospel daily within our home.

Be a Scribe For God

As mothers, we can impart our faith as we encourage our children. We can do so by writing notes, cards, and messages to our children, filled with prayers, Scriptures, and encouraging devotional readings. We can stick a note on their bathroom mirror, put a message in their lunchbox, or even send them a text! In doing so, we are, in a sense, a scribe for God within our children's lives.

Michael and I have been blessed to have mothers and grandmothers who passed on their faith through the words of Scripture. Whenever we would tell them what was going on in our family or at church, they would immediately take it to the Lord in prayer. Within a few days, we would receive a note or card in the mail with copies of devotionals, prayers, scriptures, and words of encouragement that were just what we needed. Those words of encouragement mean more to Michael and me than our loved ones will ever know!

Every Christmas, Michael's mom and grandma both have made sure that we received a classic Christian book to inspire and grow our faith in Christ. Though Grandma McClure is now with the Lord, we still hold onto those precious gifts and run to them often for words of encouragement. Grandma, though gone, is still "speaking" her faith into our lives.

When I graduated from High School, my mother-in-law, Jean, gave me a copy of *Streams in the Desert* by Mrs. C.H. Cowman—and what a treasure it has been in my life! I have gleaned wisdom from this devotional that has been a gold mine since the first time I read it. What a legacy of faith I have been given by my precious mother-in-law, who has served as God's scribe in my life.

Who Are You Following?
When Jesus first met his disciples, He asked them to leave their careers, their families, and their community to follow Him (John 1:43). If we want to be a disciple of Jesus, we must be following Him, first and foremost. Paul, a disciple of Jesus, said in his letter to the Corinthians, "Imitate me, just as I also imitate Christ" (1 Corinthians 11:1). Our supreme objective, as women of faith, must be to follow Christ with our life.

Who could have ever predicted that, today, millions of people would "follow" other people via the internet! Today, we follow famous movie stars, bloggers, decorators, and so many others. However, we should only be following imitators of Christ, and we should be able to see Jesus through them. Who are you following? Remember, your children are watching!

A Vision of Mother
Years ago, I was at a conference where Anne Graham Lotz shared a memory of her mother, Ruth Bell Graham. As a child, Anne would go up to bed, while her mother would pore over the Scriptures at her desk for hours. Her light would shine out of the living room windows and radiate into Anne's bedroom window—declaring her mother's devotion to God. This memory made a huge impact upon Anne, and it shaped and inspired her to labor over God's Word as well!

Rachel-Ruth, Anne's daughter (who also shared at the conference), said it was her mother Anne's faith that inspired her to labor over the

Scriptures. Ruth Bell Graham inspired her daughter, who then inspired her granddaughter to a life of faith and love for God's Word!

This story impacted me greatly. I went home and purchased a desk at a second-hand store, which I could use to do my daily, morning Bible reading. I wanted my children to receive a vision of their mother laboring over the Scriptures.

Are you laboring over God's Word? Or, are you laboring over something else? We need to be careful of what the little eyes are gleaning in our homes. How will your children remember you? Will they remember you always being on your phone? Working around the house? Sleeping? Or, spending time in God's presence, pouring over the Scriptures?

Authentic Devotion

A few years ago, we studied the life of David in our Women's Bible Study. My daughter Hannah, who was nine at the time, wanted me to bring an extra copy of the weekly study home so she too could study the life of David. One morning, while she was sitting in my bed doing her "homework" alongside me, she answered this question: "Who has been an example to you of authentic devotion?" She wrote, "Mommy—to read my Bible everyday."

What if I had been too busy in my season of mothering to do my Bible study? My precious Hannah would not have been sitting with me on my bed, dedicating time to the study of the Bible; nor would she have seen me as an example of devotion to God. Praise God for His grace that has enabled me to walk in faith and obedience—because my children are watching. Truly, faith is caught, not taught!

A Mother's Influence

G. Campbell Morgan, a profound British preacher in the twentieth century, influenced millions with his preaching, teaching, and writing. He had four sons who all became pastors. One day, when his youngest son, Howard, finished preaching, a reporter asked him, "Since you have five pastors in your family, who is the greatest preacher?" Expecting the son to give the honor to his father, Howard surprised the reporter by saying, "My Mother!"[15]

When a mother is completely committed to Christ and His Word— and lives a life that daily demonstrates her faith—watch out! Don't underestimate the power of your faith and the importance of investing it into your children's lives. Your children's faith and future depend upon it.

Questions to Consider

1.   How does your life demonstrate an active faith?

2.   Do you spend time in prayer and God's word daily? If not, how can you rearrange your schedule to make spending time with God a priority in your life?

3.   Is attending church a priority in your home? If not, what can you do to ensure it becomes one?

4.   Who do your children see you following—intentionally or unintentionally?

5.   Do you have a mentor? If not, how will you go about getting one?

6.   Have you been too busy for God? How might Jesus's example help you make God more of a priority in your life?

7.   When your children are grown, how will they remember you? Will they remember you as a woman who spent time poring over the scriptures or in prayer?

Notes

---

[1] Elisabeth Elliot, *The Shaping of a Christian Family* (Grand Rapids, Michigan: Fleming H. Revell, 1992), 96.

[2] Mrs. Charles E. Cowman, *Streams in the Desert* (Grand Rapids, Michigan: Zondervan Publishing House, 1925), 11.

[3] F.B. Meyer, *Through The Bible Day By Day,* Volume VII (Philadelphia: American Sunday-School Union, 1918), 114.

[4] Cowman, *Streams in the Desert*, 396.

[5] C.H. Spurgeon, quoted in Streams in the Desert, 73.

[6] Greg Laurie quoted in Harvest Virtue Studies, *"The Rebuilt Life," Session 10* (Redlands, California:Harvest Christian Fellowship, 2017-2018), 3.

[7] Elliot, *The Shaping of a Christian Family*, 68.

[8] Matthew Henry, *Matthew Henry's Commentary of the Bible, Volume II* (New York: Fleming H. Revell Company, 1708), 282.

[9] Cowman, *Streams in the Desert*, 204.

[10] C.H. Spurgeon, quoted in Cowman, *Streams in the Desert*, 380.

[11] Mrs. Charles E. Cowman, *Devotions for Morning and Evening* (New York: International Press, 1925), 350.

[12] C. H. Spurgeon, "The Child Samuel's Prayer," The Metropolitan Tabernacle Pulpit contains Sermons Preached and Revised by C.H. Spurgeon During the Year 1864. (Pasadena, Texas: Pilgrim Publications, 1991), 477.

[13] Roy Hession, *The Calvary Road* (Fort Washington, PA: CLC Publications, 1950), 24.

[14] C.H. Spurgeon, quoted in Ray Comfort, *How To Bring Your Children to Christ and Keep Them There* (Bartlesville, Oklahoma: Genesis Publishing Group), 48.

[15] Paul Fritz, "The Best Preacher In The Family," Sermon Central, November 29, 2001, accessed on July 19, 2019, https://www.sermoncentral.com/sermon-illustrations/4796/the-best-preacher-in-the-family-by-paul-fritz

Pearl of Wisdom #2

Love Your Children

Follow God's example, therefore,
as dearly loved children and walk in the way of love,
just as Christ loved us and gave himself up for us as a fragrant offering
and sacrifice to God.

Ephesians 5:1-2

Hannah demonstrated her love for Samuel every year by stitching him a new coat. Year after year, she would visit the Tabernacle to demonstrate her faith in God as she offered the yearly sacrifice and brought a new coat she had made for Samuel. She would offer two sacrifices: one to God, and then, one to Samuel. What love! "Moreover his mother used to make [Samuel] a little robe, and bring it to him year by year when she came up with her husband to offer the yearly sacrifice." (1 Samuel 2:19)

Imagine what that coat must have meant to Samuel! He must have looked forward to his mother's yearly visit, waiting for his new coat with such expectation. Throughout the year, Hannah's love for God and Samuel would be displayed through the sacrifice she made over that precious, hand-stitched coat. When we sacrifice our time and energy to love our children, we are worshiping God and offering Him a sweet-smelling aroma.

Faith Clothed in Love

As mothers we must realize that the most important aspect of our lives is our faith clothed in love. As Galatians 5:6 clearly states: "For in Christ Jesus neither circumcision nor uncircumcision avails anything, but faith working through love." Hannah's faith was clothed in love, as we see in her gift to Samuel, a hand-stitched coat. F.B. Meyer writes of Hannah's loving and sacrificial gift: "Thus parents still make the clothes that their children wear. The little ones almost unconsciously become arrayed in the character that is constantly being shown before their quick and inquisitive eyes." [1] Our sweet little ones watch us, looking for a loving example to follow. He goes on to say:

> *By their behavior to each other and to their children; by the ordering of the home-life; by their actions, more than by their words; by the way in which they speak, and spend their leisure hours, and pray—men and women are making the little coats which, for better or worse, their children wear ever after, and perhaps pass down to after generations.* [2]

Our faith, clothed in love and lived out within our home, is where our children learn their habits. Our habits are the clothing of their inner life.

Where are our habits formed? F.B. Meyer explains that our habits are formed: "Not in the mid-passage of life, but at its dawn, not in great crisis, but in daily circumstances; not in life's arena but in the home, amid the surroundings of earliest childhood."[3] Our children looking at and mimic us. Who they are is formed before our very eyes—and everything we do needs to be clothed in God's love, for it is fashioning their very being! Henry Ward Beecher states, "The mother's heart is the child's school-room." So true!

The Power of Love

We cannot underestimate the power of a mother's love. The love of a mother has the power to transform a child! It has been said: "When people are inspired and loved, they will do most anything."[4] History proves this true, time and time again—and we see it demonstrated, here, in the life of Samuel.

Why must we love our children? So, the Word of God might not be blasphemed, or spoken evil of! In Titus 2:4-5, Paul exhorts the older women in the church to "to love their husbands, to love their children... that the word of God may not be blasphemed." Our love represents Christ to those around us; and as mothers, we are the fragrance of Christ to the world. Our lack of love enables the world to speak evil of God and His Word.

As Christian mothers, love should be the supreme characteristic displayed in our life, in our home, with our children—as love is the fruit of God's Spirit at work in us and proof that we are disciples of Jesus Christ. John writes, "By this all will know that you are My disciples, if you have love for one another" (John 13:35). Love is so important that Paul states that—even if we have all the faith in the world—without love, we are nothing (1 Corinthians 13:2).

The most important reason for us to love our children is so we can demonstrate the power of the gospel. God is love, and we are commanded to abide in His love (1 John 4:16). First John 3:16-18 states: "By this we know love, because He laid down His life for us. And we also ought to lay down our lives for the brethren...My little children, let us not love in word or in tongue, but in deed and in truth." As mothers, we have the great honor of being able to influence our children into the love of God. This is our highest calling!

Amy Carmichael, a Christian missionary to India, was involved in rescuing little girls from temple prostitution. She ended up with an orphanage full of girls and, later, boys, where she ministered to children day in and out. This experience provided her with a great understanding of the power of love in raising children for Christ. She writes:

> *What I specially want to bring you is this: Young children and all who do not know our Lord have only one way of knowing*

how loving He is. They look at us. If there be any flaw in our love, if we fail them at any point, we make it just so much the harder for them to see, to know, to apprehend, His love. Do not let us fail our children. Love through me, Love of God.[5]

We are the hands and feet of Jesus, and the love we display towards our children should represent His love!

At the end of his life, D.L. Moody said, "If I could relive my life, I would devote my entire ministry to reaching children for God."[6] He realized that, in their youth, people are spiritually hungry. Children accept the gospel more easily than adults do, and the gospel has the power to mold and shape the rest of their life! As mothers, we have this high calling within our home: to display the gospel through our love for our children.

God's Sacrificial Love

What does God's love look like? It is a sacrificial love. John 3:16 tells us: "For God so loved the world that He *gave* His only begotten Son, that whoever believes in Him should not perish but have everlasting life." God's love for us compelled Him to give us up His greatest treasure, His Son, so we might be reconciled to Him. Then, Jesus's love for the Father and for us led Him to give up His life as a sacrifice— so our sins would be paid in full. And, we are called to love in this same way: "Follow God's example, therefore, as dearly loved children and walk in the way of love, just as Christ loved us and gave himself up for us as a fragrant offering and sacrifice to God." (Ephesians 5:1-2) We, as mothers, follow God's example of sacrificial love when we love our children sacrificially. Our love for God should compel us to give our time, energy, and resources, so that our children might be trained in the love of God.

Remember, we are raising prophets for the Lord, like Samuel. If we are to accomplish this great task, we have to love our children enough to make sacrifices that will benefit their soul. Henri Didon, a French preacher, wrote: "We have a great need nowadays of self-sacrificing souls to teach the young generation by their very lives."[7] We must be willing to sacrifice our very lives for the benefit of our children.

What do these daily sacrifices look like? Recently, I asked my six oldest children (since they are the ones who can talk), "How do you know that I love you?" All of them said, "Because you cook for us"—apparently, cooking goes a long way! They also said, "Because you..."

- Tell me everyday.
- Hug and kiss me.
- Pray for me.
- Are nice to me.
- Smile at me.
- Made a school for me.
- Listen to me—most of the time.

- Spend time with us.
- Discipline us.[8]

Each of these reasons are little, sacrificial acts of love. Often, they cost us nothing; yet these little sacrifices, which are so very difficult to give at times, enable our children to experience God and His love!

Selfish Love
Notice what sacrificial love is not: It is not laying down your life to fulfill the whims and desires of your children. It is not an overly idolatrous affection towards your children, where a mother desires to make her children happy and satisfied by indulging them, purchasing them lots of things, or going on expensive and elaborate vacations. This is a selfish love. Our desire should not be to make our children happy so they will love us.

Andrew Murray, in *How to Bring Your Children to Christ*, writes how selfish love is wanting our children to know Christ so they can be happy—not holy! Selfish love says, "I want my children saved, but I don't want them to go into ministry or do anything drastic, like become a missionary to Africa!"

Rather, our love should be sacrificial. Sacrificial love desires our children to know Christ so they will be holy. It wants God to use them to accomplish His work in His kingdom. Sacrificial love has no place for self; rather, it requires a complete abandoning of our desires for our children in favor of God's desire for their life. In describing a sacrificial love, Andrew Murray urges parents to completely surrender their self-interest in the raising of their children to Christ and His Spirit and service. He writes:

> *We have no conception of the extent to which self-interest weakens faith and self-sacrifice strengthens it. If I know I am seeking the salvation of my children for their own and for my sake, I will not be able to believe that God will give me the grace for training my child. But, if I lose all selfish thought of myself and my children and place them at God's disposal, then I am sure that my Father will give me grace for the work I do for Him."* [9]

Loving our children sacrificially is not easy, as we must not take our own lives into consideration. We must be focused on our mission, to be able to fulfill the great call God has placed upon our lives- raising children to transform this nation for His glory.

Love Without Limits
Thinking about God's incredible love and our responsibility as ambassadors of His love can be overwhelming. However, we don't have to be the ones mustering up God's love to give our children. Rather, it is

God, through us, who enables us to love our children sacrificially. How, you might ask? As we spend time in God's presence, we receive His love. As we are filled with His love, it then spills over into our children's lives.

We are commanded to—by faith—be rooted and grounded in love, so we can comprehend the "width and length and depth and height—to know the love of Christ which passes knowledge; that you may be filled with all the fullness of God" (Ephesians 3:17-19). And, as we experience the fullness of God, our children will experience His love, as well.

We see the characteristics of the love that God desires for our children fleshed out in 1 Corinthians 13:4-8. God's love, through us, suffers long with our children, is kind towards them, and does not envy when they are successful or have gifts that we don't. It does not behave rudely, nor does it seek our interests. Instead, it lays them down for our children's interests. God's love does not cause us to provoke our children or think the worst of them; it does not rejoice in their sin, but rejoices when they do what is right. God's love enables us to bear all things—even the unbearable things about our children. It believes that they can and will do what is right; it hopes—even when everything screams of hopelessness; and it endures no matter what. God's love, in us, should never fail our children.

Just as God's love is without limits, our love for our children should be without limits. In Romans, Paul tells us that nothing can separate us from the love of God: "For I am persuaded that neither death nor life, nor angels nor principalities nor powers, nor things present nor things to come, nor height nor depth, nor any other created thing, shall be able to separate us from the love of God which is in Christ Jesus our Lord" (Romans 8:38-39).

And, similarly, nothing should be able to separate our children from our love. We must remember that God's love sent Christ down to die for us while we will still in our sin. Before we were reconciled through Christ, God's love came down! God's love was and always is unconditional—whether or not we choose to receive His love and forgiveness, He sacrificed His life for us. If we are to successfully love our children, as God desires, our love must come down, too. We must not allow anything to separate—or keep—us from loving our children.

Too often, I find that parents, especially when children are older, become upset or offended at their children for not doing something they expected them to do or for saying something hurtful to them. However, our job is to love our children unconditionally, as Jesus loves us. Our children will hurt us—unintentionally and, sometimes, intentionally. However, our love cannot change. Our love towards our children must not based upon what our children deserve, what they do, or who they are. It must be based upon God's sacrificial love towards us. When we embrace this truth in light of our relationship with our children, everything changes—our love needs to be without limits!

Love Is A Choice

Being a mom of little ones can be super demanding and tiring. But, we must not forget that our little ones are watching—and our life is a living example to them. The season of motherhood is a high calling, as it is one of preparing our children for their eternal destiny. As a result, our perspective and attitude in our home is very important.

With all the demands and challenges that come with being a mother, we have a choice to make each day. Will we grumble, complain, respond in selfishness, and so on? If we chose to approach parenting with a bad attitude, our children will think of themselves as a burden without value. They will not feel your love—or God's love.

However, when we choose to love our children no matter what and see the little sacrifices as a blessing and a joy, our children will believe they are a blessing. And more importantly, they will receive God's love! As mothers, we must remember, as Amy Carmichael encourages us: "A cup of sweet water could never spill a drop of bitter water, no matter how heavily it was jolted." [10]

Enjoy Our Children

We live in a culture where children "get in the way." They are not valued or enjoyed or loved. As mothers, we need to do things that enable our children know that we enjoy them. We can play their favorite board game, read them a book, care about what they say, read their latest essay, watch a video they created for school, ask them how their day was, and so much more. We need to take interest in the things that interest them. Again, I am not talking about being overly consumed with your children and their life- I am talking about valuing your children and taking interest in their life.

We need to enjoy our children for who they are and delight in the different personalities and quirks that God has given each of them. We can give them winks and smiles and laugh at their jokes—even if they are not very funny. We can sit and talk to them about whatever they want to talk about. Put simply, we need to take delight in our children's lives.

When I asked my children how they know I love them, one of their responses was "because you smile at me." I was amazed how powerful a simple smile can be! A smile demonstrates that you enjoy and find pleasure in your children and the things they do.

Let your children have fun! Don't get mad at them for making forts, laughing, playing games, or chasing each other. Don't get me wrong, you need to have rules in your house—however, your home needs to be a place where your children feel valued and treasured. They need to see it as a place they can have fun, not as a place of rules and regulations where they are always in trouble.

A few years ago, one of my neighbors was moving away, and the perspective buyer asked about the rest of the families in the neighborhood. They wanted to know more about our house, especially, as they had found out that we had six children. "Are they noisy?" they wondered. My neighbor responded, "The only noise I hear from that house is laughter!" Your house should be a house of laughter and fun. Be willing to play with your children—for hours—and allow them to have fun!

Leaving Things Undone

Kay Smith, the wife of Pastor Chuck Smith, used to say over and over that she wished she did not spend so much time fussing about the house when her children were young. Similarly, I have to constantly remind myself of Proverbs 14:4: "Where no oxen are, the stall is clean; but much increase comes by the strength of an ox." This verse reminds me that, if I am going to raise children to do the work of God's kingdom, I am going to have to endure messes.

I remember talking to a friend, one day, who was one of five children. I asked her if she had loved having so many siblings. She said, "No!" When I asked her why, she stated, "My mom was always stressed out because of the house." A mother should never be more concerned for her home than for ensuring that her children know she enjoys them. This woman's perspective really affected how my friend thought about children once she was grown.

In her book *Prayer that Works*, Jill Briscoe wrote that in order to make God a priority, "We have to learn the art of leaving things undone."[11] This quote has really stuck with me through the years. It has impacted not only my time with God, but it has also enabled me to have time to spend with my husband and children. Don't get me wrong: I love a cute, organized, and clean house as much as anyone, but I am not going to lose my joy or sacrifice valuable time with my family over a messy house. (I might have taken this quote a little too far—notice I am not writing a book on how to keep a tidy house!)

Cooking Meals

One day, as I was cooking in the kitchen and talking to my children, I asked them if they felt that they were missing out because they do not get everything their friends do. Josh, one of my middle boys said, "No, we aren't missing out. We are spoiled." I asked Josh, "How are you spoiled?" He said, "You make us the yummiest food." Preparing and serving delicious food is one of the greatest way we can demonstrate our love for our children. In fact, when we cook food they enjoy, they feel spoiled.

Taking the time to plan out our meals, shop, and prepare food for our families shows them that we are spending our time and energy thinking about and caring for them. This makes our children—and husbands—feel loved in a very practical way.

Since I have had to work at our school the past few years, I often double or triple a recipe on the days I am home. Then, on the nights I work, we only have to heat up leftovers. We have also had seasons where we have eaten a lot of spaghetti and meatballs—as this meal is cheap and easy. Your children will not care what you cook, as long as you prepare it with love.

I know that many women today have not learned the skill of cooking, and some do not have any desire to learn. If this is you, you are living in the best age. Today, you can purchase pre-made meals or meals that you can easily throw together at inexpensive prices. I know one mom who uses a meal service that delivers ingredients and step-by-step instructions to her door—and her family is so happy!

Love Has No Favorites

One very important thing to remember is that love has no favorites. In Scripture, we see what having favorites does within a family: it divides and creates intense jealousy. Consider Jacob and Esau. Isaac preferred Esau, and Rebekah preferred Jacob. Their favoritism towards certain children created disunity within their family—forever!

Many times favoritism is not obvious to parents. However, when you do one thing for one child and not another, your child will see this as favoritism—even if you do not see it this way. For example, paying for one child's car and not another's is favoritism. Allowing one child to live at home rent free and not another is also favoritism. As mothers, we should not put one child's picture on our screen saver and leave the others off. Do not do one thing for one child without doing it for your others.

Life is not fair, but we can do our best to be as fair as we can with our children. Don't compliment one child over the another. Don't compare your children with one another. Don't talk behind one child's back to their sibling. And most importantly of all, do not take sides! This is especially important when your children are little: always make sure that each child apologizes for whatever the other feels they did wrong. It doesn't have to always be an accurate picture—we must strive to always stay neutral!

Your love should unify your children and give them a strong, common bond. Your children should trust you and know that you love each of them, intensely! I find, by watching many older couples near the end of their life, that having their children united is very important. At the end of your life, your children should all feel so loved that they think they must have been the favorite.

Love In Word and Deed

We can also show our love for our children through our words. When I asked my daughter, Abby, how she knew I loved her. She responded with, "You tell me everyday." I have spoken with many grown women who don't remember their mother ever telling them—or rarely telling them—that they loved them. What a shame, as the words "I love you!" are powerful!

Words of affirmation can go a long way in your child's life. We are told to "not withhold good from those to whom it is due, when it is in the power of your hand to do so" (Proverbs 3:27). Tell your children that they did a good job, that you are so proud of them, how thankful you are for them, what an answer to prayer they are, and how wealthy you are because of them. They will live up to your compliments and desire to please you all the more!

You might be in a situation where you have a hard time recognizing any of the positive attributes of your children. This is not as uncommon as you think. Ask God to show you positive characteristics in your child's life that you can praise them for. And then, start sharing these with them. Or, perhaps you can write them a note or a card or send them a text.

Notes of encouragement mean so much to our children. At the start of every school year, at Back to School night, we ask parents to write a special note to their child. This note is left on their desk for them to find the next morning. Michael and I usually divide and conquer—he writes notes to half of the children, and I write notes for the the others. In them, we tell our children how much we love them, how proud we are of them, that we are praying for them, and of course, that we are expecting them to have a great year. Those notes mean so much. Our children usually keep them in their school binders throughout the year as a reminder of how much mom and dad love them.

However, we must remember to love our children not only with our words, but also through our deeds. In 1 John 3:18, we read, "My little children, let us not love in word or in tongue, but in deed and in truth." The little, sweet things we do for our children mean so much to them. Hugs and kisses mean a great deal! We can also show our children affection through small acts of kindness, such as reading aloud to them, playing their favorite game when they don't have anyone else to play with, preparing a cup of tea for them when they are sick, placing a freshly cut rose by their bed, or having a fresh batch of cookies ready to eat when they come home from school. Small acts of kindness go a long in demonstrating your love for your children.

Cultivate An Atmosphere of Love

As mothers who are full of faith and the Holy Spirit, we must cultivate a home filled with an atmosphere of love—as love is a fruit of the Spirit, and our home is a picture of God's love to the world. Our children should grow up in the love of God. How can we accomplish this task? We train our children to love one another by covering one another's sin, being long-suffering with one another, forgiving one another, doing unto others as we want them to do unto us, and so on.

It is our job as mother to roll up our sleeves and get dirty in this area. When we see our children fight, we must call it out. If one child hits another, we must discipline them promptly. If a child yells at someone, we must send them to their room and talk to them about it. We must make sure that our children apologize to and hug each other—don't give them a choice. This faithful training produces a harvest of love within our homes.

The best training ground for life happens at home. We need to show our children how to love others and how to be a friend by teaching them to love their siblings. Their relationships with their siblings will be the longest friendships they will ever have on this earth, and it is to our benefit to ensure that these relationships are good ones. If we don't, divided children today will usually mean divided children as adults.

A few years ago, we were celebrating one of my son's birthdays. As we went around the table and shared what we loved about my son, one of my daughters started crying. And then, she said, "So and so is mean to me. I don't have anything nice to say about him." That was a great wake up call for Michael and I to start working on that relationship! Praise God that it has been mended. But, if we, as parents, had not been willing to get dirty and help our children, we cannot assume that they would have worked out their differences if we had not gotten involved.

In our home, we don't allow sarcasm, as it is hurtful and rude. Too often, sarcasm is used as a justification for being mean to someone else— in the name of a joke. Sarcasm can especially sting because there is usually a little truth within it. We do not allow our children to tease or be mean toward one another, as it is hurtful and does not cultivate an atmosphere of love.

We also remind our children over and over again that our home is a refuge from the world. It is so important that all of our children feel loved and valued in our home. Because of this, we do not allow any of our children to make one of their siblings feel like they are not loved, welcomed, or accepted. As a mother, it is my job to make sure that our home is the most loving place on earth. Will you do your part in making your home a love-filled refuge?

Love Covers
One really important aspect of love is that it covers. The Bible teaches that "He who covers a transgression seeks love, But he who repeats a matter separates friends." (Proverbs 17:9) As mothers, we need to purposefully cover our in-laws, cover our churches, cover our teachers, cover our neighbors, and so on. Allowing ourselves to cling to the idea of justice and have a critical attitude is so deadly! Our children will quickly pick up on it, and a critical spirit is such a horrible habit to break. Continuously judging everyone around us is the opposite of being a person of love.

What does covering offenses with love look like? When your children come home from school and tell you about something hurtful a friend did, don't say, "How mean!" Instead, tell them that they probably did not mean to hurt you. Encourage them forgive their friend. Or perhaps, a teacher gets upset at your children, who were wrongfully blamed for something. Tell your children that everything is going to be okay and that being blamed unjustly is a part of life. If something happens at church that you don't agree with, don't get mad and make a big scene- cover it! If something needs to be addressed, pray and address it with love.

When we jump in to rescue our children and try to get justification for all the wrongs committed against them, we are training our children to be men and women who cause division in their homes, workplaces, and churches. I have seen so many damaged homes and relationships because parents did not train their children to cover people with love. Remember, love keeps no record of wrong. If we keep such records, our children will, too. After all, they mimic us.

Years ago, someone I went out of my way to bless, offended me greatly. I was so hurt, so I was praying about what to do. I really just wanted to go and tell this person how wrong they were. However, as I sat in church one morning, my husband read from the Proverbs 19:11, "The discretion of a man makes him slow to anger, and his glory is to overlook a transgression." That morning, God told me, "Brenda, you can talk to this person and, perhaps, you can get this issue resolved. However, if you want to glorify Me, you must cover her!" When we cover others, we not only glorify God, we also seek love (Proverbs 17:9).

We also need to encourage our children to cover their siblings in their home. In times past, it has been said of the home: "The only place on earth where the faults and failings of humanity are hidden beneath a mantle of charity."[12] Our children need to be trained to cover their brothers and sisters through the "mantle of charity." When we train our children towards this end, we will find that our children will consider their home a refuge and a place they desire to be as they grow.

As we make a habit of covering those around us in love, our children will also end up covering others and us with love. We all need covering! We must show them how to do so through the way we live our life and treat others.

Imparting Truth

As mothers, we are called to "[speak] the truth in love" so that our children "may grow up all things into Him who is the head— Christ" (Ephesians 4:15). Our desire should be for our children to grow in their relationship with Christ. Therefore, we must speak truth into their lives in love. When our children miss the mark, we need to lovingly tell them they were wrong and share with them how they could have handled the situation differently. This is part of "teaching our children to obey his commandments" as we are commanded in the great commission. (Matthew 28:19-20)

Over the years, I have found that many parents neglect the imparting of wisdom in their children's lives- as they don't want to take the time or don't want to get their children upset at them. Yet, this is how we pass down our values and our children "grow up in wisdom." In many cases, we as parents assume our children children will just gain wisdom as they get older. But, unless we actually take time to impart the wisdom, show them, talk to them, teach them, break it down for them during teachable moments, that wisdom is not going to come by itself.

Imparting truth in love looks different in each season of our children's lives. When they are younger, we are able to teach and train them liberally. As they grow older, we need to use the truth to guide our children as circumstances deem it necessary. We need to love our children enough to be truthful without being nit picky or critical. And, regardless of which season our children are in, we cannot worry about about whether they like us or not. We must not set aside truth as we train them for life. If we want them to be a joy and delight to our soul, we must speak the truth in love.

Tough Love

Love requires standards. In John 14:15, Jesus states: "If you love Me, keep My commandments." If we desire to have children who love God, we must hold them to the commandments found in Scripture. We also need to love them more than we love ourselves—and take the time to discipline them. It takes a lot of tough love to stop what we are doing and take the time to train our children every time they fall short. However, we must love our children enough to do so.

Which commandments should we hold our children accountable to? The Ten Commandments given by God to Moses in Exodus 20 are a great place to start. We must expect our children to put God first, to not take His name in vain, to work hard and also keep the Sabbath day, to honor those in authority, to not hurt others, to not take things that do not belong to them, to not lie and always tell the truth, to not whine for something they don't have, and so forth. God's standards must be our standards for our children's behavior—and we must hold them to it. This is tough love. And as mothers, we need to do whatever it takes to make sure that our children's hearts are right before God in every season of parenting.

Our children will fall short of our expectations, which are outlined in Scripture. When this happens we must remember that God disciplines those He loves (Hebrews 12:6), and the best way we can show our love for our children is as we discipline them. We will speak more about how to do this in the chapter on discipline, but it is important to know that loving our children does not mean being a doormat or letting them do whatever they please—as that is what so many in our culture today believe. Remember, we are training our children to be disciples of Jesus. Our guide must be God's Word, and we must love our children enough to hold God's standard for them.

Love Your Parents and In-Laws

Around the time I gave birth to my fourth son, I realized that I would one day be a mother-in-law to four daughters! As I pondered this, I knew that I needed to make sure that I was being the type of daughter and daughter-in-law I wanted my future daughter-in-laws to be toward me.

And if I wanted my children to treat their in-laws well, they needed to learn to do so from me. As mothers, we need to love our parents and in-laws, treating them how we want to be treated by our children and children-in-law in the future.

Our children are always watching us, and they learn how we want them to treat us by our actions. Over the years, I have met many women who are training their children to be mean towards them because of they way they treat their in-laws. We need to remember to love our parents and in-laws for who they are, not who we expect them to be. We must not talk badly about them in front of our children, and we should never punish them by refusing to let them see their grandchildren, especially during the holidays. Instead, we should do unto them as we desire our children to do unto us.

As mothers, it is our job to make sure that our children honor our parents and in-laws. We must encourage our children to give them kisses and hugs, love and respect whenever they are with them. We should also expect them to write thank you cards whenever they receive gifts. Our children will only know how we want to be treated someday by watching us as we interact with our parents and in-laws. We must lead by example!

Special Traditions

Having special traditions in the home can create a really loving atmosphere. What do your children look forward to every year on their birthday? How do you celebrate Easter, Thanksgiving, and Christmas? The answers to these questions will be the precious childhood memories your children will look back on with fondness.

We have a very special birthday tradition in our home. We celebrate each child's birthday with a breakfast tea party. We use our nicest dishes and enjoy tea, scones, sausages, and eggs. We also go around the table, sharing what we love about the person whose birthday we are celebrating. We do not just share one thing; we share everything we love about them! Then, we anoint and lay hands on the child, and everyone takes turns praying for them. Each one of my children looks forward to their their tea party every year. The tea party itself is not much of a gift anymore; it is the love each child receives from their parents and siblings through the words of affirmation, the anointing, and the prayers that is the true gift.

I do not remember how this tradition was started, though it was years ago when one of our children was little. It has not been easy for me to throw birthday tea parties for every child each year—especially in the spring, when we celebrate five birthdays! However, the time I have had to sacrifice to make this tradition happen is more than worth it. I am humbled and awed every time I hear my children praise God for their sibling and ask Him to use their sibling to build and conquer God's kingdom. Ladies, we need to do our part to make memories and create traditions that will impact our children's lives, forever!

Christmas is also a very special time in our house. Every October, our children beg for us to play Christmas music, to turn on the heater, and to begin decorating the house. We are all sorts of Christmas crazy— and we should be! Jesus' birthday is coming, and my children want to start celebrating! Every year, our family gets our Christmas tree the day after Thanksgiving, and we hang ornaments of birds, crosses, angels, mangers, and hearts on it. We listen to Christmas music every second of December, make Christmas cookies, watch *It's A Wonderful Life* and *The Man Who Saved Christmas*. Every morning, our children sit on the heaters with their blankets, reading their Bibles to the glimmer of lights of the Christmas tree.

With the arrival of each new baby, I have hand-stitched a velvet Christmas stocking for each my children. Over the years, these stockings have become extremely sentimental. On Christmas morning, we open our stockings during a tea party we hold for Jesus, as it is His birthday. We also take the time to say what we love about Him, read the Christmas story, and have a time of prayer and thanksgiving, praising Jesus for all He has done for us. By the time our tea party has finished, our hearts, which are ready to open gifts, are thankful to even get a gift on Jesus' birthday!

Crazy Love

Years ago I read a book on mothers of famous men. After reading about the lives of ten famous men and their mothers, I realized that there was a common theme of all the mothers. They all had great faith in God, and their faith compelled them to some huge act of sacrifice. Whether it was working three jobs to put food on the table, getting up early each morning to bring her child before the Lord in prayer, or living without so her son could be educated- these moms thought nothing of their comfort and ease, as they were willing to do almost anything to see that God would be glorified in their children's lives.

Sometimes our love for our children enables us to do crazy things. Often, they are things we would never choose to do, but sacrificial love compels us to! This is how I felt when my husband asked me to start a school for my children. I loved being at home, managing my own schedule and homeschooling. However, it didn't take long for me to realize that the home-school environment was not the best choice of schooling for our family, being we had tons of boys and I could not be in more than one place at at time. However, we couldn't afford to send our children to private school, and public school was not an option. Even if we could afford a private school, we couldn't find any that lined up with our values: discipleship, classical curriculum, and God's Word integrated throughout every subject. This led me to obey God, and my husband, and start a school. My plan was to be at home and to not work, but my love for God and my children compelled me to pick up my cross and follow Him. It hasn't been easy, but the fruit is worth it! When I asked one of my sons how he knew I loved him, he stated, "You started a school for me!"

There might be something that God might be asking you to do out of love for your children. You might think it is crazy- but the eternal destiny of your children is worth any sacrifice. It might mean you get a job to put them in private school, homeschool your children, or give up on some dreams so God might fulfill His purpose in your children's life. This is crazy love, and when you display this type of love to your children, they will realize that God is worth anything!

What Do You Need to Sew?

Every year, Hannah sewed a little coat for Samuel. What love Samuel must have felt for his mother as he wore the coat his mother had made for him daily. When we do little deeds of love—like Hannah sewing a coat for her son—we demonstrate our love for our children, as well. I am not talking about living a life of service for our children; I am talking about all the little acts of love we do that shine forth God's love to our children.

As I have been writing this book, my son Josh has been asking me to sew up a hole in his favorite shorts. How convicted I have been by this chapter and Hannah's example—sewing Josh's shorts took me all of five minutes! There are many small acts of kindness I can do to express my love for each of my children. They do not cost me money, just time. However, giving up a bit of my time to work on the little things my children need is worth far more than I realize. One day soon, my children will be grown and gone, and I will wish for a pair of shorts to sew.

What do you need to sew for your children? Is there a book they have been asking you to read aloud to them? Are there cookies to bake? Perhaps, a hair style to do? What do you need to give up to ensure these things get done? Amy Carmichael writes, "You can give without loving, but you cannot love without giving." What little, thoughtful, sweet, sacrificial acts of love can you do today that will minister God's love to your children?

"Love Through Me, Love of God"

The most valuable work a mother can do to demonstrate her love for God is to minister to her children, Jesus's precious lambs. A mother's love for her children has the power to change the world! Mother Theresa writes: "If you want to change the world go home and love your family." So often, mothers lose perspective on how important their role is and long for a ministry outside of their homes. Perhaps they were used to praise and acclamation from jobs held before they had little ones, or maybe they have gifts that they have to put on hold while they are tending to their children. It is really easy for mothers to lose perspective of how important their role is!

Helen Keller wrote: "I long to accomplish a great and noble task, but it is my chief duty to accomplish small tasks as if they were great and noble."[13] Molding and shaping our children can be humbling. Cleaning throw-up, wiping noses, soothing fussy babies with upset tummies, getting cups of juice and water all day long, disciplining a child for the same behavior over and over again, etc. can be humbling. However, when we do these things unto the "least of these," we are doing it unto the Lord (Matthew 23:40)—and serving Him is the most noble task in all the world. Children are considered by some to be the "least of these." But to Jesus, they are heirs of the kingdom, whom He loves and desires to spend all of eternity with. There is no greater honor we can ever have than molding and shaping the next generation by our love.

As a mother of seven, there are times when I am so exhausted, I don't know if I can press on. In being involved with our church and partnering with parents at our school in the raising of their children, there have been many times that I have not had an ounce of anything to give to anyone. During one of these times, I read this passage by Amy Carmichael:

> *Often there is nothing of sacrifice in our task of bringing up children. But our Lord Jesus knew what it would cost Peter to feed His lambs, and He knows what it will cost some of us. He overlooks nothing, forgets nothing. And He says to each hidden sacrificial act, You have done it unto Me (Matthew 25:40).* [14]

What a wonderful reminder that there is a cost in raising the next generation to be God's prophets. However, God sees our sacrifices. They please Him, and He will reward us for our faithfulness. In Matthew 10:42, Jesus says: "And whoever gives one of these little ones only a cup of cold water in the name of a disciple, assuredly, I say to you, he shall by no means lose his reward." God is faithful to keep His promises, and He guarantees a reward for us when we faithfully love our precious children. Not only will we be rewarded with godly children who are a blessing, but we shall also receive a reward in the life to come in glory. Paul encourages us to "not grow weary while doing good, for in due season we shall reap [a harvest] if we do not lose heart" (Galatians 6:9).

Have you lost perspective? Has your love had limits? Are you offended by your children? Are you failing to allow God's love to flow through you? If so, may this prayer by Amy Carmichael be yours:

> *Love through me, Love of God;*
> *There is no love in me.*
> *O Fire of love, light Thou the love*
> *That burns perpetually.*

Love Your Children

Flow through me, Peace of God;
Calm River, flow until
No wind can blow, no current stir
A ripple of self-will.

Shine through me, Joy of God;
Make me like Thy clear air
That Thou dost pour Thy colors through,
As though it were not there

O blessed Love of God,
That all may taste and see
How good Thou art, once more I pray:
Love through me—even me. [15]

Questions to Consider

1. What is your attitude towards your children? Do your children see God's love through you? How could you begin demonstrating God's love in your daily life?

2. Ask your child(ren): "How do you know I love you?"—and see what they say!

3. What special traditions do you have in your home that are fond memories in your child's life?

4. Are you offended at one of your children? How can you allow God's love to come down through you into their life? What could you do to demonstrate His love?

5. Is there someone who has offended you that you could cover? If so, how do you plan to go about this? Do you need to do anything to ensure your children know you are going to love this person and no longer criticize them?

6. What have your children been asking of you that would only take a little time, yet demonstrate how much you love them?

Notes

[1] F.B. Meyer, *Through the Bible Day by Day,* Volume II (Philadelphia: American Sunday-School Union), 53.

[2] F.B. Meyer, *Samuel the Prophet* (CrossReach Publications, 2017), 12.

[3] F.B. Meyer, *Our Daily Homily,* accessed August 3, 2019, https://www.christianity.com/devotionals/our-daily-homily-fb-meyer/our-daily-homily-february-23-11529520.html

[4] R.B., "Wisdom Quotes," accessed July 19, 2019, https://lamplighter.net/c/resources/wisdom-quotes/

[5] Amy Carmichael, *Edges of His Ways* (Fort Washington, Pennsylvania: Christian Literature Crusade, 1955), 146.

[6] D.L. Moody, "Good Reads," accessed July 19, 2019, https://www.goodreads.com/quotes/4196903-if-i-could-relive-my-life-i-would-devote-my

[7] Amy Carmichael, *Whispers of His Power* (Fort Washington, Pennsylvania: CLC Publications, 1982), 218.

[8] Every time Michael or I discipline our children, we tell them that it is because we love them.

[9] Andrew Murray, *How to Bring Your Children to Christ* (Pittsburgh & Colfax Streets: Whitaker House, 1984), 159.

[10] Amy Carmichael, *If* (Fort Washington, Pennsylvania: Christian Literature Crusade, 1938), 46.

[11] Jill Briscoe, *Prayer That Works* (Colorado Springs, Colorado.: Tyndale House Publishers, Inc., 2000), 5.

[12] Wayne Erbsen, *Manners and Morals of Victorian America* (Asheville, North Carolina: Native Ground Books & Music, 2009), 60.

[13] Helen Keller, "Good Reads," accessed on July 19, 2019, https://www.goodreads.com/quotes/17302-i-long-to-accomplish-a-great-and-noble-task-but

[14] Carmichael, *Whispers of His Power,* 218.

[15] Carmichael, *Edges of His Way,* 110.

Pearl of Wisdom #3
Teach Your Children How to Pray

*"For this child I prayed, and the LORD has granted me
my petition which I asked of Him."*

1 Samuel 1:27

*"Moreover, as for me, far be it from me that I should sin
against the LORD in ceasing to pray for you..."*

1 Samuel 12:23

Hannah was a woman of heartfelt prayer. At the Tabernacle, she prayed earnestly for a son, and God heard her prayer (1 Samuel 1:10-20). In fact, she named her longed-for son Samuel, or "Heard of God." Samuel's very name was a testimony to her answered prayer!

As Hannah dropped off her son at the Tabernacle, she worshipped God with a glorious prayer (1 Samuel 2:1-11)—with Samuel right beside her. I can only imagine that the coat Hannah brought to Samuel each year was also saturated in prayer.

Scripture tells us that Samuel was a man of prayer from the time Hannah "called his name Samuel" (1 Samuel 1:20), to his old age. What began at his mother's knee during his three precious years at home culminated in a life in constant communication with God. In fact, Samuel was so committed to prayer that he told the children of Israel, "Moreover, as for me, far be it from me that I should sin against the LORD in ceasing to pray for you" (1 Samuel 12:23).

Samuel's relationship with God was ignited through his mother's prayers, and cultivated over time in God's presence and through His Word. If we desire to raise children who know how to fellowship with God, move the heart of God, and intercede for others, we need to teach them how to pray.

How Do We Pray?
When it comes to prayer, many women feel inadequate. I know I do! We think that, unless we pray in a dark closet for an hour every day, we fall short. However, this attitude is the wrong one for us to have—and a big hindrance to prayer, in general. We must cultivate a relationship with God through prayer, and then do whatever we can to teach our children to pray as well.

We must also realize that God is not just someone to go to when we are in need of something. Yes, He is there for desperate times or when we need help; but, He is also there to be glorified, magnified, and exalted for who He is. God is worthy of our praise!

So, how do we pray? Jesus's disciples did not know how to pray, so they asked Him to teach them to pray. Jesus's response is recorded in Matthew 6:9-13:

> *In this manner, therefore, pray:*
> *Our Father in heaven,*
> *Hallowed be Your name.*
> *Your kingdom come.*
> *Your will be done*
> *On earth as it is in heaven.*
> *Give us this day our daily bread.*
> *And forgive us our debts,*
> *As we forgive our debtors.*
> *And do not lead us into temptation,*
> *But deliver us from the evil one.*
> *For Yours is the kingdom and the power*
> *and the glory forever. Amen.*

Jesus's prayer sets a wonderful pattern for us to follow when we pray. The pattern can be summed up by the acronym A-C-T-S:

A stands for Adoration—"Our Father in heaven, hallowed be Your name" (Matthew 6:9). We are called to adore God, as we worship Him for who He is and all that He stands for! A great way to adore God is by reading through the Psalms, as they turn our mind and thoughts towards God. The Psalms also magnify His wonderful attributes:

> *Give unto the LORD, O you mighty ones, give unto the LORD glory and strength. Give to the Lord the glory due to His name; worship the LORD in the beauty of holiness.*
>
> *— Psalm 29:1-2*

C represents Confession—"forgive us our debts as we forgive our debtors" (Matthew 6:12). We are called to confess any sins we have committed, knowingly or unknowingly, asking for God's forgiveness:

> *Who can understand his errors? Cleanse me from secret faults. Keep back Your servant also from presumptuous sins; let them not have dominion over me. Then I shall be blameless, and I shall be innocent of great transgression.*
>
> *— Psalm 19:12-13*

T is for Thanksgiving. We are to thank God for the many blessings he has given us: our salvation, our freedom, our families, our children, our homes, our jobs, and so forth.

Oh, give thanks to the LORD, for He is good! For His mercy endures forever.

— *Psalm 107:1*

S represents Supplication—"Give us this day our daily bread...And do not lead us into temptation, but deliver us from the evil one" (Matthew 6:11, 13a). We are to bring our requests to God, asking Him to meet our needs and the needs of others, fulfill our desires, bring revival, and, most importantly, save and protect our children!

Call to Me, and I will answer you, and show you great and mighty things, which you do not know.

— *Jeremiah 33:3*

We don't have to follow this patten perfectly every time we pray. There are times when we are so desperate that we cry out to God like Hannah did when asking God for a son. Sometimes, we are so in awe of God that we break out in praise, worshiping God as Hannah did when she gave up Samuel as a sacrifice. During our prayer times with God and our children, however, the A-C-T-S prayer model is a great example to follow. Our goal should be to simply pray to the living God, and help our children through our example to develop their own prayer relationship with Him.

Kingdom Prayers
Our prayers should always be kingdom-minded. So often, when we pray, we think only of ourselves, our comfort, and our ease—or the comfort and ease of those we love. These prayers are not necessarily wrong; but, when we consider the bigger picture of the kingdom of God, our prayers will change quite dramatically.

When we experience difficulties and trials, we need to realize that God is doing something so much bigger than our comfort and ease, healing or prosperity. During those times, we need to lean and press into God. Kingdom-minded prayers will ask God to teach us through our difficulties and trials rather than asking Him for deliverance. What a huge difference! Building the kingdom of God should always be our highest aim:

Your kingdom come.
Your will be done
On earth as it is in heaven.

For Yours in the kingdom and the power
and the glory forever. Amen.

Praying for Our Children

As parents, we should pray for our children often. But, what should we pray? Below, you will find a few of the requests I have made of the Lord on my children's behalf over the years. I have prayed that:

- God would give Michael and me wisdom in knowing how to raise our children for His glory.

- God's Word would fill, mold, and shape their lives.

- They would come to know God at a young age.

- They would hear His voice early in their life—like Samuel!

- They would be Spirit-filled.

- God would reveal His plan to each of them at a young age.

- God would empower them for His service.

- Their lives would build God's Kingdom.

- They would not be attracted to the world, but be drawn to Christ.

- They would be a blessing to others.

- They would be a godly husband or wife.

- Their marriages would glorify God.

- My boys would be leaders of their homes, and good fathers.

- My girls would be virtuous, building their homes, churches and communities for God's glory.

These prayers are not comprehensive; we should also pray for every pressing need that arises as we raise our children. These needs could be our children's classwork, friendships, character traits that need improvement (such as lying, laziness, meanness, etc.), or emotional states. We should also pray that our children will not believe the lies of the enemy, that they will flee bad relationships, and so much more! Our children should know that we are praying for them, and seeking God on their behalf. They should see that we have a daily prayer time and know that we are praying for them throughout the day.

If we do not pray with and for our children, then who will? Do you remember what Samuel told the children of Israel as he ushered in the new kingdom? He stated, "Moreover, as for me, far be it from me that I should sin against the LORD in ceasing to pray for you..." (1 Samuel 12:23). Samuel considered it a sin to cease from praying for those whom he was responsible for. As mothers, we do not want to sin against God by ceasing to pray for our precious children that God has gifted to us.

Praying with Our Children

From the youngest of ages, our children are ready to be brought to Christ. In Matthew 19:13-15, several people brought their children to Jesus, so "He might put His hands on them and pray" (verse 13). Jesus disciples', though, rebuked the people for bothering Jesus with their children. But, Jesus declared, "Let the little children come to Me, and do not forbid them; for of such is the kingdom of heaven." Then, He laid His hands on the children and blessed them.

Mothers, we need to bring our children to Jesus—so that He can bless and reveal Himself to them. In fact, Jesus wants us to bring our children to Him. When we pray with our children, we bring them into the very presence of Christ. And there is nothing more important we can do as mothers! By bringing our children to Christ through prayer and in teaching them to pray, we show our children how to cultivate their own relationship with God.

How do we teach our children to pray? By praying with them. When our children are infants, we pray over them. Then, as they start talking, we have them repeat our prayers. Then, as they grow older, we pray and then give them the opportunity to pray. By demonstrating how to pray, guiding our children through prayer, and then giving them the opportunity to pray, our children learn to pray. How often should we pray? As often as we can. In fact, Scripture states that we are to "pray without ceasing" (1 Thessalonians 5:17).

It is so important that we, mothers, realize that we do not have to be experts in prayer to teach our children to pray. If we just pray as we are able, our children will follow our example. There are ample opportunities every day to take our children to God through prayer—and the younger the child, the better! We can start teaching our children to pray while they nurse in our arms, and as soon as they can utter, "Amen." When else should we pray? We should pray:

- When our children are sick.

- When they are sad or lonely.

- At mealtimes.

- When our children don't know what to do.

- When we don't know what to do.

- When our children are burdened, worried, or stressed.

- When they have been hurt by others.

- When our children have friendship issues. (See Luke 6:28.)

- When they are being disciplined.

Bedtime is probably the most important time of the day to pray with our children—as the day is settled, and we have the time to sit on their bed and pray. Children are always ripe for spiritual things at night. Often, they don't want to go to bed, so we have a captive audience! I know how exhausted we, as parents, are at night. It can be hard to get little ones to bed, but bedtime prayers are so important. They are a sacrifice that we must make for God and our children! I would like to encourage moms who are too sleepy at night to make a cup of tea or coffee an hour before bedtime (to get you through), or have your husband pray with your children. Do whatever it takes! Prayer time is a habit you cannot afford to ignore! Everything hinges on evening prayer time—in fact, several of my children came to Christ as they prayed before bed. Our children are so trained to pray before bed that they don't let Michael and me get away with not praying. In fact, they are more disciplined than we are: our girls will not go to bed unless we pray with them. What a wonderful habit!

By making prayer a habit, we teach our children how to handle the difficult things in life: by casting their cares upon the Lord, and allowing Him to work through the difficult situations in their lives. The goal is for our children to make prayer second nature in their life.

On my way home from school, my daughter Abby and I talked about her teacher's upcoming wedding that Saturday. She had planned an outdoor wedding, and the forecast was calling for rain! Abby immediately said, "We need to pray that it doesn't rain." Rather than worrying, Abby saw a need, and the first thing she thought to do was pray —which is the goal of teaching our children to pray!

What should we do when our children do not have the answer, find themselves in a difficult circumstance, or are in need of provision? We should not fix the situation immediately—which is our natural tendency. Instead, we should take our children into the presence of God through prayer and allow Him to work out the difficulty in their life.

My children all have needs, wants, and desires that Michael and I cannot meet — a pilot license, medical school, cars, camps, guitars, music lessons, etc. — so they faithfully take them to God. I don't know how God will provide for all these needs, but my children have learned early in life to look to God for provision rather than their parents.

Heartfelt Prayers

So often, parents and children get into the habit of praying rote prayers that are mere words with no meaning. In Matthew 6:7, Jesus teaches us about prayer: "And when you pray, do not use vain repetitions as the heathen do. For they think that they will be heard for their many words." Instead, we must ensure that our prayers are heartfelt, especially when we pray with our children. C.H. Spurgeon lays out what he believes to be the best plan for teaching children to pray in his message on "The Child Samuel's Prayer":

> *I take this to be the best plan. Let the Christian parent explain to the child what prayer is; tell him that God answers prayer; direct him to the Savior, and then urge him to express his desires in his own language, both when he rises, and when he goes to rest. Gather the little ones around your knee and listen to their words, suggesting to them their needs, and reminding them of God's gracious promise. You will be amazed, and, I may add, sometimes amused too; but you will be frequently surprised at the expressions they will use, the confessions they will make, the desires they will utter; and I am certain that any Christian person standing within ear-shot, and listening to the simple prayer of a little child earnestly asking God for what it thinks it wants, would never afterwards wish to teach a child a form, but would say, that as a matter of education to the heart the extemporaneous utterance was infinitely superior to the best form, and that the form should be given up for ever.[1]*

Spurgeon encourages parents to allow their children to use their own language, and speak from the heart, rather than using a specific or rote prayer. The "form" he refers to is the religious prayers of the Anglican church, which were prayed word for word rather than from the heart.

Any prayer we pray over and over again can easily become rote. So, we must make sure our prayers are heartfelt and passionate. After all, we are speaking to the living God! We cannot help but utter heartfelt words of praise and thanksgiving when we really comprehend to Whom we direct our prayers.

When We Don't Feel Like Praying

In our home, Michael and I tell our children, "When you don't feel like praying, that is when you need to pray the most!" So, when our children say they don't want to pray, we tell them they have to—and they do! We want to teach our children to pray even when they don't feel like praying. It only takes a few times of requiring our children to pray before they realize that they have to do so.

We have so much working against us whenever we go to pray—it is one of the hardest things to do! Jill Briscoe says, "Prayer that works, takes work!" How true! Yet, like most things in life, the things that are the most valuable are the hardest to do. We will never regret spending time in prayer.

When we—or our children—are not in the mood to pray, C.H. Spurgeon encourages us to pray however we can. He states:

> There is no more subtle hindrance to prayer than that of our moods...When you cannot pray as you would, pray as you can. If I feel myself disinclined to pray, then is the time when I need to pray more than ever. Possibly when the soul leaps and exults in communion with God it might more safely refrain from prayer than at those seasons when it drags heavily in devotion.[2]

When we don't feel like entering into fellowship with God, we need to pray the most—so we must simply "pray as [we] can."

Persevering Prayer

It is so easy to give up on prayer.   Too often, we begin to pray for something, and—after a few days, weeks, or months without an answer— we give up and cease to pray. Yet, in Luke 18:1, Jesus tells us "that men always ought to pray and not lose heart."   Furthermore, James 5:16b says, "The effective, fervent prayer of a righteous man avails much."   In her book, *Streams in the Desert*, Mrs. Charles Cowman writes:

> The man who forms the habit of beginning without finishing has simply formed the habit of failure. The man who begins to pray about a thing and does not pray it through to a successful issues of answer has formed the same habit in prayer. To faint is to fail; then defeat brings disheartenment, and unfaith in the reality of prayer, which is fatal to all success.[3]

How long should we pray? Until we have received an answer from God or an assurance in His word that we have our answer.

Prayers of Faith

Children have the ability to pray the most amazing prayers of faith—I cannot begin to tell you of the many, amazing prayers of faith our children have prayed—and that God has answered.   Michael and I are often amazed when our children ask the impossible of God, and He answers their prayers.   In Mark 11:24, Jesus tell us, "Therefore I say to you, whatever things you ask when you pray, believe that you receive them, and you will have them."   It is the faith of a child that moves the heart of God!

When I was pregnant with my fifth child, my four boys prayed for a little sister. The whole family was ready for a girl - especially my eldest son, Daniel.   He was six at the time, and every evening before bed he prayed for a baby sister! Daniel was convinced that I was going to have a little girl.

Well, the time for my ultrasound came. For some reason, Daniel came with me to find out the baby's gender. The doctor announced that I was pregnant with another boy. When Daniel heard the news, he told the doctor, "You are wrong! We are having a girl! God is giving us a girl!" The doctor sweetly smiled, but I was so embarrassed. As we left the doctor's office, Daniel kept insisting that we were having a girl and that the doctor was wrong. That afternoon, he got a good talking to, and later I spoke with Michael about Daniel's embarrassing behavior. That night and every night that followed, Daniel continued to pray for a sister—and I planned for another boy.

Three months before Elijah Thomas was to be born, I had another ultrasound. As the doctor looked at the screen, he asked, "What did I say you were having?" "A boy," I replied. He then said, "Well, I was wrong. You are having a girl." I didn't believe the doctor, and scheduled another, high-level ultrasound to be sure. And sure enough, I was pregnant with a little girl, our Hannah Carol! Daniel was right. God had heard my son's prayer of faith, and confirmed it in his heart—and he wasn't going to take no for an answer!

Answered Prayer
Every mother loves it when she gives something to her children, and they say, "Thank you! I appreciate you!" It is the same with God and answered prayer. When God answers our children's prayers, it is so important that we recognize His answer, and take the time to celebrate it with our children. Not only does He deserve our praise, but this acknowledgement also affirms our children's faith! As parents, it is so important that we teach our children to thank and praise God for every answered prayer in their life.

Anointing with Oil
James 5:14 asks, "Is anyone among you sick? Let him call for the elders of the church, and let them pray over him, anointing him with oil in the name of the Lord." In our home, the elders are our children—as they are all in training as prophets for God. Anytime someone is sick, our family grabs the anointing oil, lays hands on one another, and prays!

Sunday Evening Prayer
It has been said that a family that prays together stays together. Prayer really does bond families together in a unique way—and Michael and I can attest to the truth of this saying. On Sunday evenings, our family partakes in family devotions and family prayer time. In fact, it is our favorite service of the week! It has been so special to watch my children mature in their faith as they pray together.

Our family devotion time has changed over the years. It started with Michael reading from *Streams in the Desert for Children* before we transitioned into reading the regular *Streams in the Desert*. Now, our Sunday evenings begin with worship, led by one of the boys who play guitar. The four boys take turns leading the devotions, which they glean from their personal time with the Lord. Often, we take time to discuss the devotion with one another. We share prayer requests for our home, church, and school—and then, we pray. Each child prays, and their prayers are precious, heartfelt, kingdom-minded prayers. We end our time together by singing "I Love You, Lord"—a song that Michael and I have sung with our children every night before bed since they were babies!

There is power when a family prays together. Years ago, I heard a message by Jon Courson on prayer. He shared how, when his children ask for something, he thinks about it. But, when all five of his children persistently ask him for the same thing, it is much harder to resist giving it to them. The same is true of God, our Father! He delights in blessing His children—just as we do—and does not want to withhold anything good from our lives. We must consistently come before God with our children and pray with perseverance if we want to move the hand of God!

The Blessings of Prayer

When we pray with our children, we not only teach them how to pray, we also show them what we value. Then, when they start to pray on their own, they will pray for the same things we do.

One Sunday evening, the Lord really brought this truth to my attention. My sweet daughter, Abby, was praying, as it was her turn. She asked God for four things: (1) to help her be a blessing to her teachers and friends, (2) to make her a virtuous woman, (3) for her husband to love God more than anything in the world, and (4) for their children to bring Him glory. What seven year old prays for these things? A seven year old, who has been taught how to pray!

Abby has not only learned how to pray, but God will also answer these prayers in her life. She will be a blessing to those around her, as well as a virtuous woman with a godly husband. Through prayer, my daughter is realizing her responsibility at school, who she needs to be, and the type of husband she needs to look for one day.

When we pray with our children, we get to hear about the important things on their heart—and God often uses these things to move our hearts! After hearing our Abby pray for a dog for a few years, Michael and I were determined that we needed to do our part in answering that prayer.

Whenever we drive to school or church, we always pray as a family. When Michael or I forget, our children are so trained that they remind us it is time to pray! On Sundays, we ask God to anoint their daddy, and use him to bless the body of Christ. We also ask that they will be a blessing to the church, and that the people who come will be refreshed, blessed, and encouraged!

When my children were young, Michael would spend a lot of time in the boys' room, talking to them about God's Word, and praying with them. He trained them how to pray, and spoke about the importance of prayer. Now, my boys are old enough to pray together without our direction. All four boys share the same room, and they take turns praying together before singing "I Love You, Lord"—every night. Hearing them pray and sing is the most precious thing ever!

I cannot overstate the blessing a parent experiences when they have children who pray! When we have needs within our church, our children pray for them. One of my children is currently praying for revival in our church—and I am getting ready for it, as God answers the faithful prayers of my children. When I am sick or having a hard day, I have a powerhouse of prayer warriors, who pray for me, and their prayers are full of faith.

I remember one Mother's Day—when I was so depressed, exhausted and weary—that I could not even get out of bed. Michael brought the children into our room, and they laid hands on me. They blessed me, praised God for me, and then prayed for my healing. As mothers, we don't want to miss out on these blessings by not teaching our children to pray!

Egwin

Years ago, my children were playing in the backyard with their cousins, when they ran screaming into the house with a little turtle. They had found him randomly in our backyard, and my son, Josh, asked to keep him as a pet. He named the turtle Egwin.

Egwin was about six inches in length, and he was Josh's pride and joy. One day, Josh took his turtle outside for some exercise and sunshine. While turtles are slow-moving and little, if you leave them alone long enough, they can get far enough away that you lose them—and that is exactly what happened. Egwin was lost in the backyard!

Josh looked for Egwin for hours, and those hours turned into days and days. His devastation led him on a prayer journey, and every night, he would pray earnestly that he would find Egwin again.

For two years, Josh prayed for his turtle. Josh's ninth birthday was approaching, and my husband was ready to take action. Michael was convinced that there would be no better birthday gift for Josh than a turtle. So, he went to the pet store to try and buy him another turtle—as the only thing our son wanted for his birthday was Egwin! The lady at the local pet store informed Michael that he could not purchase a turtle like Egwin, as they were illegal to buy in California. She, then, explained to my husband that Egwin was a water turtle, and there was absolutely no way he could have survived in our backyard for two years. In fact, she said it was a mystery how my children found the turtle in the first place. Regardless, my husband came home severely disappointed.

Two days after Josh's birthday, our children were playing in the backyard with friends, and soon enough, they all ran into the house screaming. They had found Egwin! It was and still is unbelievable! God had answered Josh's prayers, and given him the most wonderful birthday gift ever. What Michael could not do for Josh, God did! What a wonderful reminder for our children. Not only did Josh's answered prayer build up his own faith, but it built up the faith of our whole family.

Teaching our children to come to God in prayer is one of the most important things we can do for them. Prayer helps them develop and deepen their relationship with Him, and they will need this relationship throughout their lives. It teaches our children to rely upon God, and enables them to intercede for others. Prayer is also a powerful tool to impact this world for God's kingdom. As our children grow, they will no longer need our aid as they pray. Instead, they will have a vibrant prayer life that will bless not only them, but also those who are fortunate enough to be on their prayer list. As mothers, we do not want to miss out on the blessings of teaching our children to pray.

Questions to Consider

1. Do you pray with your children daily? If not, when would be a good time in the day to start?

2. What routines (e.g., mealtime, morning, bed time) do you have with your children that enable you to teach them how to pray?

3. What values are you communicating to your children when you pray with them? Do your prayers line up with God's Word?

4. Listen to your children pray. Are they praying kingdom prayers? If not, how can you go about teaching them to pray kingdom prayers?

5. What do your children currently need? How can you help them to take these things to the Lord in prayer?

6. Do you help your children go to the Lord in prayer for their daily needs? If not, how can you cultivate a habit of doing so in your own life, as well as in their lives?

7. Make a list of kingdom prayers that you and your children can pray for on a daily basis. Make sure they line up with God's Word! Consider noting a motivating Bible verse next to each prayer.

Notes

[1] C. H. Spurgeon, "The Child Samuel's Prayer," The Metropolitan Tabernacle Pulpit contains Sermons Preached and Revised by C.H. Spurgeon During the Year 1864. (Pasadena, Texas: Pilgrim Publications, 1991), 475-476.

[2] C.H. Spurgeon, quoted in Mrs. Charles E. Cowman, *Devotions for Morning and Evening* (New York: International Press, 1925), 340.

[3] Mrs. Charles E. Cowman, *Streams in the Desert* (Grand Rapids, Michigan: Zondervan Publishing House, 1925), 150-151.

Pearl of Wisdom #4

Fight to Keep Your Children Before God's Presence

Meanwhile, the child Samuel grew before the Lord.

1 Samuel 2:21

Thou wilt show me the path of life: in thy presence is fullness of joy; at thy right hand there are pleasures for evermore.

Psalm 16:11

When Hannah brought Samuel to the Tabernacle, she was bringing her son to be raised in the very presence of God. As a boy, Samuel slept just outside the Holy of Holies—only a curtain separated him from the Ark of the Covenant, where God's presence dwelt. He was as close to the presence of God as one could be without being killed. In 1 Samuel 2:21, we are told that "Samuel grew before the Lord." He was, literally, molded and shaped by the power of God's presence!

Our homes need to be a Tabernacle, so our children can grow before the presence of God, as Samuel did. As mothers, it is our responsibility to bring the presence of God into our children's lives as much as possible. Then, we need to fight to keep our children in His presence so that they too, can be molded and shaped by the Spirit of God. Then, our children can become men and women, fashioned by God, able to hear His voice, and prepared for the work that He has called them to do.

God's Voice within His Presence

The contrast between the darkness of the times in which Samuel was living and the brightness of his upbringing in God's presence is seen in the setting given to us in within Scripture. Scottish theologian Alexander Maclaren paints a beautiful picture of this scene:

> Samuel slept in the 'Temple of the Lord, where the ark was.' The picture is much more vivid and tender, if we conceive of the dim-eyed old man, lying somewhat apart; of the glimmering night, nearly extinct but still faintly burning; and of the child laid to sleep in the Tabernacle. Surely the picturesque contrast between the sanctity of the ark and the innocent sleep of

childhood is meant to strike us, and to serve as connecting the place with the subsequent revelation. Childlike hearts, which thus quietly rest in the 'secret place of the Most High,' and day and night are near His ark, will not fail of hearing His voice.[1]

When God's word was about to go out in Israel, He spoke to Samuel. This was a direct result of Samuel dwelling in God's presence. Even though the world was dark and God's word was hidden, Samuel was able to hear God's voice, His very word!   If we want our children to be Samuels, prophets, and priests in this world, we must allow them to dwell in God's presence as Samuel did- so they, too, can hear His voice.

Created to Be in His Presence
We were all created to dwell in God's presence. When God created Adam and Eve, He placed Him in the garden, and His desire was to enjoy fellowship with them in the midst of paradise. Yet, this perfect setting was sullied by the devil, who disguised himself as a snake and deceived Adam and Eve, tricking them to eat from the tree of the knowledge of good and evil. At that moment, sin entered the world and separated man from God. Ashamed, Adam and Eve "hid themselves from the presence of the LORD God among the trees of the garden" (Genesis 3:8).   Since that day, mankind's natural state - and where we drift back toward - is separation from God and His presence, as a Holy God cannot dwell with sinful man.

From the moment Adam and Eve sinned, God embarked on a quest to redeem His people. He established a sacrificial system as a way to cover the sins of His people, so He could have fellowship with man, once again. It was through the tabernacle that God once again dwelt with His people.

The Tabernacle
The Tabernacle was a portable "tent of meeting" that God asked Moses to make so that He could dwell amongst His people. God wanted to have fellowship with the Israelites, and to communicate with them as He once communicated with Adam and Even in the Garden.

The Tabernacle was constructed according to a pattern that God designed.   Every article within the Tabernacle—the altar, laver, lampstand, table of showbread, altar of incense, and Ark of the Covenant —pointed to God, and were ways to commune with Him.

God's presence dwelt in the Holy of Holies, within the Ark of the Covenant, separated from man by a curtain. No one was allowed behind the veil, for if they trespassed, they would die. This was because our holy God could not dwell with sinful man.

It was within this Tabernacle that Hannah's precious son lived, slept, learned, and worked throughout his childhood. It is where he grew before the very presence of God.

The Power of His Presence

There is transforming power in the presence of God. Consider Moses, whom God had used to deliver the Israelites out of slavery in Egypt. Moses asked God to allow him to see His glory, but God refused. He told Moses that no man could see God's face and live. However, if Moses hid in a cleft of the rock, God would walk by, and when He walked by, God would put out His hand to cover Moses, so he could experience God's presence and live (Exodus 33:17-22). When he went down the mountain after "seeing" God, Moses's face shone, radiating the glory of God (Exodus 34:29). Moses was transformed by the very presence of God.

We, too, can be transformed by God's presence. In 2 Corinthians 3:18, we are told:

> But we all, with unveiled face, beholding as in a mirror the glory of the Lord, are being transformed into the same image from glory to glory, just as by the Spirit of the Lord.

Because of Christ's sacrifice, God's Spirit can dwell within us, and we can enter into God's presence at any moment, and dwell there. When we enter into His presence, we behold His glory, and He transforms us more and more into His image. However, to experience His presence, we must live a life set apart. As 2 Corinthians 6:16-7:1 states:

> For you are the temple of the living God. As God has said: "I will dwell with them and walk among them. I will be their God, and they shall be My people." Therefore come out from among them and be separate, says the Lord...Therefore, having these promises, beloved, let us cleanse ourselves from all filthiness of the flesh and spirit, perfecting holiness in the fear of God.

To experience God's glory, we must first be holy. Remember, our sin separates us from God, who commands us to pursue holiness, "without which no one will see the Lord" (Hebrews 12:14b). What is holiness? Holiness is living a life "set apart" for God. In Leviticus 20:7, God declares, "Consecrate yourselves therefore, and be holy, for I am the LORD your God." This means that we—and our children—cannot simply do whatever the world is doing. We must cleanse ourselves of all filthiness of the flesh and spirit, so we can be holy and seek God, and when we "see" Him, He will transform our lives. Once we are transformed, like Samuel, God can use us to transform the world. Pastor Robert Murray M'Cheyne valiantly declares, "A holy minister is an awesome weapon in the hand of God."[2]

It is not an easy thing to dwell in the presence of God. Yet, as mothers, our job is not only get our children before God's presence, but fight to keep them there- so they can be molded and shaped by the power of God. It is said that "Christ becomes more real to the one who persists in the cultivation of His presence."[3] We must faithfully allow our children to experience Christ by placing them before God's presence throughout their growing years.

The Church: God's Tabernacle

Samuel was three years old when he was sent to live at the Tabernacle in the presence of God. Like Samuel, our children should be raised in His presence as much as possible. Today, that means keeping them at church as much as possible! In *Raising Them Right: A Saint's Advice on Raising Children*, we read: "The Church, its life, and the Holy Mysteries are like a tabernacle (tent) for the children, and they should be under it without leaving it. Examples indicate how saving and fruitful this is (such as the life of the Prophet Samuel.)"[4]

It is so important that we make church a priority in the lives of our children. We need to get them to church at every opportunity, so they can dwell in the presence of the Lord and hear His voice. Whenever our church doors open, we need to be there, ready to participate in every event, activity, Bible study, camp, and missions trip. We need to help our children to love going to church, and make them feel like church is a second home.

One way we can encourage active participation in church is by attending a church close to home. With modern-day transportation, families can attend a church anywhere. While this convenience allows us to be very specific about the church we attend, it can also hinder us from being an active part of the church community.

My husband's grandparents, John and Carol McClure, lived around the corner from their church, which allowed them to become involved at their church. In fact, Carol ran the prayer ministry for over thirty years; and John was a part of the church board, always running to and from church to sign checks and attend to various services. Being an active part of the church was so important to them that they always encouraged their family members to do the same. I also know a pastor's wife who told me that she wished she had lived closer to church while her children were growing up. Instead, they lived so far from church that her children were not able to make friends or get plugged into the church community. When we make the decision to live near our church, we minimize the hindrances—like traffic or a long commute—that keep us from being a part of our church community.

As our children grow older, there are so many new things competing for their time. Over the years, I have seen a troubling pattern: children stop going to church in their teen years. The reasons vary—they are plugged into another para-church organization, such as a private, Christian high school; they get a job, and have to work on Sundays; they begin playing on a competitive sports team. Once a teenager stops going to church, it is very difficult to get them plugged back into it.

Similarly, some parents let their children decide if they want to go to church. Yet, they are the parents, and the choice should be theirs. Children do not know what is best for themselves, which is why God gave children parents. As parents, it is our job to help our children obey the fourth commandment: "Remember the Sabbath Day, to keep it holy" (Exodus 20:8). Most likely, there will come a time when our children will challenge our requirement for them to go to church. Unless we are diligent to hold the line, one missed service will soon turn into two and three and four, until our children no longer attend church at all.

Michael and I are so blessed to have been raised in Christian homes. Both of our parents had a rule: If we lived in their home, we had to go to church, no matter the circumstance. If we did not, then we were no longer welcome in our parents' homes—even if it was a job that kept us from attending church.

No matter the situation or age of our children, as parents, we must resolve now, "as for me and my house, we will serve the Lord" (Joshua 24:15). Remember, the choice to serve the Lord or spend time in His presence is not our children's—it is ours! And, it is a decision we must one day give account for. We need to teach our children to trust God: if He gives us a command to obey, then He will provide the means to obey it. If a job would like us to work on Sundays, we must trust that God will either change our boss's heart, provide enough money that we do not have to work on Sundays, or provide another job that will allow us to obey Him.

One of the great heartbreaks within the church today is the burden fathers and mothers have for their unsaved or backslidden children, who refuse to attend church. Some children will go to church on Mother's Day or other holidays, but their hearts are far from God. As parents, the decisions we make today will impact who our children are as adults. We must decide going to church is not an option. As long as our children live at home—even if they are past the age of eighteen—they must attend church. Going to church is a discipline we must purpose to cultivate in the lives of our children. And, if we attend a Spirit-filled church that teaches the Word, the chances are that God will get ahold of their heart.

Our Children's Schools: God's Tabernacle

Another way we can keep our children in God's presence is by enrolling them in a school where the Holy Spirit flows through the teachers and the curriculum brings students' thoughts towards God throughout the day. Finding a school like this can be difficult, but it is imperative if we want our children to dwell in the presence of God as much as possible. If we cannot find this kind of school, then we should consider homeschooling, so that our children can be kept in God's presence as they learn.

Our church school has been such a blessing for my family. In fact, most weeks, my children are at church every single day of the week! I remind them often that they are just like Samuel—dwelling in God's Tabernacle in a day when the Word of the Lord is rare—so they can be trained up as God's prophets to transform the nation for His glory (I can hear them now, "There goes mom again!").

Our Homes: God's Tabernacle

Our children should not just experience God's presence at church and school; they should also experience it at home. In fact, our homes should be a place where God's presence reigns! Just as the Tabernacle was filled with articles of the faith, our homes should be filled with elements of the faith, too: worship, prayer, the reading of God's Word, the leading of the Holy Spirit, the washing and cleansing of our sins, sacrifices made on behalf of others, and so forth.

Our job, as mothers, is to make God real to our children within our homes. We need to work towards providing opportunities for our children to hear God's voice, experience His presence, and enjoy His blessings! Brother Lawrence, author of *The Practice of the Presence of God*, writes: "There is not in the world a kind of life more sweet and delightful, than that of a continual conversation with God; those only can comprehend it who practice and experience it."[5]

How do we bring a "continual conversation with God" into our children's lives? We play worship music, talk about God, read and discuss God's Word, pray with our children, enjoy the beauty of God's creation, read good books, listen to audio dramas like Lamplighter Theatre or Adventures in Odyssey, which focus our children's minds on God.

Our homes should be sanctuaries, where God's presence resides and praises and worship are on the lips and hearts of those who dwell there. Peter Marshall, former chaplain of the Senate, described a lovely home he once visited:

I was privileged, in the spring, to visit a home that was to me and I am sure to the occupants—a little bit of Heaven. There was beauty there. There was a keen appreciation of the finer things of life, and an atmosphere in which it was impossible to keep from thinking of God.

The room was bright and white and clean, as well as cozy. There were many windows. Flowers were blooming in pots and vases, adding their fragrance and beauty. Books lined one wall —good books—inspiring and instructive—good books— good friends. Three bird cages hung in the brightness and color of this beautiful sanctuary, and the songsters voiced their appreciation by singing as if their little throats would burst.

Nature's music, nature's beauty—nature's peace...It seemed to me a kind of Paradise that had wandered down, an enchanted oasis—home.[6]

Wouldn't it be wonderful if our homes were "atmospheres in which it is impossible to keep from thinking of God?" For this to be true, we must purge our homes from anything that distracts us or draws us away from the presence of God, and then cultivate the presence of God in our homes.

Hindrances to God's Presence

In *The Magician's Nephew*, C.S. Lewis wrote, "I will not live at the mercy of the telephone!" Mark Hamby, remarking on Lewis' quote, stated, "I think he would have added email and Facebook!"[7] Prior to modern technology, some common distractions that kept us from God's presence were not-so-good books or magazines or friends with bad influences. However, with the onset of the radio, television, and the internet, the amount of information and entertainment that invades our home and influences our children is exploding. Today, there is an overwhelming presence of audio and visual technologies that are hindering the presence of God in our lives.

Daily, our children are drawn to connect with the world through modern technology. Let's face it: screens are mesmerizing! And now, more than ever, our children are being drawn away from the presence of God into an enticing cyber world that offers them whatever their heart desires—social networking, games, movies, music, and streaming services—at their fingertips.

These modern forms of entertainment are molding and shaping our children according to the pattern of this world. Francis Schaffer eloquently stated that, "Whoever controls the media controls the culture." Years ago, before the invention of internet, Walt Disney famously said, "Movies can and do have tremendous power in shaping young lives...."[8] And, it is not just movies anymore: it's music, video games, social media, and everything available on the internet. We must remember that the making of man is the culmination of everything that has been put into him throughout his growing years!

We are just beginning to discover the effects of technology on our children. In the book, *Screens and Teens*, by Kathy Koch, we learn that technology is to our children as air is for us to breathe. And because of that constant usage, their brains are being rewired. We can find that because of technology, our children are more impatient, have a need to multitask, experience sleeplessness, are complaining, feel entitled, are apathetic, and suffer from boredom.[9]

We are also told that video games are rewiring our children's brains, so that when our sons see pornography, they will immediately become addicted to it![10]

What's alarming is that our children are replacing their desire for God with technology. In doing so, technology has become an idol in our children's lives. Kathy Koch, author of *Screens and Teens*, writes about how children try to fulfill their deep, core needs with technology, which is being used as a counterfeit to God. Only God can fulfill our core needs of security, identity, belonging, purpose, and competence.[11]

How can we help our children find fulfillment in God rather than technology? Our children will naturally turn to what is easy, to something they don't have to work for. When they are having a hard day, they will want to run to technology to console them, to escape. When they are feeling unworthy, they are going to look to technology to discover their purpose. As parents, we must fight to keep our children in God's presence, so that He is filling their deepest needs. Rather than technology, our children should be turning to God and His Word for comfort, assurance and fulfillment.

Fight for Your Home

Fifty years ago, no one could have imagined how the enemy would captivate the hearts and minds of our children with devices like phones, tablets, and computers. Yet today, he is using them to mold and shape our children according to a pagan culture.

I can tell you story after story of how a child has been seduced by technology and then taken captive. Whether through social media, video games or pornography, our children are daily being drawn into an enticing world that will draw them away from Christ.

We must remember our vision for our children! Do we want grown adult children who are addicted to technology and captivated by the enemy? Men who are ignoring their wife and children to pursue their own lusts? Or do we desire children who are God's voice to His people bringing repentance to a nation through His powerful word, who are led and guided by His Holy Spirit! Remembering who we desire our children to be and what God has called them to be will enable us to fight for our children.

Consider Nehemiah as he worked to rebuild the wall of Jerusalem, which had been destroyed at the start of the Babylonian captivity. When the enemies in the land heard what Nehemiah and the Israelites were doing, they began to plot an attack against them. Those who were building grew weary and discouraged, but Nehemiah said to them, "Do not be afraid of them. Remember the Lord, great and awesome, and fight for your brethren, your sons, your daughters, your wives, and your houses" (Nehemiah 4:14). Then, Nehemiah required them to hold a weapon in one hand and a tool of building in the other; and the people continued building.

Our children were created to build God's kingdom, to repair the ruins. And, the enemy is after them! Our job, as mothers, is to fight for our sons and daughters and homes, just like the Israelites of Nehemiah's day. We must not allow the enemy to enter our homes and take your children captive!

Mother: The Gatekeeper

As mothers, we are the gatekeepers of our homes. In Proverbs 31:27, a virtuous woman is described as one who "watches over the ways of her household, and does not eat the bread of idleness." A wise women watches over her home and does not allow anything to enter it that will influence her family away from God. A Proverbs 31 woman does not idly watch as her children are taken captive by the philosophies of this world.

One way we can watch over our home is to carefully filter the things our children watch and give their time to. Handing our children a phone, tablet, or computer with unlimited access to the internet is not the best decision—especially when they are young! As mothers, we must help our children navigate the technological world. We must remember that the mind is the window of your soul. If our children are looking at things that are not pure, "then what is not pure will apply of its own accord to be looked at, and will soon demand an entrance at the door."[12] Our eyes can quickly influence our whole body as there is, indeed, a very real connection between the lust of the eyes and the lust of the flesh. As mothers, it is our responsibility to help filter what our children are looking at as we are training them for life. Psalm 101:2b-3 states: "I will walk within my house with a perfect heart. I will set nothing wicked before my eyes; I hate the work of those who fall away; It shall not cling to me." Our homes should be places where God's presence reigns supreme, and our children are free from the temptations of the world that comes through their eyes.

In our home, we consider Philippians 4:8 anytime we make decisions about what we take part in:

> *Finally, brethren, whatever things are true, whatever things are noble, whatever things are just, whatever things are pure, whatever things are lovely, whatever things are of good report, if there is any virtue and if there is anything praiseworthy—meditate on these things.*

When Michael and I decide what our children can watch or participate in, we use this verse as our filter. What does this look like in practice? If we want to watch a movie, we ask ourselves: "Is it true? Is it noble? Is it just? Is it pure? Is it lovely? Is it of good report?" If so, we watch and enjoy it. However, if it does not pass the Philippians 4:8 test, we skip it! The same is true for music: Do the lyrics lift me up and encourage me in my walk with God? If not, then I will not bother to mediate upon those things. We need to encourage our children to meditate on things that cultivate a relationship with God.

As far as video games are concerned, we have chosen to not allow our children to play them, because they are not true. Take Minecraft, for example—the entire game if focused on building a false world. Michael and I believe the enemy is using video games like Minecraft to get our children to leave reality and become attracted to a false world. Through video games, our children are literally building lives in false realities, rather than building this world for God's glory.

Being a gatekeeper does not just mean filtering what our children watch, listen to, or play. It also means making wise choices with our children's time. 1 Corinthians 10:23 states: "All things are lawful for me, but not all things are helpful; all things are lawful for me, but not all things edify." In other words, just because we can do something, doesn't mean we should! Just because we can, doesn't mean we are going to better off for it! We should keep in mind the old saying: "Good, better, best. Never let it rest. Until your good is better and your better is best!"

As the gatekeeper of the home, mothers have the ability to make wise choices regarding their children's time. When the family jumps in the car, do the children watch a movie or play video games on a tablet? Or, do they talk to each other, pray, listen to worship music, look at God's creation, listen to a Lamplighter or audio book as a family? The choice in how your family and children spend time is yours.

When your children come home from school, do they run to play on a video game or watch a television show? Do they turn on their computer and plug in earbuds? Or, do your children work on their homework, do their chores, or put on an apron to help with dinner?

Not too long ago one of my sons came home from school, and wanted to play chess with his friends online. However, we have a chess set at home, and he has four siblings who also love to play chess. We could have allowed Micah to play chess with his friends; but if we had, we would have never gotten him off his computer. Instead, we told Micah, "Play chess with your brothers and sisters." Sometimes, we have to make unpopular choices like these on behalf of our children, since we are the gatekeepers of our homes.

Having taught junior high for a number of years, I cannot tell you how many of my students have told me that they need help keeping distractions out of their life. They were praying for help to chose to do their homework over playing on their phones or giving their time to video games. Children desire boundaries, yet too often, their parents do not set limits for them. We must realize that it is our responsibility to set boundaries that will help our children be successful in life. We must remember that they can't do this in their own strength or on their own—they need us to help them!

When we do set boundaries for our children, it is so important to explain why we have set them. Understanding our reasons will help our children develop habits for their own life. Eventually, they will agree with us and become advocates among their friends. Our children have become so trained that—if they are watching a movie that starts to go south—they turn it off themselves. If they walk in a room at someone's house and see something they know doesn't please the Lord, they either walk out of the room or ask their friend to change the channel.

I find that so often we start off strong with boundaries, and then through the pressure of our children or those around us, we slowly loosen them and allow the enemy to take ground. Or, perhaps we hear a great message or sermon and we make a commitment to set boundaries and then over time, we end up in this place that we don't know how we arrived. That is okay! All we have to do it tell our children, God is showing me that what our family is doing is not pleasing to him, we have to restructure our home to make it more pleasing to God. Your children might kick and scream, but after about a week, they will rest under your new rules. We must remember, that our children want to see that we have a faith that is real! If God is showing us something, and we are restructuring our home to be more aligned with His word, they will respect us for it. They might not like it now, but they will appreciate it later. Remember, our job is not the happiness of our children, it is their holiness! We want them to be holy so they can be "set apart" enough to see and experience the living God.

One time, Michael and I were eating dinner with our oldest son, Daniel, and several of his friends. He was explaining that he wasn't allowed to have a phone until he was seventeen and could afford to pay for it himself. His friends, who were twenty-two and twenty-six at the time, told him, "You have no idea how blessed you are! If our parents had kept us from wasting our time or exposing ourselves to so much garbage, our lives would be much better off." Mothers, we must love our children enough to do whatever it takes to be the gatekeepers of our homes and our children's hearts!

The Blessing of a Small Home

I want to just briefly touch on the blessing of having a small home. When my children were little, I had a friend, who encouraged me to be thankful for our small house. She told me that, when she moved from a tiny home in Willow Glen to a larger home in Almaden, her family became isolated from each other. She didn't realize how much of a blessing it was to live in a small home with everyone always in each other's business—which leads to great accountability! After the move, her son got into a lot of trouble. He was checking out inappropriate books at the library, and she didn't realize it until it was too late because his room was at the other end of the house.

Cleaning up My Home

When I first studied the life of Hannah and her relationship with Samuel, my head spun. The idea that Samuel had lived before the presence of the Lord as a child hit me like dynamite! In fact, when I studied the life Hannah years ago, I went through a purging of our home and got rid of anything I felt was keeping my children from the presence of the Lord— for one, video games.

When my son, Daniel, was little, he loved video games. It started with a little green Leapster, which was a handheld device he received when he was only about three. It only allowed you to do math and drawing, but he would play that thing for hours. Eventually, I became so fed up with him and his brothers fighting over it that I took it away. Every time they found it and started using it, it was like their flesh came out, and they were always fighting. I also didn't like how they tuned everyone out, and just went into their own world.

Then, Daniel received a game cube for his birthday. He would ask me to play every day, and I got so exhausted from him constantly asking that Michael and I decided that he could only play them on Saturdays. After that, Daniel would play for hours and hours every Saturday, and as his brothers grew older, they began to play them together. But I noticed something happening—after they finished playing, they would whine and complain and be mean to each other. It took me a while to figure out that it was the hours of video games that caused them being so agitated and mean to each other. Well, I didn't know what to do about this problem until I did my study on Hannah. After reading about Samuel growing in God's presence, I felt like God gave me permission to clean up my home of everything that kept my children from His presence- and that was exactly what I needed.

And then we found ways to keep my children constantly before God's presence using Philippians 4:8 as our filter for what our children watch and hear. Our children have spent hours playing legos on the living room floor listening to audio books, praise music, Lamplighter theatre, the KIDS bible, and Adventures in Odyssey. My sweet girls love to listen to Lamplighter theatre every night before they go to bed.

Michael and I are very passionate about only using technology as a tool in our home, not for entertainment. As parents, we are accountable for our children's time—and we don't want to look back and see that our children wasted their childhood on television, movies, video games, or surfing the internet. Our children are not allowed to have a phone until they actually need one, or can pay for it themselves. And, once they can have a phone, it doesn't come with internet access! Our children don't own a smartphone or tablet of any kind. We only have one television in the entire house, and we don't have cable. Our children are not allowed to use the family iPad or pick up one of our phones—unless there is a necessity.

As a result, our children have a lot of time on their hands. And, they have used that time to teach themselves how to crochet, trap and skin animals, cook, bake, make board games, and so much more. They have learned the crafts of sewing and woodworking; they learned how to complete so many other projects. Many times, they have used the internet to find specific instructions, but they have not spent time just browsing around online. It is this lack of purpose that gets a lot of children into trouble. Occasionally, we watch a family movie or two together on the weekend, or if Michael and I are out on a date, our children can watch a movie together if their homework is done. However, this movie has to be pre-approved; our children are not allowed to browse around to find a movie to watch. In requiring our children to use technology purposefully, Michael and I are training them for life!

Similarly, anytime our children invite friends over, we require their friends to leave their phones in a basket by our front door. This rule protects our children from being exposed to things that are not pleasing to God, and it ensures that the children actually play together. We really want to avoid our children inviting friends over, and then, having them play on their phones the entire time.

Setting technology boundaries is not easy—but it is so worth it. My children have wonderful relationships with each other because they have spent so much time together. They have made memories and established relationships that will last a lifetime through endless hours of playing games and school, making lemonade stands or Lego stop-motion videos, starting a rubber band gun business, and so on. Even more, these boundaries have allowed God's Spirit to rule and reign in our home. And, we have kept the family unity, which is so important to Michael and me.

One evening, our family invited our neighbors over for dinner. Afterwards, they sat on our couch and kept telling us, "Your home is so peaceful. This is what a home should be like!" By the end of the evening, the husband turned to us and asked, "Where is your television?" It was hiding in the armoire in the living room. Do you desire peace in your home? Allow God's presence to reign supreme, rather than the latest technology.

I encourage each of you to talk with your husband about setting technology boundaries. Spend time in prayer together, asking God how you can make your home a place where your children grow before His presence. Ensuring God's presence reign's supreme will look different in each home, as we are all different people with different strengths and weaknesses. I know many moms, who manage all of their children's electronics, which is great! However, as a mom of seven, I hardly have time to manage my own technology use, let only my children's. What really matters, is that we all do our job as the gatekeeper of our home, and fight to keep our children in God's presence.

Fullness of Joy

I think one of the big lies of our culture is that, if we "set apart" our homes as God's Tabernacle, our children will miss out. Our children face so much pressure from the world and their friends to engage in activities that draw them away from Gods's presence. Yet, people were raised for thousands of years without these modern influences, and they turned out just fine—in many cases, they turned out better!

We must remember that the enemy is constantly trying to lure our children away to follow after and shape them according to the pattern of this world. Remember the Sirens of ancient Greek mythology? They were gods who sang bewitching music that enticed sailors to their destruction. Earlier, we looked at how Odysseus ordered his men tie him to his ship's mast before plugging their ears with wax, so he could hear the Sirens' music without being destroyed.

Well, there is another hero in Greek mythology, named Jason, who was able to withstand the enticement of Sirens. But, he was only able to do so with the aid of Orpheus. As Jason's ship sailed past the island of the Sirens, Orpheus drew out his lyre, and played a song that was more beautiful than the one the Sirens sang. His music kept Jason and all of the sailors safe.

What a wonderful lesson for us! When we raise our children in the presence of God, they will realize that all that the world has to offer cannot compare to the fullness of joy they experience in Christ. What Christ offers us is more pleasing and fulfilling than what the world has to offer. The world and its pleasures leads only to death and destruction. God and His presence leads to life, eternal! Psalm 16:11 declares, "Thou wilt show me the path of life: in thy presence is fullness of joy; at thy right hand there are pleasures for evermore." When we make God's presence the most important thing throughout our children's growing years, they will be able to withstand the pressure of the world and the enticement of its gods.

Our children do not miss out when they grow before God's presence. Instead, they are filled with joy and pleasures insurmountable. I recently asked my children if they felt like they were missing out on anything because they don't have phones, play video games, or own all the latest and greatest things. They all said, "No, we have the best life ever! We have so much fun: we get to shoot BB Guns, ride our bikes, play board games, do fun activities, and not waste our time." Clearly, our children have enjoyed their childhood!

When we allow our children to grow in God's presence, they develop godly character. Then, when we start to give them more freedom—especially with technology—they have discipline, self-control, and discernment, which allows them to filter the garbage that comes with it. Technology is not going away, nor are any of the temptations that attempt to lure our children away from God. The biggest gift we can give our children is character to navigate through this world to the glory of God.

A Blessed Home

When we make God's presence the most important thing in our home, not only are our children blessed, but our home and everything within it is blessed, too.

When David became King of Israel, one of the first things on his agenda was to bring the Ark of the Covenant back to Jerusalem. He had the ark placed in a cart; and as he and his men traveled, the oxen pulling the cart stumbled. Uzzah, one of the drivers, reached out to steady the ark, and he was instantly struck dead because he had touched it. The ark represented the presence of God, and no one who touched it could live. Uzzah's death caused King David and the people of Israel to fear God - so much so, that David decided to leave the ark at the the house of the Obed-Edom, while he contemplated what to do with it. In 2 Samuel 6:11, we are told: "The ark of the LORD remained in the house of Obed-Edom the Gittite three months. And the LORD blessed Obed-Edom and all his household."

Obed-Edom, his family, and his home were blessed because God's presence dwelt there. What a wonderful lesson for us! If we want our household to be blessed—our children, ourselves, and everything we have —we must allow God's presence to rule and reign in our home.

When we raise our children in God's presence, He becomes the most important thing in their life. They will not only experience "fullness of joy" and "pleasures for evermore" (Psalm 16:11), but they will continue to reap them in this life and for eternity. And like Samuel, your children will be molded and shaped by the presence and power of God, ready to do the work that He has called them to do!

Questions to Consider

1. Is your home a Tabernacle, a place where God's presence reigns supreme? What elements of the Tabernacle are missing from your home?

2. What is preventing you or your children from getting plugged into your church? What can you do to become more involved?

3. Is there anything in your home that prevents your children from growing before God's presence?

4. What boundaries have you created that enable you to be the gatekeeper of your home? Is there anything else you can do to ensure God's presence reigns supreme?

5. Is there anything in your home that does not pass the Philippians 4:8 filter? If so, what can you do to fix it?

6. What can you do to cultivate God's presence in your home?

Notes

---

[1] Alexander MacLaren, *MacLaren's Expositions of Holy Scripture, Volume 1* (Grand Rapids, Michigan: WM. B. Eerdmans Publishing Co., 1959), 269.

[2] Robert Murray M'Cheyne quoted in Warren Wiersbe, *On Being a Servant of God* (Grand Rapids, Michigan: Baker Books, 1993), 45.

[3] Mrs. Charles E. Cowman, *Streams in the Desert* (Grand Rapids, Michigan: Zondervan Publishing House, 1925), 174.

[4] Elisabeth Elliot, *The Shaping of a Christian Family* (Grand Rapids, Michigan: Fleming H. Revell, 1992), 68.

[5] Brother Lawrence, *The Practice of the Presence of God with Spiritual Maxims* (Grand Rapids, MI: Spire Books, 1958), 44.

[6] Carolyn Mahaney, *Feminine Appeal* (Wheaton, Illinois: Crossway, 2003), 113-114.

[7] Mark Hamby, "Wisdom Quotes," accessed July 19, 2019, https://lamplighter.net/c/resources/wisdom-quotes/

[8] Nancy DeMoss Wolgemuth & Dannah Gresh, *Lies Young Women Believe* (Chicago: Moody Publishers, 2008), 156.

[9] Kathy Koch, *Screens and Teens* (Chicago: Moody Publishers, 2015), 35.

[10] Trent Auguston, "Gaming, Pornography, and the Masculinity Crisis," June 10, 2015, accessed July 19, 2019, https://onepeterfive.com/gaming-pornography-and-the-masculinity-crisis/

[11] Koch, *Screens and Teens,* 15.

[12] Bramwell Booth, *Bible Battles-Axes* (St. Albans: The Salvation Army Printing Works, 1915), 78.

Pearl of Wisdom #5

Saturate Your Children in God's Word

Then the LORD appeared again in Shiloh.
For the LORD revealed Himself to Samuel in Shiloh by the word
of the LORD. And the word of Samuel came to all Israel.

1 Samuel 3:21

Samuel was a boy raised in the presence of God, and as a result, he was able to hear God's voice in a day when the Word of the Lord was rare. First Samuel 3:21 declares, "For the LORD revealed Himself to Samuel in Shiloh by the word of the LORD." What did Samuel do with this revelation? He shared God's Word with all of Israel (1 Samuel 4:1). Samuel heard God's Word, shared it with the people, and all of Israel was blessed as a result!

We, too, are living in a day when the Word of the Lord is rare. Like Samuel, our children need to grow up in the presence of God, saturated in His Word. In John 8:31-32, Jesus stated, "If you abide in My word, you are My disciples indeed. And you shall know the truth, and the truth shall make you free." When our children have been saturated in God's Word, God will reveal Himself to them. They will become His disciples, and they will be blessed to walk in the truth all the days of their life. There is nothing more powerful, instrumental, mind-shaping, or character-developing than God's Word in the life of a child!

Beholding His Glory

A.W. Tozer writes, "What comes into our minds when we think about God is the most important thing about us." What we think about God determines who we are, how we live, and how we treat others. So, where do we learn about God? We discover Him in His Word.

The world has all sorts of ideas about who God is—and most of them are lies! If we want our children to know the true character of God, they must spend time in His Word. As they spend time in the Word discovering who He is, our children will behold His glory and become transformed by the power of His presence. "But we all, with unveiled face, beholding as in a mirror the glory of the Lord, are being transformed into the same image from glory to glory, just as by the Spirit of the Lord" (2 Corinthians 3:18).

Benefits of God's Word

Books have been written about the benefits of God's Word, as they are endless. God's Word is the beginning of all wisdom. It reveals our sinful heart and keeps us from sin. It washes and cleanses us, molds and shapes us. It leads, directs, inspires, corrects us; it lights our path and enlightens our eyes. God's Word revives us, strengthens us, and empowers us. It makes us wise. It is a mirror into our soul, and it reveals the thoughts and the intentions of our heart. God's Word is living and powerful, sharper than a two-edged sword. And when it becomes the most important thing in our life, it makes our ways prosperous, as Joshua 1:8 proclaims: "This Book of the Law shall not depart from your mouth, but you shall meditate in it day and night, that you may observe to do according to all that is written in it. For then you will make your way prosperous, and then you will have good success."

Of the power of God's Word, Martin Luther brilliantly writes, "The Bible is alive, it speaks to me; it has feet, it runs after me; it has hands, it lays hold of me."[1] In describing the benefits of God's Word, the writer of Psalm 119 says, "I have rejoiced in the way of Your testimonies, as much as in all riches." God's Word is a treasure mine—in it, we find everything we need for life! We should rejoice with the psalmist "at [God's] word as one who finds great treasure" (Psalm 119:162).

Devouring God's Word

When Michael and I were first married, we purchased matching Cambridge Bibles. I changed Bibles after a few years, as this King James version was a bit much for me. However, Michael has used his for over twenty years—and it has been a very good friend to him.

When our dog, Mercy, was just a puppy, she got ahold of my husband's Cambridge Bible. She chewed the leather cover, and tore apart the first third of it. Michael was devastated, as this Bible was his most precious treasure. Fortunately, we were able to send the destroyed Bible and my old, matching copy to a book binding company who was able to merge the two together.

When we look back upon this incident, it is a great reminder to us about how God desires us to approach His Word. As Christians, we are called to not just read God's Word, but devour it! Jesus reminds us in Luke 4:4, "That Man shall not live by bread alone, but by every word of God." Similarly, C.H. Spurgeon writes:

> *Oh, that you and I might get into the very heart of the Word of God, and get that Word into ourselves! As I have seen the silkworm eat into the leaf, and consume it, so ought we to do with the Word of the Lord—not crawl over its surface, but eat right into it till we have taken it into our inmost parts. It is idle merely to let the eye glance over the words, or to recollect the poetical expressions, or the historic facts; but it is blessed to eat into the very soul of the Bible until, at last, you come to talk in*

Scriptural language, and your very style is fashioned upon
Scriptural models, and what is better sill, your spirit is favored
with the words of the Lord. [2]

Faithfully reading the "Verse of the Day" that is delivered to your email inbox does not give enough of God's Word to enable us to talk in "scriptural language" and fashion our lives after "scriptural models." We must devour God's Word! As Christians, we need to cultivate the attitude of Jeremiah, who wrote: "Your words were found, and I ate them, and Your word was to me the joy and rejoicing of my heart; for I am called by Your name, O LORD God of hosts" (Jeremiah 15:16).

God's Word as Authority

As we teach God's Word to our children, it is vital that we let them know that God's Word is truth and our absolute authority. Studies show that when our children are taught to believe that part of God's Word is not true (such as the creation account or Jesus' miracles), it undermines everything else that God says. When God's Word becomes "questionable," so does its power! Remember, all of God's Word is worthy to be trusted: "*All* Scripture *is* given by inspiration of God, and *is* profitable for doctrine, for reproof, for correction, for instruction in righteousness, that the man of God may be complete, thoroughly equipped for every good work" (2 Timothy 3:16-17).

When we teach our children that God's Word is truth, we have given them the greatest gift. The world is constantly searching for truth. Remember, God's Word says, "If you abide in My word, you are My disciples indeed. And you shall know the truth, and the truth shall make you free" (John 8:31-32). We don't want our children to live a life questioning which part of God's Word is truth. Instead, we want them to live a life of victory and freedom that only comes through the knowledge that God's Word is truth.

Taking God's Word Literally

God's Word must be more of a reality to our children than the tangible world—and this perspective takes calculated training and teaching. In God's economy, what is real is unseen, and what is seen isn't real. As 2 Corinthians 4:18 states, "For the things which are seen are temporary, but the things which are not seen are eternal." Our children need to know God's Word inside and out and take everything it says literally.

When my son, Sam, was entering seventh grade, he had a question for Michael and me one evening: "How can I honor you and dad more?" I asked him why he wanted to know. He replied, "I want to make sure I live as long as I possibly can. And the Bible says that if I honor you, I will live a long life. So, how can I honor you more?" When we teach God's Word to our children, and it becomes a reality to them—watch out!

Teaching God's Word: Our Duty

We recognize the importance of reading and knowing God's Word, but whose responsibility is it to teach God's Word to our children? According to Deuteronomy 6:4-9, it is our duty as parents:

> *Hear, O Israel: The LORD our God, the LORD is one! You shall love the LORD your God with all your heart, with all your soul, and with all your strength. And these words which I command you today shall be in your heart. You shall teach them diligently to your children, and shall talk of them when you sit in your house, when you walk by the way, when you lie down, and when you rise up. You shall bind them as a sign on your hand, and they shall be as frontlets between your eyes. You shall write them on the doorposts of your house and on your gates.*

As parents, we are commanded by God to teach His Word to our children all day long, everyday!

In the past, obeying this commandment was a fairly easy task. Families worked alongside one another on the family farm or in the family business. They spent their days together, ate meals together, and gathered around the evening fire together. Often, fathers would use this time to read the family Bible aloud before leading the family in a time of prayer. However, times have changed.

Today, family members are isolated and segregated from one another. Precious family time that was once centered around God's Word has been replaced with many other things: activities, sports, art classes, foreign language classes, play dates, modern technology, television, video games, social media, and more. In and of themselves, none of these things are wrong. But when they take precedence over family time and time spent in God's Word, it presents a huge problem that has become detrimental to our children.

Even though it has become harder than ever to fulfill God's command in Deuteronomy 6:4-9, parents still have a duty to teach God's Word to their children every day. How, you might ask? Parents need to talk about God's Word with their children whenever they can—when they get ready for the day, when they eat breakfast, when they are in the car, when they sit down for meals, when they go on walks, when they prepare for bed. God's Word should be the most important topic of conversation every day.

It is not only our responsibility to teach our children God's Word at home, but we are also responsible for ensuring that our children learn God's Word at church and at school. Our children's lives should be so saturated with God's Word that it fills their thoughts at every moment and changes the way they view things.

Teaching God's Word at Home

The home is the very first place that God's Word should be taught, as it is a parents' responsibility to bring their children to Christ. There is no better way to bring our children to the Savior than through the sharing of God's Word.

In Proverbs 8:17, God says, "I love those who love me, and those who seek me diligently will find me." C.H. Spurgeon expounds upon this: "Our business is to seek Jesus early in life. Happy are the young whose morning is spent with Jesus! It is never too soon to seek the Lord Jesus. Early seekers make certain finders."[3] Children should be introduced to God's Word on the laps of their parents at as early an age as possible. On training little ones in God's word, Spurgeon advises:

> Let us expect our children to know the Lord. Let us from the beginning mingle the name of Jesus with their ABC[s]. Let them read their first lessons from the Bible. It is a remarkable thing that there is no book from which children learn to read so quickly as from the New Testament: there is a charm about that book which draws forth the infant mind. But let us never be guilty, as parents, of forgetting the religious training of our children; for if we do we may be guilty of the blood of their souls.[4]

God's Word should be the first book we exalt to our precious little ones. We should give our children Bibles when they are young, and spend time reading and talking about its stories every day.

When our children were little, Michael would spend hours in our children's bedrooms, telling them Bible stories every night. He must have told the story of David and Goliath to my boys hundreds of times! Michael would read a children's Bible to them, and they would all sing the "B-I-B-L-E" song, rejoicing over God's Word together. One book my husband read over and over to our children is Ken Ham's *A Is For Adam*. In this book, the whole story of the Bible is explained, from creation all the way to the fire judgment. It is a fantastic way to give our children sound theology of our sin and the need for a Savior from infancy.

Once our children learned to read, Michael and I gave them a Bible storybook to read every morning. My husband grew up reading Elsie Egermeier's *Bible Story Book*, so that is the one we use.[5] This book has given our children a wonderful outline of God's Word when they were young. Then, when they have jumped into the actual Bible, they have had a great frame of reference to draw from.

Michael and I have made morning Bible reading a daily task on our children's chore charts. Once reading the Bible became a "chore," our children began reading God's Word everyday—they had no other option but to obey. This decision has transformed our house! Michael and I have also decided to give our children $150 every time they read through the entire Bible—$100 for the Old Testament, and $50 for the New best investment we, as parents, can make in the lives of our children. For when they read it, they discover God. So, as a result, not only do we have six children reading God's word every morning, at the moment four of them are reading through the Bible in a year! (I only wish we had required it of my two oldest boys earlier!).

Hanging verses on the walls of every room is a great way to saturate a home with God's Word. When you walk into the McClure home, you will see verses everywhere. In our main bathroom, we have placed the Ten Commandments where they can be easily seen and memorized by anyone using the room. In the boys' bathroom, we have hung Philippians 4:8 above the toilet, so the boys will be reminded to think about things that are true, noble, just, pure, lovely, and of good report.

Dinnertime is a great time to talk about God's Word and how to apply it. When we sit down to eat, we love to talk about current events as a family, and look at what God's Word has to say about things happening in the world. Besides our family devotional time, these discussions are probably the most important way we communicate God's Word in our home.

One thing we must remember is that a love for God's Word is caught, not taught. If we want our children to love God's Word, we have to love it, too. We need to constantly proclaim its magnificence, its power, and its wisdom in our own life. Our children need to see us spending time in God's Word, and we need to tell them what God is teaching us through it. Our children need to see God's Word transforming our life. Remember, it is alive and living and works mightily in our life if we spend time in it.

Imparting God's Word with our children does not end when they move out of the house, get married, or have children of their own. As parents, we are commanded to share the truth declared in God's Word throughout the entirety of our children's life. And then, we are to share it with our grandchildren. God's Word is a rock in our life, and it should be the cornerstone of our children and grandchildren's life, too.

Teaching God's Word at Church

Our children only spend an hour or two a week in God's house—if they faithfully attend church every Sunday. So, it is very important that their time at church is full of calculated training in the Word of God. Studying a single Bible verse or watching a Veggie Tales film is not enough to teach our children God's Word.

Attending a church that teaches the Word of God to its children is an absolute must! Most children who attend Sunday services, do not go to a Christian school, where they are taught God's Word everyday. So, the time they spend is church is even more valuable, and it must be spent actually teaching them the Bible.

At our church, our children study the entire Bible twice beginning in kindergarten and ending in fifth grade. We use a curriculum that not only teaches students key themes throughout the the Bible, but also teaches them apologetics and core theology of the Christian faith.

Controversial issues are brought up and taught on at length, including creation, the fall of man, sin, the flood, dinosaurs, the Trinity, and more. What is even more exciting is that the gospel message is woven throughout the entire curriculum just as it is woven throughout the entire Bible. How amazing!

Not too long ago, I spoke with a friend, who had recently walked by the Jr. High youth room at her church. The students were all playing video games, and secular music was blaring over the speakers! She told her children that they would not be going back to the church's youth group because they needed to spend time in God's Word, not on idols like video games and secular music. Unfortunately, this in not the first time that idols have been found in the church.

Most likely, your children will want to go a youth group like the one at my friend's church, as it looks more fun and attractive. Many churches today are doing everything they can to lure children to church, even if their methods are not pleasing to God. As parents, we must ensure that God's Word being taught to our children and youth. It must be taught as absolute truth, and it must be a priority in our church—our children's souls are at stake!

Teaching God's Word at School

Saturating our children in God's Word should not just happen at home and at church. It should also happen at school. Children spend more than 30 hours a week and more than 16,000 hours of their life at school, and they are all being taught a worldview of some kind.

A Christian worldview is only created by spending time in God's Word. If a teacher does not know or teach through the lens of God's Word, our children will leave school with a non-biblical worldview. The only way we can ensure our children view the world through the lens of God's Word (rather than man's word) is to saturate them in God's Word at home, at church, and at school.

When Daniel was two years old, Michael and I started praying about his future education. At the time, I spoke with a girlfriend about different schooling options, and she mentioned that she read a book called *The Lost Tools of Learning*. She recommended I read Douglas Wilson's book, and I did. This book transformed the way I thought about education! In it, Wilson stated that it was the parents' responsibility to ensure their children fulfilled the greatest commandment: "And you shall love the LORD your God with all your heart, with all your soul, with all your mind, and with all your strength. This is the first commandment" (Mark 12:30). How do we love God with all our heart, soul, mind, and strength? By guiding our children to love God with all their heart, soul, mind, and strength all day long— especially with their mind!

If teachers do not believe in God or know His Word, our children are not learning to love God with all their mind—no matter what subject is being taught. Their minds are not capable of making connections between God's Word and the things they learn in history, science, or math by themselves. They must be trained to do so, and this training requires them to learn everything through the lens of Scripture. Our children will only love God with all their mind when His Word is the consuming occupation of their life and education.

As parents, we can no longer afford to be ignorant in this area—we are losing our children to the philosophies of this world because they are not being taught a Christian worldview at school. Adolf Hitler, leader of the Nazi uprising during World War II, stated, "He alone, who owns the youth, gains the future."[6] He understood that, if he could use the government schools in Germany to train students in his political philosophies, he could win over the whole country - and all of Europe, for that matter. Hitler knew exactly what he was doing when he used the schools to indoctrinate children to the point that they did not question his "final solution" to the "Jewish problem". The result: the deaths of millions of Jews, and a second world war with millions of casualties. Hitler proved Theodore Roosevelt was right when he stated that, "To educate a man in mind and not in morals is to educate a menace to society."[7] Our government schools have an agenda, and it is not teaching our children through the lens of God's word so they can build His kingdom for His glory!

What is our solution today? We must ensure that God's Word is the center of our children's education. Martin Luther once wrote about the importance of teaching God's Word in schools. He said, "I am afraid Schools will prove the very gates of hell, unless they diligently labor in explaining the Holy Scriptures and engraving them in the heart of the youth."[8] Since the expulsion of God's Word and prayer from public schools in 1962, schools have proven to be the gate through which so many of our children walk away from their faith in Christ! What solution do we, as parents, have? God's Word must be the center of our children's education—every subject must be taught through the lens of scripture.

Unfortunately, even many Christian schools today are Christian in name only. So, parents must work to make sure that God's Word is the center of their children's school. If it is not, then they need to consider finding a new school, or homeschooling. It is not worth sacrificing our children to a school system not rooted on the Bible, let alone one so opposed to its principles as today's government schools!

At our church school, students study God's Word in depth. They study all of the Old and New Testament in kindergarten and first grade. In second to third grade they use a children's Bible to do their nightly reading. From second to sixth grade, they study the Bible a second time, and learn its entirety through song. In seventh and eighth grade, they read through the entire Bible again. Students study the Bible and learn to apply it in greater depth in high school.

Yet, that is not enough! We teach every subject through the lens of God's Word. And, we have come to realize that when students attend a school full of Spirit-filled teachers teaching the best curriculum, the world had better watch out! The students are transformed!

Michael likes to note that—with all the teaching of God's Word that happens at our school—one teacher can accomplish in one year what it takes him twenty years to accomplish on a Sunday morning! Theodore Roosevelt once stated, "A thorough knowledge of the Bible is worth more than a college education."9 As parents, ensuring our children have a deep understanding of God's Word is the best gift we can ever give them!

Hiding God's Word

The great heartbreak of today is that as a culture we are not only neglecting to teach God's word, but we are literally hiding God's word from our children. Psalm 78 explains that we should not hide God's Word from our children; instead, we must tell them of the "praises of the Lord, and His strength and His wonderful works that He has done" (vs. 4). In doing so, our children will "not be like their fathers, a stubborn and rebellious generation, a generation that did not set its heart aright, and whose spirit was not faithful to God" (vs. 8). Teaching God's Word to our children not only keeps them from walking away from God, it also ensures they know Him, and learn from the mistakes of those who have gone before them.

Yet, the Enemy is adept at finding ways to keep us from saturating our children in God's Word. As the great reformer Martin Luther declared, "All the cunning of the devil is exercised in trying to tear us away from the word."10 If Luther's statement was true in the days of the Reformation of the church, how much more is it true today?

King Josiah

The Bible told us of a time in Israel's history when God's Word was hidden from the people. When King Josiah took the throne at the age of eight, he had never heard God's Word (2 Kings 22-23, 2 Chronicles 34-35). There he was, the King of Israel, and he did not know God's Word. Yet, he wanted to follow after God, and to please Him - like his forefather, King David - except he did not know how!

During Josiah's reign, the Israelites worshipped God in all sorts of crazy ways—heaping judgment upon themselves—because they did not have God's Word to guide them. They worshipped God in the high places, which they were forbidden to do. They ran after false gods, hoping to fulfill their lusts. Their homes and communities were filled with idols; and even worse, God's Temple was filled with idols, too.

King Josiah commissioned a renovation of the Temple. He sent his scribe, Shaphan, to the High Priest, Hilkiah, with instructions to restore the Temple. In the midst of the renovations, Hilkiah found a book, the Book of the Law, God's Word, which had been hiding in the Temple.

When Josiah heard God's Word for the very first time, he tore his clothes and wept over the sins of his people. Then, Josiah went up to the Temple, gathering all the leaders of Judah and inhabitants of Jerusalem to himself. There, he had the Book of the Law read to the people and made a covenant to follow God and obey His Word from that day forward.

Because Josiah read the Word of God, he recognized that his kingdom was full of idols. In his obedience to God, he destroyed all the idols in the public squares, in homes, and most importantly, in the Temple! He put to death the priests of the high places, and he had altars destroyed throughout the entire country. Some of these altars had been in use for hundreds of years! He also outlawed child sacrifice by destroying the altar of Molech.

Then, Josiah worshiped God according to God's Word—not in the way the people had assumed they should worship God, based upon their own ideas and customs. Josiah reinstated the Passover celebration, and "[s]uch a Passover surely had never been held since the days of the judges who judged Israel, nor in all the days of the kings of Israel and the kings of Judah" (2 Kings 23:22). What was Josiah's legacy? In 2 Kings 23:35, we are told: "Now before him there was no king like him, who turned to the LORD with all his heart, with all his soul, and with all his might, according to all the Law of Moses; nor after him did any arise like him." But as righteous as Josiah was, it was too late for Josiah and the kingdom of Judah!

Because of the sins of the people—and the sins of Josiah's grandfather, Manasseh, who created altars to false gods, sacrificed his son to Molech, and committed evil in the sight of the Lord—God had to judge the kingdom of Judah. Josiah was killed when Assyria and Egypt joined forces to war against Judah in the valley of Meggido.

After Josiah's death, the nation fell back into idolatry. Twelve years later, Jerusalem fell to King Nebuchadnezzar, and the people of Judah were taken into captivity by the Babylonians. For centuries, God had sent His prophets to warn His people of an impending judgment if they turned their hearts away from Him to follow after idols—and with the Babylonian captivity, God was faithful to His word!

When we consider the reign of King Josiah, there is a lot for us to learn. The state of our own country parallels the state of the kingdom of Judah in many ways. Today, we are hiding God's Word from our children! We need to rediscover the Word of God, read it, and realize that we have been seeking after false gods. In Exodus 20:5, God commands us not to worship idols, because He is "a jealous God," and if we do, then we—and the generations after us—will end up reaping severe consequences.

Our homes, churches, and schools should be miniature Tabernacles, where God's Word is the priority—not hidden. When we hide it, we end up with children who worship God in ways that are completely pagan and idolatrous. Our children will suffer because they do not know God's Word, they do not know what idolatry is, and they do not know how God desires to be worshipped. And, if they do not know the Word of God, they cannot know or obey Him. As a result, our children will turn to idols in an attempt to satisfy the emptiness and longing of their heart. Hiding God's Word from our children also means that they will face an impending judgment—like the one that awaited Josiah and the kingdom of Judah due to their disobedience.

If we want our children to transform the culture, we must make God's Word the priority in our children's lives—at home, church, and school. In my experience, an explosion happens in the hearts and lives of children who learn God's Word at home as they are discipled by their parents, attend a Spirit-filled church that teaches the power and authority of God's Word, and are educated in a school centered around the truth of scripture. Such a saturation is like dynamite!

The Power of God's Word

One morning, when my son, Josh, was in seventh grade, he casually told me that he only had a couple chapters to go before he finished reading through the Bible. I didn't even know he was reading through the entire Bible! As I mentioned earlier, Michael and I had decided to give our children $150 every time they read through the Bible completely. When Josh told me he had almost finished, I was actually teaching his seventh grade class at school. Then, the Lord gave me an idea—I told my students that if they read through the entire Bible by the end of the school year, I would extend on the "McClure Family Deal" to them, and pay them $150, too. That day, I paid Josh cash in front of the class so that they could see that I meant business!

We live in Silicon Valley, and everyone is all about making investments, always looking for the next best thing. So, when my students wanted to know why Michael and I were willing to spend so much money on them, I told them that the best investment Pastor Mike and I could make was God's Word in them. Our investment of $150 would pay off in eternal dividends!

The entire class took up the challenge—all twelve students. In the end, eight of the twelve read through the entire Bible by the end of the school year, and earned awards for their amazing accomplishment. (I had secret deals with the remaining students to get them to finish by the end of the summer).

At our school, we have an end-of-the-year tradition. Our teachers put together binders full of pictures, quotes, poems, writing assignments, and projects for each student. The first page is usually a questionnaire that each student fills out as they reflect upon the things they did and learned during the school year. Here are some of the questions and responses given by the twelve students who took up my challenge to read the entire Bible:

What is the greatest lesson I learned this year?
Reading the Bible pays off, literally!

What was my favorite book I read this year?
Three students wrote:
> *The Bible. It teaches how I should live.*
> *The Bible. It keeps me accountable.*
> *The Bible. I feel wiser after reading it!*

What was my biggest accomplishment this year?
Five students wrote:
> *Reading the entire Bible!*

As the school year ended, one of my students said, "Mrs. McClure, you are having to pay out, like, $1500—that is way too much money!" I reminded my student that if I was concerned about money, I wouldn't be teaching at our school—I would be working down the road, at Apple! God's Word in my students was the the best investment I could make, as it molded and shaped them. It will continue to be instrumental in the decisions they make throughout their whole life!

What I haven't told you yet was how nervous I was to teach this class of twelve at the beginning of the year. The students, who all had very strong personalities, had a history of making life difficult for their teachers. Around December, I was exhausted. Classroom management had never been something I really had to work at; but with this class, I had to be on it all the time.

But, in the New Year, everything changed. I started to see hearts softening, and my students began to respond to correction. They desired to please and wanted to do what was right. I spoke with other teachers, and we all wondered what was going on with this class. Towards the end the year, I told the class that I had seen a transformation in them during the school year. One of my students, Evan, told me, "Mrs. McClure, it's because we were all reading the Bible like crazy over Christmas break, and during the rest of the year." You know what? He was absolutely right! God's Word transformed the lives of my middle school students. And it was nothing short of a miracle!

When I shared this story with my mother-in-law, Jean, she loved it so much that she shared it with some women at a Bible study she was teaching at the time. She hoped it would inspire them to read God's Word, and to encourage their children to read it, too. Afterwards, one of the ladies came up to Jean, and asked her, "Do you think I can pay my nineteen year old to read the Bible?" This question reminded me that we only have a small window of time to inspire our children to read God's Word and allow it to mold and shape them. If we miss this window, we will regret it for the rest of our life!

There are so many parents in our church with young adult children, who grew up in the church, but are not interested in God at all because they never read or learned God's Word themselves. And, what is worse, their children's children are not interested in God, either. Today, these parents would give anything to go back and make sure that their children knew God, and were saturated in His Word.

God's Word: An Ancient Landmark

Reading God's Word has been an ancient landmark within our country for hundreds of years. It used to be said that, in the New World, two books could be found in every home: *Pilgrim's Progress* and the Bible. The Bible has been called "The Greatest Book There Has Ever Been"—and rightly so.

However, over the years, we have slowly removed this ancient landmark from our homes, churches, and schools. Yet, we were warned against this very thing! Proverbs 22:28 tells us, "Do not remove the ancient landmark which your fathers have set." Recently, I came across the following story in *Devotions for Morning and Evening*:

Among the property owned jointly by two young brothers who were carpenters was the old tumbledown place of their birth. One of the brothers was soon to be married and the old house was to be torn down and a new one erected on its site. For years neither of the brothers had visited the cottage, as it had been leased.

As they entered now and started the work of demolishing the place, again and again floods of tender memories swept over them. By the time they reached the kitchen they were well-nigh overcome with their emotions. There was the place where the old kitchen table had stood—with the family Bible—where they knelt every evening. They were recalling now with a pang how in later years they had felt a little superior to that time-honored custom carefully observed by their father.

Said one: "We're better off than he was, but we're not better men."

The other agreed, saying, "I'm going back to the old church and the old ways, and in my new home I'm going to make room for worship as Dad did." [11]

Today, we might be better off than those who have gone before us, with our new technological advances and progressive thinking, but we are not better men! We need to go back to the old ways, and make God's Word the center of our homes, our lives, and our children's lives.

Have you removed this ancient landmark from your home? Has God's Word been hidden from your children? My encouragement to you, as gatekeepers, is to make your home a Tabernacle, holy and pleasing to God. Take down your idols and replace them with the Word of God.

Saturate your children in God's Word, so they can commune with the living God!

Abraham Lincoln once said, "The strength of a nation lies in the homes of its people."[12] Imagine if God's presence reigned supreme and His Word was honored above all in every Christian home in our country. How our nation would be affected!

Josh's Bible

When we make God's Word the most precious treasure in our homes, our children will esteem God's Word, as well. Last year, my son, Josh, came to me one morning. He told me, "Mom, look! The pages of my Bible are not white; they are turning yellow. I want to show my grandchildren my Bible someday, and tell them that I have read this book a hundred times." God's Word is Josh's greatest treasure! C.H. Spurgeon writes, "A Bible that's falling apart usually belongs to someone who isn't."[13]

There is no greater joy than seeing our children delight in God's Word. Whatever it takes, we must make God's Word the priority of our children's lives—and the sooner the better! When we saturate our children in God's Word, they will not only know the living God and be changed by His power, but they will, like Samuel, be prepared to transform this world for His glory!

Oh! give me Samuel's mind,
A sweet unmurmuring faith,
Obedient and resigned
To Thee in life and death;
That I may read with child-like eyes
Truths that are hidden from the wise.[14]

— J.D. Burns

Questions to Consider

1. Ask your children to describe God. Are the characteristics they list and the thoughts they have about God biblical or based upon man's ideas and lies?

2. Take an inventory of your home. Is there anything taking the place of or tearing you away from God's Word? What idols do you have in your home?

3. What would your children say is the most valued treasure in your home? Is it God's Word? Why, or why not?

4. What worldview are your children being trained in at school? Do they view things through the lens of God's Word or man's word?

5. List the ways your family worships God. Are there any ways that are not pleasing to Him? If so, do they stem from a lack of understanding of God's Word?

6. Are your children reading God's word on a daily basis? How might you encourage them to do so?

Notes

[1] Martin Luther, quoted in Warren Wiersbe, *On Being a Servant of God* (Grand Rapids, Michigan: Baker Books, 1993)104.

[2] Ray Rhodes, Jr., *Susie: The Life and Legacy of Susanna Spurgeon* (Chicago: Moody Publishers, 2018), 52-53.

[3] C.H. Spurgeon, *Cheque Book of the Bank of Faith (Great Britain:Christian Focus Publications, 1996)*, 236.

[4] C.H. Spurgeon, quoted in Ray Comfort, *How To Bring Your Children to Christ and Keep Them There* (Bartlesville, Oklahoma: Genesis Publishing Group), 49.

[5] Ibid.

[6] There are so many wonderful Bible storybooks for children of every age. Just be sure to choose one that is biblically accurate and theologically sound!

[7] Theodore Roosevelt, "Good Reads," accessed July 19, 2019, https://www.goodreads.com/quotes/663600-to-educate-a-man-in-mind-and-not-in-morals

[8] Martin Luther, "Brainy Quote," accessed July 19, 2019, https://www.brainyquote.com/quotes/martin_luther_151405

[9] Theodore Roosevelt, "Good Reads," accessed July 19, 2019, https://www.goodreads.com/quotes/711431-a-thorough-knowledge-of-the-bible-is-worth-more-than

[10] Martin Luther, "Good Reads," accessed July 19, 2019, https://www.goodreads.com/quotes/26856-all-the-cunning-of-the-devil-is-exercised-in-trying

[11] Mrs. Charles E. Cowman, *Devotions for Morning and Evening* (New York: International Press, 1925), 50.

[12] Abraham Lincoln, "Good Reads," accessed July 19, 2019, https://www.goodreads.com/quotes/9681700-the-strength-of-a-nation-lies-in-the-homes-of

[13] C. H. Spurgeon, "Good Reads," accessed July 19, 2019, https://www.goodreads.com/quotes/397346-a-bible-that-s-falling-apart-usually-belongs-to-someone-who

[14] F.B. Meyer, *Samuel the Prophet* (CrossReach Publications, 2017), 14.

Pearl of Wisdom #6

Cast a Vision for Your Children's Lives

Therefore I also have lent him to the LORD;
as long as he lives he shall be lent to the LORD.

1 Samuel 1:28

For we are His workmanship,
created in Christ Jesus for good works,
which God prepared beforehand that we should walk in them.

Ephesians 2:10

Samuel's life and destiny was fixed before conception. He was to be a servant and priest of God all the days of his life, as Hannah vowed at the Tabernacle in her prayer to the Lord. Hannah's vision for Samuel's life began with her vow to God, and was then confirmed with the naming of her son, her intentional training while at home, and finally by the giving of Samuel to the Lord.

In 1 Samuel 1:28, Hannah declared, "Therefore I also have lent him to the LORD; as long as he lives he shall be lent to the LORD." It wasn't Samuel's choice to belong to God; it was Hannah's! Hannah's son would be a servant of God, and she would do everything in her power to enable this to happen. Samuel was created for God's glory from the moment he was born—and he knew it! His training at home and in the Tabernacle was all focused towards this end.

Our children's destiny is fixed, too. They were created to glorify God. As parents, we need to cast a vision for our children's lives in the same way Hannah cast a vision for her son's life. From birth, our children should understand Who created them, why they were created, and for what end they were created. All of the training in our children's lives should point towards this end.

The Importance of a Name
Casting vision for our children begins with their name. Hannah named her son Samuel—"Heard by God"—because she had asked for him from the Lord, and He had heard her prayer (1 Samuel 1:20). As he grew,

Samuel's name declared to him and everyone else that he was an answer to prayer. How powerful!

Today, we do not often think about the importance of a name. But, when we name our children, we should declare who they are or what their destiny is. Often, people really do end up becoming who their name declares them to be. A name fitly chosen and taught to our children really can send them on a quest to fulfill their name's great call!

Proverbs 22:1 states, "A good name is to be chosen rather than great riches, loving favor rather than silver and gold." It is very important that we pray over the names of our children and seek God about His vision for our children—before they are even born! We then need to name our children according to God's desires—rather than choosing a name that sounds pretty, or adheres to the latest fad.

Michael and I chose all of our children's names through prayer and confirmation found in God's Word. God gave each of the names to us before our children were born—and many times before they were even conceived! Our children's names are:

Daniel John — *God is My Judge, God is Gracious*
Micah James — *Who is Like God?, Heel Catcher*
Joshua Philip — *Yahweh is Salvation, Lover of Horses (He
    Likes Fast Things)*
Samuel Aaron — *Heard of God, Enlightened One*
Hannah Carol — *God is Gracious, Song of Joy*
Abigail Jean — *Joy of My Father, Gift of God*
Ruth Marguerite — *Friendship, Flower*

It is amazing how each of our children fit their names so perfectly! Michael and I constantly remind our children of the meaning of their name and how it is their destiny to fulfill it. In fact, we have set up email addresses for each of our children based on the meaning of their Hebrew name. These email addresses are just another way that Michael and I remind our children of who they are in Christ. There is power in a name!

Of course, a child's destiny is not dependent on their name. Many great men and women of faith had names that had nothing to do with God or His Word, yet they still did mighty things for His kingdom. Conversely, there are some children, who have great names but consider it a shame to be identified with God. Sometimes, as we see with Samuel, however, a name can become a catalyst for life of service to the glory of God.

Identity Crisis
It doesn't take much contemplation to realize that children raised in today's culture are suffering an identity crisis. They are being raised without knowing the answers to fundamental questions about life:

> Why was I created?
> How was I created?
> What is the purpose of my life?
> Where am I going?

Modern biographer and speaker Eric Metaxas gave a message at Harvest Christian Fellowship, explaining that his education at Yale College, though exemplary by the world's standards, was lacking in a major way.[1] It did not prepare him to for the fundamental questions about life. He left Yale with a prestigious degree, yet he could not answer these questions:

> Why am I here?
> Where did I come from?
> Is there a purpose for my life?
> Where am I going?

Yale was founded in 1701 by colonial clergymen. The college was founded upon the motto *Lux et Veritas*—"Light and Truth." The school's main goal was to proclaim the light and truth of God's Word! Yale's college laws declared: "Every student shall consider ye main end of his study to know God in Jesus Christ and answerably to lead a Godly sober life."[2] The goal of this college was for every student to know their Creator and live a life that would please and honor Him. Yet, today, young adults leave Yale and other colleges and universities not knowing these fundamental truths about life.

Since the first colonists immigrated to our country, American children used to grow up knowing the answers to the fundamental questions about life. Colonial children were taught from a little, blue book known as *The New England Primer*. This "textbook" was created by the Puritans of New England for the express purpose of educating all American children in letters, numbers, and moral truths.

The New England Primer was used in American schools for over two hundred years! Its influence has had a lasting impact on the moral landscape of America. This little book was the original "common core" curriculum.

When children first learned the alphabet, they learned little rhymes that also taught biblical truths: "A — In Adam's Fall, We Sinned all," and so on. *The New England Primer* also included stories of famous men, who fought for religious freedom, though it is best known for its infamous Catechism. The Catechism contained over one hundred questions about fundamental biblical truths. A teacher would call out a theological question, and students would respond with a scripted answer. The first question that students of every age were expected to answer was: "What is the chief end of man?" Their response: "To glorify God and enjoy Him forever."

For hundreds of years, every American student grew up with the understanding that they were created for God's pleasure and purpose—not their own! Today, few children understand this fundamental truth, including those growing up in Christian homes. Yet, the destiny of each child has been fixed from the foundation of the world. Our children were all created by God for His glory, and they are destined to enjoy Him forever.

As parents, we must pray and ask God to reveal what He has called our children to do, rather than questioning if He has called them to do something at all. Once we have identified their calling, our job is to teach our children and remind them of the special vision that God has for their life.

In our home, our children do not have an option to serve God with their lives or not—they were created to glorify God. The question is how they will glorify Him: What occupation will they have? How will they use their gifts?

Since they were little, Michael has asked our boys, "What are you going to be when you grow up?" They respond, "A man of God." Michael continues, "What are you going to do as a man of God?" Their reply: "A pastor." "A doctor." "A missionary pilot." "An evangelist." Our girls' answers are nearly the same. They are going to be: "A woman of God," who is also "A mom and teacher." When your children's vision is to be men and women of God, their careers will be ones that enable them to be men and women who make a difference in this world for the glory of God.

Our Mission

God has called every believer to build the world for His glory. Spurgeon writes, "Our business in this world is to conquer it for Jesus."[3] This is not only our business; it is also the business of our children! Our children were designed to conquer the world for Jesus Christ. How can they do this? They must live a life that builds God's kingdom and declares God's love to a lost and dying world!

I believe this desire to conquer the world for Christ is innately found within every person, although they don't necessarily realize or know how to accomplish it. This desire is displayed in our children's lives in a variety of ways due to a lack of direction and training from parents. For example, many young boys are addicted to video games, which "fulfill" their need to conquer a kingdom. Yet, a video game cannot truly satisfy—it is only a fantasy. Many young girls want to be part of God's glorious story, but they are "satisfied" and enamored with movies that only replicate a portion of the Great Story we find through the gospel of Jesus Christ!

What is this Great Story? A perfect King created a perfect and beautiful world, full of creatures and plants. He desired fellowship, so He created mankind, whom He could commune with and love. However, this perfect world was marred when the devil, disguised as a snake, deceived mankind, who disobeyed their loving King. The Result: Man became separated from their holy and glorious King! This King embarked on a quest to reconcile mankind to Himself, which resulted in Him sending His most precious treasure, His perfect Son, His One and Only Son, into the fallen world, so He could defeat the devil, conquering sin and death. This Son took upon Himself the sins of the world, dying on the cross of Calvary. Through His blood, mankind would be washed and cleansed of their sin, and be reconciled to their King. And one glorious day, He will live in paradise with His creation, and live in eternal bliss. This gospel message is the Great Story. Our world and children need to hear this message, and allow the gospel to transform their lives!

Our children all have a desire deep within themselves to be a part of God's Great Story, and to do their part in conquering this world for their King. They innately know their destiny. Our job, as parents, is to train and inspire our children to become a part of that Great Story—and build God's kingdom on earth, for His glory!

Identity
Before we can cast a vision for our children's lives, they must first know who they are, and where they have come from. Our job is to help our children find their identity in Christ as early as possible. This is absolutely necessary, as our children receive many confusing and contradictory messages from today's culture!

Casting vision for our children starts with the beginning. In Genesis, God created man in His own image. Man did not evolve over billions of years; he was created by God. Woman was then created from man, in order to complete him—as "[i]t is not good that man should be alone" (Genesis 2:18). God created man and woman as two distinct beings (Genesis 1:27). He, then, gave them their mandate: "Be fruitful and multiply; fill the earth and subdue it" (Genesis 1:28). Basically, man and woman were to enjoy the amazing relationship—marriage (Genesis 2:24)—given to them by God. They were to have lots of children, and conquer the world for God's glory. This vision is glorious!

But today, the enemy has crept into our culture, and done a great job of demonizing the role of man, devaluing the role of woman, and even blending their identities! As parents, it is imperative that we share the truth about our children's identity with them through faithful Bible reading and apologetics. We must teach our children that they are created in the image of God, distinctly male or female, and then inspire them to fulfill their God-given mandate through their role.

Because today's culture is uncertain of the beginning, they are also uncertain about what it means to be male or female. God created man and woman to be different, with two distinct bodies and personalities. Yet, boys are being de-masculinized today. Rather than allowing them to fight with swords and guns, embrace logic, and be protective, we are training boys in the art of feelings and emotions. Girls are being encouraged to set aside godly submission to become independent, take on the man's world, and not become burdened with children. And, as if that is not enough, kindergarten students in our public schools are being taught that they can decide whether they are a boy or a girl. Furthermore they can choose to "like" a boy if they are a boy, or a girl if they are a girl —or, even worse, both!

The world is molding and shaping our children, pressuring them to adhere to these new gender standards. As our culture grows increasingly godless, we will find see an increase of the world's influences in public schools, movies, social media, and more. In fact, I can't even take my children to the mall without them seeing advertisements with so many mixed messages.

The world will try to force these godless behaviors on us at the most shocking times and in the most shocking ways. A few years ago, we took our children to a G-rated movie. As we waited for the movie to start, we saw a preview that was very shocking and alarming. My husband yelled to our children, "Cover your eyes! Don't watch this garbage!" The whole theatre turned and stared at us—but we refuse to allow the world to mold and shape our children's values by desensitizing them to wickedness.

As parents, we must push worldly influences aside and cultivate our children's identity in Christ. But, what do we do when the culture creeps in to our homes? Hold the standard. The biggest way moms and dads can adhere to God's standard is to celebrate the roles that God has given to them. How you and your husband treat each other is so important, as it demonstrates to your children and the world what God desires for the Christian home. Your marriage and relationship is a reflection of God's love for His church, as well as a testimony of His plan for all the families in this world.

As parents, we must be very intentional about celebrating and rejoicing in the roles that God has given us. Michael and I do this in a number of ways. Our girls can't cut their hair short like a boy, and they must wear a dress to church on Sunday—dad's orders. Our boys cannot dress like a girl. Birthday and Christmas gifts for our girls include: baby dolls, strollers, cookbooks, teacher desks, pencils and pens, chalkboards, and other things that will inspire our daughters to cultivate a home and nurture the next generation. Our boys's gifts include guns, knives, bows and arrows, legos—all things suited for young men, who are designed to build and conquer a kingdom for God's glory.

We must realize, as parents, that our children don't just come out of their room one day dressed like the opposite sex, or desiring a relationship with someone of the same sex. It is the things we have allowed into their lives that allow them to reach this point. Every decision we make must be intentional from the moment our children our born! We are all raising our children to follow a model. The question is whether or not that model is godly and counter-cultural. We must do everything we can to help our children find their identify in Christ as early as possible!

Cast a Vision

In C.S. Lewis's book, *The Voyage of the Dawn Treader*, Reepicheep the Mouse was given a prophecy while he was in his cradle. The prophecy was a song, and it went like this:

> *Where sky and water meet,*
> *Where the waves grow sweet,*
> *Doubt not, Reepicheep,*
> *To find all you seek,*
> *There is the utter East.*[4]

This prophecy drove Reepicheep his entire life to search out the Utter East. This was his life quest, this prophecy that he meditated on drove his every decision until it was fulfilled.

When we speak God's Word, and cast a vision over our children's lives while they are young, it will shape their destiny—and they will also do whatever it takes to fulfill it!

In 1 Timothy 4:14, Paul encourages Timothy: "Do not neglect the gift that is in you, which was given to you by prophecy with the laying on of the hands of the eldership." A prophecy was spoken over Timothy's life, and Paul encouraged Timothy to fulfill it. As parents, we are not only speak prophecy over our children lives, but we should also encourage them to fulfill it. Prophecy is simply the Word of God.

When we speak God's Word over our children's lives, it can really change their destiny. A prophecy can be general: "You were created to glorify God." Or, God may give us a specific word for our children during times of Bible reading and prayer. And, if He does, we should share this word with them. God has given me specific "words" for my children through the years. Before Daniel was born, God told me that he was going to be "filled with the Holy Spirit, even from his mother's womb", like John the Baptist (Luke 1:15), and that he would grow "in favor with God and men", like Jesus (Luke 2:52). When I was expecting Josh, the Lord told me that he was going to be "zealous with [God's] zeal", as Aaron's grandson Phinehas was. God has also given me many different words of prophecy for my children as I have prayed for them throughout their childhood.

Build God's Kingdom

Casting a vision for our children's lives, and inspiring them to conquer the kingdom for God must be done within the context of a family that has the same vision. When a family is united in building the kingdom of God, children will naturally receive the vision and desire to continue it! A family whose purpose is to build God's kingdom is a powerful force to the glory of God!

A mother teaches her children that the most important thing in life is to build God's kingdom through her example. We are all called to "seek first the kingdom of God and His righteousness" (Matthew 6:33), yet so many moms are building their children's kingdom rather than God's. This happens when they pour their time and energy into their children's achievements, friendships, and activities, rather than kingdom business. Is it any wonder that our children are not interested in building God's kingdom when they are older?

I have searched throughout scripture, looking for a word from the Lord that would encourage moms who work tirelessly to build up their children's lives. The Lord keeps bringing me back to: "Then Jesus said to His disciples, 'If anyone desires to come after Me, let him deny himself, and take up his cross, and follow Me'" (Matthew 16:24). We are not called to follow our children; we are called to follow Jesus! We must work tirelessly and sacrificially to follow God, not our children.

As moms, our greatest goal should be, first, to build God's kingdom, and, second, to encourage our children to build God's kingdom with us. There is so much work to be done in the kingdom of God. I am not talking about participating in missions trip here and there or an occasional Sunday School service. No, I am talking about a life poured out for the kingdom of God! What does this look like? Take on a ministry at your church as a family. You could oversee the nursery, bless the elderly, or disciple middle school children. Every church is full of needs! Be purposeful about sharing the gospel with neighbors; supporting local and overseas missionaries; praying for the persecuted church, and for revival within your home, church, and city. Be on the look-out for needs where you can shine God's love within your sphere of influence. When we make building God's kingdom our priority in our lives and homes, our children will naturally seek to build God's kingdom. They will also want the kingdom to come because their whole life has been focused towards that end.

Each of our children has a dream for their life. They are all different —a doctor, a missionary pilot, a pastor, a businessman/philanthropist/ evangelist, a mom, and a teacher. Yet, while these career paths may change, my children each have a vision of how they can build God's kingdom. Michael and I pray that, whatever field our children go into one day, they will pursue it with the sole purpose of building God's kingdom on this earth. Have you communicated the importance of building the kingdom of God to your children? Do they want to live a life poured out for Him and His glory?

Raise the Standard
As I wrote this chapter, I asked my son, Daniel, why he and his siblings are so kingdom-minded. I wondered why they each have such huge visions for their lives. He told me, "Mom, you expect so much more from us than all of our friends' parents expect of them. And, as your children, we want to meet your expectations!"

Mothers, we must realize that our expectations have consequences. Studies show that, when parents or teachers raise their expectations, children will rise up to meet them. Expectations are often a self-fulfilling prophecy. If we expect our children to eat junk food, be selfish and lazy, play video games, and not turn in their homework, that is exactly what we will get! As parents, we must raise the bar for our children, then encourage them to meet it. This idea is biblical. Consider 1 Corinthians 10:31, which states, "Therefore, whether you eat or drink, or whatever you do, do all to the glory of God."

Over the past one hundred years, the expectations parents have had for their children have lowered dramatically. Children are no longer seen as an asset necessary to help support the family, work on the family farm, or take over a business. Today, children are rarely expected to serve or give towards something bigger than themselves. Instead, they are consumers and takers. Statistics and the evidence of our own eyes testifies to the result of lowered expectations—especially in the teenage years. Our culture expects teenagers to be lazy, rebellious, and expensive. However, our children don't have to become another statistic. As parents seeking to raise godly children, we do not need to conform to the patterns of this world. Our culture has a vision for our children; they want to tell our children how to think, act, talk and what to wear, buy, and so on! As moms, we need to set new standards in our homes.

Our children can transform this world for Jesus Christ, but we need to first cast a vision, and inspire them to do so. We must raise the standard for our children if we want them to do great things for God. Henry Ford, founder of the Ford Motor Company, said, "Whether you think you can, or you think you can't—you're right." Our job is to inspire our children to "think they can." Hudson Taylor wrote, "Commonly there are three stages in a work for God: Impossible, Difficult, Done!"[5] As we raise the standard for our children and inspire them to meet them—God can and will accomplish the impossible through our children's lives!

Children will naturally take the easy road and do what is comfortable. We must not allow them to do so; instead, we must remind our children why they were created. I have found that the most important thing I can do is to constantly share scripture with my children, then guide them to greater and higher things. What does God's Word say about picking up their cross, being lazy, wasting time, not being disciplined with their time, not saving their money, and more? A true man or woman of God will say no to what is comfortable and easy, so that they can work to conquer this world for Jesus Christ.

One thing that really bothers me is when my children waste their time. Time is one of the most precious gifts we have been given, and once it is wasted, we can never get it back! Donald Miller, CEO of StoryBrand, writes:

No culture in history has been more distracted. If you are wondering why there are no more C.S. Lewises in the world, no more stories as good as Tolkien's, no cathedrals as great as the gothic, no music as moving as Pachelbel's, it may be because the writers of these books, the tellers of these stories, architects of

these buildings and the composers of these symphonies are
sitting on their couches watching television. I wonder what's on
tonight.[6]

Just think: If the men in times past spent all of their time watching
YouTube, playing video games, or surfing the internet, we would not have
these wonderful books, beautiful cathedrals, or amazing symphonies to
inspire us! If we want our children to be men and women who transform
this world for God's glory, we cannot allow them to waste their time. We
must train them to not only be disciplined, but to also make wise
decisions with their time.

Stir Up Their Gifts

A few years ago, I read C.S. Lewis's *The Lion, the Witch, and the*
Wardrobe with my seventh grade class. We reached the part where
Father Christmas gives the Penvensie children gifts—all of which were to
be used to battle the White Witch. As we discussed these gifts, my
students and I talked about how God has given each of us gifts to use in
fighting for His kingdom. I asked each of the children what their gifts
were, and I realized that most of them had no idea what gifts they could
have that God would want to use!

One student, who knew God's Word, and had parents who had
explained the gifts of God to him, said that he had the gift of evangelism,
discernment, hard work, discipline, and so on! He was a student who
had had a vision cast for his life by his parents. He knew where he was
going! As parents who are raising our children to know the things of
God, we don't want them to flounder, wondering what God has called
them to do. All of God's children have been "created in Christ Jesus for
good works, which God prepared beforehand that we should walk in
them" (Ephesians 2:10). God has called every one of our children, and
He has given them each gifts to use for His glory. Our job is to help our
sons and daughters understand what their gifts are.

It is not enough to simply point out our children's gifts; we must also
encourage them to use the gifts that God has given them. This does not
mean setting everything aside to allow our children to build their
academic portfolio. Rather, it means we acknowledge and cultivate the
gifts we see in our children's lives, so they can use them to build God's
kingdom.

Romans 12:6 teaches us that we all have "gifts differing according to
the grace that is given to us," and so, we must "use them." These gifts
include: prophecy, teaching, leadership, mercy, hospitality, love, faith,
healing, exhortation, help, and more. If we seek to disciple our children,
we must do our part in recognizing their gifts, then encouraging them to
use them.

This encouragement starts when our children are little. For example,
our sweet Ruth loves babies. Whenever she sees one, she screams,
"Baby!" even if they are across the room! If she is near the baby, she sits

down on the ground and pats her legs, asking the mom to let her to hold the baby. For Christmas, Michael and I bought her a baby doll and stroller—and she is having the time of her life caring for it!

Cultivating gifts in our children can be that simple. Do they love to build? Purchase Legos! Do they love to worship God? Enroll them in music lessons. Are they gifted at writing? Give them good literature to read, to nurture their imagination. Are they good at math? Find board games (like chess) that cultivate calculating skills. Do they like to cook? Purchase a special cookbook and stock your cupboard with ingredients. Do they love school? Allow them set up an area in your house as a school, so they can teach their younger siblings as they nurture their desire to invest in the lives of others.

When your children come home from school with an award-winning paper, or a Student of the Month nomination, encourage them in their skills and character. If their teacher praises them for an act of service, praise them, and affirm their gifts. Remember, we are called to "stir up the gift of God" (2 Timothy 1:6) in our children. Stirring up our children's gifts does not mean that we set out to make every opportunity a possibility for them. It simply means seeing what opportunities might arise for our children to use their gifts for kingdom work.

Each year, on our children's birthdays, everyone goes around the table, sharing what we love about each other. Most of the time, we are just calling out the gifts that God has given them. Our children say things like, he is compassionate, generous, a good artist, good at math, loves to read, makes good board games, is funny, is always thinking of others, and so forth. Then, we pray, thank God for these gifts, and ask God to use them as we anoint our children and pray for them! These words of affirmation are really a self-fulfilling prophecy! Not only are our children's gifts identified, but we are praying for this gifts to be used to build God's kingdom.

Forward Thinking

Once we have given our children to God, cast a vision for their life, and declared and cultivated their gifts; we need to make decisions with a long range vision in mind—rather than what will make our children happy for a moment. For example, if your child wants to be a doctor, then he or she must learn to be disciplined with their time now. If God has called your child to be a missionary in Africa, then your son or daughter needs to learn to live without. We must make decisions today that train our children to be the men and women God has called them to be.

So often, parents have great visions for their children, but they are not making decisions with this vision in mind. If we desire godly children, we must build their character now, instilling in them a work ethic and a love of service. We can't expect our children to be productive adults if they spend all their time playing video games or only thinking about themselves. When we revolve our lives around our children, or strive to make them happy all the time, giving our children an easy life—

we cannot expect them to live a life of self-sacrifice for the kingdom of God! Our children will not be able to do hard things for God if we do not train them to lead a disciplined life in their youth.

This kind of training can be very hard, especially when we decide to raise our children differently than their friends are being raised. However, our mission is clear: we must keep our vision before us, and not allow ourselves to be swayed by what others are doing. Raising children according to the pattern of this world does not work. It is only in following God's Word and the pattern He has laid out in it that we will be able to raise godly children.

Remember, we are "a chosen generation", called by God "to proclaim the praises of Him who called you out of darkness into His marvelous light" (1 Peter 2:9). If we truly believe what this verse says, we will do things differently from the world and other families, who might find what we do very peculiar! We cannot be God's light to a dark world—who desperately desire answers when it comes to raising children—if we let the pressures of others drive us to make decisions that do not honor or please Him.

Introduce Them to Great Men

One powerful way we can inspire our children to be used by God for His glory is by introducing them to "great men." When our children read the biographies of men and women of faith, they are encouraged in their own walks with God.

A.W. Tozer writes, "Next to the Holy Scriptures, the greatest aid to the life of faith may be Christian biographies."[7] I heartily agree! In fact, Michael and I have seen firsthand the power of a Christian biography in the lives of our own children and the lives of students at our church's school. These books are transformative! They not only provide a wonderful example of a life of faith, but they are also a continual source of inspiration for the rest of their life. In fact, it was a biography on Nate Saint that inspired my son, Josh, to decide to become a missionary pilot when he was in fourth grade.

Introducing our children to great men and women of the faith—like the ten Boom sisters, C.T. Studd, David Livingston, and more—helps to mold and shape their values as it gives them a vision for life beyond themselves. Ransome W. Cooper, a British pastor, wrote:

The *reading of good biography forms an important part of a Christian's education. It provides him with numberless illustrations for use in his own service. He learns to assess the true worth of character, to glimpse a work goal for his own life, to decide how to best attain it, what self-denial is needed to curb unworthy aspirations; and all the time he learns how God breaks into the dedicated life to bring about his own purposes.*[8]

Reading biographies of men and women of faith can truly transform our lives.

Last year, Michael and I had a very difficult time with our son, Josh. He would not do his homework, he had a bad attitude, and he was not making the best choices. As we discipled him, we realized that Josh was feeling a bit hopeless—he didn't enjoy school and felt overwhelmed with life. Michael and I prayed for wisdom, and the Lord gave us a plan. We decided to homeschool Josh two days a week, and give him projects that he could do with his hands, so he could feel the sense of accomplishment. Then, we put him on an aggressive reading program. Josh read biographies about ten heroes of the faith—C.T. Studd, George Mueller, Hudson Taylor, David Livingstone, Eric Liddell, and other missionaries. Within a month, we received our son back!

Josh not only accomplished many woodworking projects, but he also had a fresh vision for his life. One of his projects was to make a rubber band gun from scratch. In the middle of the project, Josh got stuck; he couldn't figure out how to make the gun's lever. He had just finished a biography about George Mueller, so he decided to do what George Mueller did about everything: pray. Josh prayed that God would help him figure out what to do, and to his astonishment, God answered his prayer! When he proudly shot his gun for the first time, he smiled, and joyfully proclaimed that God had shown him how to build the lever—just like God had faithfully helped George Mueller in his times of need! Josh needed the examples of "great men" to rekindle his passion for God, and to renew his vision for his life!

He Must Increase

Today's youth have an unhealthy obsession with fame. Many of our children who do desire to serve God think they are going to do something great for God by becoming famous. Then, through their fame, they will have a platform to glorify God.

A couple years ago, I taught a discipleship class for our junior high girls. At the end of the year, each student was asked to write down all the dreams they had for their life. After their list was complete, they were asked to spend time with God before filtering their dreams through the His Word. Afterwards, they needed to share their dreams with their parents and with the other girls in the class. Their dreams: becoming an Oscar Award recipient; becoming an Emmy Award recipient; being a famous soccer player; and lastly, being a wife, mom, and teacher.

Each of these girls desired to glorify God with their life, but most of them thought the best way they could do so was to first become famous. I was rather taken aback, as I had never imagined being famous as a young girl. Yet, the need to be famous is the message our children get from movies, sports, social media, and modern entertainment. Our children genuinely believe that they can give more glory to God if they are famous, but this thinking is not biblical! We must teach our children that we need to become nothing, so that God can become everything.

We see this truth exemplified in the life of John the Baptist. God sent the angel Gabriel to tell Zacharias that he would have a son, whom he was to name John because he would "be great in the sight of the Lord" (Luke 1:15). John's God-given mission was to prepare the world for the coming of the Savior, Jesus Christ. His message to the people was that "He [Jesus] must increase, but I must decrease" (John 3:30). After John's death, Jesus said that "there is not a greater prophet than John the Baptist, but he who is least in the kingdom of God is greater than he" (Luke 7:28).

The message here and throughout scripture is clear: if we desire to be great in the sight of the Lord, we must decrease, and God must increase. After listening to a message given at a Christian rock concert, my son, Sam, said, "I couldn't understand what the preacher was saying. All I could see was him and his clothes. I like preachers who disappear when they preach, and all I can see is God!" To glorify God, we must disappear —and we must teach our children to understand this message!

Throughout history, we see many examples of men and women, who became nothing so that Christ could have accomplish His will through them. Oswald Chambers wrote, "They laid their lives on the altar, so God could be seen in their life. Their heart's cry was, 'It is no longer I who lives, but Christ who lives within me!'" But, this is not the message your children hear on Instagram, Pinterest and YouTube! The heart's cry of our children should be like that of the psalmist: "Not unto us, O LORD, not unto us, but to Your name give glory," (Psalm 115:1).

Our Example

God has called each of our children to a specific work, and our job, as moms, is to help our children recognize God's call for their life, remind them of the vision, and encourage them to walk in it!

There is no greater example of a man who fulfilled God's vision for His life than Jesus. The name Jesus means "Yahweh is Salvation." It was God's vision—before the foundation of the world—that Jesus would come into the world to reconcile it to God and mankind from their sin. And, He fulfilled the Father's mission. Jesus set His face, like flint, to the cross —and on the way the cross, He told the Father, "I have finished the work you have called me to do" (John 17:4) Then, as Jesus hung on the cross, He said, "It is finished" (John 19:30), as He completed the vision God had for Him.

There is no greater inspiration we can give our children than a vision of Jesus' life, death and resurrection. In fact, it has been a source of inspiration for countless men and women throughout the centuries! C.H. Spurgeon remarks:

> There is one great event, which every day attracts more admiration than do the sun, the moon, the stars, when they march in their courses. That event is the death of our Lord Jesus Christ. To it, the eyes of the saints who lived before the

Christian era were always directed; and backwards, through the thousand years of history, the eyes of all modern saints are looking.[9]

When we get our children' eyes off of themselves and onto the Lord, there is no stopping what God can do in and through them.

On being asked about how he wrote his "Hallelujah Chorus," Handel, composer of *Messiah*, remarked, "I did see God on His throne."[10] When our children see God on His throne and lose all thoughts of themselves, God can inspire them to do great things for His glory.

There is an old saying, "Some people are so heavenly minded that they are no earthly good."[11] This is absolute rubbish! A man who has his thoughts and mind fixed upon God and His kingdom makes decisions that affect all of eternity! C.S. Lewis once wrote, "Aim at Heaven and you will get Earth 'thrown in': aim at Earth and you will get neither."[12] The vision we cast for our children's life needs to be aimed at focusing their minds on God.

When our children receive a clear vision from God, there is no stopping what God can do in and through them. History is filled with men and women who received a vision for their life, and worked tirelessly to fulfill that vision. Of their example, C.S Lewis writes:

If you read history, you will find that the Christians who did the most for the present world were just those who thought most of the next. The Apostles themselves, who set on foot the conversion of the Roman Empire, the great men who build up the Middle Ages, the English Evangelicals who abolished the Slave Trade, all left their marks on Earth, precisely because their minds were occupied with heaven.[13]

It was David Livingston who wrote: "If a commission by an earthly king is considered an honor, how can a commission by a Heavenly King be considered a sacrifice?"[14] God, our King, has commissioned our children to do His work. Regardless of their future occupation, our children are called to be men and women of God, who are His voice to a lost and dying world. God has a mighty task for each of our children, and we must encourage and inspire them to fulfill His great call.

A Mother's Influence
During the 18th century, a Quaker family lived in the backwoods of Pennsylvania. The youngest son of ten children, Benjamin West grew up to be a world-renowned painter. His source of inspiration: his mother.

One day, when Benjamin was just a boy, he watched his baby niece as she slept. Admiring little Sally's face, he became so moved by her expression that he decided to sketch it. When his mother came home, she was so awestruck by his drawing that she said, "Why, bless me, it is a picture of little Sally." Then, she threw her arms around Benjamin's neck and kissed him.

This kiss from his mother was such an encouragement to Benjamin that, later in life, he stated, "A kiss from my mother made me a painter."[15] Sarah West remained Benjamin's source of encouragement his whole life. Not only did she recognize her son's God-given gift early in his life, but she also continued to encourage him to fulfill God's vision for life as long as she lived.

As mothers, we have great influence over the destiny of our children's lives. We must purposefully cast a vision for their lives, stir up their gifts, raise the standard, and make decisions that will enable them to be prepared to answer God's call. We must do everything in our power to encourage our children to be the men and women that God has called them to be so they can transform this world for His glory!

Questions to Consider

1. Do your children know why they were created? How can you ingrain in them a vision for their life?

2. When was the last time you spoke or prayed a prophecy over your children's lives? When might be a good time to do this?

3. Do your children know what their gifts are? How are you cultivating these gifts within their lives?

4. What expectations do you hold for your children? When was the last time you shared these expectations with them?

5. What vision do you have for your children? Are you making decision now that will enable your son/daughter to fulfill this vision? Are any of you decisions having the opposite affect?

6. Do your children desire fame? How can you encourage them to lose their identity in Christ?

7. Have your children write out all of their dreams and desires. Then, listen to them. — Are their desires pleasing to God? If so, affirm and encourage them in their heart's desires. If they are not pleasing to God, work on helping your children see what a life that is pleasing to God looks like.

Notes

[1] Eric Metaxas, "Message by Eric Metaxas," November 6, 2016, Harvest Christian Church, accessed August 3, 2019, https://harvest.org/resources/webcast/message-by-eric-metaxas/

[2] Dan Oren '79, '84MD, "Stamp Of Approval" Yale Alumni Magazine, March 2001, adapted from *Joining The Club: A History of Jews and Yale,* Second Edition (Yale University Press, 2001), accessed July 20, 2019

[3] C.H. Spurgeon, *Cheque Book of the Bank of Faith* (Great Britain:Christian Focus Publications, 1996), 328.

[4] C.S. Lewis, *The Voyage of the Dawn Treader* (New York, New York: Harper Collins Publishing, 1952), 1.

[5] Hudson Taylor, quoted in Mrs. Charles E. Cowman, *Devotions for Morning and Evening* (New York: International Press, 1925), 390.

[6] Donald Miller, "Good Reads," January 7, 2011, accessed July 9, 2019, https://www.goodreads.com/author/show/4829.Donald_Miller/blog?page=129

[7] A.W. Tozer, *Let My People Go: The Life of Robert A. Jaffray* (Camp Hill, Pennsylvania: Wing Spread Publishers, 1948), preface.

[8] Ransome W. Cooper, quoted in Oswald Sanders, *Spiritual Leadership* (Chicago: Moody Press, 1976), 105.

[9] C. H. Spurgeon, *Spurgeon's Sermons*, Volume 4 (Woodstock, Ontario: Devoted Publishing, 2017), 59.

[10] George Frederick Handel, quoted in Cowman, *Devotions for Morning and Evening*, 393.

[11] Oliver Wendell Holmes, Sr. "Good Reads," accessed July 20, 2019, https://www.goodreads.com/quotes/687900-some-people-are-so-heavenly-minded-that-they-are-no

[12] C.S. Lewis, "Good Reads," accessed July 20, 2019, https://www.goodreads.com/quotes/82131-aim-at-heaven-and-you-will-get-earth-thrown-in

[13] C.S. Lewis, "Good Reads," accessed July 20, 2019, https://www.goodreads.com/quotes/451775-if-you-read-history-you-will-find-that-the-christians

[14] David Livingstone, "Good Reads," accessed July 20, 2019, https://www.goodreads.com/quotes/805628-if-a-commission-by-an-earthly-king-is-considered-an

[15] Benjamin West, quoted in Debroah Hamby, *Mothers of Famous Men* (New York: Lamplighter Publishing, 1999), 96.

Pearl of Wisdom #7
Teach Your Children to Serve

But Samuel ministered before the Lord, even as a child,
wearing a linen ephod.

1 Samuel 2:18

After Hannah dropped off Samuel at the Tabernacle, what did he do? He ministered to the Lord! Can you imagine a little boy of three, serving God by working in the the Tabernacle? I can just picture him closing and opening the doors of the Tabernacle, lighting the candlesticks in the late afternoon, baking bread for the table of showbread, preparing the lampstand, washing the altar, cleaning the water in the laver, and doing all the little chores about the Tabernacle—like taking out the trash, sweeping the floors, washing the utensils, and so forth.

Samuel is such a wonderful example for us moms. Our job is to rightly teach and demonstrate to our children the purpose and joy of serving—and then, to allow them, like Samuel, to serve God from a young age. As mothers, we need to cast a vision for our children's life, and train them to be servants of the living God, so they can fulfill the vision that He has given them!

Why Work?
The ability to work is a gift given to us by God: "For we are His workmanship, created in Christ Jesus for good works, which God prepared beforehand that we should walk in them" (Ephesians 2:10). When God created man, He placed him in the Garden of Eden, and put him to work! Adam's job was to tend the Garden and name the animals.

Work is a gift that God gives to His people. It is an opportunity for us to take part in His creation. "[T]he heavens are the work of [His] hands" (Hebrews 1:10), and the work of our hands is one way we can take part in His glorious creation.

God worked six days, when He created the earth, and then He rested on the seventh. We, too, are commanded to work six days and rest on the seventh. In Exodus 20, God gave Moses the Ten Commandments. His fourth commandment states:

Six days you shall labor and do all your work, but the seventh
days the Sabbath of the LORD your God. In it you shall do no
work...For in six days the LORD made the heavens and the
earth, the sea, and all that is in them, and rested the seventh

day. Therefore the LORD blessed the Sabbath day and hallowed it.

— Exodus 20:9-11

Clearly, we were created to work. God gave each of us gifts to use for His glory. He intends for us to use them to bless others and build His kingdom.

When God wanted an ark built, he used Noah and his sons (Genesis 6). When He wanted a Tabernacle built, he used the skilled workers of Bezalel and Oholiab and their assistants (Exodus 36:1). When Jesus miraculously fed the five thousand, He used the hands of His disciples for the distribution of the bread and fish (Matthew 14:19). He also used the lips and tongues of His disciples for the preaching of the gospel (Luke 9:1-6). Whenever God wants to get work done in this world, He chooses to work through us by the Holy Spirit.

One day, when our work on earth and our life is over, we will enter into glory—and what will we be doing? Working! Revelation gives us a glimpse of this heavenly scene: "And there shall be no more curse, but the throne of God and of the Lamb shall be in it, and His servants shall serve Him." (Revelation 22:3) When we are in glory for all eternity, we will be free from the curse of sin, and we will be given the joy of serving the Lord forever. Our children need to become "servants of God" here on this earth, so they will be prepared to serve Him for eternity. And if they serve God now, they will reign with Him "forever and ever" in glory (Revelation 22:5)!

Our service now determines our future role in the kingdom of God. In other words, the work we do here on this earth and how we do it will be rewarded—and determine where we will work in God's coming Kingdom. Amy Carmichael notes, "We will have all eternity to celebrate our victories, but only a few short hours to win them." Work is a glorious privilege!

The Curse
Because of sin, there are all sorts of distortions surrounding work. After the Fall, work became more difficult. This is a result of the curse God placed upon mankind after Adam and Eve's sin in the Garden of Eden:

Cursed is the ground for your sake; in toil you shall eat of it all the days of your life. Both thorns and thistles it shall bring forth for you, and you shall eat of the herb of the field. In the sweat of your face you shall eat bread till you return to the ground, for out of it you were taken; for dust you are, and to dust you shall return.

— Genesis 3:17-19

Elisabeth Elliot shares her father's insight on why God made work much harder after sin entered the world:

My father believed that when God ordained hard work for man after he sinned, God knew that his wandering thoughts and imagination would need to be kept in check and his mischievous hands would need to be kept busy. If there were no need to earn money, each man would be a law unto himself, and we would soon have chaos instead of the large measure of order that we do have.[1]

Not only has our work become more difficult, but our attitude towards work has also become distorted. Rather than praising God for an opportunity to take part in His creation, we see work as a means to an end, a necessary evil to be endured Monday through Friday. Rather than viewing work as a glorious honor and privilege, we believe it is a depressing burden, the pits. What a distortion!

This distortion is not only seen in our own attitude toward work, but also in the way we train our children. Children today are not taught that work is a trait to be cultivated; they are being taught the opposite. Rather than being trained to serve, our children are conditioned to *be* served. Instead of making a transition from servant to trainer, mothers often continue to serve their children throughout their life—believing the lie that the more they do for their children, the more love they express, and the better mom they become. Many mothers believe that requiring their children to work will deprive them of their childhood.

Culturally, we have lowered our expectations for our children. Children who were once producers—valuable assets to the family, home, and business—are now just consumers. In most homes today, when a child is asked to do something, they start complaining—especially if the task gets in the way of what they were already doing. Household chores have become a thing of the past, as playtime and activities have taken precedence. Many children no longer get jobs as teenagers, babysitting, working paper routes, or serving at a local restaurant. Instead, their achievements, sports, and social events have taken priority. Mothers have encouraged this shift by revolving their lives around their children, and by making sure they get every opportunity—especially if the opportunities are ones they didn't get as a child.

For a family of nine, it is always a lot of work to get groceries, pack them into the car, and then unload them at home. Anytime I go to Costco, I always take a child or two with me to help. On one occasion, I took my son, who was in sixth grade at the time. He pushed and filled the cart for me as I directed where to go and what to buy. While we were in the store, we saw one of his schoolmates. He was sitting in his mother's cart, playing a video game. What a perfect picture of what is happening with children in our culture! Rather than training our children to work, or allowing them to learn the blessing of service, or contributing towards the family, we are giving them a life of aimless leisure.

As mothers, we must restore the value of work in our families, training and inspiring our children to live a life of service for the glory of God! We must remember the vision we have cast for our children, and spend the rest of their growing years training them towards that end. There is nothing more glorious than working towards building God's kingdom!

Children at Work

God has given us the ability to work, and the sooner our children learn to serve, like Samuel, the better! We can start training our children to serve by teaching them that the world does not revolve around them. The easiest way to do this is by putting them on a schedule from birth. Babies think only of themselves and their needs. However, if they are on a schedule, they will soon learn that they are not in charge—their parents are! And, their parents are in control of what they get, and when. A schedule is a great way to teach children early on that they are created to serve, not to be served.

Around the age of two to three, we can begin to train our children to serve practically within the home. Two to three might sound very young to us, but we must remember Samuel—he was three years old when he began serving the Lord in the Tabernacle! If we do not teach our children to serve as young children, they are not going to wake up one day as teenagers with a sudden desire to start working.

We must train our children to work from a very young age, so that work will be a natural part of their life as they grow older. Now, I am not suggesting that we reestablish nineteenth century workhouses, or reverse child labor laws. No, instead I am talking about teaching our children the importance and virtue of hard work, as well as the vices of idleness and laziness. We need to teach our children the joy of serving others, the importance of doing our best, and the privilege of taking part in building this world for God's glory!

I am not suggesting we replace work with play, as play is such a valuable part of a child's life. Rather, we must add service and work into their life, as part of their training. M. A. Stodart talks about the blessings of a child who works in her poem, "One Thing at a Time:"

> *Work while you work, play while you play.*
> *That is the way to be cheerful all day.*
> *All that you do, do with your might.*
> *Things done by halves are never done right.*
> *One thing each time and that done well*
> *is a very good rule as many can tell.*
> *Moments are useless trifled away; so*
> *work while you work, and play while you play.*[2]

As parents, we need to remember and teach our children the age-old adage, "Work hard; play hard." When our children are trained to work, and to work hard, they will enjoy their time of play so much more! Play is the reward we receive from work. The writer of Ecclesiastes states: "So I commended enjoyment, because a man has nothing better under the sun than to eat, drink, and be merry; for this will remain with him in his labor all the days of his life which God gives him under the sun" (Ecclesiastes 8:15). Play is a gift from God. Yet, when our play is interspersed with work, it brings so much more joy! And there is no better time for our children to learn to work hard than when they are children.

Serving Others

Our role as moms is to teach our children to serve others. In order to do this, we must require them to serve. To enable this to happen, our service towards our children has to transition from servant to trainer. So often, I find that we as moms have a hard time making this transition. However, if we want children who treat other people with love and respect—and eventually, that means us—we need to teach them to think of others above themselves.

Recently, I went to a coffee shop, and noticed a man wearing a leather crown as a hat. It is a real crown, of sorts. As I pondered why this man would wear a crown, I was reminded that, in general, people in our culture think much too highly of themselves. Our entitlement culture tells them they should be served, rather than being the one serving.

As Christians, we are not to think highly of ourselves; rather, we are told to esteem others above ourselves (Philippians 2:3). I am so grateful that Jesus, the true King, became a man, taking on the form of a humble servant, so he could become nothing, and die on the cross to save our souls. Jesus is the greatest example of serving others: "For even the Son of Man did not come to be served, but to serve, and to give His life a ransom for many" (Mark 10:45).

Because of Jesus, we are in debt to the world around us for His sake. Our love for Jesus should motivate us to serve others. In 1 Corinthians 9, Paul declares that he was motivated to serve others because of Jesus and for the sake of the gospel. In verse nineteen, he writes, "For though I am free from all men, I have made myself a servant to all, that I might win the more." As mothers, it is our duty to train our children to put others before themselves, and to serve them in love. We have all been given liberty in Christ, but we must follow Jesus's example by denying our flesh and serving one another in love (Galatians 5:13).

How do we serve others in love? We do unto others as we want them to do unto us. We are courteous and kind towards them. We treat them as we want to be treated. We think of them more highly than ourselves. We attend birthday parties and showers. We send out thank you notes, and greet people when we walk into a room. We sit and talk with our grandparents when they come over, giving them hugs and kisses and thanking them for visiting. We make sure we are the last ones to eat, so others have priority! None of these actions are natural for children, who only want to do what their flesh desires. However, if we want to train our children to serve others, we must require them to do things that their flesh doesn't want to do—to bless others!

Often, I find that we give our children the choice to be a blessing or not. If they are shy, they don't have to say hello. If they don't feel like going somewhere to help others, they don't have to. We must beware of allowing our children to make decisions based upon their feelings. Rather, we need to train our children to deny themselves to do what the need is. Our children should not have an option in this area—we need to train our children to deny themselves, pick up their cross, and follow Jesus by serving other people in love! Our children were created to serve. They were not created to live for their own interests, but for the interests of others (Philippians 2:4).

Serving others is a sign that we are followers of Christ. John 12:26 states, "If anyone serves Me, let him follow Me; and where I am, there My servant will be also. If anyone serves Me, him My Father will honor." Jesus also tells us that "whoever desires to become great among you, let him be your servant" (Matthew 20:26). This command explains why Paul, James, Peter, and Jude all opened their epistles with a "servant of God and the Lord Jesus Christ." Each of these men could have boasted about their credentials in Christ; but for them, their greatest honor was to be called a "servant of God."

There is a certain joy that comes through serving others. As a young child, I learned about the acronym J-O-Y: **J**esus, **O**thers, **Y**ou. To receive real joy, we must put *Jesus* first in our lives, consider *others* second and *you* last. When we put these three in the right order, we receive real joy!

Serving at Home
The training ground for serving others is the home! There is definitely something to be said for a family farm or business, as every member works together to survive. Today, more than ever, we have to work to train our children to serve one another in the home—modern conveniences and technology have taken so much work out of the home! Yet, there is still so much we can do to teach our children to serve within our homes.

So, how do we teach our children to serve? We know that when our children are born, they are not able to do anything. We are their servants —they need us to feed them, comfort them, cuddle them, change them, bathe them, and so forth! However, as they start to become independent, we can start training them to serve. Around the age of two, our children can pick up toys, throw out their trash, put their shoes away, and more. At three, they can start getting their own water and putting their plate on the counter until, eventually, they become teenagers who are able to cook, clean, do laundry, serve at church, do their homework independently, and hold a job. It is fascinating that today, when many people think of a teenager, they think of a season of rebellion, laziness, and non-productivity. However, we must remember, that the term teenager is a modern day term given to us by affluent culture. Elisabeth Elliot wrote about a time when she and her five siblings were the age of teenagers today:

> We never were teen-agers. I can't help being thankful that the term had not been thought of in my day. I think it spared us some silliness and some real pain. It has become an accepted label for a stage in life usually dreaded by parents and relished by children as a time when anything goes. But this is an invention of modern times and affluent societies. Jesus, at the age of twelve, deliberately set about His Father's business. Jewish boys at thirteen mark a clear transition from child to adult in the Bar Mitzvah. King Josiah was eight years old when he began to reign, and at sixteen the Bible says that he began to seek the God of his father David. At twenty he took strong and sweeping action against the idolatry rampant in Judah at the time...There was no time or inclination for doing nothing. [3]

As mothers, if we want to raise men and women set-apart, molded, and shaped by the power of God and His Word, we do not have to adhere to the world's standards for our teens by allowing them to do nothing. In fact, we shouldn't! We should expect far more of our children, especially in their teenage years. By the time they are adults, they will have all the necessary skills to leave our homes, and be launched into the world for a lifetime of service.

As a mom, I really erred in the area of service when my children were young. I honestly felt, the more I serve my children- the greater I became. It sounds biblical, doesn't it? However, I was dead wrong! In serving my children to the point of exhaustion, I was teaching my children to be selfish. I wanted my children to have a fun, carefree childhood, where all their dreams came true. Since this was my vision, I did everything around the house—all the cooking, cleaning, laundry, etc. —and I was exhausted!

One Sunday evening, Michael was at a prayer meeting, and I put the children to bed. Afterwards, I walked into the living room, and became so overwhelmed and frustrated at the messy house. I wanted to burst into tears. In my exasperation, I went into the boys' room, and yelled at them to get out of bed and clean up the house! They immediately jumped up, and went to work. Later that evening, my son, Josh, told me, "Mom, all you had to do was ask us to clean up, and we would have done it. You didn't have to get upset!" He was absolutely right! However, at the time, I was drowning, and I didn't really know what to do or where to start to fix the problem.

What really opened my eyes was *Parenting by the Book*, by John Rosemond. After reading it, I realized that I was creating entitled kids by not teaching them to serve at home. Things were not working at home; and once I realized that service is actually a blessing for children, and it was my responsibility to teach my children to serve, Michael and I sat down and listed out all the household chores on a piece of paper. Then, we divided up the list up between our six children. We made chores charts to keep each of them accountable to their new "jobs." We laminated and hung the charts on a board in our hallway. Assigning chores not only made our household run smoother, it also allowed our children to experience the blessing of serving their family.

Working together as a family brings about so many blessings! Today, our children do the majority of the household work, as Michael and I manage our home. In the evenings after dinner, the children clean up the dishes, while the two of us take the baby and dog for a walk, or simply visit in our bedroom. Having our children serve has been such a blessing in our lives. Often, people ask me how I manage to do life with seven children. I am so grateful for each of my children, who all do the bulk of the work. Granted, there are more bodies in my home, more groceries to purchase, more laundry to sort; but the pressure, exhaustion, and overwhelming feelings have been eliminated as my children work together and serve within our home.

Getting your children to serve at home can be a daunting task for some moms, especially when they think of all the training and messiness involved. As I write this chapter, my husband is making a run to the hardware store to fix a drip line that our son broke while planting a new tree. My kitchen is a disaster because one of my daughters has just made banana bread for dessert, and the other has broken a cup and spilled milk while setting up our tea party.

When we train our children to serve, we are going to have broken drip lines in the yard, dishes shattered in the kitchen, and favorite dresses or sweater ruined in the laundry! Yet, the small sacrifices and momentary disappointments are worth the blessings of having help around the house and children who have learned the skills they need for life.

Chore Charts
What really transformed our home was chore charts. Today, my children help keep our home running smoothly, rather than just consuming. What a gift to Michael and me! It took us awhile to figure out the best plan for children and house, as there are so many ways to create a chore chart. I have found that the best ones are different for every family; it all depends on the mom's personality, and her ability to train her children.

Michael and I are casually organized, and our chore charts are not super detailed—but our training and organization works well for our family. There are many more efficient ways to do chores than the way they are done in the McClure household, but I hope that our chore charts can be a help to those who are just starting to create their own.

Michael and I are casually organized, and our chore charts are not super detailed—but our training and organization works well for our family. We began by listing all of the chores in our house on a piece of paper. Then, we decided who would do which chore on what day and hung the list in a place where everyone could see it. Once we established the list, we created an individual chore chart for each of our children, which has their specific chores listed every day. If our children do not do their chores for the day, they lose a part of their allowance—for us, it is 25 cents. Our boys only earn $5 a week, so losing 25 cents a chore adds up quickly! (Note: Losing 25 cents a chore does not make sense mathematically with the number of chores each child has, but it is easy to manage).

Michael and I do not switch out our children's chores often. It takes time to train our children to do a job, and we don't have time to retrain someone else the following week. This might not be the best in the long run for our children, but it works for our home. Eventually, our children will all know how to do the dishes; but for now, the younger ones have other chores. Our children each cook a different meal for breakfast. For example, Hannah cooks French toast; Daniel cooks waffles; Micah, pancakes; Sam, scrambled eggs, and so on. They all cook their meals on specific days.

Once Michael and I completed the chore charts, our children knew what our expectations were, and there was no arguing or complaining about who was going to do what. This was revolutionary in our family! A lot of my earlier frustration with my children came from the things I wanted and expected them to do—without ever communicating these things to them. Our children are not going to naturally see a need and fill it. They must first be trained to serve.

Michael and I are not good at paying our children on a weekly basis, but they are still faithful to do their chores—as it keeps the family and house running smoothly. We usually end up paying them every few months, and our children keep track of how much we owe them. Praise God that our children are gracious with us. We also switch up the chores every few months, as the little ones grow older and are able to take on new chores.

Obviously, there is no one way to organize a home or chore chart. Simply create or choose one that works best for your family. What matters most is that our children must be trained to serve. They not only need to know the expectations we have for them, but we also need to follow through and hold them accountable to our expectations.

Serving at Church
Our children should not just be serving at home, however. It is imperative that they begin serving at church from a young age. This concept is huge for my husband. He believes that the younger children are when they start serving at church, the sooner they will build a life-

time habit and make church an important part of their life—like it was for Samuel!

Serving at church is more important than ever. Today, many children (and adults) go to church expecting to be served. When their needs are not met, they run from church to church; or as we are finding more and more often, many leave the church altogether.

When we train our children to serve at church from a young age, they will not have this entitled attitude towards church. They will look for ways to be a blessing to others rather than wondering how their needs will be met by their church. Imagine what would happen if everyone you know came to church with this type of attitude!

It is not enough for our children to be serving God individually at church. The entire family should be serving the Lord together. They could work in the Children's Ministry once a month; serve on the worship team together; head up the meals ministry, youth ministry, hospitality ministry, or start a ministry for an unmet need.

So often, children who do not grow up serving in their church do not see the value or necessity of serving when they are older. But, when a family decides to make serving a priority, the children grow up knowing that it is a valuable part of their life. Then, when they are raising their own children, they will make serving a priority as well! Additionally, serving together at church is a great way to impart your biblical values to your children.

Next to the family, the church is the most important institution God has created and ordained for Christians to be a part of. Not your sports league, your children's school, or another para organization, but the church. The church should be a very important part of our lives and our children's lives—an extension of the family, if you will!

Recently, a mom told me, "My family is the priority in my life, not church"—and granted, it is important that you do not neglect your family to serve at your church, as that will make your children resent it. However, it is so important that families do not make their children's sports games, social lives, or family activities more important than church. Remember, it is easy to wrap our lives around building our children's kingdoms; but in doing so, we indirectly teach our children that their life is more important than God's kingdom! Rather, as a family, we should be making sacrifices for the Kingdom, which teaches our children that there is nothing more important than serving God. Children will grow up making sacrifices for the kingdom of God as well!

When my children were young, and Michael and I were new to the ministry, we read a profound piece of advice from Warren Wiersbe's book *On Being a Servant of God*. In it, he spoke about the relationship between the family and the church. He stated:

The best thing my wife and I could do for the churches we served was to build a good home and raise children who were a credit to the Lord and to the church. And the best thing we could do for our home was to build good churches for our children to attend. The two became one....

He goes on to say:

When our children understand that everybody in the family is a part of the ministry, and that together we are all building the church and building our home, we have a common outlook to help us in making decisions. It isn't an either/or situation; it's both/and.[4]

This has meant that sometimes our children have to sacrifice for the church. And what a wonderful lesson for them to realize that serving God requires sacrifice. But other times, we have had to let things go undone for our family to be rightly ordered. As there is no greater sermon that Michael can preach than to have a family rightly ordered.

Ever since our boys were very little, Michael would tell them how God asked Noah to build the ark because of the coming judgment—and He didn't just ask Noah. He also asked his sons. Michael would tell our boys, "There is a coming judgement, and God has asked Daddy to build an ark, His church. You are my sons, and He is asking you to help me build it, too!" Then, Michael would remind them on Sunday morning, "Remember to help Daddy build the ark today!" When our boys were naughty at church, he would come home and tell them, "You did not help Daddy build the ark today," and they would get in trouble!

Michael insists that all our children serve at church. The younger ones serve in the nursery or with the toddlers, while the older ones work in the elementary—with the students, running technology, leading worship, or even teaching. Our church staff know that, when there is a need, they can call upon our children to fill it.

When one of our sons was in junior high, he struggled with a bad attitude. He would complain every day about nearly everything. Michael and I prayed about what to do. Michael asked our Assistant Pastor to talk to him. So, he took our son to lunch. He gave our son a Giants hammer to remind him that his job was to build the ark—and that his attitude could build or destroy it. Their talk (and the hammer as a visual) really did its work, giving my son a much-needed perspective!

Our goal is to raise up children who serve in the church no matter what occupation the Lord calls them to or where He sends them. We want our children to build the church, and to be a blessing to their church family. They should not only be servants within the church, but also raise up the hands of their pastor and his family, supporting them as they do the work of the ministry. Someday, when Mike and I visit our children and their churches, and we meet their pastors, we want them to say: Micah is my best man, he is such a blessing to our church; I don't know what I would do without Josh; Hannah just builds our church, and supports other women and their families. This is the result of children who grow up making serving church a priority throughout their life.

There are many blessings that come from serving at church. Michael and I have noticed through the years that whenever families are busy serving at church, they get to know other people, and use their gifts to be a blessing to others—as they serve, meet needs, and support their church staff. We have also noticed that when families are busy serving at church, they are not as critical of the church. So often, the things that bother us at church are needs that God has given us the gifts to fill, if we would just roll up our sleeves and get dirty. And when we fill the need, it can change our whole perspective!

School Work

One important area of work our children need to learn to do well is their school work, as they are going to spend the majority of their growing years in a school setting. We have all sorts of ideas about how our children should approach their school work, and there are just as many educational philosophies to choose from—from unschooling to a very rigid approach. Yet, we can glean some practical insights from God's Word regarding our children and school work, regardless of the philosophy we hold.

First off, it is God's will that our children attend school. School work can become real drudgery when our children enter their teen years; however, we must remind them that God has required this work of them. We must encourage them to persevere through it.

At school, our children are prepared for the work that God has called them to do. School is not something they can bypass; instead, it something they must submit to and learn all they can from. Often, children say, "I am never going to use this subject again in my life." However, we must remember that our Lord and Savior was the "Special One," who knew everything; yet, He was not able to escape the childhood responsibilities that all children have to endure! Scripture states that "Jesus grew in wisdom and statue, and in favor with God and man" (Luke 2:52). If Jesus lived at home and subjected himself to his parents authority, our children can do this as well! God is molding and preparing our children for the work He is calling them to do, and school is a big part of this process.

Another important thing to remember is that our children need to approach their school work with an attitude of doing their best as unto the Lord. Their best might mean that they get all C's in school, but it is still their best. We need to teach our children to "do all to the glory of God" (1 Corinthians 10:31).

Education is a gift from the Lord, and should be treated as such. As parents, we need to constantly praise God for the education that our children receive. If we take the time to declare the many benefits of their education, they will catch on, and believe it is valuable, too. Often, when we talk or pray together, my children will randomly say, "We go to the best school ever." Now, they did not decide by themselves that they go to the best school, they have been told that by their parents, their teachers, and their friends! Going to "the best school ever" does not mean their school is easy; instead, it means that the engaging atmosphere, love for learning, and Spirit-filled environment are contagious!

Helping our children get a good perspective in this area can really motivate them to faithfully persevere through their time in school. This perseverance will help them build character, and enable them to do the work that God has called them to do in the future.

Beware of Idleness

When we train our children to serve, we must beware of idleness, as it "is a sort of commercial traveller for the devil."[5] Idleness introduces evil thoughts, and clears the way for little sins to enter our lives. We are told that the sin of Sodom was idleness—"pride, fullness of food, and abundance of idleness" (Ezekiel 16:49). J.C. Ryle warns parents about idleness in his book, *Duties of Parents*: "Idleness is the devil's best friend. It is the surest way to give him an opportunity of doing us harm. An idle mind is like an open door, and if Satan does not enter in himself by it, it is certain he will throw in something to raise bad thoughts in our souls."[6]

I can honestly tell you that when I have too much free time, the enemy attacks my mind! How much more does he attack the minds of our children? Bramwell Booth, leader of the Salvation Army, warned his officers, "The idle, the easy-going, the nothing-particular-to-do-just-now Officer always goes down."[7]

Theodore Roosevelt once said, "Never throughout history has a man who lived a life of ease left a name worth remembering." When we are idle, the enemy not only attacks our mind, but also hinders us from accomplishing anything of value with the time we have. And, if we want to accomplish much for the Lord, we have to work!

Our children naturally want to do what is comfortable and easy. So, we must teach them about the vices of laziness. God's Word declares that a lazy man chases after fantasies or frivolities (Proverbs 12:11). How are our children chasing fantasies today? They chase after get-rich-quick schemes so they can get out of working. They read endless books, watch YouTube videos or Netflix, waste their time on video games about fantasy worlds rather than working or engaging in reality. These things—and more—are the vices of laziness. Our children must be trained to avoid them and be wise with their time.

One of our sons used to have a real problem with laziness. Whenever he would hear that something needed to be done, he would literally run in the opposite direction, and hide. Michael and I had him memorize Proverbs 13:4, "The soul of a lazy man desires, and has nothing; But the soul of the diligent shall be made rich." For years, we had to constantly remind him of this verse! However, when he went to Junior High Camp, God spoke to him about serving his family—and my son's life was transformed. Now, whenever he sees a need, he fills it, rather than running away.

So, what is the remedy to an idle life? Bramwell Booth has an answer: hard work! "It is a friend of the soul, the guardian angel of the conscience, medicine for the body, and a panoply and protection against all sorts of temptation."[8] Work is a great preserver of life as it really does keep our heart and body rightly ordered.

My children learned a lesson about work from *Duck Tales*, a TV show they used to watch: "Work smarter, not harder"—and this lesson is one we talk about all the time! Michael and I always seem to work harder, and our children are always thinking of ways for us to work smarter! They offer us ideas about how to make our home more efficient, how to make investments to pay bills, and so on. Working smarter is not being lazy, it is wise—and if our children are blessed with wisdom, then we are going to grab ahold of it!

Hard Work

If we want our children to be future leaders, we need to teach them how to work, and work hard. Preacher Alexander MacLaren assures us that, "The secret of success in everything is trust in God and hard work."[9] This world is a very hard one, and there is so much work to be done! Oswald Sanders writes in his book, *Spiritual Leadership*:

> *The Spirit of the welfare state does not produce leaders. If a Christian is not willing to rise early and work late, to expend greater effort in diligent study and faithful work, that person will not change a generation. Fatigue is the price of leadership! Mediocrity is the result of never getting tired.*[10]

As parents, we are training future leaders, so we must train our children to work hard! Ecclesiastes 9:10 exhorts us, "Whatever your hand finds to do, do it with your might"—and our children must learn this from their youth. If we do not train our children to work hard when they are young, they will not suddenly become hard workers when they are an adult. Hard work is something we need to, first, model for our children, then train them to do. In this way, when they have work of their own, they will be prepared.

Too often in our culture today, we are warned against working too hard. Being tired out is seen as a bad thing. But, Bramwell Booth has a different perspective:

> *Do not be afraid of being tired out. I sometimes hear people say, "I am so tired," with as much agony and horror as if they had the cholera! To be thoroughly weary in every muscle and sinew and serve is a grand experience, and a true help to keep the body in its right place.*[11]

Serving God with all our might is something to aspire to, rather than run away from. Amy Carmichael, missionary in India, once wrote, "I would rather burn out than rust out." Colossians 3:23-24 exhorts us: "And whatever you do, do it heartily, as to the Lord and not to men, knowing that from the Lord you will receive the reward of the inheritance; for you serve the Lord Christ." We must not grow weary of working hard in this life, as God is going to reward us for the work that we have done. C.H. Spurgeon attests, "God deserves to be served with all the energy of which we are capable," He goes on to say,

> *If the service of God is worth anything, it is worth everything. We shall find our best reward in the Lord's work if we do it with determined diligence. Our labour is not in vain in the Lord, and we know it. Half-hearted work will bring no reward; but, when we throw our whole soul into the cause, we shall see prosperity.[12]*

As C.T. Studd, missionary to Africa and China, so eloquently stated: "Only one life, 'twill soon be past, only what's done for Christ will last."[13]

Faithful Service
Faithfulness in work is such a valuable lesson to teach our children. What is faithfulness? It is "strict adherence to injunctions, and to the duties of a station; as the faithfulness of servants or ministers." In today's culture, it seems like faithfulness to work—seeing a task through from beginning to completion—has become a virtue of the past.

As parents, we need to teach our children the importance of being faithful in the little things—cleaning, picking up, organizing, and such. As Elisabeth Elliot put it, "Ordinary work, which is what most of us do, most of the time, is ordained by God every bit as much as is the extraordinary. All our work done for God is spiritual work and therefore not merely a duty but a holy privilege."[14] It doesn't matter if we are mopping the kitchen floor or organizing an evangelistic crusade; both are important to God, and deserve our faithfulness!

It is often easier to serve when people are around to praise us, or when things are going well. But, when serving gets "bumpy", and no one is around, that is when the rubber meets the road. In Luke 12:43, Jesus encourages us to be faithful because, "Blessed is that servant whom his master will find so doing when he comes." We need to teach our children to serve faithfully when others are not looking, because they are working "as to the Lord and not to men" (Colossians 2:23). J.R.R. Tolkien writes in his *Lord of the Rings Trilogy*, that "...the deeds will not be less valiant because they are unpraised."[15] We must never forget that God is always watching us, and will award us accordingly.

Why is it important for our children to be faithful in their work? Their faithfulness determines their reward in heaven! In Luke 19:12-26, Jesus explains that we are each going to be rewarded in heaven according to our faithfulness in serving God and using the gifts He has given us for His glory. Ecclesiastes 12:14 tells us that "God will bring every work into judgment, including every secret thing, whether good or evil." And, He will not forget our work or our faithfulness, as Hebrews 6:10 proclaims: "For God is not unjust to forget your work and labor of love which you have shown toward His name, in that you have ministered to the saints, and do minister."

Mother Theresa once stated, "God did not call me to be successful. God called me to be faithful." No matter what task God puts before us, He has called us to be faithful in completing it. And, if we teach our children the virtue of faithfulness, they will be like Joseph, who started as a slave, and ended up running the country. Or, like Daniel, who was set apart by God, found favor in the court of a pagan king, and ended up ruling the world.

We do not want our children to miss out on the blessings that come from being faithful to their jobs, to their spouse, to their family, to their church, to the community, and in friendships that God has given them. Faithfulness is best learned when our children are young. Let us strive to instill faithfulness in our children!

Work: A Glorious Privilege
It is a glorious privilege to be part of God's work in this world! No matter what field we are in, we have the ability to use our work to build God's kingdom and give Him glory.

In the sixteenth century, Johannes Gutenberg used the technology of his day to advance the gospel of Jesus Christ in a way that changed the world forever! He has been called "The Man of the Millennium." After inventing the printing press, Gutenberg was able to publish around 200 copies of the Bible at a reasonable price. Previously, God's Word was painstakingly copied by hand by monks in monasteries. It took a single scribe over a year to copy a Bible, which resulted in a limited number of Bibles being available. The thought of owning a family Bible in your own language was unheard of, unless you were an extremely wealthy individual. With the invention of the printing press, God's word was able to be read by common people in their own language.

This glorious invention transformed the world as we know it. When asked about his printing press, Johannes explained his vision:

Yes, it is a press, certainly, but a press from which shall flow in inexhaustible streams, the most abundant and most marvelous liquor that has ever flowed to relieve the thirst of men! Through it, God will spread His Word. A spring of truth shall flow from it: like a new star it shall scatter the darkness of ignorance, and cause a light heretofore unknown to shine amongst men.[16]

Through Johannes Gutenberg's work, God's Word has been spread throughout the world. Today, it will take the hard work of our children to transform this world for God's glory!

There is so much work to do in the kingdom of God, especially in our current culture. As parents, we must faithfully do our work: casting a vision for our children, and teaching them about the glorious privilege it is to work together to build God's kingdom!

> *A vision without a task is but a dream.*
> *A task without a vision is drudgery.*
> *A vision and a task are the hope of the world.*

> —*Inscription on a church wall in Sussex, England (c. 1730)*

Questions to Consider

1. Have you bought into the lie that the more you do for your children, the better a mom you are? If so, how is this being displayed in your home?

2. How do you and your children serve at church? What can you do to make serving at your church more of a priority?

3. How do your children serve at home? How can you give them more opportunities to serve there?

4. What attitude do your children have towards school work? How can you encourage them to do their work for the glory of God?

5. Is serving others a priority in your children's lives? How can you train your children to put other people's interests above their own?

6. Have your children succumbed to the trap of idleness? What adjustments can you make so they have less idle time?

Notes

[1] Elisabeth Elliot, *The Shaping of a Christian Family* (Grand Rapids, Michigan: Fleming H. Revell, 1992), 156.

[2] Bob Schultz, *Created for Work* (Eugene, Oregon: Great Expectations Book Co., 2006), 9.

[3] Elliot, *The Shaping of a Christian Family*, 180.

[4] Warren Wiersbe, *On Being a Servant of God* (Grand Rapids, Michigan: Baker Books, 1993), 97.

[5] Bramwell Booth, *Bible Battles-Axes* (St. Albans: The Salvation Army Printing Works, 1915), 80.

[6] J.C. Ryle, *Duties of Parents,* quoted in Elliot, *The Shaping of a Christian Family*, 160.

[7] Bramwell Booth, *Bible Battles-Axes*, 80.

[8] Ibid.

[9] Alexander MacLaren, *MacLaren's Expositions of Holy Scripture, Volume 1* (Grand Rapids, Michigan: WM. B. Eerdmans Publishing Co., 1959), preface.

[10] Oswald Sanders, *Spiritual Leadership* (Chicago: Moody Press, 1976), 119.

[11] Booth, *Bible Battles-Axes*, 80.

[12] C.H. Spurgeon, *Cheque Book of the Bank of Faith* (Great Britain: Christian Focus Publications, 1996), 48.

[13] C.T. Studd, "The Master's Seminary," accessed July 20, 2019, https://www.tms.edu/blog/only-one-life/

[14] Elliot, *The Shaping of a Christian Family*, 157.

[15] J.R.R. Tolkien, "Good Reads," accessed July 20, 2019, https://www.goodreads.com/quotes/752104-a-time-may-come-soon-said-he-when-none-will

[16] Johannes Gutenberg, quoted in Stephen Abbott Northrop, *A Cloud of Witnesses: The Greatest Men in the World for Christ and the Book* (Fort Wayne, Indiana: The Mason Long Publishing Co., 1 894), 202.

Pearl of Wisdom #8
Teach Your Children To Live Without

And those who are Christ's have crucified the flesh with its passions and desires.

Galatians 5:24

At the Tabernacle, Samuel lived without. He did not have the luxuries of home: his mother's comfort, his father's guidance, home-cooked meals, family fellowship, or the knowledge that his parents would provide whatever he needed. Samuel learned that serving God required sacrifice. In fact, he had just one coat, made yearly by his mother. This coat was something he needed, and God provided it through his mother.

It is critically important that our children realize that living for God requires sacrifice. Living for God means that we don't get to do what others do, we don't get to buy the things that other people buy, and so forth. Understanding this truth is huge in a culture where children rarely live without.

If we desire children who will transform this world for God's glory, then they are going to have to learn to give up the luxuries of this life for the kingdom—which takes self-discipline! If we don't train them to say "No!" to their appetites and desires by allowing them to go without, then they will not have the necessary self-control to be disciplined with their time, money, appetites, etc. As followers of Christ, our children must learn to "crucify the flesh with its passions and desires" (Galatians 5:24). Without this sacrifice, our children will not have the self-discipline they need to live a life fully for Jesus Christ.

Beware of Indulgence
In our culture, parents see to it that their children lack nothing! Whether it's the latest video game, smartphone, or gadget—children today do not go long without it. If they beg and pressure their parents long or hard enough, they get it. Or, if their parents say no, they just have to work on their grandparents until they get what they want. In his book *The Making of a Man*, Alan Redpath said, "By self-indulgence a man's character is wrecked, or by self-discipline a man's character is made."[1] We may not realize it, but the more we give in to the whims of our children, the more we ruin their character!

We have come quite a long way since the early days of our country when children had to make their own toys and amuse themselves. Consider Laura Ingalls Wilder, who made her own corn husk doll in *Little House in the Big Woods*. Today, anything our children could desire is at their fingertips, and they have suffered as a result.

As parents, we must remember that, just because we have the means to fulfill the every whim of our children, it doesn't mean we should! Looking back at history, it is easy to see that children today are indulged at an unprecedented rate—and this indulgence has created a sense of entitlement in our children.

In *The Shaping of a Christian Family*, Elisabeth Elliot gives us a glimpse into her childhood, as she shares the following:

> *Compared to the immense piles of toys many children accumulate today, our toys were very few. There were several reasons—far fewer were manufactured. We hadn't money to spend on many toys. Our parents did not believe happiness lay in the possession of things. People did not shower us with gifts.*[2]

Unlike the era in which Elisabeth Elliot was raised, many parents today believe that "happiness [lies] in the possession of things." As parents, we must ask ourselves, "What are teaching our children when we shower them with an abundance of things?"

Whether we realize it or not, we are teaching them that purchasing things will satisfy their longings. We must remember that "the indulgence of one lust often strengthens the power of another."[3] Similarly, "sin is an endless chain."[4] We do not want to indirectly train our children to live only to satisfy their lusts; instead, we want them to be self-disciplined, able to say "No!" to their flesh and "Yes!" to God.

In Scripture, we are commanded by God to love and train up our children. However, loving them does not mean buying our children whatever their hearts desire. Yet today, many parents believe that they are expressing their love for their children when they buy things for them. Even children recognize that our love is not measured by the things we give them. When you ask children, "How do you know that your parents love you?"—they rarely say, "Because they buy me whatever I want." What these parents do not realize is that they are actually doing their children a disservice. Because they don't want their children to "miss out" on something, they sacrifice valuable opportunities for character building.

If our children are going to be men and women who hear God's voice and proclaim it to our culture, they will have to make sacrifices. It will be much easier for our children to learn to live without now than to have everything they want, then have to give it all up as an adult! Our goal in life is not the same as *The Game of Life*: it is not dying with the most luxurious cars, the greatest amount of money, the biggest houses. In God's economy, the goal of life is completely different. Warren Wiersbe writes, "In spite of what some 'success preachers' say, God's goal for our lives is not money but maturity, not happiness but holiness, not getting but giving."[5]   We bless our children by not only teaching them these values, but also training them to live by them.

Treasures In Heaven

God's Word is clear, we are not to be storing up our treasures on this earth, but in heaven. Matthew 6:19-21 commands us:

> *Do not lay up for yourselves treasures on earth, where moth and rust destroy and where thieves break in and steal; but lay up for yourselves treasures in heaven, where neither moth nor rust destroys and where thieves do not break in and steal. For where your treasure is, there your heart will be also.*

The things of this earth are temporal and will be destroyed, but when we invest in heaven, it will last forever. Not only that, our hearts are turned toward where we are investing our time and energy. If we are consumed with purchasing things for this life, that is where our heart will be. However, if God's kingdom is the most important mission of our life, our hearts will be consumed with God, and we will reap treasures that will last forever!

Jesus Is Enough

Our children will lack nothing if we faithfully love them, and give them the most important gift: Jesus Christ! Our children's greatest source of wealth can be found in the person of Jesus Christ. All they need can be found in Him. Colossians 2:3 tells us that "in [Christ] are hidden all the treasures of wisdom and knowledge."

Giving our children what they need is different than giving them what they want. Often, what a child wants is very different from what he needs. We must remember that God, our perfect Father, gives us what we need, not all that we want.   Philippians 4:19 proclaims, "And my God shall supply all your needs according to His riches in glory by Christ Jesus." We will never lack anything with Jesus as our Savior. Romans 8:32 also reminds us that "He who did not spare His own Son, but delivered Him up for us all, how shall He not with Him also freely give us all things?" Considering all that Jesus, our Savior, gave up for us to have all that we do is quite humbling.

Jesus is all we need and want—we just don't realize it!   Speaking about this truth, C.H. Spurgeon writes: "Whatever thou art, and wherever thou art, remember God is just what thou wantest, and just where thou wantest and He can do all thou wantest!"[6] As parents, we must follow God's example, and give our children what they need—being careful not to get caught up in giving them what they think they want. So often, the things our children want are detrimental to their character.   We must hold fast to our vision for our children—Samuels—and allow it to help us navigate their wants and desires.

Being Grateful
When we indulge our children, giving them too much, they become ungrateful. Studies have shown that—rather than feeling more loved and more satisfied with an abundance of things—the more children have, the more ungrateful they become. John Rosemond has written a *Bill of Rights for Children*, which states, "Children have the right to learn to be grateful for what they receive, therefore, they have the right to receive all of what they truly need and very little of what they simply want."[7] As parents, we must decide to give our children what they need (rather than what they want) to foster gratitude in their hearts.

Our children should be grateful for everything they are given, no matter how little! As parents, we need to realize that the more often our children receive a blessing, the less special it becomes. If our children are always eating out, participating in activities, getting the newest gadgets, then they will be less grateful for these things. Conversely, the less often we indulge our children in these things, the more grateful they will be for the blessings they do have.

Godliness and Contentment
Contentment is one of the best character traits we can cultivate in our children. It only comes as a result of living without and finding our satisfaction in Christ—rather than in an abundance of things. If we really stop to think about it, all the desires we attempt to fulfill in life can be filled in the person of Jesus Christ! In the words of C.S. Lewis: "All that we call human history— money, poverty, ambition, war, prostitution, classes, empires, slavery—is the long terrible story of man trying to find something other than God which will make him happy."[8]

Happiness is not something we receive as we get things. C.H. Spurgeon writes, "If you are not content with what you have, you would not be satisfied if it were doubled."[9] Too often, the moment we receive the thing we thought would make us happy, we begin to desire something else that will make us happy. Even Epicurus once wrote: "Do not spoil what you have by desiring what you have not; remember that what you now have was once among the things you only hoped for."[10] Happiness is something we cultivate in our life as a result of having a right relationship with God—not in getting things.

The pursuit of wealth can easily destroy a man's life. Paul warns us in 1 Timothy of the snares of wealth:

> *Now godliness with contentment is great gain. For we brought nothing into this world, and it is certain we can carry nothing out. And having food and clothing, with these we shall be content. But those who desire to be rich fall into temptation and a snare, and into many foolish and harmful lusts which drown*

men in destruction and perdition. For the love of money is a root of all kinds of evil, for which some have strayed from the faith in their greediness, and pierced themselves through with many sorrows.

— 1 Timothy 6:6-10

When we chase after riches to obtain things to satisfy our lives, we so often can drown in our own lusts, which end up turning us away from Christ. Yet, we are reminded that we brought nothing into this world, and will not be able to take anything out! And if we have just food and clothing, we should be content.

Allowing our children to live without teaches them early in life that their happiness does not depend on things. Our church is so blessed to support a church and school in Entebbe, Africa. I have visited the mission field there several times; every time I go, I am amazed at how happy the children are. They have nothing, yet they are the most happy children I have ever seen! C.S. Lewis once said, "Don't let your happiness depend on something you may lose." We must remember—and help our children remember—that everything we own is temporal. It will not last. Our joy comes from our relationship with Christ, not from what we own. If our children learn from an early age that "godliness with contentment is great gain" (1 Timothy 6:6), then they will be blessed indeed.

Delayed Gratification

Blessings in life and eternity depend upon delayed gratification. We must have the ability to deny ourselves for a moment to receive a greater blessing later. For example, saving money for a car, a house, or retirement may mean doing without something we want. Other examples include saving our sexual appetites for marriage, or serving God without expectation of reward on earth. Each of these things requires the discipline of self-denial in the present, so we might be blessed in the future. C.H. Spurgeon describes this self-denial as "pawning the present for the future." He says:

Dear brethren, this is exactly what we have to do, we have to pawn the present for the future. We must be satisfied to give up anything which Christ may require of us for the sake of that which is to come. Our inheritance is not on this side of Jordan. Our joy is yet to be revealed. I grant you that we have much thrown in, for the Lord is a good paymaster; but on the road to heaven he gives us only our spending money.

As parents, we must train our children to say "No!" to their desires now, so they can be blessed in the future. We must remember God's promise in Psalm 84:11b, "No good thing will He withhold from those who walk uprightly." If we can train our children to say "No!" to their flesh—to save their money, be disciplined with their time, tithe to the Lord, give the last piece of cake to a sister, etc.—we are giving them a tremendous gift!

If we want our children to have a blessed marriage, to be the best employee at their job, to save their neighbors by their loving example, to love and train our grandchildren to walk with God, we must train them to do without now. If we give them everything they want, we will end up with selfish, indulged children, who think only of themselves and their own personal happiness.

Buy It Yourself

When we teach our children to live without, they become good stewards of what they have. In the McClure home, our children get money by fulfilling their chore charts, on their birthdays, and when they complete small jobs for people. Other than these occasions—and some infrequent splurges for donuts, Jamba Juice, or coffee—our children have to buy things for themselves.

Children are never too young to learn the value of a dollar. A few years ago, our whole family listened to Dave Ramsey's *Financial Peace University* as we traveled in the car to and from our family vacation. Dave said something that stood out to all of us: you will find that rich people don't know who the latest Survivor is on television. This statement stuck with one of my children, and ever since, he has had no desire to watch T.V. or movies. My son honestly believes that if he watches T.V., he will be poor! How incredible to be so disciplined at such a young age.

After learning about commissions from Dave Ramsey, Michael and I purchased six large Mason jars, and put our children's names on them. Then, we allocated a price for each job on their chore charts. By not handing our children money whenever they need or want it, they are motivated to do their chores. Not only are they motivated to do their chores, but they all have an entrepreneurial spirit. Each of my children have things they want but cannot get from mom and dad—therefore, they are always thinking of new ways to work and make money. The blessings children receive from a commission are endless!

When my children were little, I did not like to take them shopping, as they always asked for everything. All I would hear the whole time was, "I want this! I want that! Can you buy this for me?" Shopping was super stressful. So, a few years ago, I took my children to Target—which I hadn't done for some time. After leaving the store and getting into my car, I realized that they had not asked or pressured me for anything. I remarked, "You guys didn't ask me to buy anything." One of my sons said, "That's because we have our own money, and if we want something, we can buy it ourselves." How revolutionary! By making our children work to earn money, they felt liberated—and so did I!

I have found that, when my children buy their clothes and the things they want for themselves, they not only learn the value of money, but they also make sure they are getting the best deal possible. I am no longer wasting money on petty things my children won't care about five minutes later!

A few years ago, rolling, ZÜKA backpacks were the rage at our school. It seemed like every parent was buying them. My children wanted to join in on the fun, so they ended up spending all of their birthday money from us and their relatives on a backpack. One by one, each of my children purchased a ZÜKA for their birthday, only to realize later that it really wasn't worth the money they had paid for it. What a great lesson for them to learn! One of the greatest gifts we can give our children is teaching them how to manage their money from a young age.

Christmas Pressure

So often, people ask me, "How do you do Christmas with seven children and a ministry salary?" The answer: we keep Jesus at the center! Our family has fun traditions that do not depend on things; instead, they focus on building memories. Too often people get caught up in giving and receiving gifts at Christmas, forgetting that we are actually celebrating Jesus' birthday.

So, how do we keep Jesus at the center? We read the Christmas story, have a tea party for Jesus, listen to music celebrating His birth, attend every church service and event. We enjoy a warm, decorated home, yummy food, and the love of friends and family. We have wonderful memories of homemade stockings filled with inexpensive treats, watching *It's a Wonderful Life*, and going to watch *A Christmas Carol* at a local theater. On Christmas day, Michael and I mostly give our children what they need— socks, underwear, new jeans, jackets, new shoes, and of course, pajamas—and a little of what they want—purses, baby dolls, rubber band guns, knives. We try to keep it really simple.

Amy Carmichael writes, "Do not forget what Christmas cost Him— Gethsemane and Calvary."[11] Christmas cost our Savior so much. How amazing that our Savior gave to us on His birthday! We should focus on sharing this message with our children every Christmas—that we get anything on His birthday is amazing! Pastor David Jeremiah writes:

> *Christ chose a stable so that he could identify with the least of us, with the poor and the vulnerable. He demanded none of the world's comforts nor protections. Jesus came exposed, from the first moment, to all the dangers the world could offer. And so he remained until they led Him to the cross. He chose the least so that you might have. He entered by the stable so that you might dwell forever in the palace.[12]*

The true message of Christmas is Christ and His sacrifice. Jesus didn't go without so we can indulge our children at Christmas. He went without so our hearts could be right before Him. We cannot allow the world to push into our homes, making Christmas less powerful and more superficial.

Keeping our Christmas centered around Jesus allows our family to be free from the Christmas pressure so many parents experience around Christmas time.

Michael and I have dear friends in the ministry who established a "three gifts was good enough for Jesus, it will be good enough for you" policy in their home. Our friends gave their children one gift they needed, one they wanted, and one that was a surprise from mom and dad.

(Our children have never watched commercials, and they rarely look through catalogs with advertisements. So, when Christmas rolls around they often have a difficult time thinking of things they want. It is hard to want something they have never seen!)

Birthdays
In our home, we love to celebrate our children's lives, but we don't want to pressure our friends to come to another birthday party and give more gifts. Thankfully, we have enough children in our family to turn a birthday into an instant party—just add a cake and a handful of gifts! Because of this, we have not had many birthday parties for our children where we invite their friends or go somewhere elaborate.

When my daughter, Hannah, was in second grade, she wanted very badly to have a birthday party. So, we had a tea party, and invited all the girls in her class at school. The party was super sweet, but afterwards, she had so many gifts they couldn't even fit in her room! In fact, she never even opened most of them. After her party, Michael and I decided that—if any of our children ever had a birthday party again—no gifts would be allowed! Some of my children's friends have had parties where the guests bring money to donate towards a cause or canned food for a shelter, in place of a gift. What a wonderful idea!

While we may keep our children's birthdays simple, they are still a big deal in our family. We start the day with birthday tea party full of prayer and love. Then, my children get to eat a dinner of their choice with their family and top off their night with a homemade cake! Michael and I give each of our children $100 that they can spend on a gift or receive as cash. Recent gifts have included: ear piercing, new shoes, a leather Bible, an old-fashioned typewriter, new clothes, a bathrobe and slippers, and so on.

Identity in Christ
Today, many parents wrap up their identity in what they can give to their children. Often, they felt slighted as a child, and want to make sure their children have every opportunity possible. Or, they measure how well they are fulfilling their job as parent with the activities, opportunities, skills, grades, and careers of their children. However, as parents, our identity needs to be rooted in Christ. Our goal should be to raise children who are prepared and trained to do a work for the kingdom of God. This

goal will sometimes mean that our children do not get to do all that their friends get to do.

I remember when Hannah was around eight years old, I took her with me to get a pedicure. My first pedicure was before I was married at twenty, and I always thought how fun it would be to have a daughter to take with me to get our toes done. As I was on my way, I told my mom where I was going. She said to me, "Training her to be a princess, are you?" I thought, "No. We are just getting a pedicure." However, as I thought about this, I realized- I was indirectly training her to be a princess! A pedicure is a luxurious treat that I can hardly find time for. It is not super cheap. Hannah would be much better off saving for a pedicure herself, or only going on special occasions, like a birthday gift.

When my oldest son, Daniel, was preparing to go into high school, we started praying about where to send him to school. At the time, our school went up to only eighth grade. Michael and I were considering the other private high schools in the area, as they provided every opportunity imaginable. I was thinking, "I don't want Daniel to miss out on any opportunities that he could have by keeping him home or in a smaller social setting." However, as we prayed, the Lord clearly spoke to my heart, and specifically said, "Keep him in my Tabernacle." Looking back, I see how these opportunities were not necessarily what Daniel needed. Rather, he needed discipleship, character building, and to live without- so he could learn to work hard, and become dependent upon God.

The big lie is that if we don't provide opportunities, experiences, the latest gadgets, the most-expensive schools, and the latest in fashion for our children, they will grow up and not be prepared for life or miss out on their childhood. However, it is quite the opposite! So often, these gifts we give to our children become indulgences that our children become dependent upon as they get older. And it starts when our children are little.

We need to realize that it is okay to not buy toys that our children ask for in a store. It is okay to miss their sports games. It is ok for our children to wear hand-me-downs. It is okay if we don't celebrate their birthdays on their actual birthdays, or give them birthday parties every year. It is okay if we don't attend their school field trips, don't buy them a drink when we go out for coffee, don't get them everything on their Christmas list, don't see the latest movie in the theater, and don't go to Disneyland every year. In fact, it is probably better if we don't. If we do all these things and more, we are setting our children up live a life of unrealistic expectations—expectations that they will transfer onto their spouses, employers, and even God! We should want our children to be people who are willing to give up everything they have and want for a life of dependency upon God.

Giving It Up For Christ

We must realize that, if we desire our children to serve God, it is going to cost them something. Jesus could not have been any clearer when he stated, "If anyone desires to come after Me, let him deny himself, and take up his cross daily, and follow Me" (Luke 9:23). Elisabeth Elliot expounds upon this idea:

> *To be a follower of the Crucified Christ means, sooner or later, a personal encounter with the cross. And the cross always entails loss. The great symbol of Christianity means sacrifice and no one who calls himself a Christian can evade this stark fact. It is not by any means an easy thing to recognize, within a given instance of personal loss, the opportunity it affords for participation in Christ's own loss.[13]*

The cross can be something that is taken up or left behind, the choice is ours! Our children must each decide if they want to deny themselves to follow Him. Are we willing to train up children who choose to deny self and follow God? If so, we must train them to live without! Jesus, our example, made Himself poor, so we could become rich. We, too, have an opportunity to make ourselves poor, so others can become rich. In fact, Proverbs 13:7 tells us, "There is one who makes himself rich, yet has nothing; and one who makes himself poor, yet has great riches." In God's economy, wealth is not measured by what you own, but by what you can live without.

Hudson Taylor, famous missionary to China, left behind an incredible legacy: the China Inland Mission. Before he left for China, Hudson Taylor wanted to make sure he was prepared to live a life totally dependent upon God—as he knew he was going to have to live without on the mission field. In preparation for this work, he decided to give up earthly luxuries to help him adjust more easily to life abroad. He gave up the comforts of food, money, a soft bed, and modern conveniences, training himself to depend completely upon God. He wrote in his journal:

> *Having now the twofold object in view (he recalled) of accustoming myself to endure hardness, and of economizing in order to help those among whom I was laboring in the Gospel, I soon found that I could live upon very much less than I had previously thought possible. Butter, milk and other luxuries I ceased to use, and found that by living mainly on oatmeal and rice, with occasional variations, a very small sum was sufficient for my needs. In this way I had more more than two-thirds of my income available for other purposes, and my experience was the less I spent on myself and the more I gave to others, the fuller of happiness and blessing did my soul become.[14]*

Hudson Taylor found himself satisfied with the living God rather than luxuries like milk and butter. In fact, he stated that, in living without, "the fuller of happiness and blessing did my soul become." It was through sacrifice that Hudson Taylor was happy and blessed.

Now, we do not have to make such an extreme sacrifice, giving up the luxuries of milk and butter like Hudson Taylor. However, when we consider all that this famous missionary learned, I am sure we can see how we might be indulging our children in some way.

Reflecting upon Hudson Taylor's journal entry in *Hudson Taylor's Spiritual Secret*, Howard and Geraldine Taylor wrote:

> *For God is no man's debtor, and here in his solitude Hudson Taylor was learning something of what He can be to the one who follows hard after Him. In these days of easy-going Christianity, it is not well to remind ourselves that it really does cost to be a man or woman whom God can use? One cannot obtain a Christlike character for nothing; one cannot do a Christlike work save at a great price. "Can ye drink of the cup that I drink of, and be baptized with the baptism wherewith I am baptized?"15*

When we give up the things of this world to gain Christ, God can work through us in ways we never thought possible. In Hebrews, we are told that Moses understood that Christ was worth far more than any material possession:

> *By faith Moses, when he became of age, refused to be called the son of Pharaoh's daughter, choosing rather to suffer affliction with the people of God than to enjoy the passing pleasures of sin, esteeming the reproach of Christ greater riches than the treasures in Egypt; for he looked to the reward.*
>
> *— Hebrews 11:24-26*

Moses was willing to suffer affliction because the "reproach of Christ" was worth more to him than all of Egypt's treasures. Moses was a man who was used mightily by God—he was "God's Voice", and the means of deliverance to His people, who had spent years in bondage—yet it came at a great cost!

As parents, we must realize that training our children to answer the call of the living God is going to cost something—from us and from them. So, our training should prepare our children to pay this cost by allowing them to live without.

Children Who Depend on God
When we allow our children to live without, they learn to depend on God for things. The result? Their faith is increased as they watch God provide for their needs and, sometimes, their wants. What did Samuel do when he was in need? He couldn't just go to His parents for provision —he had to go to the Lord! Our children need to learn to do so, too.

I cannot count the number of times God has provided for my children when Michael and I would or could not provide for them. However, one time stands out above all the rest. My children's school had an American Girl Doll club for a time. Girls who attended the club, would bring their dolls, which were the rage of every little girl. But, these dolls are very pricey, and not something to purchase on a whim. At the time, I had my heart set on buying a Kit Kittredge doll of my daughter, Hannah, but I had no idea how God would provide.

Around that time, our family went on a yearly outing to the city-wide Los Gatos garage sale. Every year my children would find inexpensive treasures as well-off people gave away their nice, barely-used belongings for practically nothing. At one house, my son, Daniel, spotted an American Girl Doll for sale. And it wasn't just any doll, it was Kit—in perfect condition for only twenty dollars! What a find!

We went home with Kit, and proclaimed to all our friends what God had done for us. And, God's provision did not stop there! When a sweet friend heard about our new treasure, she gave us some old American Doll clothes that her daughter no longer needed, that were being stored in her garage. They included a cast for a doll's leg and a beautiful evening gown.

A week later, a group of moms and daughters from our school and church headed up to Palo Alto to attend an American Girl Fashion Show. We were able to go, too. Another girlfriend gave us her expensive tickets, since she no longer could attend the event. Hannah and I went to the American Girl Fashion Show, basking in God's goodness, as we brought along Kit, decked out in her cast and evening gown. But, God's grace did not stop there!

My sister, who also attended the event, purchased twenty raffle tickets, and gave five to Hannah. (At this time in our life, five dollars for five raffle tickets was a big deal.) The grand prize was all of Sage's accessories, which included her painting set. As the evening drew to a close, the time for the raffle came. The smaller raffles passed, and when they brought out the grand prize basket, whose number do you think they called? My Hannah's!

There Hannah was, with a huge basket she could hardly hold at an American Girl Fashion Show with Kit decked out in her new clothes, smiling from ear to ear! She did not realize what God had done for her at the time, but I knew! I could never have provided any of these things for her. Yet, God could!

Each of my children have so many things they are looking to God to provide because they have been trained to realize that Michael and I are not the source of their provision. Remember, our goal is to raise children who are dependent upon God, not us. The sooner we train our children to look to God—by allowing them to live without—the better prepared they will be to do a lasting work for His kingdom!

Questions to Consider

1. Consider this past year. How many things did you purchase for your children because they pressured you?

2. What do you purchase for your children that you could require them to start purchasing for themselves? Remember, we want our children to learn the value of hard work and the dollar!

3. Are there any areas you might be indulging your children?

4. How can you enable your children to become more self-disciplined?

5. Reflect on how your family celebrates Christmas. Does the message of Christmas gleam through your family's traditions? Or, are your children consumed with gifts?

6. Do your children look to you or to God to fulfill their desires? How can you encourage them to take their desires to God more than to you?

7. What have your children given up for Christ in the past months?

Notes

1 Alan Redpath, *The Making of a Man* (Grand Rapids, MI: Fleming H. Revell, 1962), 33.

2 Elisabeth Elliot, *The Shaping of a Christian Family* (Grand Rapids, Michigan: Fleming H. Revell, 1992), 163.

3 Bramwell Booth, *Bible Battles-Axes* (St. Albans: The Salvation Army Printing Works, 1915), 78.

4 Ibid.

5 Warren Wiersbe, *On Being a Servant of God* (Grand Rapids, Michigan: Baker Books, 1993), 51.

6 Mrs. Charles E. Cowman, *Devotions for Morning and Evening* (New York: International Press, 1925), 311.

7 John Rosemond, "Bill *of Rights for Children,"* tuscaloosanews.com, *March 19, 2002, accessed on July 19, 2019,* https://www.tuscaloosanews.com/news/20020319/john-rosemond-rosemonds-bill-of-rights-for-children

8 C.S. Lewis, "Good Reads," accessed July 19, 2019, https://www.goodreads.com/quotes/401009-all-that-we-call-human-history--money-poverty-ambition-war-prostitution

9 C.H. Spurgeon, "Good Reads," accessed July 19, 2019, https://www.goodreads.com/quotes/189188-you-say-if-i-had-a-little-more-i-should

10 Epicurus, "Good Reads," accessed July 19, 2019, https://www.goodreads.com/quotes/169009-do-not-spoil-what-you-have-by-desiring-what-you

11 Amy Carmichael, *Edges of His Ways* (Fort Washington, Pennsylvania: Christian Literature Crusade, 1955), 187.

12 David Jeremiah, *Why The Nativity* (Orange, California: Yates & Yates, 2006), 54.

13 Elisabeth Elliot, "Good Reads," accessed August 10, 2019, https://www.goodreads.com/quotes/255854-to-be-a-follower-of-the-crucified-means-sooner-or

14 Dr. & Mrs. Howard Taylor, *Hudson Taylor's Spiritual Secret* (Chicago: Moody Publishers, 1989), 27.

15 Ibid.

Teach Your Children to Discern God's Voice

*Now the LORD came and stood and called as at other times,
"Samuel! Samuel!" And Samuel answered,
"Speak, for Your servant hears."*

1 Samuel 3:10

My sheep hear My voice, and I know them, and they follow Me.

John 10:27

One night, as Samuel slept in the Tabernacle, in the very presence of God, he heard someone calling him. He immediately thought it was Eli, so he ran to Eli—three times, in fact—until Eli realized that it was God calling to him. After his realization, Eli told Samuel, "Go, lie down; and it shall be, if He calls you, that you must say, 'Speak, LORD, for Your servant hears'" (1 Samuel 3:9). So, Samuel did as Eli commanded. When the Lord called him again, Samuel answered, and said, "Speak, for Your servant hears" (1 Samuel 3:10). God then gave Samuel a very hard message to deliver to Eli regarding his sons. Samuel faithfully delivered the message, and thus began Samuel's ministry as a voice of God to His people.

Like Samuel, our children are never too young to hear the voice of God. If our children are going to be modern-day prophets to a complacent and corrupt culture, as Samuel was, then they must learn to discern and obey the voice of God from their youth. In fact, the sooner our children learn to discern His voice and obey it, the more blessed they will become.

One of the blessings of discerning God's voice as a child is they "escape the scars and sorrows of a life wrongly begun." In the words of Matthew Henry:

God calls each child in our homes as truly as He did Samuel. From each the same obedience is asked. Each may, like the boy in the Tabernacle, grow up "in the nurture and admonition of the Lord," and so escape the many scars and sorrows of a life wrongly begun. Let parents see to it that they think rightly of their work, and do not content themselves with conveying information, but aim at nothing short of helping all their children to hear and lovingly to yield to the gentle call of the incarnate God![1]

What a gift we have given our children when they can grow up learning to discern God's voice and obey it! As Oswald Chambers states, when our children "[g]et into the habit of saying, 'Speak Lord,' [their] life will become a romance."[2]

A Mother's Duty

When God called Samuel, the young boy did not recognize God's voice—Eli had to help him discern it (1 Samuel 3:8-9). While our children are never too young to hear God's voice, we must first teach them to discern it. In fact, the sooner we do so, the better! Alexander MacLaren, an English minister, writes:

What higher service can any man do to his fellows, old or young, than to help them to discern God's call and to obey it? What nobler conception of a teacher's work is there than that? Eli heard no voice, from which we may probably conclude that, however real the voice, it was not audible to sense; but he taught Samuel to interpret and answer the voice which he heard, and thus won some share of a prophet's reward.[3]

As mothers, it is our duty to teach our children to discern God's voice—it is not the job of our children's schools, Sunday school teachers, or youth pastors. And when our children learn to hear His voice and respond to it, as mothers, we shall reap the rewards of their work.

The Power of God's Voice

The voice of God is a very powerful thing. It spoke the world into existence. Psalm 29:3-4 declares: "The voice of the LORD is over the waters; The God of glory thunders; The LORD is over many waters. The voice of the LORD is powerful; The voice of the LORD is full of majesty." When we understand the power, glory, and majesty of God's voice, it is humbling to think that He is constantly speaking to His children, leading and guiding them.

Once we come into a relationship with Christ and respond to His call to salvation, the Holy Spirit begins to draw and call and lead us. This guidance is the voice of God. In John 10:27, Jesus said, "My sheep hear My voice, and I know them, and they follow Me." When our children come to Christ (or are born again), He becomes their Shepherd, and they become one of His sheep. Then, when God speaks to them, they hear His voice and follow Him.

God's voice has been leading and guiding His children from the beginning of time. He spoke to Abraham, calling him out from Ur to a "city whose builder and maker is God" (Hebrews 11:10). God's voice spoke to Moses from the burning bush, sending him to free the children of Israel. God's voice called Gideon to free the children of Israel from the Midianites. It spoke to Samuel, and gave him the words to lead, guide, and draw the children of Israel to repentance. God's voice anointed and confirmed Jesus's ministry, when He was baptized by John the Baptist in the Jordan River. God's voice called out to Saul on the road to Damascus, commissioning him to carry the gospel to the Gentiles. It also calls out to our children today.

On our way home from school, I once asked my two younger boys if they had ever heard God's voice. They told me, "All the time." I asked how they heard it? Their reply: "Through God's Word." I then asked them what God's voice told them. My son, Josh, said, "He mostly convicts me of my sin, and tells me how to live." Wow! God's voice is powerful in the life of a child! The voice of God will transform the life of a child, so the earlier they can discern it, the better! If our children do not recognize God's voice, they will not know His will for their lives, and they will miss out on the calling He has prepared for them.

Hearing His Voice
When God's Word was about to depart from Israel, God spoke to Samuel. How was Samuel able to hear God's voice? Alexander MacLaren paints a beautiful picture of the atmosphere that allowed it:

> *Samuel slept in the "Temple of the Lord, where the ark was." The picture is much more vivid and tender, if we conceive of the dim- eyed old man, lying somewhat apart; of the glimmering light, nearly extinct but still faintly burning; and of the child laid to sleep in the Tabernacle. Surely the picturesque contrast between the sanctity of the ark and the innocent sleep of childhood is meant to strike us, and to serve as connecting the place with the subsequent revelation. Childlike hearts, which thus quietly rest in the "secret place of the Most High," and day and night are near His ark, will not fail of hearing His voice.*[4]

Samuel dwelt in God's presence day and night, which allowed him to hear God's voice even though the world was very dark.

God's voice is a still small voice—and He is always speaking to His children by His Word. Martin Luther wrote, "Let the man who would hear God speak read Holy Scripture."[5] I have found that there is a direct correlation between hearing the voice of God and the amount of time we spend in God's presence: reading His Word, worshiping Him, and talking about Him with others. The same is true for our children. If we want them to be modern-day Samuels—prophets and priests in today's world— we must teach them to discern God's voice as they spend time in His presence. Their prayer and ours should ever be, "Speak Lord, for your servant hears" (1 Samuel 3:10).

Unclogging Our Ears

God is always speaking to His children—however, they can't always hear Him. There are so many distractions and hindrances in today's world that drown out God's voice, including the many things that entertain and keep our children busy.

This past year, my son, Sam, had a hard time hearing. His ears hurt, but he never ran a fever. So, we took him to the doctor to figure out what was wrong. When the doctor looked in his ears, she couldn't even see his eardrum! Sam had used a Q-tip to dry his ears out, and in the process, he had shoved all of his ear wax against his ear drum. He had trouble hearing because there was too much wax! As soon as the doctor flushed out the wax, Sam could hear.

Our children's spiritual ears can likewise become so clogged up with distractions that our children have trouble hearing God's voice when He speaks to them. As parents, we must figure out what is clogging our children's ears, and do whatever it takes to flush out the wax! Often, we may need to free up our children's schedules so they have time to hear God's voice.

Turn Down the Noise

How can our children hear God's voice if it is being drowned out by other voices? Today, voices come at us faster and louder than ever before. From where do these voices come? The world, the flesh and the devil! Anytime our flesh desires something, the devil is right there, saying, "Go for it! You will be satisfied if you fulfill your desire"—but, God's Word tells us not to listen to the lies of the Enemy. Our job, as parents, is to help our children turn down the noise of these voices, so they can discern God's voice in the midst of all the other noise.

When did Samuel hear God's voice? He heard it in the middle of the night, as he rested outside the Holy of Holies—not while he was watching television or playing video games. If we want our children to hear God's voice, we must turn down the noise in their life. Otherwise, they will have a hard time hearing Him.

The Devil

In the Garden of Eden, Satan, disguised as a snake, deceived Eve, who disobeyed God by eating of the fruit of the Tree of the knowledge of good and evil. How did the devil deceive Eve? He took God's words, and twisted them into a lie, which Eve believed and acted upon. Emboldened by Satan's lies, she encouraged Adam to eat of the fruit, as well, ushering sin into the world.

Satan, the enemy of our souls, is still up to the same old tricks. He attacks our mind by throwing lies at us all day long. These lies, which twist God's Word, not only lead us into sin, but also keep us from knowing and obeying God's will. Satan never speaks the truth—"there is no truth in him...for he is a liar and the father of it" (John 8:44).

Sometimes, it can be hard to detect the lies of Satan—so we must always be on our guard.

Satan—"the accuser of the brethren" (Revelation 12:9-10)—does not simply want to deceive us; he also wants to destroy our children. He wants them to believe that God could never forgive their sins, by reminding them of all they have ever done wrong. He wants them to think that God could never love them, that they have no gifts of value, and they could never use their gifts for His kingdom. Satan wants to discourage our children, and make them ineffective for the kingdom. He wants them to feel isolated, alone, separated. He wants to sow discord in the church, so that our children will have a bad taste in their mouth for God and His people.

One of the Enemy's greatest tactics is to puff up pride, and stir up a desire for recognition. Satan fell from heaven because, in his pride and discontent, he wanted to be like the Most High (Isaiah 14:12-21). Too often, he creeps close, and whispers lies in our ears—"They don't realize how great you are! They don't recognize how much you do!"—in hopes of puffing up our pride and discontent. He wants us to harden our heart against God, so he can use us to do his bidding. We must keep in mind that Satan's goal is to destroy our life. When we listen to his lies, they soon control our thoughts and actions, leading to bad habits which destroy our character, life, and God-given destiny.

The Devil's Mouthpiece: The Internet

Today, the Enemy uses technology—especially the internet and social media—to mold our children into the pattern of the world, destroy their life, and propagate his lies. If you don't believe me, consider the children you know.

Many children today are deeply troubled—and usually, there is a direct correlation to the amount of time they spend on the internet. In fact, studies have revealed that social media has led to decreased mental health and increase in youth suicide.[6] We can no longer afford to be ignorant of the devil's tools and schemes. He is lying to our children as they surf the internet, with the sole purpose of their destruction and death.

In her book, *Screens and Teens*, Kathy Koch discusses five lies the internet feeds to our children:[7]

Lie #1	I am the center of my own universe.
Lie #2	I deserve to be happy all the time.
Lie #3	I must have choices.
Lie #4	I am my own authority.
Lie #5	Information is all I need, so I don't need teachers.

Each of these lies go against the teaching of God's Word. How?

Truth #1	God is the center of the universe, not me.

Truth #2   I can have joy in every circumstance, even
             unhappy ones.
Truth #3   I need to commit my choices to God, and obey His will.
Truth #4   God calls me to submit to authority.
Truth #5   I need to seek God, and listen to godly counsel.

We must realize that the internet feeds lies to our children—not truth! Yet, we allow them to constantly run to the internet to find "truth." Do we want the devil's mouthpiece to shape our children? Or, do we want God's Word to mold them more and more into the image of Christ? The internet not only feeds our children's insecurities, it also draws them away from God, and drowns out His voice in their life.

When Facebook first came out, I was so excited to catch up with old friends. It became a way for me to "leave the house" without actually having to leave—especially with lots of little children at home. Soon, I realized that Facebook was not the best use of my time. I would jump on to Facebook when I had five minutes to spare, and then be on it for hours! My children were babies at the time, and I would totally ignore them. What is worse, I became really discontented with my own less-than-perfect life, and I always wanted more. So, I made the decision to only go on Facebook a couple of times a year to catch up with friends.

Last year, I received a Facebook notification from an old friend in my email inbox. The subject line was "Crater Lake," and as I had never seen Crater Lake, I was curious. I opened Facebook, and found my friend's post. Twenty minutes later, after spending time looking at her posts from the past year, I had been taken captive by the following lies:

1. My husband doesn't make enough money.
2. My husband doesn't get enough time off.
3. Our family lives in a horrible area.
4. We never go anywhere.
5. I work too much, and don't have time for myself.

It took me fully two weeks to unwind these lies, reprogram my heart, and be content with what God had given me. It is hard enough to fight the daily lies of the Enemy; I can't imagine what kind of mess I would be in if I made social media and the internet a priority in my life!

I have a precious friend who realized that Satan was using social media to feed her daughter's insecurities. Wanting to help her daughter, my friend realized that she could not get rid of her daughter's accounts unless she was willing to do the same herself. The two went off social media together, and her daughter is doing so much better spiritually! Too many parents today allow their children to spend their growing years listening to the lies of Satan. Technology, social media, and the internet are molding and shaping their character and destiny into the patterns of this world. But, we don't have to let them!

Battling for the Truth

Once we have identified how the devil is tempting our children, we must help them engage in battle. How do we battle Satan? We use the Word of God, as Jesus did in Luke 4:1-13.

After His baptism, Jesus was filled with the Holy Spirit, who led Him into the wilderness. There, He was tempted for forty days by the devil. Satan tempted Jesus three times—and every time, he took God's Word out of context, twisted it, and appealed to His flesh. How did Jesus respond? With God's Word, saying, "It is written..." (Luke 4:4, 8, 10).

We must teach our children to respond to the lies of Satan by declaring God's Word in context. In Ephesians 6:17, we are told that God's Word is "living and powerful, and sharper than any two-edged sword, piercing even to the division of soul and spirit, and of joints and marrow, and is a discerner of the thoughts and intents of the heart" (Hebrews 4:12). It is also "the sword of the Spirit," meant to engage the Enemy in battle (Ephesians 6:17). In other words, the Word of God not only helps us detect the lies of the enemy, but it also helps us defeat them.

We have victory over the devil's lies when we meditate on and declare God's Word over our life, asking God for deliverance. When the battle in our thoughts is really strong, it often helps to speak God's Word audibly, or share our struggles with someone who can join us in prayer over the situation. We must not think, "Oh, the struggle will go away." Instead, we must set out to do battle for our minds, and take every thought captive. Remember, Satan's goal is to destroy our lives, so we cannot neglect this battle!

Taking Our Thoughts Captive

The human mind is astounding! It stores facts, impressions, and emotions—and can recall them years later. Our memory allows us to reach into the past and, through our imagination, into the future. Our thoughts affect our feelings and actions. Proverbs 23:7 declares, "For as [man] thinks in his heart, so he is." So, it is very important that we teach our children to take their thoughts captive to the obedience of Christ. After all, our warfare is spiritual, not carnal! Second Corinthians 10:3-6 offers us insight into the battle we face:

> For though we walk in the flesh, we do not war according to the flesh. For the weapons of our warfare are not carnal but mighty in God for pulling down strongholds, casting down arguments and every high thing that exalts itself against the knowledge of God, bringing every thought into captivity to the obedience of Christ, and being ready to punish all disobedience when your obedience is fulfilled.

Whenever a thought goes against God's Word, we must take it captive, making it submit to Christ as we declare the truth of Scripture over it.

I have met people whose thought-life was so out of control that the things they believed in their mind was more true to them than reality! These people, who have bought into the Enemy's lies, do not believe God when He tries to speak to them. We must remember: "Carelessness with thoughts is as dangerous as toying with explosives! Bolt that door!"[8] If we do not teach our children to take their thoughts captive, then they will buy into the lies of Satan to their destruction.

As mothers, we also need to help our children recognize the difference between God's voice and their feelings. Our feelings are not truth. Often, when a child feels bad or angry or discontent, they have grabbed hold of a lie, meditated on it, and allowed it to drive their emotions and, ultimately, decisions. Then, they jump from emotion to emotion—and their whole life is centered around how they feel in the moment.

Our job is to teach our children to discern the difference between truth and lies. Only then will our children be able to escape the snare of the devil! When they have been taken captive by Satan's lies, we must teach them to free their thoughts—rather than do the Enemy's bidding by feeding his lies. Second Timothy 2:24-26 declares our role when our children have been taken captive:

> *And a servant of the Lord must not quarrel but be gentle to all, able to teach, patient, in humility correcting those who are in opposition, if God perhaps will grant them repentance, so that they may know the truth, and that they may come to their senses and escape the snare of the devil, having been taken captive by him to do his will.*

As moms, we must patiently and humbly teach our children the truth of God's Word, so they can come to their senses and repent their wrong thinking. In doing so, we help our children escape the snare of the devil!

It is essential that we recognize why the devil wants to take our children captive: he wants to use them to do his will rather than God's will! For example, any time our child believes a lie and becomes offended, the Enemy encourages them to lash out, retaliate meanly, gossip, etc.—all of which cause division and tear down God's kingdom. When we see the Satan's plan in this light, we recognize the importance teaching our children to discern God's voice.

Defeating the Lie
Even when we do our best to turn down the noise in our children's lives—by freeing them from distractions, and ensuring they spend time in God's presence—we still have to battle the lies of the Enemy. They cannot escape them: Satan is out to get our children! How do know our children are listening to and believing his lies? They will say things like:

- Nobody likes me.
- Everyone hates me.
- My teacher hates me.
- My parents don't love me.
- No one will ever love me.
- Nobody cares if I live.
- I want to kill myself.
- I'm ugly.
- I'm not smart.
- I will never accomplish anything.
- I can't do anything right.
- I'm not good enough.
- I'm worthless.
- God can't forgive me.
- God doesn't care about me.
- God doesn't want me to be happy.
- I have time to get my relationship with God right.

Matthew 12:34b states, "For out of the abundance of the heart the mouth speaks." In other words, the things our children say reveal what is in their heart and their thoughts. Comments like the ones listed above, tell us that our children are listening to lies—because these comments are not based on truth.

It is our job to discover the source of the lies our children believe, then battle the lies by speaking the truth of God's Word into our children's life. We must ensure that we ourselves are in God's Word, so we have it in our arsenal when we do battle to help our children.

When we hear these lies, we must not grab ahold of, feed, or respond to them. For example, if my daughter says, "I don't have any friends at school. I don't have anything in common with them. Nobody likes me!", as a mom, I must check my first response. I should not feel sorry for my daughter, dwell on the lies, or make a big deal of the situation. I should not get mad at the other girls in the class, call her teacher and demand a solution, or transfer her to a different school so she can have a better group of friends. So, what should I do?

I should tell my daughter: "I am so sorry you are sad about your friends. However, you must realize that what you feel is not true. In fact, it is a lie from the enemy! Dad and I love you! Your brothers and sisters love you. Your teacher loves you. You have so many precious friends at school. Last week, Sally came over, and you had the best time ever! Remember, Jesus is a friend that sticks closer than a brother. He loves you so much that he died for you! You can always run to Him whenever you need a friend, and He will meet your needs. If you feel like you don't have any friends, why don't you try being one? Why don't you reach out and talk about things they are interested in? Remember what God's Word says, 'A man who has friends must himself be friendly, but there is a friend who sticks closer than a brother' (Proverbs 18:24). Let's pray, and ask God to help you be a good friend to others!"

One of the greatest shortcomings of the church today is that people do not realize when the devil is at work. Rather than focusing on the real Enemy, and doing battle using God's Word, we attack those around us because we think they are the problem. Ephesians 6:12 describes our true Enemy: "For we do not wrestle against flesh and blood, but against principalities, against powers, against the rulers of the darkness of this age, against spiritual hosts of wickedness in the heavenly places." Satan is at the root of most of our problems!

Sometimes, we do not recognize the devil's lies because he disguises himself as an angel of light. However, it is vital that we see through his deception, like Jesus did when Satan tempted him in the wilderness. Bramwell Booth, second General of the Salvation Army, expounds upon this need:

> *Jesus treats the devil as the tempter all the way through. He calls him Satan. It is one of the strong advantages that Jesus had in the conflict, that He recognized His enemy. It will be a great strength to you, my comrade, to attribute to the devil at once the temptations which assail you. When the evil thought comes to you, say to yourself, "That is of the devil." Do not on any account listen to the twaddle which would make it appear that evil is nothing but an influence around you—a sort of disagreeable gas! It may be an influence, perhaps, but it proceeds direct from that old serpent, the devil! When you listen to the suggestions of evil you are really listening to him; when you yield to that influence you are yielding to the great destroyer himself.[9]*

We must not only be on guard against the lies of the Enemy, we must name them as lies as soon as we hear them.

When I was younger in the faith, I used to think that Christians were overly concerned with the devil, as our flesh and the world are very strong. However, since my youth, I have been schooled in spiritual warfare—in ways I would never want to relive—and acknowledge that Satan is, indeed, "like a roaring lion, seeking whom he may devour" (1 Peter 5:8). I have also realized that, whenever lies or temptations come, the Enemy has something to do with it!

At the start of *Screwtape Letters*, C.S. Lewis opens his book with a note to readers about the two main misconceptions people have about Satan: some do not believe he exists, while others have an over fascination with him![10] As Christians, we must recognize that the devil is always on the move, seeking to destroy our lives. We must be sober, vigilant, and alert—especially if we desire to train up train up godly children. And, if Satan can't get us to fall into his traps, he will go after our children.

There is nothing our Enemy hates more than children who are set apart for God and trained to build His kingdom. The most important thing we can do for our children is to train them to discern God's voice and recognize the devil's lies.

Proclaiming Truth

If we do not want our children to be fed lies, we must surround, inspire, and train them with the truth of God's Word. As moms, we must proclaim the truth of Scripture all day long: "God is so good! Look at the beautiful world God created! You are such a blessing and gift from God! Praise God for His wonderful provision! We are so blessed to go to such a wonderful church! You won't believe what God showed me in the Bible today!" When we constantly proclaim God's Word, our children will be so used to hearing truth that they will not only be able to recognize a lie, but will also be ready to counter it with Scripture.

Betsy ten Boom, who died in a Nazi concentration camp, once said, "There is no pit so deep that God's love is not greater still." I often share this quote with my children because I want them to know that—no matter where Satan may take them in their mind—God's love is rope that can get them out of the depths of despair. There is always hope!

Discovering God's Voice

How can we help our children discover God's voice for themselves? We can take them to Bible studies. We can read or listen to good books together. After church, we can ask them questions: "What did you learn today? What was the lesson about? What stood out to you? What do you think God was trying to show you?" We can also help our children by making connections to their life: "Did you hear what he pastor said today? He was talking about honoring your parents, and that is exactly what we have been talking about at home."

It is important to note that, when we hear God's voice, we must pay attention—and we must train our children to pay attention, too. If God speaks the same word to us again and again, then we must make sure we are listening!

Confirming God's Voice

When we think God has spoken to us, how do we know it was indeed Him? We can confirm we are hearing God's voice if the word we received passes the following tests:

1. God's voice will be confirmed in His Word.

2. God's voice will always lead us to glorify God.

3. God's voice will always give us peace.

4. God's voice is always confirmed in His presence.

5. God's voice usually leads us to deny ourselves.

It is important to note that God's voice rarely confirms what we feel, and it rarely leads leads us to a life of comfort and ease. Remember Samuel's call. God asked Samuel to deliver a really hard message to Eli, regarding the demise of his sons. What a hard word from the Lord!

Considering Samuel, F.B. Meyer explains how we can discern God's voice for ourselves:

> *We may test God's call by its effect on us. Does it lead to self-denial? Does it induce us to leave the comfortable bed and step into the cold? Does it drive us forth to minister to others? Does it make us more unselfish, loving, tender, modest, humble? Whatever is to the humbling of our pride and the glory of God, may be truly deemed God's call. Be quick to respond, and fearlessly deliver the message the Lord has given you.*[11]

Often, God's voice leads us to deny ourselves to bring glory to God. The question is, will we obey?

Obeying God's Voice

Our children's future hinges on their ability to discern and obey God's voice. As Christians, God promises to bless us when we hear and obey His voice. Deuteronomy 28:1-2 promises:

> *Now it shall come to pass, if you diligently obey the voice of the LORD your God, to observe carefully all His commandments which I command you today, that the LORD your God will set you high above all nations of the earth. And all these blessings shall come upon you and overtake you, because you obey the voice of the LORD your God...*

While there are many blessing for those who obey God's voice, there are also curses in store for those who disobey it:

> *But it shall come to pass, if you do not obey the voice of the LORD your God, to observe carefully all His commandments and His statutes which I command you today, that all these curses will come upon you and overtake you...*

> *— Deuteronomy 28:15*

Our obedience to God's voice determines the blessing we receive from Him. Many times, God's voice speaks to us, and we forsake complete obedience to God for what we think will make God happy. However, halfway obedience is not obedience.

When King Saul was ruling over the Israelites, God commanded him to conquer the Amalekites and "utterly destroy all that they have" (1 Samuel 15:3). After their victory in battle, Saul and his men spared King Agag, as well as the best of the sheep, oxen, fatlings, lambs, and all that was good. King Saul spared them because he desired to give them as a sacrifice to God. However, that is not what God asked him to do. In His wrath, God had Samuel deliver this stern message to King Saul:

> *Has the LORD as great delight in burnt offerings and sacrifices, as in obeying the voice of the LORD? Behold to obey is better than sacrifice, and to heed than the fat of rams. For rebellion is as the sin of witchcraft, and stubbornness is as iniquity and idolatry. Because you have rejected the word of the LORD, He also has rejected you from being king.*

> *— 1 Samuel 15:22-23*

God desires our obedience before our worship. Because Saul did not obey God completely, the kingdom was taken from him. The rest of his life was filled with misery, wars, jealousy, and torment. It is so important that we teach our children to not only discern God's voice, but learn to obey Him completely, as well!

Complete Obedience

There is no greater example of complete obedience than that of Jesus Christ. Obeying God's voice, Jesus forsook His feelings as He walked in obedience toward the cross. Scripture tells us that Jesus did not want to embrace the cross; His flesh did not want to endure the pain and suffering that was to come. And yet, He willingly endured the cross because it was the will of His Father. In fact, He lived "to do the will of Him who sent Me, and to finish His work" (John 4:34). His love for God compelled Him to obey. And, what did He do in the midst of His suffering? He prayed for and forgave those who were responsible for His pain, turmoil, humiliation, and death. Jesus was never more in the will of God than when he hung from that cross- yet I can guarantee you that his flesh despised every moment of it. God called Jesus to a monumental task, and He obeyed. What an amazing example we have in Jesus Christ!

As parents, we need to follow Christ's example, by training our children to do the will of the Father, too. We do not want our children to miss out on the blessings of a life lived in obedience to God's voice. We need to help them build habits of obedience that are stronger than their feelings and emotions. As they learn to recognize and do God's will above their own, they will grow in character, saying "no" to their flesh and "yes" to God. In *My Utmost for His Highest*, Oswald Chambers writes, "The proof that your old life is dead, having been 'crucified with Christ' (Galatians 2:20), is the amazing ease with which the life of God in you now enables you to obey the voice of Jesus Christ!"[12] May our children obey the voice of Jesus Christ, putting to death the flesh to the glory of God!

David Livingstone
The life of David Livingstone was not an easy one. God called him to serve as a missionary, explorer, philanthropist, scientist, medic, and anti-slavery campaigner in Africa during the nineteenth century. In Africa, Livingstone encountered all kinds of obstacles, from disease and famine to being mauled by a lion, and having his very life threatened by local tribes.

God's voice, through His Word, was Livingstone's guide throughout his "thirty years of wearied effort in evangelizing the continent of Africa."[13] On one occasion, when Livingstone's life was in danger, the missionary wrote in his diary:

> Evening. *Felt much turmoil of spirit, in prospect of having all my plans for the welfare of this great region and this seeming population, knocked on the head by savages tomorrow. But I read that Jesus said: "All power is given unto me in heaven and in earth. Go ye therefore, and teach all nations...and, lo, I am with you always, even unto the end of the world!" It is the word of a Gentlemen, of the strictest and most sacred honor. So there's an end of it! I will not cross furtively tonight as I intended. Should such a man as I flee? Nay, verily, I shall take observations for latitude and longitude tonight, though they may be the last. I feel quite calm now, thank God!*[14]

Because Livingstone heard the voice of the Lord, he did not flee from those who threatened his life. Instead, he determined to keep doing the work that God had commissioned Him to do.

If he had not heard or heeded the voice of God, David Livingstone would not have been able to accomplish the work that transformed the entire continent of Africa. And, without the ability to discern God's voice for themselves, our children will not be able to accomplish the work that God is calling them to do! While our children may not be threatened in quite the same way as Livingstone, they will face the very grave dangers of today's progressive world. Our children will not be able to navigate through this life or to be God's mouthpiece to the world if they cannot hear His voice. As parents, we must teach our children how to discern God's voice—especially if we want them to be like Samuel, declaring God's voice to His people.

Questions to Consider

1. Have your children given their hearts to God? If not, how will you introduce them to God?

2. What could be drowning out God's voice in your children's life?

3. How are you training your children to discern God's voice?

4. Are your children on social media? Have they bought into any of the five lies? If so, how can you counteract these lies with the truth?

   Lie #1   I am the center of my own universe.
   Lie #2   I deserve to be happy all the time.
   Lie #3   I must have choices.
   Lie #4   I am my own authority.
   Lie #5   Information is all I need, so I don't need teachers.

5. Does your child say things that are not true? How often? How do you respond?

6. When your children speak lies, do you attribute it to the Enemy, or have you attributed it to specific people and situations? Why is it so important to identify the Enemy?

7. Consider your children's thought life. What lies have they grabbed ahold of? How can you help them discern truth and lies in the future?

Notes

[1] Ibid., *274-275*.

[2] Oswald Chambers, *My Utmost for His Highest* (New York: Dodd, Mead & Company, 1935), 30.

[3] Alexander MacLaren, *MacLaren's Expositions of Holy Scripture, Volume 1* (Grand Rapids, Michigan: WM. B. Eerdmans Publishing Co., 1959), 269.

[4] MacLaren, *MacLaren's Expositions of Holy Scripture,* 269.

[5] Martin Luther, "Good Reads," accessed July 19, 2019, https://www.goodreads.com/quotes/854796-let-the-man-who-would-hear-god-speak-read-holy

[6] David D. Luxton, PhD, Jennifer D. June, BA, and Jonathan M. Fairall, BS, "Social Media and Suicide: A Public Health Perspective," PMC, May 2012, accessed July 19, 2019, https://www.ncbi.nlm.nih.gov/pmc/articles/PMC3477910/

[7] Kathy Koch, *Screens and Teens* (Chicago: Moody Publishers, 2015), 3551-200.

[8] Mrs. Charles E. Cowman, *Streams in the Desert* (Grand Rapids, Michigan: Zondervan Publishing House, 1925), 196.

[9] Bramwell Booth, *Bible Battles-Axes* (St. Albans: The Salvation Army Printing Works, 1915), 32-33.

[10] C.S. Lewis, *The Screwtape Letters* (New York, New York: Harper Collins Publishers, 1942), preface.

[11] F.B. Meyer, *Daybook of Promise: Classic Selections From Every Century and Tradition of the Church* (Brentwood, Tennessee: Worthy Media, 2014), 203.

[12] Oswald Chambers, *My Utmost for His Highest* (New York: Dodd, Mead & Company, 1935), *358*.

[13] David's Livingstone's Tombstone, Westminster Abby, London.

[14] Mrs. Charles E. Cowman, *Devotions for Morning and Evening* (New York: International Press, 1925), 412.

Allow Your Children to Develop Their Character

...but we also glory in tribulations, knowing that tribulation produces perseverance; and perseverance, character; and character, hope.

Romans 5:3-4

Samuel's time at home with his mother, as well as his years spent in the Tabernacle, were instrumental in the building of his character. At home, Hannah spent three precious years training Samuel in obedience, worship, discipline, and respect for others. We know this because, when Samuel was dropped off at the Tabernacle, he worshiped God. Additionally, when he later heard God's voice in the middle of the night and thought it was Eli's, he ran to see what Eli needed. This reaction is how a child of character responds in moments of trial and need.

Samuel not only worked in the Tabernacle, living without his family and the comforts of home, but he also grew up alone, surrounded by Eli's wicked sons. As a young child, he endured hardships, and bore the yoke of suffering—for God had asked something very hard of Samuel. When God spoke to Samuel in the middle of the night, he asked him to share a vision with Eli, regarding the sin and future destruction of his family. This vision was a very hard message to receive, and Samuel was afraid to tell Eli. What a heavy burden for such a small boy to carry! Matthew Henry reflects upon the importance of this burden: "It was a terrible message to give to a child; but Samuel's calling was to be the guide of Israel in a period of transition, and he had to be broken early into the work, which needed severity as well as tenderness."[1]

Despite the difficult message, Samuel obeyed God and told Eli everything. He held nothing back. 1 Samuel 3:8a, 19 reads: "Then Samuel told him everything, and hid nothing from him...So Samuel grew, and the LORD was with him and let none of his words fall to the ground." Samuel had to make a habit of doing hard things to be prepared for his lifework. Those years at home and in the Tabernacle were years of training for Samuel—training of character for a lifetime of service to God's glory! F.B. Meyer remarks on the character of Samuel:

Samuel was not a prophet in the sense of foretelling the long future, and was not possessed of Isaiah's genius and eloquence;

his only contribution to his age was a saintly character, and it was by the saintliness, the moral grandeur of his character, that he arrested the ruin of his people.[2]

Meyer compares Samuel to other prophets, noting that because of his character, God used him to bring repentance and revival to His people! Samuel lived in an era full of challenges—and the same is true of our children. We are handing them a really hard world, and they are going to need character to make a difference in it. F.B. Meyer explains the importance of being men and women of character in today's culture, a culture like Samuel's. He writes:

We too may be called to face an era of change; our eyes may have to witness the passing of the old and the coming of the new; it may be that in our time also the Lord will shake once more, not earth only, but Heaven, that the things which cannot be shaken may remain; in our time also ancient landmarks may be removed, as familiar and sacred as the tabernacle of Shiloh, and the Ark of the Covenant to Israel. But there is one property within our reach need never pass away, which shall remain unimpaired and radiant through the years and that is an unblemished character a soul stainlessly arrayed, and a holy life in which these shall be embodied.[3]

We are facing an era of change. Our landmarks are being removed, and we are witnessing the passing of the old and the coming of the new. We need to train our children to be men of women of conviction, who have been tested and tried—so they, too, can "arrest the ruin of our people."

What Is Character?
In the 1828 Webster's Dictionary, Daniel Webster defined character as: "By way of eminence, distinguished or good qualities; those which are esteemed and respected; and those which are ascribed to a person in common estimation." In summary, character is the good qualities we esteem and respect in a person. These qualities include honesty, kindness, hard work, diligence, faithfulness, self-control, perseverance, generosity, and more. D.L. Moody defines character as ""what a man is in the dark."[4] It is something that is tested when no one else is looking. In *Mere Christianity*, C.S. Lewis writes, "Surely what a man does when he is taken off his guard is the best evidence for what sort of man he is."[5] Character is doing the right thing, even when everything screams otherwise.

How does one develop character? Character begins to grow through an intentional training in morals, rooted in God's Word. It flourishes as one perseveres through hardships.

A few years ago, our family visited Capitola, and we were shopping in a cute French shop. While we were looking at their cosmetics, there was a lip balm that said, "Try Me." My son, Sam, who was ten at the time, had chapped lips. So, he put his finger in the container, scooped out a huge chunk, and liberally coated his lips. The owner of the shop, who watched this happen, rebuked Sam for taking too much. My son apologized, but he felt really bad. Sam looked at the price of the container and, then, shopped around the store to find something to buy that would compensate the owner for the amount of lip balm he took. He ended up buying a lavender soap. When we left the store, he gave the soap to me as a gift. I was touched, and thanked him. He told me that he wanted to buy something from the store to make up for his blunder. This is what character looks like in a child.

Theodore Roosevelt once stated, "Character, in the long run, is the decisive factor in the life of an individual and of nations alike."[6] If we overindulge our children, they become materialistic, selfish, and consumed with their own desires. They will not be concerned with the welfare of others or the spiritual climate of their country. Our children must have character if they are going to transform this world for God's glory!

Choosing Character

Choosing to develop the character of our children is a choice we must make as parents. Our children will not grow character by chance—it takes work to instill character in a child! We must begin molding and shaping our children into the men and women we want them to be when they are still young. J.C. Ryle writes about the need for childhood training in his book, *Thoughts for Young Men*: "Youth is the seed-time of full age, the molding season in the little space of human life, the turning-point into the history of man's mind."[7] In other words, the training our children receive in their growing years determines who they are going to be their entire life.

In today's culture, many parents are replacing character building with entertainment, activities, and achievements. The result: children grow increasingly selfish. They constantly think about how to make themselves happy, how to entertain themselves, and how to get out of doing hard things. C.H. Spurgeon writes "Better far to have the young heart trained to bear the yoke than to fill the childish head with knowledge, however valuable. An ounce of obedience is better than a ton of learning."[8]

As mothers, we need to decide if we want children of character or children of accomplishment. Would we rather have children who put others first, say "Please" and "Thank you!," and are kind to others? Or, do we desire children who learn how to read, play instruments, and join a competitive soccer league by Kindergarten? If we really think about it, we will get children of accomplishment if we take the time to develop children of character first. Children of character work hard, persevere through trials, and put others before themselves—all things necessary to accomplish great things in life. But, if we forgo character development in favor of raising children of accomplishments, we will not necessarily receive children of character.

The goal of Christian parenting is to instill Christian character in our children. We want our children to serve others and be a blessing—now and when they are thirty. We want them to become parents of character, who raise up grandchildren of character. The choices we make today will determine who our children become as adults.

Character Training

Character is developed through intentional training. If we want children who are honest, loving, kind, hard working, diligent, generous, and more, we must first teach them to behave. Matthew Henry writes: "Teach young people what they shall say, for they cannot order their speech by reason of darkness."[9] In other words, we cannot expect our children to behave if we have not taught them how to do so. When our children ask for something, we must teach them to say, "Please." When they get something, they need to say, "Thank you!" If we do not train our children to do these things, they won't know any better.

What should we do when we see behavior that is not pleasing to God? We must correct the behavior, sharing with our children how they should act according to God's Word. What does this look like practically? If our children interrupt us, we need to let them know they are being rude, then train them to politely wait until we are finished talking. *Parenting with Scripture* by Kara Durbin is a wonderful resource in this area, as it uses God's Word as a source of truth and guidance as it builds character. Sometimes, our children's behavior will require additional discipline— perhaps our children hit a sibling or scream, "No!", when we ask them to do something. If we don't take the time to address misbehavior and train our children to behave well now, they will not naturally absorb character as they grow.

I remember when my son Sam was in first grade, and cheated on his spelling test. He had dyslexia, and could not spell, no matter how hard he tried. In a moment of frustration and desperation, he folded up the words to the spelling desk, tucked them under his desk, and was copying them during his test. His teacher found out, and sent him to the principal's office. Now, Michael and I had such compassion for him. However, we could not let our feelings get in the way of training our child in what we knew was right! If we did not discipline Sam for lying, he might be tempted to repeat this sin throughout his life. We made it a big deal, and he was punished. As a result, Sam is a very honest child. He will keep his word, even to his own hurt! We look back at this incident as a gift from God, as it was an opportunity for us to train Sam to be a man of character.

Character training really begins in our children's thought life. So, we need to carefully consider what we allow our children to be exposed to. The writer of Psalm 19:14 encourages us: "Let the words of my mouth and the meditation of my heart be acceptable in Your sight, O LORD, my strength and my Redeemer." We need to make sure we surround them with truth that will inspire and train their thought life, rather than allowing them to be fed lies. Consider this well-known poem:

> *Watch your thoughts, they become words.*
> *Watch your words, they become actions.*
> *Watch your actions, they become habits.*
> *Watch your habits, they become character.*
> *Watch your character, it becomes your destiny.*

As parents, it is really important that we discipline our children's thoughts, words, and actions. Our children will say what they think, and if we don't correct their thinking, they will end up acting upon false ideas. And if we don't correct their actions, they will form bad habits that will corrupt their character and end up destroying their destiny.

For example, when our children say something that is not right, we need to correct them—and, then, share the truth with them. For example, after we discipline or talk sternly with our children, they may say that we don't love them. We need to tell them, "No, I love you! I disciplined you because I love you. The Bible says that if I didn't love you, I would not discipline you." This is intentional character training that must begin when our children are young.

We must also consider how to stimulate our children to love and good deeds (Hebrews 10:24). How can we help our children love those around them? We can encourage them to do loving acts that build character, like giving their brothers and sisters hugs, or doing something kind and generous. We should point out needs in our home, church, school, and neighborhood and work to fill it with the help of our children.

Great Books

Reading great books also helps develop character in our children. In fact, great books can have great power in their life. Ralph Waldo Emerson once said, "Many times the reading of a book has made the future of a man."[10] Why are books so powerful? When our children read a well-written, classic story, they learn valuable lessons, and develop character without actually enduring the situations in the books themselves. Take *Robinson Crusoe*, for example. Children learn the importance of obeying their parents—unless they want to end up "shipwrecked on an island" for thirty years! They learn the valuable lessons of friendships and self-sacrifice as they read about Frodo and Sam's journey to Mordor in Tolkien's *The Lord of the Rings*. As they read great books, our children experience the pressure of great responsibilities and the glory of accomplishing an impossible task—without having to go through it personally.

Books have transformed the lives of men and women throughout history. Five books made up the education of Abraham Lincoln. In a tiny log cabin in the backwoods of Kentucky, a young Abe educated himself, by reading the Bible, *Pilgrim's Progress*, *Aesop's Fables*, *Robinson Crusoe*, and *Arabian Nights*. These five books formed the character of our sixteenth president, launching him into the world, and transforming it.

What great books should our children read? There are too many to list! In our family, we often refer to *Honey For a Child's Heart* to find new books to read. Also, we can't get enough of *Lamplighter Theatre*, which is an absolute delight for our whole family! Their books and audio dramas build character, and inspire our children to take on hard things for the glory of God!

Building Character Through Suffering
If want our children's character to grow, we have to allow them to endure hard things. Lamentations 3:27 tells us, "It is good for a man to bear the yoke in his youth." Spurgeon expounds upon this verse:

> *Men who rise to eminence without a struggle usually fall into dishonor. The yoke of affliction, disappointment, and excessive labour is by no means to be sought for; but when the Lord lays it on us in our youth it frequently develops a character which glorifies God and blesses the church.* [11]

Hard things are a gift from God. They not only help our children grow in character, but they also prepare them to be used more effectively for His Kingdom. When our children endure a hard thing, they will remember that God gave them the grace to get through it. Then, when they face another obstacle, they will trust that He will help them get through it, as well.

Watching our children suffer—knowing that God is working out something glorious in their life—is not easy, by any means. However, it is necessary if we want our children to be God's ministers to this lost and dying world. Allowing our children to suffer does not mean allowing them to walk into danger or harm's way. No, our job is to protect our children. Rather, it means allowing them to endure personal struggles and suffering so they become men and women of character, who trust in God:

> *The most illustrious characters of the Bible were bruised and threshed and ground into bread for the hungry. Abraham's diploma styles him as "father of the faithful." That was because he stood at the head of his class in affliction and obedience. Jacob suffered severe threshing and grindings. Joseph was bruised and beaten and had to go through Potiphar's kitchen and Egypt's prison to get to his throne. David, hunted like a partridge on the mountain, bruised, weary and footsore, was ground into bread for a kingdom. Paul never could have been bread for Caesar's household if he had not endured bruising,*

whippings and stonings. He was ground into fine flour for the royal family.[12]

As parents, we need to allow our children to suffer, so they will have what it takes to persevere and faithfully do the work God calls them to do.

Coddling

One of the greatest reasons children lack character today is moms' unwillingness to let their children suffer. As mothers, we want to coddle them, keeping them safe like we did while they were in our womb. So, we set up the perfect environment of comfort and ease, helping them grow and flourish in the sunshine of life. As wonderful as this life sounds, we must realize coddling our children will result in underdevelopment of the coping skills needed for life.

> *If the parent is always there to clean up a child's mess—or prevent the problem in the first place—how does the child ever learn to cope with loss, disappointment, or failure? Studies have found that helicopter parenting can make children feel less competent in dealing with the stresses of life on their own.*[13]

Coddling our children is a new phenomenon in parenting—consider how our grandparents and great-grandparents walked miles in the snow each winter day to get to their one room school house! And, they made this trek after getting up early to take care of the animals and complete their household chores. Our grandparents and great-grandparents were men and women of character! They were people who worked hard, kept their word, and were continually made sacrifices for others—especially the next generation! They are considered "The Greatest Generation" for the hardships they endured and the sacrifices they made for others.

C.H. Spurgeon reminds us that character is not developed during times of ease and comfort:

> *Why the Lord always trains His soldiers, not by letting them lie on feather beds, but by turning them out, and using them to forced marches and hard service. He makes them ford through streams, and swim through rivers, and climb mountains, and walk many a long march with heavy knapsacks of sorrow on their backs. This is the way in which He makes them soldiers— not by dressing them up in fine uniforms, to swagger at the barrack gates, and to be find gentlemen in the eyes of the loungers in the park. God knows that soldiers are only to be made in battle; they are not to be grown in peaceful times. We may grow the stuff of which soldiers are made; but warriors are really educated by the smell of powder, in the midst of whizzing bullets and roaring cannonades, not in soft and peaceful times.*[14]

Coddling our children—"letting them lie on feather beds", or "dressing them up in fine uniforms"—does not prepare them to be soldiers in the Lord's army! We are handing our children a really hard world, and we need to prepare them to do serious battle!

What is so heartbreaking about our culture today is the number of adolescents taking antidepressants, addicted to drugs or alcohol, and committing suicide because they cannot cope with life. Let that not be said of our children! As mothers, we need to allow them to grow their character, so that they can not only learn to cope with life, but also become the ones who transform it!

Meddling

When our children experience hard things, it is so tempting to meddle with what God is trying to do in their lives. Many moms today pride themselves in being "mama bears"- ready to take on anyone or anything that might harm our children. In doing so, we are rescuing our children from trials that are meant to grow them. It is imperative that we allow our children to not only reap the consequences of their actions, but to also endure life's unjust treatment as a results of sin in the world—so that God can produce character in their life!

As mothers, we don't want our children to suffer at the hands of mean children, unjust policies, favoritism, or unfair teachers. However, when our children valiantly endure hardship, character is produced—a character that can endure more difficulty and more pressure than one could ever imagine!

Do you want children of character? Then, you must allow God to have His way in your child, no matter how painful it is to watch! Stephen Merritt encourages us in this area. He writes:

> *Cease from meddling with God's plans and wills. You touch anything of His, and you mar the work. You may move the hands of a clock to suit you, but you do not change the time; so you may hurry the unfolding of God's will, but you harm and do not help the work. You can open a rosebud, but you spoil the flower. Leave all to Him. Hands down. Thy will, not mine.*[15]

Psalm 25:12 reminds us, "Who is the man that fears the LORD? Him shall He teach in the way He chooses." We do not get to choose how our children will be trained by God. We need to step aside, allow God to work, and do our best to guide our children along the way. When they experience hard things, we must realize, as Corrie ten Boom declares, that: "God has plans, not problems for our lives. The life of a Christian is an education for a higher service. God is training you for something."[16] God is training our children. As parents, we should not try to stop His work—especially if we want children of character, who can accomplish His plan for their life.

When our children do hard things—read a really difficult book, or tackle an impossible assignment—they feel accomplished. Then, when the next hard thing comes their way, they will choose to face it head on, rather than squirming or running away at the sight of it. Amy Carmichael declares: "All life's training is just exactly what is needed for the true Life- work, still out of view but far away from none of us. Don't grudge me the learning of a new lesson."[17] Moms, don't grudge your children the learning of a new lesson. We must look at their struggles from God's perspective—and refuse to prevent them from learning and growing through the difficulty.

Giving Perspective

When our children endure hardships, our role as mothers is to help them navigate through it by giving them perspective, rather than feed the injustice. I remember a time when I was in sixth grade. There was an eighth grader in my school who wanted to beat me up. I didn't even know her, but she always gave me dirty looks. I was devastated. After a couple of weeks, I talked to my mom about the situation, and she told me that people didn't like her when she younger, either—and in the scheme of life, it really doesn't matter what people think about us. What a relief! My mom helped me gain perspective on the situation. She also taught me how to navigate the situation: "Be nice anyways!"

As moms of faith, it is our duty to pray for our children when they go through hard times. We should be sharing scripture with our children, giving them insight on their situation in the light of God's kingdom and His word! If our children know the Lord, they have the Holy Spirit inside them, and we can encourage them that God will comfort them and be with them throughout their day! As mothers, we need to help our children learn how to seek God and His will within the trials so they can someday learn to navigate through their trials without us.

As the world grows more and more complicated, our children will have to navigate through harder and harder difficulties. We need to fight the temptation to rescue them, or to take the situation into our own hands. Instead, our children need our wisdom as we speak truth into their life, bringing perspective found in God's Word, allowing their character to grow as they face life's challenges.

Perseverance

Our culture does not value perseverance through suffering. When things get hard, it tells us to jump ship—in all areas of life! For example, when it is time to check out at Costco, I always examine all the lines, trying to choose the one that I think will go the fastest. Then, if the checker is slow, I jump from line to line until I find one that can check me out quicker. While this may seem like a natural response, it is not what God wants us to do when we experience trials. Romans 5:3-4 reminds us that persevering through trials builds our character: "...but we also glory in tribulations, knowing that tribulation produces perseverance; and perseverance, character; and character, hope."

Too often, when we experience trials, we jump out of them because we don't like suffering or experiencing pain. When we have troubles with a friend, we just write them off. Or, if we have a conflict with our church, we decide to leave and find a new one. If we get a bad review at work that we do not feel we deserved, we go find a new job, where people will appreciate us. But, bailing out should not be a pattern in our lives. As Christians, God calls us to glory in our sufferings. When we persevere and endure trials, we grow—into men and women of character!

The fruit of persevering is not only true for us, but it is also especially true for our children. Persevering grows habits that will help them grow into the men and women God has called them to be. In today's culture, children jump from job to job, church to church, and relationship to relationship. There is no loyalty anymore. Recently, I listened to Dennis Rainey (*Family Life Today*) speak about launching his children into life. The one thing he wished he and his wife had done differently as they raised their children was to teach them to persevere through trials in their jobs, churches, and relationships.[18]

We need to realize that allowing our children to escape trials actually does them a disservice. They learn that it is okay to jump from job to job when their boss is mean, when they can't get the right hours, or when they are not treated fairly. We should not be surprised when they do not have a job in the future because they lack a good work ethic. If we jump from church to church with our children in search of the perfect worship service and pastor, we should not be surprised if our children end up as church critics, or not attending church at all. When we tell our children it is okay to leave friendships or relationships because things grow difficult, we should not be surprised if they end up divorced.

We must teach our children to persevere through trials. *Devotions for Morning and Evening* offers some perspective:

> As Dr. Hillis said: "He who would ask to be relieved from suffering would take the winter out of the seasons, the glory of the night out of the round day, the cloud and rainstorms out of the summer; would expel the furrows from the face of Lincoln; would rob Socrates of his dignity and majesty, would make Saint Paul a mere esthetic feeling; would steal the sweetness from maternity; would rob the Divine Sufferer of His sanctity."[19]

We are called by God to persevere through trials, knowing that He is doing a work in us that can only be accomplished in our suffering. James 1:2-4 tells us: "My brethren, count it all joy when you fall into various trials, knowing that the testing of your faith produces patience. But let patience have *its* perfect work, that you may be perfect and complete, lacking nothing." When circumstances in life get hard, it is so important that we stay under the trial, no matter how terrible the pressure is. Trials grow our character and help transform us into the image of Christ! *Streams In the Desert* describes the beauty that comes when we persevere:

> *He that is mastered by Christ is the master of every circumstance. Does the circumstance press hard against you? Do no push it away. It is the Potter's hand. Your mastery will come, not by arresting its progress, but by enduring its discipline, for it is not only shaping you into a vessel of beauty and honor, but it is making your resources available.*[20]

I have also found in life that, if I am going through a struggle, but do not learn what was needed in it, or escape the trial, God gives another trial packaged with new people and a different circumstances, so I can learn the same lesson. And, if I don't learn it this time, He will continue to give me the trial over and over again! We have all met people who just never get it. They have gone to ten churches, can't hold a job, and are always frustrated with people. Wouldn't it be such a blessing if we could help our children navigate through their trials, so they can grow their character, and always be learning new and greater things so they might men and women of character—prepared to do a great work!

What if we had the attitude of a servant, and chose to persevere in our trials, believing that doing our job faithfully could make our company more efficient and successful? What if we allowed Christ's love and grace to fill our hearts, and were generous and gracious to those in our churches? What if we were generous with our love and forgiveness when we have been wronged or hurt by those closest to us? Remember, God does not call us to be like the world, escaping hardships when they come; instead, He calls us to embrace them, allowing them to prepare us to demonstrate Christ's love to the world! Remember, Jesus did not feel like going to the cross, yet He did it anyway! Our children will not naturally want to walk through a hard situation, yet when they do, they will reap the blessing of godly character!

When is it ok to leave the pressure of a situation? When your commitment is over, or when God has worked out circumstances where you can leave in a way that blesses the other party involved. God will lead you by His peace. Not the peace that you receive from escaping your trial, but a peace that says God is glorified, I did what was right, and I left in a way that pleases God and blessed the other person or community I was part of. This might mean you have to change, apologize, or humble yourself. Remember the goal is that you learn and grow your character through God being glorified in your life.

Reap What You Sow

Galatians 6:7 states, "Do not be deceived, God is not mocked; for whatever a man sows, that he will also reap." When our children sin, we need to let them suffer the consequences, or reap what they sow. Today, many parents rescue their children, and keep them from paying the consequences of their sin—whether they realize it or not.

In our children's life, consequences are gifts from the Lord! They teach valuable lessons that build our character. Samuel Rutherford once declared, "O, what I owe I to the file, to the hammer, to the furnace of my Lord Jesus!"[21] God teaches us many lessons through our afflictions, as C.H. Spurgeon also attests:

> *I bear my willing witness that I owe more to the fire, and the hammer, and the file, than to anything else in my Lord's workshop. I sometimes question whether I have ever learned anything except through the rod. When my schoolroom is darkened, I see most."*[22]

What does this look like practically? When your children accidentally break your window with a BB Gun bullet, let them pay to replace it. When their teachers send a note home because they were messing around in class, discipline them. When they break their friend's phone, have them pay for it. And then there are the little things, when your child forgets their lunch, homework, or jacket. I think all moms feel bad when their child forgets their lunch, however, if it is done repeatedly, the only way for them to learn is when they are taught to reap what they sow. When we allow our children to reap what they sow, their character will grow, and they will be a blessing to us and the world around them.

Let Your Yes Be Yes

When we are training our children to be men and women of character, we must remember to teach them to honor their commitments no matter what. We have all made commitments only to find out later that something more pressing or attractive required our time. But, we need to teach our children that when they commit to doing something—whether they promised or not—they need to follow through, even if it means they miss out on something more appealing! James 5:12 states: "But above all, my brethren, do not swear, either by heaven or by earth or with any other oath. But let your "Yes" be "Yes," and your "No," "No," lest you fall into judgment."

Being a man or woman of your word is a virtue of the past; but for Christians, our word should be held to a higher standard. Remember our Savior: He holds His word above His own name! And, His standard should be the standard for our word, as well.

When our children complain bitterly about a commitment they have made, we must not allow them to break it. We have all met adults who do not honor commitments, especially when things get hard. Do we want our children to be like them?

Life Is Not Fair
Growing up, when I would complain about something, my mother used to say, "Life is not fair." And it is so true! The sooner our children learn to take what life hands them and make the best of it, the better off they will be. As mothers, our job is not to right all the wrongs that our children suffer. We must help them realize that life is full of injustices. We can feed life's injustices, or we can help our children understand that unfair things happen—but, how we deal with these things is a choice we each have to make.

In this life, we will be wronged over and over again. How will we respond? As moms, we must fight the temptation to right the wrongs in our children's life. We give them a gift when we teach them to forgive others and show grace, even when it is not deserved. Reflecting on this truth, Charles Wagner writes:

> *In the very depths of yourself, dig a grave. Let it be like some forgotten spot to which no path leads; and there, in the eternal silence, bury the wrongs that you have suffered. Your heart will feel as if a weight had fallen from it, and a Divine peace come to abide with you.*[23]

Our children need to learn to set aside the wrongs they have suffered, and to allow God's peace to fill them. We need to train them to live like Christ in a fallen world, by being gracious, and by forgiving others when they have wronged us. When our children overcome life's injustices, and see them as stepping stones to greater things, they will be given a great gift!

Taking on Our Children's Offenses
In times past, when children would get in trouble, parents would discipline them, and thank the person who was responsible for pointing out their bad behavior. Both parties desired the child's character to grow.

Often, when children get in trouble today, parents take on their children's feelings—and become offended—because their children's feelings trump their misbehavior. How unfortunate! Then, when the children are no longer upset, or the situation is no longer an issue, the parents still hold a grudge or desire compensation for the wrong they feel was committed. Rather than helping their children develop their character or learn to deal with conflict, parents end up making the situation bigger as they take on the offense and, often, blow the issue way out of proportion. Amy Carmichael inspires us to not take on offenses easily. She writes: "If I take offense easily; if I am content to continue in a cool unfriendliness, though friendship be possible, then I know nothing of Calvary love."[24]

As parents, it is truly important that we support the people who are authority figures in our children's lives—even when they are making decisions we do not agree with, or are not the people we would choose to have in authority. Or, perhaps we don't agree with how a situation was handled. God requires us to respect those in authority, and we need to teach our children to do so, too. We are commanded in Romans 13:1 "Let every soul be subject to the governing authorities. For there is no authority except from God, and the authorities that exist are appointed by God." Our children have many authorities in their lives, and they need to learn to support and respect them. We need to teach our children the importance of submitting, honoring, and obeying the people God has placed over us—as there is great blessing in store for those who do!

We must remember—and teach our children—that God uses those we believe are against us to accomplish His will in our lives and develop our character. Amy Carmichael writes, "The effect of man's sin or mistake, temptation or discouragement about ourselves, all limitations and frustrations, and all trials of the flesh and spirit, are really "under-smiths and servants" working together for good to us who love God."[25] The author of Romans so gloriously reminds us: "And we know that all things work together for good to those who love God, to those who are the called according to His purpose." (Romans 8:28)

Mothers, we need to guide our children to see circumstances through the lens of God's word. We need to teach them to be gracious, and to make sure their own heart is right before God before they would ever judge others, or demand that their wrongs be righted. As Thomas à Kempis so eloquently writes: "In judging others a man labors in vain, often errs and easily sins, but in judging and examining himself, he always labors fruitfully."[26]

Often, I find in these situations that we have a piece of the story, and then the enemy takes hold of that piece, twists it, and creates the rest of the story in our minds; then, we moms dwell upon it, and end up being taken captive by the enemy. So often, the story is not as bad as we have made it out to be. And, if we would only examine our own hearts in the situation, we would find ways we could improve, rather than making things so much bigger than they need to be.

In situations that comes up in our children's lives, we must remember that we should "do unto others and we want them to do unto us." Why? Because so often, with what we measure to others, it will be measured back to us. If we want others to be gracious with us, we must remember to be gracious ourselves. A few years back, I was on a bike ride with our eight graders from our school in Los Gatos. On our way back, I was so far behind the front of the group that I didn't realize that I had lost two of the children. They were in the downtown area, and had to each find a shop to ask to borrow a phone to call their parents, who called the school, to call me, to tell me they were lost! Our vice-principal had to drive over and pick them up. What a humbling moment! I am so grateful that these parents were gracious with me! We must remember to be as gracious with others as we want them to be towards us when we fail- as it is only a matter of time until we do!

What happens when you have a situation that clearly needs to be addressed? There will be times where you will need to deal with a conflict in your children's lives- yet it must be done in a way that pleases God. If there is a situation you need to address for the sake of the community, we should go directly to the person, in love, and address the situation; hopefully they will apologize or explain, which will clear things up. If that does not happen, then we are told in Matthew 18 to get another person, and then address the situation. The goal is that the other person will be right before God and others, and will be restored from the error of their ways. As so often, people don't realize that what they have done was wrong until someone loves them enough to tell them in love and humility.

Conquering Giants

When the children of Israel came to the border of the Promised Land, they sent a team to spy out the land. When the spies came back, they reported, "There we saw the giants" (Numbers 13:33). Some of the people became afraid, and did not want to enter the land, while others wanted to go and claim it. It took Joshua and Caleb reminding the people that God was bigger than the giants in the land for the people to persevere in pursuing God's promise. These two men of faith were confident that the Israelites would "eat up" the giants like "bread" with God's help (Numbers 14:9).

While we do not face literal giants today, we do face great difficulties —and these are everywhere. They are in our families, churches, social life, and our very own hearts. We must overcome our giants, or they will swallow us up!

Our children also have giants in their life: glasses, lisps, stuttering, anxieties, learning disabilities, friendship issues, deaths of a loved one, and more. We must teach our children to face these giants, after all: "Blood marks stain the steps that lead to thrones. Scars are the price of scepters. Our crowns will be wrested from the giants we conquer. Grief has always been the lot of greatness."[27] When our children overcome giants, they forge determination and character, which will empower them to persevere for the rest of their life. As moms, we must realize that the greatest blessings are not wrapped in pleasant packages.

Five of my children struggle with the same giant: the gift of dyslexia —though two have very severe cases. I call their dyslexia a gift for two reasons: their brains work outside the box, and it has given them perseverance. My children all attend a rigorous, classical school, and they have had to learn to work around their dyslexia, as we have never made a big deal of it. At first, we gave them outside tutoring, or made small adjustments to their twenty-word spelling lists. But, they have all learned to work harder than everyone else in their class to succeed. The result: all five of them can read, and they all know how to work diligently and persevere.

Our Example

It is overwhelming when we think about all that Jesus had to endure as a result of man's sin. And God the Father sent Him to us anyways! Jesus suffered greatly— ridicule, gossip, jealously, persecution, mocking, scourging, and ultimately, death—at the hands those He came to save. At any point, God could have intervened and said, "You cannot treat my Son this way!" Yet, He didn't! God's love for you and me was greater than the temptation toward what was comfortable or easy.

Because Jesus walked the road He did, we can take the road He calls us to, knowing He has trodden the path before us. If He can endure it, so can we, because the same power that was in Jesus is within us, now!

On the eve of His greatest trial with the cross awaiting Him, Jesus prayed to His Father, pleading with Him: "Now My soul is troubled, and what shall I say? "Father, save Me from this hour"? But for this purpose I came to this hour. "Father, glorify Your name." (John 12:27-28a) Jesus's prayer was one of submission and obedience in suffering. Jesus did not feel like going to the cross, yet he denied His flesh and feelings, and did it anyway! We not only need to follow His example, but we also need to teach our children to follow it. Hebrews 5:8 tells us that "though [Jesus] was a Son, yet He learned obedience by the things which He suffered." Jesus experienced depths of yielding to God that would not have been possible outside of suffering and continued obedience to the Father. Suffering does the same thing in our lives and our children's lives.

God did not save His Son from suffering, and we shouldn't save our children from it either. The cross was the only way for Jesus, the Savior of humanity, to accomplish His great mission—and it is the only way our children will be able to accomplish their mission, too. In Luke 14:27, Jesus tell us that "whoever does not bear his cross and come after Me cannot be My disciple." (Luke 14:27). As we teach our children to be followers of Christ, we cannot skip the lesson of suffering, as it is the most important lesson of their life. Remember, we are called to disciple our children, and "[t]he secret of discipleship is the Cross of our Lord Jesus Christ."[28] There are some things our children must learn that only comes by suffering. So, we must allow them to experience it and teach them to take up their cross. In the words of Amy Carmichael:

> *He calls for much; He calls for everything. He calls for the march that may have no return and can have compromise. He demands this loyalty because His enterprise is a crusade. Its method is that of the cross, and there is no other way. Because He goes that way, His disciple also must go that way.* [29]

In 1668, the imprisoned William Penn wrote a book, *No Cross, No Crown*. In his preface, Penn wrote, "Christ's cross is Christ's way to Christ's crown."[30] In other words, if we suffer, we shall reign with Christ:

The greatest helpers of humanity have been its cross-bearers. The leaders of men have suffered in loneliness; the prophets have learned their lesson in the school of pain. The corals in the sheltered lagoon grow rank and useless; those that are broken and crushed by the surf from the living rock and the foundations of continents. Ease has not produced greatness. Men who have had to struggle with an unfavorable environment, to fight cold, to buffet the storm, to blast the rock or wring a livelihood from a niggardly soil, have won character by their pains.[31]

Our children win "character by their pains." Our world is desperate for men and women of character, who know God. We desperately need men and women of character, who are willing to pick up their cross, and to persevere through hardships. Only then will they have the character they need to be God's voice in a day when the Word of the Lord is rare. Transforming this world for the glory of God is not going to be an easy task, and all our training of our children should be towards this end!

So often, I think we mothers think that it is not loving for us to not rescue our children, nor respond to their feelings of hurt of injustice. However, it is the opposite! Amy Carmichael urges us to remember: "If I refuse to allow one who is dear to me to suffer for the sake of Christ, if I do not see such suffering as the greatest honor that can be offered to any follower of the Crucified, then I know nothing of Calvary love."[32]

We must not rescue our children from the crosses only they were meant to bear. In doing so, we will not only miss out on children of character, but our children will not be prepared to accomplish God's great calling.

Martin Luther once wrote, "A religion that gives nothing, costs nothing, and suffers nothing, is worth nothing."[33] In the same vein, F.B. Meyer notes: "That which costs nothing is of small avail to the salvation and help of mankind. The souls that are set on saving themselves will never be the saviors of the race."[34]

As mothers, we cannot underestimate the importance of allowing our children to develop character! Through character, our children can become kingdom changers, who do great things for the glory of God. F.B. Meyer, again, states:

The noblest gift that any of us can make to our fatherland or age is an undefiled character and a stainless life. Let us live our best in the power of the Spirit of God, and prove the the God of Pentecost is living still.[35]

C.T. Studd, a wealthy Englishman who donated all of his wealth to live by faith on the mission field, once wrote, "Some want to live within the sound of church or chapel bell; I want to run a rescue shop within a yard of hell." What compels a man to give up a life of comfort and ease for a life of toil, hardship, and sacrifice?   Jesus Christ—and a life transformed by His suffering.

Moms, we must remember our mission: children who can hear God's voice and proclaim it to a lost and dying world! This is not an easy task, but we must allow our children to endure hardships and suffering, so they learn to persevere. Through intentional training of their character, our children will not run away from hard things, but rather embrace them as a way to glorify God and build His kingdom.

Questions to Consider

1. Is training your children's character a priority? If so, how?

2. What have you rescued your children from lately? What might they have learned if you had not interfered?

3. How can you guide your children the next time they go through something hard?

4. Are you holding on to any offenses as the result of the way your child has been treated? If so, what can you do to free yourself?

5. What giants do your children need to persevere against and conquer in their life? How can you help them overcome these giants? If they do, how will their character be developed?

6. How are you teaching your children to be faithful in their relationships, church, and work?

Allowing our children to suffer is probably the most difficult thing for us to do—after all, they are only children!

Notes

---

1 Alexander MacLaren, *MacLaren's Expositions of Holy Scripture, Volume 1* (Grand Rapids, Michigan: WM. B. Eerdmans Publishing Co., 1959), 274.

2 F.B. Meyer, *Samuel the Prophet* (CrossReach Publications, 2017), 15.

3 Ibid.

4 D.L. Moody, "Brainy Quote," accessed July 19, 2019, https://www.brainyquote.com/quotes/dwight_l_moody_379867

5 C.S. Lewis, *Mere Christianity* (New York, New York: HarperCollins, 1952), 192.

6 Theodore Roosevelt, "Good Reads," accessed July 19, 2019, https://www.goodreads.com/quotes/63681-character-in-the-long-run-is-the-decisive-factor-in

7 J.C. Ryle, "Good Reads," Thoughts From Young Men Quotes, accessed August 10, 2019, https://www.goodreads.com/work/quotes/241324-thoughts-for-young-men

8 C.H. Spurgeon, *Spiritual Parenting* (New Kensington, PA: Whitaker House, 1995), 93.

9 Matthew Henry, *Matthew Henry's Commentary of the Bible, Volume II* (New York: Fleming H. Revell Company, 1708), 278.

10 Ralph Waldo Emerson, "AZ Quotes," accessed July 19, 2019, https://www.azquotes.com/quote/531161

11 C.H. Spurgeon, *Cheque Book of the Bank of Faith* (Great Britain:Christian Focus Publications, 1996), 256.

12 Mrs. Charles E. Cowman, *Devotions for Morning and Evening* (New York: International Press, 1925), 375.

13 Kate Bayless, "What Is Helicopter Parenting," Parents Magazine, Updated: September 26, 2018, accessed July 20, 2019, https://www.parents.com/parenting/better-parenting/what-is-helicopter-parenting/

14 C.H. Spurgeon, quoted by Mrs. Charles E. Cowman, *Streams in the Desert* (Grand Rapids, Michigan: Zondervan Publishing House, 1925), 303.

15 Stephen Merritt, quoted by Cowman, *Streams in the Desert*, 109.

16 Corrie ten Boom, "Quote Fancy," accessed July 20, 2019, https://quotefancy.com/quote/789862/Corrie-ten-Boom-God-has-plans-not-problems-for-our-lives-The-life-of-a-Christian-is-an

17 Amy Carmichael, "Good Reads," accessed July 20, 2019, https://www.goodreads.com/author/quotes/3935881.Amy_Carmichael?page=2

18 Dennis and Barbara Rainey, "Putting the Finishing Touches on Character," Family Life, March 30, 2009, accused on March 30, 2009, https://www.familylife.com/podcast/familylife-today/putting-the-finishing-touches-on-charact/

19 Dr. Hillis, quoted by Cowman, *Devotions for Morning and Evening*, 415.

20 Cowman, *Streams in the Desert*, 150.

21 Samuel Rutherford, *The Loveliness of Christ* (London: Samuel Bagster & Sons Limited, 1909), 8.

22 C.H. Spurgeon, *Spurgeon Sermon Notes*, ed., David Otis Fuller (Grand Rapids, MI: Kregel Publications, 307.

23 Ibid., 427.

24 Amy Carmichael, *If* (Fort Washington, Pennsylvania: Christian Literature Crusade, 1938), 45.

25 Amy Carmichael, *Whispers of His Power* (Fort Washington, Pennsylvania: CLC Publications, 1982), 145.

26 Thomas à Kempis, *On the Imitation of Christ*, The Catholic Archive, Book 1, Chapter 14, accessed on July 20, 2019, http://catholicarchive.org/thomas_a_kempis/the_imitation_of_christ/1/14.html

27 Cowman, *Devotions for Morning and Evening*, 51.

28 Oswald Chambers, *The Best From All His Books, Volume II* (Nashville, Tennessee: Thomas Nelson Publishers, 1989), 66.

29 Carmichael, *Whispers of His Power*, 180-181.

30 Ibid., 35.

31 Cowman, *Devotions by Morning and Evening*, 434.

32 Carmichael, *If*, 66.

33 Martin Luther, "AZ Quotes," accessed July 23, 2019, https://www.azquotes.com/quote/529749

34 Meyer, *Samuel the Prophet*, 6.

35 Ibid., 15.

Pearl of Wisdom #11

Allow Your Children to Become Independent

When I was a child, I spoke as a child,
I understood as a child, I thought as a child;
but when I became a man, I put away childish things.

1 Corinthians 13:11

When Samuel was three years old, Hannah dropped him off at the Tabernacle—to live there forever! Hannah had to trust God with her son, then continue to trust Him as she allowed Samuel to grow under Eli's guidance. Hannah's faith was astonishing! She could have been full of fear, yet she was not. By faith, she dropped off her dearest treasure at the Tabernacle, and trusted God to mold and shape him into a mighty man!

At a young age, Samuel learned that he could not depend upon his mom for what he needed; instead, he had to depend upon the Lord. He could not rely upon his mother to make things happen for him; rather, he had to learn to navigate life independently. If we desire children who will do great work for the kingdom of God, we must allow them to become independent as young as possible. That way, they will have what it takes to transform this world for the glory of God!

Letting Go

When children are born, they are completely dependent upon their parents for their all their basic needs. Sometimes, as moms, we forget that our children need to grow toward independence after just a few short years of dependence. We must not resist the process of letting our children go, as that is the only way they will become mature, independent adults. If we want our children to be the leaders of their generation, we have to allow them to become independent of us as soon as possible.

As mothers, we need to get into the habit of letting our children go from the moment they are born. Yet, too often we cling onto them tighter and tighter as time passes. Corrie ten Boom once wrote, "Hold everything in your hands lightly. Otherwise, it hurts when God pries your fingers open."[1] When we fail to let our children go, God is faithful to get our children one way or another.

Releasing our children to the Lord and to His will for their lives demands great faith. So often, the reason we hold tightly to our children is because we fear for their future. The "what ifs" feel very real to moms.

However, we must remember that fear is the opposite of faith! We are not trusting God with our children when we do not allow them to become independent—and we do not allow them to see us as an example of faith. If we want our children to be God's voice like Samuel, we first need to be like Hannah, trusting God with our children and allowing them to become independent.

If we have allowed our children to develop their character, we do not have to be afraid of allowing them to become independent. Yes, they will make wrong choices, but we are there to mentor, teach, and guide them through their mistakes. If we want to launch our children into the world to do great things for God's kingdom and be as successful as they possibly can, we must allow them to become independent from us.

Micromanaging Moms
The phrase "micromanaging mom" was coined in 1969, and became so popular that it has since become a dictionary entry. It is used to describe moms who are overly involved in their children's lives, or who are "over-controlling, over-protecting, and over-perfecting, in a way that is in excess of responsible parenting."[2] These moms also take responsibility for their children's experiences, specifically their successes or failures.

There are many reasons that moms become overly involved in their children's lives. Sometimes, they feel responsible for their children's achievements and disappointments. They think it is their responsibility to help their children make it in life, often overcompensating for the things they did not get in their own childhood. Others feel pressure from others who are over-parenting. They feel like they are a bad mom if they are not overly involved in their children's lives. Regardless of why a mom micromanages, it ultimately boils down to one thing: "helicopter" moms are afraid to let their children become independent.

Studies have proven that—though the helicopter moms' intentions might be good—micromanaging leads to a multitude of problems in children's lives. These problems include: an inability to cope with the hardships of life, a sense of entitlement (due to mom revolving her life around her children), and a lack of life skills needed to live an independent life in the future. Rather than being better off, micromanaged children suffer as a result of their mom's over-involvement!

God has called us to be women of faith, not fear. Remember, fear is the opposite of faith! In fact, George Mueller writes, "The beginning of anxiety is the end of faith, and the beginning of true faith is the end of anxiety."[3] As moms, God has given us an incredible mission for our children, and we must—by faith—allow them to become independent of us.

When my children were young, the Lord spoke to me, "Brenda, if you want your children to be world changers, they have to be independent of you—or one day, they will be thirty years old, sitting in the kitchen, waiting for you to cook them a meal!" My children cannot change the world for God's glory from my kitchen. And, neither can yours.

Overcoming Fear

As moms, we must decide to live either by fear or by faith—and each choice takes our children in completely different directions. Second Timothy 1:7 reminds us, "For God has not given us a spirit of fear, but of power and of love and of a sound mind." When we live by fear, we lose our power, our love, and our sound mind. In other words, we make decisions without conviction, love, or sound judgment. Our decisions become skewed because they are made without complete trust in God. Rather than trusting Him to provide, we freak out, and take things into our own hands. Instead of trusting God to watch over and protect our children, we micromanage and over-control them, preventing them from becoming independent adults. As moms, we need to make decisions out of faith, trusting God as we walk in obedience to Him. We can rest, knowing that our children are in His hands.

I have met many mothers who regret making decisions out of fear as they raised their children. Not trusting in God's provision, they placed their children in public schools, where their children walked away from the Lord due to secular teaching or ungodly friends. Some were afraid their children would not like them, so they didn't say "no" to a relationship, job, or habit that their child pressured them to keep. Others would not let their children go to church camp because they worried—the drive was too far, or it was going to snow. As a result, children missed out on growing their relationship with God because their mothers lacked faith. And, sadly, the mothers' lack of faith limited the children's faith in turn. Remember, faith imparts faith!

So many mothers are heartbroken today because they made decisions for their children's lives out of fear. Let us pray that we will choose to raise our children by faith.

Hannah's Example

Today, many moms worry that, if they don't make life happen perfectly, their children may miss out on opportunities, which will keep them from becoming who God has called them to be. However, nothing could be further from the truth!

Consider the life of Hannah. She loved Samuel, and, for the first few years of his life, she imparted her faith, cast a vision for his life, disciplined and trained him, and taught him to pray. Then, she gave Samuel to God. Her son dwelt in the Tabernacle, surrounded by God's presence, and saturated in His word. Samuel's independence from his mother allowed him to develop his character, discern God's voice, live without, and learn to serve. And, it made all the difference in his life! God used Samuel's independence to prepare him to become the man He called him to be.

If we choose to follow Hannah's example, we, too, can have children who are independent—prepared to do all that God has called them to do!

Circles of Influence

It is important to note that Hannah did not drop off Samuel at a Philistine camp, and say, "Educate and train my son. I am no longer going to be involved in raising him." Instead, she placed him in the perfect setting for him to grow and flourish to independence—the Tabernacle! We, too, need to place our children in a perfect setting, so they can grow and flourish to independence.

The irony of our culture is that moms micromanage their children's lives, yet allow them to have choices about the big things. For example, a micromanaging mom might choose her children's friends, help with each homework assignment, and oversee every activity, but then allow her children to decide what church the family goes to, what school they attend, or what activities they participate in. These "big" decisions become tragic when her children choose to enter circles of influence that do not line up with the biblical values. It is only a matter of time before her children start to develop habits, friendships, and ideas that do not line up with the family's values.

As parents, it is our responsibility to manage the circles of influence our children are exposed to—church, school, activities—but not every detail within them. We need to let our children build relationships, do their homework independently, develop their own spiritual life, and, in the process, make mistakes and grow from them. Our job is to guide our children, and train them through situations that arise, rather than take the lead in everything. If we are training our children in godly character, we can give them the freedom to be independent within those spheres, so they can grow and learn to be independent!

One of the blessings of having a lot of children and a lot on my plate is that I can't micromanage my children's friendships, homework, activities, etc. For years, I felt guilty because I could not conform to the culture's standard for moms today—I thought I was not a good mom. Then, I read John Rosemond's *Parenting By the Book*, and I realized that I was actually doing my children a favor by not micromanaging their lives. My children had to learn to be independent from a very young age. God's ways are so much greater than our own!

Areas of Over-Control

Micromanaging moms over-control many aspects of children's lives. Here are some of the most common:

Homework

Homework seems to be a huge point of tension within homes today—and many moms micromanage it. In some schools, teachers expect parents to do homework with their children. The result: many parents not only oversee their children's homework, but they also "help" them with it, managing and correcting every assignment their children have. In fact, moms and dads who "help" in this way are deemed good moms and dads, concerned with the education of their children. Eventually, however, students will have to learn how to independently complete and keep track of their own homework—how else will they make it through college?

In my years of teaching Middle School and with my own personal experience with my children, I have found the earlier a child is allowed to be independent with their homework, the easier it is for the whole family! Many parents, though, decide to stop micromanaging, and wean their children off of homework "help" when they are in middle or high school— as homework has become quite a struggle, and a huge point of tension in their children's lives. But, their children have been trained to do homework only when their mom or dad tells them to, or makes them do so. They become codependent with their parents. In my experience, it is really difficult to wean a child from homework micromanaging during these years.

Throughout my entire education, I don't think that my mom even knew about any of my homework assignments. Not only did I get good grades, but I graduated from college with honors. As moms, we must realize that our children need to learn at a young age that they are the ones who need to work hard to make life happen for themselves. We cannot be the ones constantly propping up their grades so that they can be successful in life.

All of my children have had to learn early on in their school careers that they are the ones responsible for keeping track of and doing their homework—with seven children, it is next to impossible for me to keep track of and manage all of their assignments! For most of my children, their younger years were a little rocky; but by around fourth or fifth grade, they grew in independence, and were able to manage all of their homework completely on their own.

One day, when my daughter, Abigail, was in third grade, she woke up, walked into the kitchen, and said, "Mom, I need a soda bottle. I have a book report I have to do on Abraham Lincoln." I asked her, "When is it due?" She said, "Today!" I, then, asked her, "Did you read the book?" "No," she said, "I am going to read it later." Well, she didn't even have the book—and what made it even worse was that it was her ninth birthday! The previous night, she had watched a movie for her birthday; and the week before (which was our school's winter break), she had all the time in the world to complete her project. But, she failed to tell us!

Now, I had a choice to make between two options. One, I could have kept her home from school, figured out how to get her book report done —and take her to school later, with a completed book report. Or, I could let her face the music. I could send her to school, as the only student without the assignment completed, on her birthday, then expect her to read the book, and turn in her report late. Michael and I chose the latter.

Why? Because one day, when Abby says she is going to come over for Christmas dinner and bring a salad, I want to be able to count on her to bring the salad! Granted, she was only in third grade, but learning personal responsibility begins at a young age.

At one point or another, all of my children have experienced something similar to Abby. But, Michael and I have made a decision to not bail our children out of their personal mistakes and failures. Instead, we have allowed them to suffer the consequences, and learn from them— so they can grow their character as they learn personal responsibility!

Friendships
Another area moms micromanage their children's lives is friendships. Today, parents are very concerned with who their children's friends are, and rightfully so. After all, there are many different parenting styles and so many things our children can be exposed to if we are not careful—and it is so important that our children's friends are ones who compliment what is taught in our homes. Scripture reminds us in Proverbs 12:26, "The righteous should choose his friends carefully, for the way of the wicked leads them astray." We don't want our children to be led astray by their choice of friends.

In light of this truth, many moms today over-control their children's friendships, ensuring that their children choose friends carefully. In fact, these moms often put their children's social life above their own. They not only choose their children's friends, but they also invite them over for playdates, and manage every detail of their children's social life.

Think about it: Can you recall your parents organizing play dates for you? Or, your grandparents for your mother? My mom didn't ever seem to have time for coffee dates herself, let alone to schedule play dates for me.

Now, there is nothing wrong with inviting your children's friends over to play. However, there are some moms who literally manage every detail of their children's friendships and social activities. What kind of message are they giving their children, when they revolve their whole life around their children's social interactions?

When my children were little, their friends were the children of the women I was friends with—usually people from church. When my friend came over, she would bring her children with her. Our children would play together, and naturally become friends. Or, I would serve with a woman at church, and our children would hang out together and become friends. As my children grew older, they would ask to invite certain school or church friends to our home to play—and we would have them over occasionally. During all these years, I have never looked for friends for my children, or asked their parents if our children could get together to play. I hardly have time to manage my own social life, let alone those of my children.

Often, women at school or church tell me, "Oh, I want my child to play with your child." And, I have to tell them, "I don't have time to organize play dates for my children. But, if you want to come over for coffee, or would like me to babysit your children, you are welcome to stop by, or bring your children to my house so they can play with my children." While this is unusual by today's standards, it is how things have been done during times past.

Don't forget that if we are diligent in managing our children's circles of influence, we can give them the freedom to make choices about their friendships. Our job is simply to guide them through these relationships, not form or manage them.

Sometimes, guidance is not enough—and we need to get involved! In fact, there have been times when I have had to get involved with my children's friendships. I can think of a time when a young boy who was indulged and not disciplined at home became attached to my son. This boy always asked for my son to come over and play—and when my son came home from playing with his friend, he always acted like a different person. After trying to train my son in how to behave around his friend, I finally had to stop him from going over to his friend's house.

As mothers, we must remember that we are responsible to God for our children's character. 1 Corinthians 15:33 declares: "Bad company corrupts good morals." Many children fall away from God, or become corrupt in character, because of bad friendships. We should care more about the character of our children than about hurting another mom's feelings because we will not allow our children to play with their son or daughter.

If your children have good circles of influence, the probability of them having good friends is very high—as their friends' families should all have the same values as yours. Then, your role is simply to help your children navigate through their friendships. However, if your children are not in good circles of influence, then it will be hard for you to allow your children to be independent in this area.

Activities

Another way parents over-control their children's lives is by signing them up for too many activities. Today, many parents feel pressured to put their children into sports and competitive leagues from a very young age. They have this idea that, if they don't get their children playing the sport of their choice early enough, they will be left behind, and they won't be successful at any sport when they are older. This idea—which is now an American ideal—is a new, twenty-first century standard that our culture has placed upon parents. The reason? Many people believe it is due to the compulsory schooling laws, the self-esteem movement, and the pressure parents face to get their children into good colleges![4] As parents, we really need to think about the vision we have for our children's lives. Will sports and other activities help or hinder us in fulfilling this vision?

When we fill up our children's time with activities like sports, music lessons, foreign language classes, art classes—and do this for multiple children— our lives begin to revolve around our children's schedules. It is important for us moms to realize that life has not always been this way! The pressure to do this is a new one. One hundred years ago, moms did not sign their children up for tons of activities and spend all their leisure time watching their children perform. Today, the result is exhausted parents and entitled children.

When our own children were little, Michael and I signed them all up to play soccer. For weeks, we would spend all our free time running them to and from practices during the week, and every Saturday watching their games. The entire time I thought: I really should be home doing laundry, catching up on housework, spending time with my husband and children, etc. And, if I was too busy to go to a game, I felt so guilty! It was only after reading *Parenting by the Book* that I realized I was following the culture's standards for moms, not the biblical standard.

God's Word does not tell us to give our children every opportunity the world has to offer. Instead, it tells us to train them up in the fear and admonition of the Lord (Ephesians 6:4). It tells us to teach them God's Word and what it means to live righteously. In *Parenting by the Book*, John Rosemond writes, "Does football train up this child in the way he should go? No it does not. That training can only be properly done within what I call the 'classroom of the family.'"5

Rosemond also discusses the importance of "Team Family." As a culture, we are so focused on team sports, team activities, and team projects; but the greatest team our children can be a part of is the family. Rosemond goes on to say, "the very best of all contexts in which to learn to be a team player is within one's own family, by doing chores, by obeying the rules, by carrying out instructions properly, by sharing with siblings, and so on."6 God created the family to be the center of society— and we should not sacrifice our family time for a team sport or some other activity!

Now, I am not anti-activity! Before signing our children up for any activity, Michael and I prayerfully consider what they will be committed to—what is the purpose of the activity? Just because our children want to sign up for something doesn't mean they get to! In fact, most of the time they don't. Currently, I have two children enrolled in music lessons, so they can learn to lead worship; two of my children are training for a Spartan Race, to be physically fit; and two others play volleyball for our school team, to keep them from having idle time after school. These three activities do not take time away from our family, and they do not cause me to become a frenzied driver shuttling my children around town!

I once read a fascinating article in *Good Housekeeping,* about Shane and Julie Good, who lived in a school bus with their six children. When asked why they lived this way, Julie said, "I never saw my parents when I was growing up, because I was so busy with activities." Julie did so many activities as a child that she did not feel like she knew her parents or siblings. Now, it may seem a bit drastic for a family of eight to live in a school bus, but the point is that family matters! What is your goal for your your family and children? Do you want them to become world famous athletes? Or, do you want your sons to be husbands who love and lead their family with God's love? Or, your daughters to be wives who raise godly children? The decisions we make today for our family and our time will determine who our children will be in the future.

The *Good Housekeeping* article, Shane and Julie Good went on to say that, "The greatest lesson in our family is learning is to respect and love one another."[7] I can attest that the time Michael and I have invested into "Team Family"—spending time together and communicating our values— has enabled our children to grow very close, and to hold the same values we do! I find great peace in knowing that my grandchildren will be raised with the same values that Michael and I hold, because we have taken the time to pass these values on to our children—rather than waste all our time on meaningless activities. You cannot put a price tag on this assurance!

Screen Time

Many moms don't realize it, but too much screen time is another way they micromanage their children—as it allows them to know where their children are, and what they are doing. Many children are allowed to play video games, watch whatever they want on unlimited television, and interact with whomever they choose on the internet! The reason: the children are home, and not doing something they shouldn't be doing. A mom can feel a sort of safety, knowing her child is tucked away in their room on some sort of electronic device.

A couple of years ago, I spoke with a mom who struggled with having her children home all summer. She allowed them to play violent video games all day long because it kept them busy, and she knew where they were. One of the big lies of our culture, however, is that our children are "safe" if they are behind a screen—but nothing could be further from the truth. Whatever technology our children engage with either reprograms their brain, molds and shapes their worldview, feeds their lustful cravings, numbs them to reality, or all and above .

Not only that, screen time keeps our children from the many benefits of play. Many mothers have told me that their children have been taken captive by technology. In fact, their children don't know what to do with their free time when the devices are taken away. Not only that, they have a hard time engaging with other children their age because the only thing these children want to talk about on the playground is the latest video game or meme.

Allowing our children to become independent might mean that we are allowing them to ride bikes to the local grocery store to buy a slurpy, ride skateboards to the park to play basketball with friends, set up a lemonade stand in the front yard, or even have a nerf gun war in the backyard. When we have allowed our children to develop their character, we don't have to worry about allowing them to play like children once did in the past!

Phones

One of the biggest ways moms micromanage their children today is by giving them phones. Even young children today have phones for "safety reasons." We live in a dangerous world, and phones allow moms to track their children or get ahold of them at any moment of the day. However, I am convinced that the advantages of a phone do not outweigh the negative impact these devices have on our children.

If your children have character, they will be honest about where they are, and they will be home when they tell you they will be. Our society has functioned this way for thousands of years—and our children's lives have been better off! When we track our children's every move, they do not feel trusted, and this perceived lack of trust can become a huge frustration in our relationships with them. Trusting our children is part of allowing them to become independent.

You might be wondering, "What if something happens to my child? What if there is an emergency? If my child has a phone, I will know exactly where they are and be able to get hold of them. Or, they can get ahold of me." However, we must realize that in today's world everyone has a phone, and if something were to happen, our children would have access to a friend's or another adult's phone.

Today, many moms feel pressured to give their children phones as soon as they start school. In fact, it is almost looked down upon if her elementary students do not own a phone. But, students have been going to the school office to call their parents for years—and they can still do so today.

In our home, Michael and I allow our children to get a phone when they have need of one and are old enough to pay for it themselves. But, they are not allowed to have internet access on their phone, as it can create bad habits, and does not cultivate family relationships. Currently, our oldest son, Daniel, is our only child with a phone. He was seventeen when he began using an old cellphone to text and make calls. It cost him $15 a month to use.

As parents raising godly children in a free country, we do not want to train our children to think that the only time they are safe is when they are tracked. Think about what our culture would be like if every child was raised to believe that it is the responsibility of those in authority to track them? Sounds a bit like *1984*, doesn't it?

Getting a Job

Not allowing our children to get a job is another way parents micromanage their children today. Often, parents over-manage their children's schedules, so their children do not have time to get a job. Jobs tend to get in the way of after-school sports, activities, and homework. Studies have shown that fewer and fewer high school students get jobs during the summer, because parents are concerned that jobs will interfere with vacations, special summer schools, and other activities.

However, children who learn to balance school, work, and friendships are better prepared for life after high school.

Today, many parents give their children allowances, money, and whatever else they need—so why would they need a job? In our school and church community, families struggle to find babysitters because teenage girls no longer need a job. If they need money, their parents give it to them. These "handouts" are extremely detrimental. The girls do not learn the value of a dollar, and they do not learn to work hard to earn money. In my experience, when we cast a vision for our children's life, and teach them how to serve rather than wasting time, we won't be able to keep our children from working, as they will be filled with an entrepreneurial spirit!

My husband, Michael, often thanks my mom and dad for making me go out and find a job at the age of fifteen, because it taught me to work hard, know the value of the dollar, and learn the skills I would later need to balance our crazy life. Jobs teach our children valuable skills that they need to learn—sooner rather than later.

Life Skills

Today, many young men and women leave home unprepared for life. They do not know how to cook, clean, do laundry, or manage money, because their parents did not train them to do these things. In many cases, mom was so busy making life—playdates, sports, activities— happen for her children, that training in basic life skills was neglected.

One of my friends told me that her daughter constantly bought new clothes while she was in college, rather than going to the laundromat to do laundry. She did not know how to do laundry. She and her mom spent so much time traveling around the country for her competitive sports games that she missed out on learning the valuable homemaking and basic life sills of cooking, cleaning, doing laundry, and managing money. These are all basic skills that should be taught at home.

Making a Mess
As we allow our children to become independent, they must learn a lot of lessons—and these lessons can often become messy. Our children will spill milk, ruin laundry, break valuable treasures, and fail at projects. Things will not be done the way we want them to be done all the time. But, these messes are a necessary part of becoming independent human beings.

One of my daughters is currently learning how to cook. She received a cookbook for Christmas, and is learning to gather ingredients, follow directions, and clean the dishes. Just yesterday, she caught the oven on fire—literally! Yet, if I want her to help me in the kitchen, I have to allow her to experiment and learn, even if it is messy. Over the years, I have lost a lot of dishes. Rather than get upset, anytime one of my children breaks a china plate or cup, we store the pieces in a cupboard to someday make a mosaic.

Personal Responsibility

One of the most important things we can teach our children is personal responsibility! This life skill includes: organizing their backpack, packing their lunch, doing their homework, cleaning up their messes, doing their laundry, keeping their room clean, remembering to bring home their water bottle, and keeping track of their jacket at school. When our children come home from school, where do they put their shoes, backpacks, and jackets? Where and when do they do their homework? Our children must learn to take responsibility for these things and others from a young age if they are going to be successful in life.

As parents, it is our responsibility to train our children to take on these responsibilities, and we hold them accountable when they fail to follow through. Currently, my children owe me a dollar every time they leave their shoes on the mudroom floor rather than putting them away in their basket. These dollars are my coffee money, and the consequence motivates my children to create good habits.

Years ago, one of my children had a rotten sandwich in their backpack for quite some time, and it began to get really smelly at school. Her teacher found the sandwich in my daughter's backpack, and was afraid to tell me. She thought I would feel like a bad mother. However, when our goal is teach our children personal responsibility, we parents are freed from the guilt that comes whenever our children makes a mess, flunks a test, goes hungry because they forgot their lunch, or leaves a rotten sandwich in their backpack. These messes are how they learn.

Dealing with Conflict

One very important way we allow our children to become independent is by guiding them through personal conflict. The Bible gives us a very clear path for dealing with conflict. If we cannot cover an offense with love, Matthew 18 teaches us to go to the person who has offended us, and share the offense with them with love and humility. Most of the time, doing so will settle the matter. However, if the person gets mad, disagrees, or refuses to make things right, we are then supposed to take someone else with us to confront the person about the issue. Conflict resolution is such a wonderful gift we can give our children, as so many young adults today do not know how to deal with conflict—in fact, when it arises, they run!

Growing Their Faith

It is critical that we allow our children to grow in their faith while they are at home. Samuel could not live on Hannah's faith during his life; he needed to make his faith his own. As mothers, we need to allow our children to develop their own relationship with God. Taking our children to church and having them read the Bible on their own is important, but we must also allow them to grow in faith as they attend church events, participate in church activities, and partake in the sacraments, like baptism and communion.

When Daniel was in Kindergarten, our church had a baptism after church one Sunday. He begged and begged me, as we stood in the lobby, to get baptized. He knew what baptism meant, but I thought he was too young. While Daniel begged me, a precious saint in the church who saw what was happening proceeded to tell me, "Don't ever stop your children from doing anything that will advance their faith in God." What an awesome word from the Lord—and it has been my motto for all my children since that day! Whether it is a church camp, a bible study, or a missions trip—if God has put it on my children's heart—they are going. And, even if it is not their idea, they are going—as their relationship with God is the most important relationship they will ever develop in their life.

Going to Church Camp

Some parents micromanage their children's lives by not allowing them to go to church camp, or participate in other church youth events. Often, this decision is driven by fear—the drive to camp is too long; the weather is bad; it's too expensive; they might get sick; they don't want to go, and I don't want to force them to go, because they might resent me or God. Rather than allowing fear to rule us, we must have faith, and send our children to camp or other church events, praying and trusting that God will break through into our children's lives.

Words cannot express how impactful church camps are for our youth. These camps are times when our children can go away for a few days to be saturated with God's Word and presence. My life and my husband's life were both transformed when we attended camps as youth, and our children have experienced the same! At camp, our children have not only encountered God, but they have made Christian friends, and have become more plugged in to church.

Camp truly does change the course of a child's life! When my son Josh entered sixth grade, he had such a negative attitude, and he was really hard to be around. That year, I could not wait to send him to camp! A few days before he left, he was driving me crazy. I told him, "Josh, you had better come home from camp a different person." Well, he experienced God, and came home completely changed! Later, he told me, "I didn't know how I was going to come home different; but after experiencing God, I knew that I could." Usually, the children who do not go to camp are the ones who need it the most.

A few years ago, I taught a seventh and eighth grade combo class. One afternoon, each student had the opportunity to share their testimony. Seven out of the twelve students declared that they grew up in the church, yet it wasn't until they went to camp the summer before sixth grade that they really made their faith their own. I know it is often hard for parents to let their children go to camp—as it can be costly, and so many things can happen. However, a decision to surrender their life to Christ is priceless—especially as they enter the rocky middle school years.

I remember a time in sixth grade that I did not want to go to church. My parents insisted—in fact, they made me go to a Winter Camp, literally crying, kicking, and screaming, too! Looking back, this was one of the best decisions they ever made for my life. I met all sorts of new friends, and from then on, my parents couldn't keep me away from church. I fell in love with God, and never turned back!

Now, I am not saying that you should send your children to camp blindly. Find out where the camp is located, who is speaking, who the leaders are, etc. Talk to other children who have gone to camp before, as well as their families, to see what their experiences were. If you hear good reports, send them! And, if you send your children and they experience God, they will come back changed.

Going on Missions Trips

Another way to allow our children to become independent is by sending them on a church missions trips. Like camp, mission trips are wonderful opportunities for God to transform our children's lives. Not only will they see that others' lives are very different from their own, they will also see how they can impact the world around them for God's glory. Sending our children on missions trip with a group of people from church is a great way to help them grow in their relationship with the Lord and with others.

I recently spoke with a high school mom who would not allow her son to participate in an upcoming mission trip. She was afraid to send her son to another country—as so much could go wrong. Her response is one rooted in fear, yet she—like each of us—is called to be a woman of faith, making decisions in faith, not fear! Our children are watching, and know whether we make decisions out of faith or fear. (Since then, her son went on the missions trip, and his life was transformed!)

Launching Your Children

Launching our children into adulthood does not begin when our children turn eighteen. It begins while they become a teenager, and earlier. The teenage years are mentoring years, and the things we require of our children should help them grow to independence.

Teenagers

Today, most parents dread their children becoming "teenagers." In fact, many believe that, once their child is a teen, all they can expect is arguing, rebellion, and expense. However, this expectation is a modern one. When we raise children as Hannah did—casting a vision for their lives, training them through discipline, allowing them to serve, allowing them to live without—we can expect our children's teenage years to be years of productivity within our home, church, and community. They will be a time when we can reap the fruit of the years we have poured into the lives of our children when they were young!

Michael and I are blessed to have four teenagers in our home—with two more coming right behind them! These teenage years have brought so much joy to our home. Not only are our children working independently at home, church, and school, which is such blessing to us and to others; but they are also a joy to be around! All of our teenagers have big dreams and plans that they are working towards. These years are the years we can reap the harvest of the labor Michael and I have diligently sowed in the lives of our children!

Choices

Today, there is a lot of confusion about what we should allow our teenage children to decide. When our children are younger, we really should make all of the decisions: what they eat, where they go, who they go with, what they watch, what activities they do, etc. As they get older, we need to slowly allow our children to start making their own choices. But, parents must discipline and train their children in the early years, so that they will have the wisdom to make wise choices as teenagers.

Today, most teenagers are not making choices that will benefit them in the long run. Rather, they are making decisions that make them happy in the moment, as that is what they have been trained to do by all the little decisions their parents have allowed them to make throughout their childhood. These decisions affect how they spend their time and money, as well as how they approach their jobs, commitments, and relationships.

As parents, we must prayerfully consider what decisions we will allow our teenagers to make, which depends upon the training we have given them in their younger years. However, there are some things that are non-negotiable. If our teenagers are living at home, they must:

- Go to church and attend church camps or events
- Screen what they watch
- Get a job
- Learn to manage their money—including tithing 10% and saving
- Go to whatever high school or college you decide they will attend (especially if you are paying the bill)

We can err in two ways during our children's teenage years: continuing to micromanage our children's every move, or allowing them to make every decision for their life. During the teenage years, we we need to slowly allow our children to make decisions, as we see they are capable of making wise choices. As I wrote this chapter, I asked my teenagers which choices they are making on their own. They responded, "We don't really make any choices on our own. They have all been made for us, while we are young—and we are okay with it!" Michael and I do not have to fight with our children over the decisions they make or want to make, because they have learned to be wise about their choices. Early training has guided them in deciding what to wear, what to watch, what activities to participate in, who to date, who to hang out with, and so on. Therefore, we do not have to keep managing them as teenagers.

We should not be surprised if we have to do some training in our children's teenage years to compensate for something we missed when they were younger. For instance, if we failed to train our children to properly manage money, we will have to retrain them as teenagers. If we didn't share with them what type of person to look for in a spouse, we will need to do so before we let them start dating. This can get really messy, so we must use discernment and spend much time in prayer! As we don't want to push our children away during these years. If your child happens to come home with a tattoo, it is not the time to tell them how much we disapprove of tattoos. We should have let them know much earlier! If our children start behaving in ways we disapprove—because we failed to teach them our values—then we have to be careful about how we respond, as we can be the ones at fault- for failing to teach them! We must train our children to know our values while they are young, so they will have the wisdom to make right decisions when they are older.

If we do not allow our children to become independent in the teenage years, we cannot be surprised if they are not ready to make it once we have launched them into the world!

Personal Responsibility
During the teenage years, it is very important to allow our children to suffer the consequences of their actions. If they break their phone, have them pay to replace it. If they get a speeding ticket, make sure they pay for it. If they mismanage their money, don't bail them out—as this failure will help them become responsible and financially independent. Sometimes, our children do not deserve a situation or consequence that happened. As parents of teenagers, we need to support and be there for them, but we must not rescue them if we want them to learn personal responsibility. God may be using the situation or consequence to teach them something.

During this season, we need to really be women of prayer. We shouldn't say everything we think- as we don't want our children to run from us. We can hold a standard for the big things, the important, non-negotiables, and pray about the little things. It is important that we, as parents, do not major on the minors, nor sweat the small stuff. If our teenager does not want to iron their shirt or tuck it in, that's okay! If you don't like their hair or clothes style, just smile- as long as it is not inappropriate for your house standards. We need to maintain our relationship with our children: have fun; enjoy them! They do not want us to be constantly nit-picking and nagging them. Remember, they are growing to independence!

Dating

One of the biggest decisions our children will ever make is who they will date and, eventually, marry. So often, parents do not take the time they should to prepare their children for this monumental event.

In our home, training in this area starts early, as we cast a vision for marriage and future children while our children are young. In fact, Michael and I began praying for our children's spouses from the time they were born. As they become old enough to pray, they join us in praying for a godly spouse. Then, as our children have grown, we have pointed out good examples of boys and girls with godly and virtuous character, who would make good spouses.

We have also taken each of our children through Dennis and Barbara Rainey's *Passport to Purity,* once they have reached middle school. What we love about this series is that each child goes away with one of their parents to learn learn about what to expect in their teenage years. We discuss peer pressure, sex, and all that comes with these things. *Passport to Purity* is a great way to start a conversation about dating and marriage with your children. At the end of their *Passport to Purity* weekend, each of my boys have decided on their own that they will not date until they are eighteen—and dad and mom say they are ready to date. We have already bypassed so much drama because of this wonderful resource. I give it my highest recommendation!

After High School

I recently read an article in the *Wall Street Journal* that explored how today's parents are struggling to launch their adult children into the world. Even after college, parents are struggling to get their children to find a job and move out of the house. In fact, some parents are paying their children to leave their home. And then, when they finally do move out around the age of twenty-seven, many times they come back—they become "boomerang children"![8] Children have become an endless outflow of cash, and today's parents are wondering if they will ever be free. This failure to launch is really a recent phenomenon, and is usually a result of inadequately preparing children to be launched.

Right now, I am in the process of launching my older children. But, my parents successfully laughed three children—and I am the result. How did they do it? They started by teaching me how to live without, and letting me go while I was young. Then, when I reached high school, they made me work to pay for my own gas, clothes, food, etc. My parents made me go to college, and they let me know they were looking forward to the day I successfully moved out of the house.

It is absolutely necessary that parents have a launching plan for their children, but there is not one perfect launching plan. Your plan will depend largely upon your family values, as well as your economic status. The McClure family launching plan after high school is as follows:

- Our children can live at home as long as they go to college full-time, or are enrolled in a full-time trade school.
- They must pay for their own car, car insurance, and gas.
- They must pay for their own schooling.
- As long as they live at home, they must be home by 11 p.m.
- Our children must have a job, but they must not on Sundays—as it is the Lord's day.
- They must attend church with the family.
- They must be home for family devotion night (to keep family unity).

Once our children graduate, they are welcome to remain in our home for a specific amount of time. But, they must have a goal they are working towards, and they must be willing to pay rent.

Our launching plans should not be lists of impossible requirements, especially if our children have already learned the value of hard work, money management, and self-discipline with their time and resources! We don't want our children to find our homes too comfortable—or they will never want to leave.

Our children should know the launching plan well before they turn eighteen. We should first tell them about the plan in their childhood, so they have time to get fully onboard. Children love and need to know what is expected of them. As teenagers, our children should begin this plan by working a job, and by paying for their car expenses, their own clothes, entertainment, and such. Then, when they graduate from high school, they will already be doing much of what is required of them, just adding school tuition to their responsibilities. By clearly communicating and implementing our launching plan, our children can rest, rather than rebel, when things suddenly change at eighteen.

So, what happens when our teenagers decide they do not want to follow the launching plan? Maybe they don't want to go to church, or they decide to quit their job. If our children decide to rebel, then they are no longer welcome to live in our home. Remember Joshua, who declared, "as for me and my house, we will serve the LORD" (Joshua 24:15). If our children are going to live in our house, they must to honor God in everything! We cannot afford to let our children live by a standard other than God's, and still live in our home—as God will hold us responsible. I believe that this double standard is one of the biggest mistakes many parents are making today.

College

Let's consider colleges, particularly Christian colleges. Current statistics and personal testimonies are proving that many Christian children going to colleges today are choosing to walk away from their faith—whether they are attending Christian or non-Christian colleges! Ken Ham addresses this alarming trend is his book, *Already Gone*. He states that two-thirds of Christian children walk away from their faith after attending college. Although these statistics are not new, Christian parents spend thousands of dollars every year, sending their precious children away from home to be indoctrinated by liberal ideas and beliefs!

Unfortunately, many Christian universities have succumbed to the pressures of "political correctness" for funding or to be more attractive to more students. Professors who do not believe in miracles or the authority of God's Word are actively undermining our children's faith.

As parents, we need to decide what we desire for our children. Is their career more important than their faith? Is attending a prominent college more important than the type of person they become? We might believe our children are strong enough to not become a part of the two-thirds statistic, but they are not! At the age of eighteen, our children, still deciding who they are and what they believe, are easily influenced, and very impressionable.

In the past, when students went off to college, their faith was tested and tried in the classroom, and became strengthened—as it did for Michael and me. However, colleges today are very different than the ones we attended. Today, there is an all-out assault on the Christian faith. The pressure our children experience in college is not like anything we once experienced. And, if we have not adequately prepared them for the battle, they will fold under the pressure.

Even more alarming, many Christian children leave home to go to college, and end up unplugged from Christian community—never to go back. In *Already Gone*, children who had been raised in the church were asked why they stopped attending during or after college. Twenty-five percent stated, "I moved to college and stopped attending church." Twenty-three percent mentioned that their "work responsibilities prevented [them] from attending," and twenty-two percent stated that they "moved too far away from the church to continue attending."[9] In other words, if our children are not plugged into a church by high school, or if they move away from their home church to attend college, the chance these students will leave the church is very high. And, once they leave, they rarely come back.

Over the years, Michael and I have found that children who live in their parents' homes and stay plugged in to their church community usually have the support they need to navigate college. With the support of their family and church, they are able to identify and withstand the lies and political agenda they are constantly bombarded with in the classroom.

If you believe God has called your children to leave your home to attend college, I encourage you to pray and fast for God's confirmation. Wait to send your children until you receive a word from Him that it is actually His will for their life. Once God gives the go-ahead, take the time to openly share your concerns with your children. Let them know what to watch out for, help them find a good church community close to the school, and make sure you stay connected to your child.

As parents, we should not be afraid to send our children to college. But, we do need to retain our relationship with them. Remember, we become our children's mentors and friends during this season of their lives. We cannot disengage from our children's lives when they go to college. We must continue to be involved in their lives—calling them, talking to them about the decisions they make, asking them how are they spending their time. Our job is to keep them accountable in their church attendance, friendships, and, most importantly, relationship with Christ. Our children still need our wisdom and guidance after we have launched them—now, more than ever!

Eric Liddell

A wonderful example of a man who set out to do God's work was Eric Liddell. Not only a famous Olympic runner, he was also a missionary to China. But, he didn't become either by waiting for his parents to forge a path for him. No, they allowed him to grow to independence!

Eric Liddell did not become a famous Olympic star because his parents put him into a competitive running league or made sure he had every opportunity to become the best. In fact, they did the opposite. They sent Eric away to boarding school at the age of eight, while they served God in China. After a life of hardships, hard work, and sacrifice, Eric Liddell had the character necessary to handle the pressures of becoming an Olympic runner, and to stand by his conviction to not run on Sundays.

Though he "[felt] God's pleasure" when he ran, it was not running or becoming an Olympic star that was the most important thing in Eric Liddell's life. God was. He gave everything up to follow his parents' example, to serve God on the mission field of China.

When we look back at history, there are very few men who became world-changers because their parents paved the way for them. Eric Liddell's parents did not over-concern themselves with Eric's academic or social achievements. Instead, they believed his relationship with God was paramount. Their faith in God drove them to make sacrifices that directly affected their son's life and destiny. As moms, we must seek the kingdom of God ourselves before we train our children to know that God is more important than anything.

Remember Our Vision

In our day to day lives, we often lose sight of the vision God has given us for our children. Remember, our vision is to raise up men and women of character, who fear God and use their gifts and abilities to build the kingdom of God on earth. Our vision is children who become husbands and wives that honor and respect their spouses, and reflect God's glory in their marriage. Our vision is godly grandchildren, who desire to conquer this world for God's glory. Do not lose sight of this vision!

Our children will naturally become independent individuals who desire to be God's voice to this lost and dying world if we, as mothers, live a life of faith, love our children, teach them to pray, fight to keep them before God's presence, saturate them in God's Word, cast a vision for their life, teach them to serve, teach them to live without, teach them to discern God's voice, and allow them to develop their character.

Made to Soar

One of the most beautiful sights to behold is an eagle soaring in the sky, as Proverbs 30:18-19 attests. Yet, for an eagle to soar, it must first gain its independence from the nest.

When a mother eagle is expecting babies, she prepares a nest high up in the sky. She uses sticks, thorns, and branches to create a nest base before lining the egg-shaped bowl with Spanish moss, grasses, and feathers to create a soft cushion for her babies. For about thirty-six days, the mother eagle keeps her eggs warm and cozy, until they are ready to hatch. After they hatch, she feeds her babies, and takes care of them— but, they can't stay in the nest forever. They were made to fly!

Baby eagles fledge (or learn to fly) when they are about ten to twelve weeks old. But, an eaglet left on its own will never learn to fly. The mother eagle must encourage her little ones to jump out of the nest. She does this by first taking away the nest's warm cushion. Then, she nudges her little ones to the sides of the nest, where she pushes them out one by one. Once the eaglets are out of the nest, they learn to fly; and, once they can fly, they are soon ready to soar!

As mothers, we must realize that our children were made to soar, too. Allowing our children to become independent will take work—as it will not be natural for us. Just as the mother eagle began by making the nest uncomfortable, we will have to do the same in our homes. We might need to nudge and push our children to do things that are uncomfortable, but it is a part of growing older! Once our children are completely independent, and actively building God's kingdom on their own, we will have the joy and delight of watching them soar. And we will declare that watching our children soar is almost too wonderful for us to behold!

Questions to Consider

1. Are you a micromanaging mom? If so, what drives you to be so involved in your child's life?

2. What fears are you experiencing as you raise your children? Are they driving your decisions? How can you trust God more with your children's lives?

3. In what areas of your children's lives are you not allowing them to be independent?

4. Do your children's circles of influence reflect your family's values? How might you enable all of your children's circles of influence to complement your home?

5. How can you encourage your children to grow and develop their faith?

6. What life skills do your children need to work on to become more independent?

7. What choices are you allowing your children to make that could possibly lead to wrong choices being made as they grow older?

8. Do you and your husband have a launching plan for your children? If not, when do you think you can put one together? The sooner the better.

Notes

[1] Corrie ten Boom, "Good Reads," accessed July 20, 109, https://www.goodreads.com/quotes/28322-hold-everything-in-your-hands-lightly-otherwise-it-hurts-when

[2] Kate Bayless, "What is Helicopter Parenting," Parents Magazine, Updated: September 26, 2018, accessed July 20, 2019, https://www.parents.com/parenting/better-parenting/what-is-helicopter-parenting/

[3] George Mueller, quoted in *Streams in the Desert* (Grand Rapids, Michigan: Zondervan Publishing House, 1925), 294. 11.

[4] Hilary Levey Friedman, "When Did Competitive Sports Take Over American Childhood?" September 20, 2013, theatlantic.com, accessed July 20, 2019, https://www.theatlantic.com/education/archive/2013/09/when-did-competitive-sports-take-over-american-childhood/279868/

[5] John *Parenting by the Book* (New York, New York: Howard Books, 2007), 162-163.

[6] Ibid., 162.

[7] Cory Stieg, "This Family of 9 Calls a School Bus Home," goodhousekeeping.com July 20, 2016, accessed July 20, 2019, https://www.goodhousekeeping.com/life/a39481/housekeeping-on-edge-bus-home/

[8] Rosemond, *Parenting by the Book,* 174.

[9] Ken Ham and Britt Beemer, *Already Gone* (Arkansas: Master Books, 2009), 30.

Pearl of Wisdom #12
Discipline Your Children

Correct your son, and he will give you rest;
Yes, he will give delight to your soul.

Proverbs 29:17

God's Word does not tell us that Hannah disciplined Samuel, yet we can tell he was disciplined based upon his obedience when she dropped him off at the Tabernacle and, later, through the obedience he displayed toward Eli on the evening God spoke to Samuel. That evening, when Samuel heard God's voice, he immediately rose from his sleep, and ran to Eli. This obedience to come when called was the result of direct training. Matthew Henry writes:

> That [Samuel] had learned the spirit of true religion, is
> indicated by his instantaneous obedience, and the habit of
> obedience became a valuable guide to him in the perplexities of
> that eventful hour. He runs to Eli, and says, "Here am I, for
> thou didst call me;" and though this is three times repeated, yet
> he seems nothing loath to leave his warm bed, and run to his
> foster-father, to see if he could get him any comfort that his old
> age might require during the night, or otherwise do his bidding
> —a sure sign that the child had acquired the healthy principle of
> obedience though he did not understand the mystery of the
> prophetic call. [1]

Samuel's obedience was a sign of his character, which could only have come through biblical discipline. Though he must have been tired, he did not stumble out of bed and sleepily walk over to Eli. Instead, he ran to Eli—three times!   And then, when he finally recognized the voice as God's, he obeyed, and delivered a terrible message to Eli about the future destruction of Eli's family.   If we want our children to hear and obey God's voice, like Samuel, we must train our children through biblical discipline!

The Importance of Engaging
In contrast to Samuel and his obedience to God, Eli's two sons, who were also raised in the Tabernacle, are described as "wicked men...having no regard for the Lord" (1 Samuel 2:12, BSB). Eli's sons were known for stealing meat from the peoples' sacrifices (1 Samuel 2:13-17) and having sex with women in the Tabernacle (1 Samuel 2:22). Their sin "was very

great before the LORD (1 Samuel 2:17)—and what is worse, Eli knew about it, ignored their behavior, and failed to discipline them (1 Samuel 2:22-25). Because of Eli's lack of engagement, God's reputation was at stake: "men abhorred the offering of the LORD" (1 Samuel 2:17). Eli's failure to a discipline his sons left a sour taste for God in the mouths of the people of Israel.

Our failure to restrain our children does the same today. As parents, it is so easy to be like Eli, and ignore our children's bad behavior. However, God's reputation is at stake. When we fail to engage and discipline our children—and people know we are Christians—not only do our children suffer bad character, but God's reputation and our testimony are maligned.

Scripture does not tell us why Eli did not restrain his sons. Perhaps he was too tired to engage, or not disciplined himself, partaking in the same sins as his sons. Maybe he wanted his children to like him, and thought he would gain their approval by not restraining them. Whatever the case, Eli was honoring his sons more than he was honoring God.

In 1 Samuel 2:29, God questioned Eli, "Why do you kick at My sacrifice and My offering which I have commanded in My dwelling place, and honor your sons more than Me, to make yourselves fat with the best of all the offerings of Israel My people?" Here, "honor" means "fear." Eli feared his sons more than he feared God.

As parents, we must honor or fear God more than our children. Proverbs 29:25 states, "The fear of man brings a snare, but whoever trusts in the LORD shall be safe." A "snare" is a noose used to catch wild beasts and birds, or an iron ring put through the nostrils of a beast. When we fear our children rather than God, we are, literally, taken captive—caught by a noose of our own making or pulled along by the iron ring of our children's whims and desires like Eli. When we do not discipline our children, we suffer in our captivity, and our children (and the generations following them) suffer a life of devastation.

Proverbs 14:26 declares, "In the fear of the LORD there is strong confidence, and His children will have a place of refuge." Fearing God, enables us and our children to have a place of refuge in this unstable world. What a gift!

I am sure that Eli thought he had a good excuse for not disciplining his sons—most parents do. However, as parents, we must engage with and discipline our children. If we do not, we will reap terrible consequences. Believe me, as a mother of seven children, I know how exhausting engaging and disciplining children can be. Sometimes we are so exhausted that we just want to lie on the couch, and shout commands at our children without making sure they listen or stop what they are doing. However, parenting from the couch does not work. Even when we feel too tired to discipline, we must get up off the couch and engage. Otherwise, our children will never learn how to govern themselves.

Sometimes, bad behavior looks adorable when our children are young, but that behavior does not look so cute when they are teenagers or

adults. Bad habits, left unchecked, will always lead to destruction.
Proverbs 19:18 reminds us to "[c]hasten your son while there is hope, and
do not set your heart on his destruction." When we fail to restrain our
children through discipline and biblical training, our children are
destined to suffer. If we desire righteous children, and want our future
generations to be blessed, we must engage with our children now,
especially when they are young.

It is important to note that failure to restrain our children is not only
bad parenting, but it is also a sin on our part. Like Eli, God will hold us
accountable for our children's behavior. Our lack of discipline will lead to
punishment for our children by God, as well as our own punishment for
lack of engagement. Considering Eli and his sons, F.B. Meyer writes,
"Better to do less in the Church and the world than allow your children to
grow up a misery to themselves and a reproach to you."[2] We must
discipline our children!

Our Sinful Nature

As parents, it doesn't take long for us to realize that our children are
sinful. Even as precious babies, our children's tempers flare when they
don't get what they desire, when they want it. We do not have to train
our children to be mean, throw tantrums, or be selfish—they are born
sinful (Psalm 51:5). Scripture affirms this truth: "Foolishness is bound
up in the heart of a child; the rod of correction will drive it far from
him" (Proverbs 22:15). Discipline is a "rod of correction" that teaches our
children how to govern themselves and be wise. God's Word is very
clear: we must discipline our children if we want them to become men
and women who bring God glory and honor.

Modern psychology, which is rooted in humanism, has done a
thorough job of transforming how children are raised today. As John
Rosemond attests, many parents believe "children are fundamentally
good; that in any given situation a child is inclined to do the right thing."[3]
Furthermore, they believe that "high-self esteem is desirable— essential,
in fact, to personal happiness—and [they] should do everything in their
power to help their children acquire it."[4] Parents believe their children
are "inclined to do the right things;" and when they actually do
something wrong, discipline damages their self-esteem, which should be
protected at all costs. No wonder parenting is all over the map when it
comes to discipline.

Modern psychology demands that parents throw out many of the
traditional forms of discipline. Rather than relying on biblical truth and
thousands of years of experience, parents have decided to embrace new
ideas and philosophies. The result: rebellious children—who have no
respect for their parents, teachers, or any authority in their life—with
high self-esteem because their parents have made them the center of the
universe![5]

Many parents have bought into the great lie of modern psychology:
discipline harms children more than it causes fruit to grow in their life.

We live in a culture that shies away from discipline; and when discipline is implemented, it is not very effective. As parents, we need to take our cues from God's Word, not the world. Scripture commands us, "Do not remove the ancient landmark" (Proverbs 23:10), instead follow "the old paths, where the good way is" (Jeremiah 6:16). God's Word gives us an ancient and clear path to follow as we discipline our children—and it has proven effective for thousands of years!

What Is Discipline?
In the 1828 Webster's Dictionary, discipline means: "To correct; to chastise; to punish." It can also mean, "To instruct or educate; to inform the mind; to prepare by instructing in correct principles and habits; as, to discipline youth for a profession, or for future usefulness. " Clearly, discipline is an action word. For parents, discipline means correcting, rebuking, restraining, chastening, and instructing our children!

Why We Discipline?
The Bible clearly states that parents are to "bring [their children] up in the training and admonition of the Lord" (Ephesians 6:4). And, God has called children to "obey [their] parents in the Lord, for this is right. 'Honor your father and mother'" (Ephesians 6:1-2). God has given parents a duty: to train their children. To children, God has given them a different duty: to obey. Parents discipline, and children obey, because God has called them to do so. Both must conform their wills to obedience to God. No parent enjoys disciplining their children, but they do it because their position demands it of them.

We discipline our children because we love them. Proverbs 13:24 reminds us, "He who spares the rod hates his son, but he who loves him disciplines him promptly." Our discipline also shows our children that we love or delight in them (Proverbs 3:12).

Discipline is also a sign of legitimacy. Hebrews 12:7-8 reminds us: "If you endure chastening, God deals with you as with sons; for what son is there whom a father does not chasten? But if you are without chastening, of which all have become partakers, then you are illegitimate and not sons." In these verses, the author of Hebrews reminds us that parents discipline their children because they are their children. If they fail to do so, then they are not only failing in their duty as parents, they are also failing to treat their children as legitimate heirs. Our children will grow to despise us if we do not discipline them. They will look at their life, and wonder why we failed them—as their future success lies in the fulfillment of our duty to discipline.

The ultimate goal of discipline is for our children to become self-disciplined, "a law to themselves" (Romans 2:14). If we do not discipline our children, then we are withholding the tools they need to govern their own spirit. Therefore, they will be "like a city broken down, without walls" (Proverbs 25:28)—vulnerable to the enemy, who has footholds in their life. However, in discipling and training our children, we build up their city walls, as they learn habits of self-discipline which will cause blessing to flow into their lives.

Discipline in Love

The fundamental ingredient in discipline is love.   Remember, we discipline our children because we love them (Proverbs 13:24)—and that love should be clearly seen! We need to remind our children that we love them as we discipline them.   We are taking the time to train them because we want them to be a blessing to other people. Love is the lens through which all correction should be done.

As parents, we are a reflection of Christ to our children, and they should be able to see His love through our discipline.   Psalm 89:30-22 explains how God disciplines His children:

> If his sons forsake My law and do not walk in My judgments, if they break My statutes and do not keep My commandments, then I will punish their transgression with the rod, and their iniquity with stripes. Nevertheless My lovingkindness I will not utterly take from him, nor allow my faithfulness to fail.

God will never discipline us without love, and we need to follow His example with our own children. In a similar vein, Roy Hession, author of *The Calvary Road*, writes:

> Certainly, if we are a parent we shall often need to correct our child with firmness.   But none of this is to be from selfish motives, but only out of love for the other and a longing for their good. Our own convenience and rights must all the time be yielded. Only so will the love of the Lord Jesus be able to fill us and express itself through us."[6]

God's perfect love should be the lens through which all our correction is given. Because we love our children, we must discipline them—just as the Lord corrects us because of His great love for us (Proverbs 3:11-12). Not only do we need to demonstrate our love through hugs and kisses, but we need to remind them that we are disciplining them because we love them- every time!

Effective Discipline Must Be Painful

Discipline comes in many forms and methods in our modern, progressive world—yet few are effective.   God gives us a clear description of what discipline is actually effective in His Word, and it is the same method He uses for us. Hebrews 12:11 states, "Now no chastening seems to be joyful for the present, but painful; nevertheless, afterward it yields the peaceable fruit of righteousness to those who have been trained by it." According to Scripture, discipline has to be "painful" to be fruitful in a child's life.

You might be wondering what is painful discipline? It is discipline that stings, causing enough pain to bring about an immediate change in behavior. It might mean spanking your children on the bottom when they run into the street, or it might mean taking away their most precious possession. Discipline needs to include a painful consequence that makes a child never want to commit their sinful act again as long as they live! If discipline is not painful, it is not effective.

Today, many parents attempt to discipline their children without hurting their feelings. In the past, parents knew that, unless their children felt bad about their sin, then they would not truly repent or change their behavior. However, the progressive lie says that the most important thing a parent can do is build up their children's self-esteem—and when their feelings are hurt, our children's self-esteem lowers. Remember, we do not want to raise our children's self-esteem, as high self-esteem results in selfish children who only think about themselves. However, we want children who know that they are not perfect and often fall short. Through discipline, they should recognize that they are sinful and in desperate need of a Savior. For this realization to happen, our discipline must be painful!

My son, Josh, just reminded me that, when he was younger, Michael and I made every sin a big deal. The consequence for sinning—whether our children had lied, cheated, stolen something, made a rude comment, etc.—was big enough that they never wanted to commit that sin again. Now that our children are older, they have formed godly habits that do not include these "little," childhood sins. Often, it is easy for parents to overlook "little" sins in their children's lives; but in doing so, their children create habits of sin that grow bigger and become harder to root out in the future. Parents must be assertive with discipline, making sin a big deal, and consequences painful. Only then will they reap the fruit of godly children in the future.

The Fruit of Discipline
After we use effective discipline, we reap a harvest of fruit in our children's lives, as they become right before God! When we are faithful to discipline our children, they will:

Become Wise
Scripture tells us that children who have been disciplined become wise. They realize that hitting is mean, stealing is wrong, lying gets them into trouble, being selfish does not produce blessing, etc. Proverbs 15:5 says, "A fool despises his father's instruction, but he who receives correction is prudent."

Respect Authority
Hebrews 12:9 declares, "Furthermore, we have had human fathers who corrected us, and we paid them respect." When we discipline our children, they will not only respect us, but they will also respect the other

authorities in their life. Too often, because we desire our children to love us, we refrain from disciplining them. However, respect turns to love. If we want our children to love us as they grow older, we must gain their respect by disciplining them consistently throughout their childhood.

Become Trained in Righteousness
When we discipline our children, they are trained in righteousness. In other words, they know the right way to live. They become selfless, hard-working, kind, disciplined, well-mannered, considerate of others, and so forth. "Train up a child in the way he should go, and when he is old he will not depart from it" (Proverbs 22:6).

Bring Peace to Our Home
Disciplined children are not just a joy to be around, but they also bring peace to our home. I cannot begin to tell you how many people Michael and I have spoken to, who are reaping the consequences of not disciplining their children. They live in a home full of chaos. Remember, it is much harder to root out sin in a teenager. When our children are toddlers, we can spank, love, and restore them—and they come out of their room happy! However, discipline is not as easy when you are dealing with a teenager. Failure to discipline when your children are young can cause a lot of unrest in your home. As Proverbs 29:17 declares, "Correct your son, and he will give you rest; yes he will give delight to your soul." If you want a peaceful home, discipline your children when they are young!

Bring Delight to Our Soul
When we discipline our children, they bring delight to our soul! "The father of the righteous will greatly rejoice, and he who begets a wise child will delight in him. Let your father and your mother be glad, and let her who bore you rejoice" (Proverbs 23:24-25). Ultimately, when we are faithful to train our children, they become a blessing to us and others—someone we want to spend time with when they are adults.

Expectations
There is a lot of confusion today about acceptable behavior in children. In the past, everyone was on the same page when it came to discipline; but now, parents are all over the map in regards to their expectations for their children. Before we can effectively discipline our children, we need to have clear expectations!

In the 19th century, Robert Lewis Stevenson wrote a poem, entitled "Whole Duty of Children," which describes the expectations for children in his day. It reads:

A child should always say what's true
And speak when he is spoken to,
And behave mannerly at the table;

At least as far as he is able.[7]

Far gone are the days when a child should only "speak when he is spoken to", and "behave mannerly at the table." In many homes, manners—and expectations like these ones—have been thrown out the window!

So, what expectations should we have for our children? From where should they come? Our expectations should come from Scripture, and the Ten Commandments (Exodus 20:1-17) is a great place to start:

- Worship God.
- Do not worship false gods.
- Do not say God's name in vain.
- Go to church.
- Rest on the Sabbath Day.
- Honor your father and mother.
- Do not kill (or hurt someone else).
- Do not commit adultery (or look at pornography).
- Do not lie.
- Do not steal.
- Do not covet someone else's belongings.

To these expectations, we can add not using bad language (Ephesians 4:29), not complaining (Philippians 2:14), being kind and forgiving one another (Colossians 3:12-13), being respectful of authority (1 Peter 5:5), and more. Ultimately, these expectations and others must come from the standards found in God's Word.

It is so important that we are consistent with our expectations. Often, we have expectations for our children, yet we sometimes hold our children accountable to them, and other times we don't. To train godly children we must be consistent with our expectations, so our children will not become children of compromise.

Obedience

Once our children know our expectations, they are commanded by God to obey (Ephesians 6:1-3). Obedience is foundational to discipline. So, we must start training our children to obey when they are young. Then, we must diligently follow through in our training. For example, when we ask our children to pick up their toys, to clean their room, or to stop doing something, we must expect and require immediate obedience.

Michael and I often remind our children: "Obey...right away, all the way, and with a joyful heart!" If our children do not obey right away, they must suffer a painful consequence—so they will never want to disobey again! After all, delayed—or incomplete—obedience is disobedience.

When we are faithful to teach our children obedience, we will receive the blessing of older children who are faithful to help around the house, run errands, do chores, and more, without complaining. When Michael or I ask one of our children to do a random chore, like sweep the floor or walk the dog, they do not complain or tell me that what they are doing is more important. They have been trained to obey immediately. What a blessing!

When our children receive the gift of obedience, they easily transfer that obedience toward other authority figures in their lives, especially God. Consider Samuel: in obeying Eli, he obeyed God. Alexander MacLaren expounds on this truth. He writes:

> His service was "unto the Lord," and it was "before Eli"; that is to say, he learned his work from the old man, and in obeying him he served God. The child's religion is largely obedience to human guides, and he serves God best by doing what he is bid— a lesson needed in our days by both parents and children.[8]

We do not want our children to suffer the consequences that are the result of not obeying God. Our faithfulness in teaching our children to obey will enable them to receive the blessings that only come from a life of submission and obedience to God.

Forms of Discipline

Michael and I were both blessed to have been raised in Christian homes filled with biblical discipline. In raising us, our parents drew inspiration from God's Word, which gave them a clear pattern for discipline. Proverbs 29:15 states, "The rod and rebuke give wisdom, but a child left to himself brings shame to his mother." According to Scripture, raising wise children requires the rod and rebuke—or discipline. If we leave our children to themselves, then they will bring shame into our lives. We do not want our children to be our shame.

In *The Voyage of the Dawn Treader*, C.S. Lewis gives his readers a picture of a child "left to himself", in the character of Eustace Scrubb. Lewis gives Eustace a clever introduction: "There once was a boy by the name of Eustace Clarence Scrubb, and he almost deserved it."[9] As the novel continues, Lewis reveals that Eustace was raised with a modern education, and according to modern philosophies. In other words, he was not disciplined, which resulted in an undisciplined boy, without manners or friends. He was also selfish, rude, prideful, arrogant, and lazy. Though Eustace did not know what a dragon was (thanks to his modern education), he becomes one after "thinking greedy dragonish thoughts."[10] After becoming a monster, Eustace discovers that the true monster was himself all along. With the help of Aslan the Lion, Eustace is able to tear off his old dragon skin, and become a boy again, a new boy no longer a "shame to his mother." Eustace's life would have been so much easier—for him and everyone else—if his parents had trained him in the right way in the first place. What a grave warning!

Progressive, modern philosophies about raising children turn them into monsters! I can't imagine what C.S. Lewis would think of the generation of children being raised today. Yet, our children do not have to become our shame. If we are faithful to rebuke their sin and use the rod, then they will become wise.

Offenses

As we train our children, they will disobey—after all, they are sinners! Their disobedience will take on the form of various offenses, which will each require a different degree of punishment.

Small offenses include: bickering, fighting, meanness, sarcasm, laziness, selfishness, disruptiveness, etc. We must diligently call out these sins in our home, and rebuke our children. If they continue in sin, then the rod may become necessary. Most of the time, these small offenses can be be conquered with a rebuke and diligent training in the right behavior.

Major offenses are bigger sins. These include: dishonesty, hitting a sibling, bad language, being disrespectful, downright rebellion, and more. These sins require immediate discipline, so they will never happen again. Our children's punishment must be so painful that they will never want to pay the price for their sin again. Major offenses usually require the rod of correction. Remember, however, that painful discipline must be done in love to be effective.

Rebuke

There are many reasons to rebuke our children—they complain, use unkind words, run through the house screaming, do not stay on a task, and more. In these situations, we must correct and "rebuke with all authority" (Titus 2:15). Rebuking our children is correcting them with words, not yelling at them when they do something wrong. Remember, we are not to "provoke [our] children to wrath" (Ephesians 6:4).

Rebuking children requires authority. If we want our children to stop doing something wrong, we must speak firmly. For example, if my sweet baby, Ruth, picks up a marker, I would not say in my kindest voice, "Ruth, please put the marker down. I don't want you to draw on the walls or furniture." Instead, I should say, "Ruth! No-no!" in a mom voice, while giving her a mom look until she drops the marker. If she doesn't obey immediately, I would need to take the marker from her before giving her a swat on the hand.

Remember, small offenses can be taken care of with a rebuke. Sometimes, we can simply say our children's names, or "What did I say?" Or, we might not need to say anything—just a look might do. The mom look takes practice to master, but it can be a highly effective rebuke.

The Rod

Spanking is not encouraged in our culture today—even within the church. What was once an appropriate and effective discipline tool for thousands of years has now become "politically incorrect." Modern psychologists consider spanking an unloving act and a form of abuse.

I recently came across an article by by the National Public Radio (NPR) titled, "The American Academy of Pediatrics on Spanking Children: Don't Do It, Ever." The article states that parents should never spank their children, because it causes severe problems with brain development. The authors state, "With new evidence, researches link corporal punishment to an increased risk of negative behavioral, cognitive, psychosocial, and emotional outcomes for children."[11] They go on to say that verbal abuse (rebuking children) and physical abuse (spanking) "are adverse childhood events that can cause toxic stress that can lead to health problems as well as emotional problems as a child reaches the preteen and teen years."[12] Instead of rebuke or the rod, the authors suggest that parents reward good behavior, stay consistent with expectations, and use time-outs. The problem with these forms of discipline is that they are not effective, in and of themselves. Also, good behavior should be expected, not rewarded.

Some psychologists claim that spanking children will teach them to hit others. Yet, this "truth" is not based on observation. Children who hit others at home, in school, or in other social situations are the ones who have never been restrained or trained by their parents.

Discipline done without love has skewed society's view of spanking. Some people, who experienced abuse or discipline in anger, often see all discipline through the lens of their experience. They are allowing the sins of others to keep them from obeying to God's command to discipline their children. Whatever the reason, as a culture, we have distanced ourself from traditional discipline, and our children are reaping the consequence. Simply look at the world today and consider how children behave now compared to how they were expected to behave in the past. Clearly, the new philosophies about training and disciplining children are not working.

Elisabeth Elliot writes about the discipline she received as a child. In her day, spanking with a rod was a common practice. She writes:

> *Spanking is not child abuse. It is a deliberate measure of pain, delivered calmly, lovingly, and with self-control, on a loved child in order to deliver him from self-will and ultimate self-destruction. This is how God treats sons. My parents took their cues from Him.[13]*

She is right. God's Word has been very clear on how to discipline effectively—and it has proven to work for thousands of years. Proverbs 13:24 (NLT) declares, "Those who spare the rod of discipline hate their children. Those who love their children care enough to discipline them." Here, parents are encouraged to correct their children with "the rod of discipline." And, if they neglect their duty, God's Word declares that they hate their children.

Modern culture has interpreted this verse in many different ways to justify not using "the rod of discipline." Many people interpret "the rod" to mean, metaphorically speaking, spanking. However, if we actually look at the word in its original language, we will find that "the rod" means "a staff or branch of some kind, used to discipline a child"—which is why Michael and I believe that we should use a paddle or spoon when we spank our children, as the bible suggests. The rod is as symbol of authority, and it is such a great tool to use to promote order in the home. James Dobson, author of *Dare to Discipline*, agrees. He states:

> *I recommend a neutral object of some type...The reason I suggest a switch or paddle is because the hand should be seen as an object of love—to hold, hug, pat and caress. However, if you're used to suddenly disciplining with the hand, your child may not know when he's about to be swatted and can develop a pattern of flinching when you suddenly scratch your head. This is not a problem if you take the time to get a neutral object.*[14]

Although our culture has changed its view of the rod, God has not. His Word is clear, regarding what effective discipline is. The Bible says that parents demonstrate their love for their children as they discipline them through spanking. Proverbs 13:24 says, "He who spares his rod hates his son, but he who loves him disciplines him promptly." Furthermore, "Foolishness is bound up in the heart of a child; the rod of correction will drive it far from him" (Proverbs 22:15).

When I asked my children how they knew that I love them, a few of them responded with, "Because you spank us." As parents, we need to take our cues from God's Word, not the world. When we discipline our children, through the lens of love, they will respect, love, and grow up to thank us.

How to Use the Rod: Spanking
During the first two seasons of our children's life, spanking is usually the most effective tool for discipline, because it is quick and painful. We want our children to remember it. As they can not reason with us as children, especially as toddlers. What does this look like in practice? If Ruth ran into the street, I would say, "Ruth- don't run in the street!" Then I would run after her, swoop her up and give her two spanks on her thigh or bottom before telling her, "You can't go into the street. You might get hit by a car." Then, I would give her a hug and kiss and tell her how much I love her and don't want anything to happen to her. The next time she thinks about running into the street, she will remember the pain she experienced and, hopefully, think twice!

Between the ages of eighteen months and six years old are some of the most intense training years when it comes to discipline. Correction will involve a lot of rebukes and a lot of spankings. Michael and I first started spanking our babies around fifteen months of age on their hand or thigh. If a rebuke was not heeded, then we would follow up with a spanking. For example, if one of our babies threw their food on the floor, we would tell them, "No throwing!" If they looked at us and threw the food again, we would again say, "No throwing!" and follow up with a swat on the hand.

As our children grew a little older, Michael and I would send them to their bedroom if they needed a spanking. Then, when we had calmed down and finished whatever we had been working on, we would go to their room with the paddle or wooden spoon and follow the steps of restoration laid out later in this chapter. Our children have seldom needed a spanking past the age of ten. But, there have been times that we have given them the choice of a spanking or losing something they had been looking forward to. Sometimes, our children have chosen a spanking because it is over quickly!

As a mom, a paddle or wooden spoon is a valuable spanking tool, as it gave me authority. Just as a police officer gains authority by his weapon, a mother's authority is substantiated with her paddle. As a mother of six, I spent many years at home, disciplining young children. In fact, I used to wear an apron all day long, and place a wooden spoon in the pocket, so my children could see that I meant business. The paddle was a great tool to to help me manage my home. Whether I went to the grocery store, church or was just in the car, I would show my children the paddle and all of a sudden my children were on their best behavior. It was especially useful at bedtime. Most evenings, Michael or I would have to grab the paddle in order to get our six little ones to obey us, and get in bed.

When my four boys were little, and needed immediate training, I took care of the spankings, as I was with them all day. As they grew out of their second season, however, most of their discipline has been done by their father, after he comes home from work. If we consistently train and spank our children during their first two seasons of parenting, then we will not have to do it as often in season three. Now, as my boys are older and know that I mean business, I can simply give them a look, and they know they had better pull it together. In fact, even though I have to look up to two of them now, they still respect me as much as they did when they were three! Those years of faithful training have been so fruitful. Our children bring so much joy, delight, and peace to our home.

When I was expecting my sixth child, Abigail, I was sitting at my kitchen table with my four little boys, talking and having fun. Unbeknownst to me, my oldest son, Daniel, dared his younger brother, Micah, to dial 911. Micah did so while the rest of us talked about funny spanking stories. Micah and Daniel laughed about a time when Micah, who had been sent to his room for a spanking, put on layers of underwear in an attempt to cushion his bottom. Micah reminisced about how the spanking didn't hurt. So, after dad made him take the extra underwear off, he ended up getting more spankings!

When the story ended, I realized that someone was on the phone. Since I hadn't called anyone, I hung up. Immediately, a 911 dispatcher called the house and asked me who I was. When I told her, she asked me if I knew who had called 911. By this time, I had found out about the dare, which I told her about. She then told me that she didn't think our home was safe, so she was sending two police officers right then.

I immediately sent my boys to their room, and told them to pray—and pray hard! I called Michael, who came home from church, and we prayed together, earnestly. A few minutes later, two police officers knocked on our door. Michael opened it, and one of them said, "Pastor Mike!" Immediately, I knew that God had answered our prayers. The police officer had been in our church's youth group when Mike was the youth pastor.

I am sharing this story with you not only to demonstrate the power of prayer, but to encourage you to use discernment when disciplining your children. Today, everything we do or say is being filmed and recorded, so we must make sure we are acting in accordance with God's Word. We need to be discrete about where and when we discipline. For instance, we should not spank our children in the middle of a store or a parking lot. There are many people in today's world who think the world would be a much better place if spankings were outlawed altogether. Part of obeying God's Word when it comes to discipline is using discernment.

Time-Out
Many parents in today's culture have replaced the rod and rebuke with time-out when their children are younger. The problem with a time-out is that it is not painful—and therefore, most often, ineffective. Children, who are put in time-out will continue to commit offenses, because the consequence is not painful enough.

That being said, there is an effective time to use a time-out. For example, I send my children to their rooms for a time-out if they have a bad attitude. They can rejoin the family once they have a happy heart, as it is not fair for the whole family to endure their poor attitude. If my children are disruptive at the dinner table, I send them to their room so the rest of the family can enjoy their dinner in peace. In the past, I have also had to put whining babies into their crib until they stop complaining or fall asleep. Sometimes, my child asks for something, and I say "no," but they still keep asking. In these cases, I will send my child to their room so they can realize that I don't want to hear their request any more.

We also use time-out when a rebuke goes unheeded, as sometimes a little distance from the situation can enable our children to obey. Usually, Michael and I have our children go to their room for a time-out before we spank them. This is usually when they are in direct disobedience. The time-out enables them to "stew in their juices" for a bit—and also allows us to finish up whatever we were working on.

Taking Things Away

Taking away possessions is painful and effective form of discipline. When my children were little and would fight over a toy, I would take it away and, often, put it in the trash. If the toy was a more costly object, I would put it in time out, sometimes indefinitely. Usually, however, my children would fight over a cheap, plastic toy that really did not mean much to them. They quickly learned that I meant business anytime I got rid of the toy being fought over—and they made an effort not to fight over little things, especially if they did not want it to end up in the trash.

As our children grow older, taking away events, activities, and precious possessions (e.g., technology, favorite jackets, favorite shoes, etc.) can be a highly effective form of discipline. In fact, God uses this method of discipline with us. Psalm 39:11 (NASB) declares, "With reproofs You chasten a man for iniquity; you consume as a moth what is precious to him; surely every man is a mere breath." Having the things that are "precious" taken away from us is a very painful form of discipline.

When my son, Daniel, was little, he loved his Spider-Man costume more than anything. Michael and I had to take it away from him quite a few times, and doing so was highly effective in stopping his bad behavior. Daniel would do anything to get his costume back!

At the age of fourteen, my son, Josh, looked in the mirror one day and said, "I am too big to get spanked." His brother, Sam, responded, "That's why, when you get in trouble, mom and dad take away your money." How true! Josh loves to save his money, and nothing is more painful to him than losing some of it. So, when Josh gets in trouble, he owes us money. This consequence would not be effective for my sweet Abby, as she could care less about money. But, she cares about her stuffed animals.

Faithful Discipline

We have discussed how discipline looks different in the various seasons of a child's life. It starts with rebukes and spankings, then can grow to time-outs, extra chores and taking away precious possessions. When we are faithful to discipline our children effectively and consistently, with discernment, from an early age, it will have long term effects. Elisabeth Elliot provides us with some insight into how she and her siblings were disciplined in their teenager years:

> *Parents have asked me what sort of punishment I might recommend for children who are beyond the spanking age. They don't know what to do with teen-agers. What did my parents do? I couldn't think of a thing. I asked my sister and brothers. Nobody can remember any punishment such as "grounding," fines, withholding the car keys (we seldom got them anyway—we never had more than one car for the whole tribe), or anything else. Isn't this just "the proof of the*

pudding"? Training given early enough, consistently enough has long-term effects. It wasn't that we were "good kids." It's just that we got the message. No other explanation seems possible.[15]

The work parents do in the earlier years really does pay off when children are older. Life should not get harder in the teenage years—and it won't, if we are faithful to discipline our children with love when they are young. Then, in the teenage years, we will be blessed with children, who are a joy and delight in our home!

Now that my children are older, I hear stories of times when they were young and unjustly punished. It is amusing to see how they view things through different lenses—often exaggerating what actually happened. I hear them say things like, "You spanked me twenty times, and it wasn't even my fault!" I always remind my children that there probably was a time they deserved to be disciplined, but were not. Those times they were punished unfairly make up for the times they should have been disciplined. I also remind them that their dad and I are not perfect, and we will continue to fail them throughout their life. However, God is perfect! He is so faithful, fair, and just—and He will never discipline any of us unless we deserve it.

As you read this chapter, you may realize that you have neglected to discipline or adequately train your children during their younger years. If that is the case, then you must do whatever it takes to train them in a life of discipline today. I encourage you to talk with your husband, and get on the same page as him. Pray and put together a plan of action going forward. Then, sit down with your children, apologize for the lack of discipline, and explain your vision for them. Make your new expectations clear, as well as the consequences for their misbehavior. Remember, in doing so, you demonstrate to them that the gospel works— as it has changed and is changing you! Your children might grumble and complain, but they will end up respecting you. Eventually, that respect will turn to love.

Training through Discipline

The goal of discipline is for our children to understand that they are a sinner in need of a Savior—and ultimately, to get their heart right before God. When we discipline our children, we demonstrate to them their need for the gospel. This is why it is so important we discipline them in the right way. We don't want to push our children away from Christ; instead, we want to draw them to Him.

Children who have never been disciplined tend to think they do not need a Savior. In fact, they do not believe they are ever wrong or ever in sin. As parents, we do not want to be guilty of misrepresenting the gospel or pushing our children away from Christ.

When disciplining children, it is helpful to follow the steps below:

Identify Sin

The first thing we must do is to identify the sin committed. If one of our boys hit their brother, Michael and I would send him to his room, and ask, "Why did dad or mom send you to your room?" If he can admit his sin—"I hit my brother"—then, we ask, "What does God say about how you should treat your brother?" If he doesn't know, then we help him: "God wants you to love your brother, and hitting is not loving."

It is vital that we take the necessary time to talk to our children, explain how they sinned, and why it was wrong. Usually, Michael and I use scripture that describes the sin they committed, and explain why they were wrong. If they were being selfish, then they were not putting other people's needs before their own (Philippians 2:4). Or, if they provoked someone to anger, they are actually sinning against God—not just the person they hurt or offended. As Psalm 51:4 reveals, all of our sins is actually sin against God.

Many children will make excuses for their behavior, thinking they had a legitimate reason for their bad behavior. However, it is so important that we do not allow them to make excuses. We must lead our children to confess and forsake their sin. Proverbs 28:13 reminds us that "He that covers his sins will not prosper, but whoever confesses and forsakes them will have mercy."

Often, moms allow their children's excuses to justify why they don't punish their children—and their children grow up constantly making excuses for their sins. This bad habit does not make for a good employee, co-worker, neighbor, or spouse. Nobody wants to work with, be around, or be married to a person who is never wrong and always making excuses for their sins. We must do whatever it takes to teach our children to confess and repent of their sin.

Determine the Punishment

While identifying sin is incredibly important, "talking" to our children about it must not replace the actual consequence. Talking is not a punishment.

Because we love our children, we must determine a punishment after we identify their sin. The consequence depends on their age and the crime committed. As our children grow older, it is okay to take time to determine their punishment. Often, we will need to talk to our husband and determine what the punishment should be. It is so important that whatever the punishment is, that it is painful enough that our children never want to commit their offense again. If we decide on a spanking, we can use a paddle or wooden spoon to give them three spanks on their bottom. Or, we might decide to take something precious away.

What kinds of offenses require a spanking? Screaming, hitting, lying, disobedience, rebellion, etc. When should we take things away? If your son shoots his brother in the face with a rubber band gun, take the gun away. If he was wearing his Spider-Man costume, and ended up being too rough with their sisters, take the costume away. If a daughter gets a low grade in school, take away technology privileges until the grade improves. (For my children, this includes watching movies with the rest of the family, and listening to the Lamplighter audiobooks).

Confession and Repentance

After punishment, our children should be crying—as crying is a sign of repentance. When they are older, they just feel really bad that they have disappointed us. Then we pray. During the prayer, they should confess their sin to God, and ask Him to help them have self-control, be a better brother or sister, honor their mom or dad, fill-in-the-blank. Usually, when our children are super young, they will need to repeat their prayer after mom and dad. But, as they get older, they know how to confess and repent on their own—and we just join them in prayer.

If our children have a rebellious heart when it comes to discipline, we need to remind them that the Bible says, "Whoever loves instruction loves knowledge, but he who hates correction is stupid" (Proverbs 12:1). We want our children to love correction and become wise. They should see discipline as a gift in their life.

Restoration and Restitution

After we have identified the sin, instituted the punishment, and led our children to repent of their sins, we need to bring about restoration in their life. As parents, we do this by hugging our children and telling them how much we love them. We remind them that we do not enjoy disciplining them—but we want them to be wise and a blessing in everyone's life. Then, our children need to make the situation right, and apologize to whoever they have offended (e.g., mom or dad, a sibling, a friend, a neighbor, a teacher). When my children were young, and needed to make things right with one of their siblings, I would always have them apologize and give their sibling a hug. Requiring both of these things is one way Michael and I have cultivated love and forgiveness amongst our children.

Ineffective Discipline

Failing to follow the biblical model of discipline can have a devastating effect on our children and undermine our effectiveness as parents. Remember, the ultimate goal of discipline is to draw our children to Christ. And, if we fail to discipline our children or discipline them in a way that provokes them to wrath, then we can push them away from Christ!

Here are some common mistakes that lead to ineffective discipline:

Not Following Through

When we discipline, we must follow through with our threats, as it will teach our children we mean what we say. If we do not follow through, then we can make threats all day long—and it won't mean anything.

Have you ever heard a mom in a store or restaurant tell her child, "If you don't stop right now, we are going to leave"? Did she follow through? Most likely not. As parents, we need to make sure our threats are ones that we are willing to uphold if we want our children realize that we "mean what we say." Only then will our words have the power they need to be effective in training and discipling our children.

Disciplining in Anger

We must not discipline our children in anger—do not yell, scream, or rage! Remember, Ephesians 6:4, which says, "And you, fathers, do not provoke your children to wrath, but bring them up in the training and admonition of the Lord." When we discipline in anger, we provoke our children to wrath, which causes them to become discouraged (Colossians 3:21).

To bring about repentance, we need to discipline in love. Anytime we are tempted to discipline in anger, we must ask ourselves, "Do I want to bring about repentance in my children's life, and draw them to Christ? Or, do I want to discourage my children, make them angry, and push them away from Him?" We must purpose to use discipline to draw our children to their Savior, not push them away from Him!

Keeping Our Husband Out of the Loop

As moms, we must keep our husband in the loop when it comes to our children and their behavior. Too often, wives do not tell their husband about their children's misbehaviors, because they feel like their husband will not handle it the way they would. Bypassing your husband's authority in the home is detrimental to your children's character. Not only are you showing your children that the two of you are a divided front, you are also allowing them to impact your marriage, and get away with sin!

It is so important that wives let their husband know everything that is going on with their children. In fact, they should be making every decision about their children with their husband. Too often, moms let their emotions impair them from punishing their children, and they need their husband's logical input to make wise decisions for their children. There is a reason God created both man and women to become one flesh, and produce children to raise together.

Not Making It Painful

Whatever punishment we decide on must be painful enough to make our children decide they never want to commit their offense again. If one of our children throws a tantrum and starts yelling that they hate us, their consequence should not be a time-out. The punishment does not match the crime! If our children "hate us," they will enjoy the time-out in their room, as they will get a break from us. Our discipline must be painful enough that our child never treats us like that again. The consequence must cost our child something that really moves them enough to change their behavior.

Not Being Home to Discipline
I just recently met a mom whose twenty-two year old son does not want to get a job, because he doesn't want anyone telling him what to do. She and her husband now realize that they spent so much time helping their child keep up academically and socially that they did not take the time to actually discipline their child. Now, they are trying to figure out how they can make up for lost time with their twenty-two year old son—and they have a huge task before them.

I have found that setting aside discipline and a child's character in favor of academics and a child's social life is becoming more and more common. If parents are never home to train and discipline their children, then their children will end up bothered when people tell them what to do.

Using Talking As a Form of Discipline
Sometimes, an offense requires a rebuke. But, if it was a major offense, our punishment must fit the crime. Remember, talking is not a consequence; therefore, it's not an effective form of discipline.

Arguing with Our Children
Talking back is disrespectful, and should never be permitted in our homes. If our children are talking back, they need to immediately be sent to their room. We do not need to continue our discussion with them. We are the parents, and they are the child! Our children can come out of their room when they no longer feel like arguing.

Trying Not to Hurt Our Children's Feelings
Modern psychology tells us that we must take our children's feelings into account when we discipline them. But, how can we let our children know that their behavior was not appropriate if we are not willing to hurt their feelings? For a change of behavior to occur, parents must hurt their children's feelings. Life is hard, and our children need to get used to taking correction gracefully—even when it is hurtful, as that is how we learn and grow. We must not be over-concerned with our children's feelings; instead, we must train them to obey in spite of their feelings!

Not Being Authoritative

A lack of authority leads to ineffective discipline. Asking or suggesting our children do things gives them control. When we want our children to do something, we need to tell them in a direct, authoritative voice.

I am not suggesting that we order our children around meanly. We can be kind, yet firm. Consider the difference: "Daniel, please go clean your room." "Daniel, can you please go clean your room?" "Daniel, I would really like it if you would please go clean your room." We should give our children clear commands, not choices.

Giving in to Tantrums

When children do not get their way, they might throw a tantrum in hopes of pressuring their parents to bend to their will. Every time we, as parents, give in to our children's tantrums and whims, we train them to believe that our word is changeable. If they can just pressure us enough, then we will give them what they want for the sake of peace.

However, if we would simply discipline our children, then we could experience a lasting peace. When our children throw a tantrum in a restaurant, the answer is not to give them a milkshake or our cell phone to make them happy. Instead, we need to show them the wooden spoon that we've tucked in our purse, reminding them of the last time they received a spanking for throwing a tantrum in public.

Making Excuses for Our Children

Too often, I hear moms making excuses for their children when their children do something wrong: "Oh, he's just tired. She's just hungry." By excusing their children's sins, moms teach their children that they do not need to respect authority, confess their sins, or suffer consequences for misbehavior.

It is so important that we do not excuse our children's bad behavior—or allow them to make excuses. Sin is sin, whether our children meant to sin or not! When we fail in life, people don't look at us and say, "Oh, well, she had a bad day." No, we have to reap the consequences for our sin. Similarly, our children must learn to reap the consequences of their sin—even when they are tired and hungry.

Discipline and Our Legacy

Failure to discipline our children directly affects our legacy! Remember Eli. He knew about his sons' sin, yet he failed to restrain them—and Eli's family was judged by God forever (1 Samuel 3:13). This eternal punishment may seem harsh, but it shows us how God views lack of discipline in our children's lives. Alexander MacLaren explains God's view:

> *The sin was mainly the sons'; but the guilt was largely the father's. We may learn how cruel paternal laxity is, and how fatal mischief may be done, by neglect of the plain duty of*

restraining children. He who tolerates evil which it is his province to suppress, is an accomplice, and the blood of the doers is red on his hands.[16]

Eli's failure to restrain his sons made him "an accomplice" to their sins. And, when they were eventually judged by God, Eli was judged with them!

Eli ruined his spiritual legacy because he failed to discipline, train, and restrain his children. He had faith in and served God, but he was not willing to invest in his children. The result was devastating.

How did God judge Eli? God not only removed the priesthood from Eli's family line, but both of his sons died a tragic death as they battled against the Philistines, Israel's arch enemy. As if that wasn't bad enough, the Ark of the Covenant was captured by the Philistines in the same battle. When the news reached Eli, he was so shocked that he fell over and died. Eli died a shameful death with the knowledge that his sin—in not disciplining his sons—caused God's glory to depart from Israel. (See 1 Samuel 4.) Eli's legacy should be a warning to us all.

In contrast, Hannah—through her obedience to God in training and disciplining her son, Samuel—was able to see God's glory restored in Israel. Hannah's legacy, displayed in the life of Samuel, far surpassed her own life. We must understand that the way we raise our children today impacts our legacy—forever!

Questions to Consider

1. How have you neglected to discipline your children for the sake of making them happy?

2. Is there any evidence in your parenting that would suggest you fear your children more than obeying God?

3. Have you bought into the culture's lies about discipline? If so, how?

4. How effective is your discipline? How can you make it more effective?

5. When you discipline your children, do you take the time for restoration and teaching? If not, how might you start implementing these important steps?

6. What excuses might you be making for your children's behavior to justify a lack of discipline?

7. Your legacy hinges on your ability to discipline your children. What discipline changes should you make in your home?

Notes

¹ C.H. Spurgeon, *Spiritual Parenting* (New Kensington, PA: Whitaker House, 1995), 92-93.

² F.B. Meyer, *Samuel the Prophet* (CrossReach Publications, 2017), 14.

³ John Rosemond, *Parenting by the Book* (New York, New York: Howard Books, 2007), 49.

⁴ Ibid.

⁵ Ibid., 50.

⁶ Roy Hession, *The Calvary Road* (Fort Washington, PA: CLC Publications, 1950), 24.

⁷ Robert Lewis Stevenson, *A Child's Garden of Verses* (New York, New York: Simon & Schuster Books For Young Readers, 1999), 13.

⁸ Alexander MacLaren, *MacLaren's Expositions of Holy Scripture, Volume 1* (Grand Rapids, Michigan: WM. B. Eerdmans Publishing Co., 1959), 268.

⁹ C.S. Lewis, *The Voyage of the Dawn Treader* (New York, New York: Harper Collins Publishing, 1952), 1.

¹⁰ Ibid., 91.

¹¹ Cameron Jenkins, "The American Academy of Pediatrics on Spanking Children: Don't Do It, Ever, NPR, November 11, 2018, accessed July 20, 2019, https://www.npr.org/2018/11/11/666646403/the-american-academy-of-pediatrics-on-spanking-children-dont-do-it-ever

¹² Ibid.

¹³ Elisabeth Elliot, *The Shaping of a Christian Family* (Grand Rapids, Michigan: Fleming H. Revell, 1992), 134.

¹⁴ James Dobson, *Dare to Discipline* (Carol Stream, Illinois:Tyndale House publishing, 1970), 64.

¹⁵ Elliot, *The Shaping of a Christian Family*, 182.

¹⁶ MacLaren, MacLaren's *Expositions of Holy Scripture,* 274.

Hannah's Legacy: Samuel

Behold, children are a heritage from the LORD,
The fruit of the womb is a reward.

Psalm 127:3

As Samuel grew in the Tabernacle, the scripture tells us he "grew...in favor both with the LORD and men" (1 Samuel 2:26). He was set-apart from the days of his youth, trained in God's Word and prayer, and allowed to grow in the very presence of God. Samuel knew God and how to hear His voice. His training enabled him to fulfill the call that God had upon his life!

Because of Samuel, the word of the LORD appeared again in Shiloh, then in all of Israel:

> *So Samuel grew, and the LORD was with him and let none of his words fall to the ground. And all Israel from Dan to Beersheba knew that Samuel had been established as a prophet of the LORD. Then the LORD appeared again in Shiloh. For the LORD revealed Himself to Samuel in Shiloh by the word of the LORD.*

> *— 1 Samuel 3:19-21*

Before the kingdom was established, Samuel led the children of Israel into national repentance. He united a divided country by leading them into into a nation-wide revival, where the people abandoned their foreign gods, poured out their hearts to the Lord, and worshiped Him with burnt offerings. Then, God delivered the nation of Israel from the Philistines, and the people set up an Ebenezer stone, remembering, "Thus far the LORD has helped us" (1 Samuel 4-7).

Samuel then spoke to God on behalf of the people, who wanted a king like the other nations (1 Samuel 8). With God's leading, he anointed both Saul (1 Samuel 9-10) and David (1 Samuel 16:1-13) to be king, marking a seamless transition from the period of the Judges into the beginning of Israel's monarchy. Samuel became a counselor to kings as he continued to seek God's word for His people during the establishment of the kingdom. During all of this time, Samuel let none of God's words fall to the ground. He was faithful to reveal it to His people! Recounting the life of Samuel, F.B. Meyer writes:

It was a beautiful life—-strong in its faculty of administration, wise is steering the nation from the rule of the judges into the royal state of the kings, unimpeachably just, but blamelessly pure, towering above his contemporaries like a peak of glistening chrysolite, on which the sunlight plays, while all the valleys beneath are wrapped in scudding clouds and sweeping rain.[1]

From the very beginning, Hannah knew what the children of Israel needed, and she was willing to allow God to have His way in Samuel to make it happen. She gave up her dreams for her son, and allowed God to fulfill His purpose in and through his life. Because of Samuel, Hannah had great reason to rejoice. When we raise godly children, our hearts, too, rejoice! Proverbs 23:24-25 declares: "The father of the righteous will greatly rejoice, and he who begets a wise child will delight in him. Let your father and your mother be glad, and let her who bore you rejoice!" When we have wise children, not only are we blessed by children who love God, but those who know our children are blessed as well. Hannah's legacy was her faith, imparted to Samuel—and she has passed her legacy of faith down to us, thousands of years later.

What Is a Legacy?
The Websters 1828 dictionary describes a legacy as a "bequest; a particular thing, or a certain sum of money given by last will or testament." It can be wealth in the form of money, assets, or property bequeathed to another in a will.

As a U.S. History major in college, I learned about several fascinating legacies bequeathed by wealthy men to their children. For example, J.P. Morgan—one of the wealthiest Americans at the turn of the nineteenth century—was so wealthy he lent huge sums of money to the American government. Upon his death, he left his banking legacy to his son, J.P. Morgan, Jr. Or, consider Henry Ford, whose hard work made his dream come alive in the form of the Model T, and, in the process, greatly changed America. He created an outstanding legacy from nothing, leaving it to his grandson, Henry Ford II.

These legacies were built on the world's value system. Money, investments, companies, stocks, and land are what society values, and they are the things people often strive after in creating their legacy. While we can leave riches like these to the ones we love, no amount of wealth can guarantee a better life. It was the nineteenth century steel magnate Andrew Carnegie who remarked: "The almighty dollar bequeathed to a child is an almighty curse. No man has the right to handicap his son with such a burden as great wealth."[2]

Proverbs 13:22 states "that a good man leaves an inheritance to his children's children." This inheritance doesn't necessarily mean material wealth, though it can. Money can be a blessing as long as we have not stored it up at the expense of our children's character. Money can be the destruction of our children if we have not taken the pains to train them up to be men and woman of integrity.

As Christians, God has called us to a different value system than the world. More than money, an estate, valuable jewels, or beautiful china, we, as Christian women, have the honor of leaving a spiritual legacy to those we leave behind, especially our children. Proverbs 20:7 states, "The righteous man walks in his integrity; his children are blessed after him." Expounding on this verse, Charles Spurgeon writes: "If we walk before the Lord in integrity, we shall do more than bless our descendants than if we bequeathed them large estates. A father or mother's holy life is a rich legacy for his children."[3]

The most valuable asset we can leave our children is not a large estate, a huge sum of money, or a business empire—it is a life of faith, a life lived recklessly abandoned for God!

Our Legacy: Faith

In order to leave any kind of legacy to our children, we must first establish one. How do you build a legacy? By investing your resources into savings, investments, property, etc. Consider J.P. Morgan, who spent his whole life investing all of his resources into companies and investments in order to create a huge empire of wealth.

As Christian women who desire to leave a spiritual legacy to our children, we must purposefully invest our resources—our time, money, energy, prayers—into the kingdom of God. Having Jesus in our heart is only the beginning, the opening of our spiritual bank account. Simply believing in and knowing about the God we serve is not enough if we want to leave behind a rich spiritual legacy. We must also live a life of faith, which results in a dynamic relationship with Jesus that naturally spills over to influence and inspire others, especially our children. In the words of Spurgeon: "The upright man leaves his heirs his example, and this in itself will be a mine of true wealth. How many men may trace their success in life to the example of his parents!"[4]

How we raise our children today directly impacts our legacy. We will not get the blessing of godly children—who will raise godly grandchildren —if we are not willing to make the necessary sacrifices now to raise godly children. Our legacy hinges on our children's acceptance of Christ as their Savior, as well as their character that you have formed throughout your years of raising them.

Are we willing to make sacrifices, or investments in our children's lives, today? If we are not willing to make these sacrifices, we will pay the consequences, and our legacy will suffer.

Our Mandate: Children

One of the great heartbreaks of our culture is not just people unwilling to make investments in their children lives, but also people who do not think children are even worthy to be had. This is a modern-day lie! Since the creation of the world, and until just recently, children have been considered a blessing—and the more children you had, the more blessed you were.

It is only in looking back to Genesis that we can truly understand the value of children. When God finished creating the world and all that is in it, he did not say to Adam and Eve, "Now, go and make as much money as you possibly can, storing up wealth and treasure on this earth, because you have only one life to live." Rather, God blessed them, and said, "Be fruitful and multiply; fill the earth and subdue it; have dominion over the fish of the sea, over the birds of the air, and over every living thing that moves on the earth"(Genesis 1:28).

God commanded Adam and Eve to enjoy the relationship He had given to them, marriage, and to fill the earth with the result of their love, children. They and their children were created by God to reign over His creation and enjoy it.

Consider this: our love for our husband, displayed through sex, creates eternal beings, who bring glory to God forever. What a magnificent picture!

Our Shift in Thinking

In the ancient world, children were considered an asset, a gift and reward from God, by both their parents and the rest of their agrarian society. The more children a family had, the more blessed they were believed to be.

Today, few of us live in an agrarian society, where children are a financial asset, necessary to our survival. Instead, modern society views children as a burden, a big commitment, a financial hardship, and a liability. People today believe that parents should only have as many children as they can afford to put through private school, purchase nice cars for, and send to expensive colleges. Parents are also urged to consider how much time they have—as children will require all of their time and energy. What a giant shift in thinking!

This recent shift, due in large part to the movement away from the family farm to an urban lifestyle, as well as to the influence of progressive thought, is destroying families. What God declared a blessing, our world considers a burden. Rather than embracing children as gifts from the Lord, we take steps to prevent their conception, or to abort them with the hopes that we will have more time, more freedom, and more money— which, in the end, is only an attempt to fulfill our desire for the comfort and ease Adam and Eve experienced in the Garden of Eden, before the Fall.

Rather than turning to God's Word for wisdom, people are listening to the lies of the culture. In his book, *Postmodern Times*, Gene Edward Veith, Jr., discusses our culture's new philosophy on children:

> *The new anti-humanism is inevitably anti-child, assuming as it does that new human life is a problem, a drain on the earth and on the parent's resources. We scarcely hear the classic view*

that a child is itself a resource, a valuable addition to the human race. Thus, we have "the right to an abortion," a way to eliminate children that has become a rallying political cause.[5]

This new philosophy can be seen throughout the culture. Having delivered seven children, I have been astonished at how moms are treated during their pregnancy today. When you make your first doctor's visit, many practitioners ask if a mom wants to keep her child, rather than congratulating her new baby. The more children you have, the more persistent doctors are in encouraging women to make birth control permanent—because the mother's health is at stake or it is "the responsible thing to do". Since Michael and I are firm believers that every child is a gift of God, we chose not to have any tests done to find out if our child had any birth defects before birth. In order to opt out of the tests, we were required to sign a waiver, stating we would not sue our doctor if our child was born with any kind of abnormality. Many of today's parents do not desire the burden of taking care of a child who might need extra care. Clearly, the lies of the culture have completely encompassed how we view the gift of children.

The Blessing of Children

With all the lies streaming at us, it takes more faith than ever to have children—even one child, for that matter! Parents need to have the faith to believe their children will be a blessing, and that God will give them the strength, finances, and wisdom they need to raise their children. Our faith is strengthened when we discover how God views children. So, what does God's Word say about children?

> *Behold, children are a heritage from the Lord,*
> *The fruit of the womb is a reward.*
> *Like arrows in the hand of a warrior,*
> *So are the children's of one's youth.*
> *Happy is the man who has his quiver full of them;*
> *They shall not be ashamed,*
> *But shall speak with their enemies in the gate.*

> — *Psalm 127:3-5*

In these verses, children are described as a "heritage," "fruit," "reward," and "arrow." In other words, our children are a blessing, far greater than you might have realized!

Children As a Heritage

In Psalm 127:3, Solomon declares, "Behold, children are a heritage from the Lord." He means that children are an inheritance. They are a God-given gift, wealth we have inherited from the Lord. Do we value our children as wealth? God does.

When we truly see children as wealth—the way God does—we will not want to limit the number of children He gives to us. It would be like telling God, "We don't need ten million dollars, one million will do!" If we are honest, no one would turn down a freely-offered inheritance of ten million dollars. Yet, many people choose to turn down the inheritance God has for them—children. The question is: How wealthy do you want to be?

Children As Fruit

The word Solomon uses to describe children as "[t]he fruit of the womb" (Psalm 127:3) is the same word used to describe the fruit one would eat from a tree. In Proverbs 8:19, we are reminded that God's fruit "is better than gold, yes, than fine gold." God's fruit, which comes from our womb, is a blessing given to us by God. Children are a produce of love created for the enjoyment of others—and they are far more precious than gold!

On a walk last spring, I noticed two different trees on our block. One tree was loaded with fruit, and the fruit—which was not being picked or cultivated—was falling to the ground and rotting. The owners were not eating or distributing their fruit. The owners of the other tree daily checked on their fruit tree, and as soon as the fruit was ripe, they picked and used it. They had such an overflow of fruit, and no more time to make additional pies and jam, that they distributed fruit to the neighbors for their enjoyment. Our family was blessed with two big, delicious boxes of peaches!

As Michael and I considered these two trees, God gave us a picture of our children lives. If we were faithful to continue the work of pruning, watering, fertilizing, and carefully maintaining our children's lives (as the second set of owners did with their fruit tree), then our children, too, would be fruitful. They would be a blessing in our life and in the lives of other people. Proverbs 11:31 says, "The fruit of the righteous is a tree of life, and he who wins souls is wise." However, if we do not put forth effort to invest in our children's lives, they might end up becoming wasted fruit, rotting on the ground as our legacy suffers.

A few years ago, I woke up exhausted and overwhelmed on a Sunday morning, not feeling well. I told my children that I did not think I would be able to make it to church that morning. My son, Micah, told me, "Mom, if you don't feel like going to church, that is when you really need to go the most. That's what you always tells us." I was shocked; he was absolutely right! I had been telling my children this very thing for years, and my son had taken the lesson to heart. He had encouraged me in my walk with the Lord. That is the goal and fruit of Christian parenting, and it is worth more than gold!

Children As a Reward

Not only are children a fruit, but they are "a reward" (Psalm 127:3). Here, reward is the same word used for wages—meaning wealth.

Whenever God wanted to bless someone, we are told in scripture, "And God blessed *so and so*, He gave him (or her) *this many* sons and daughters." We see this in the life of Hannah, as 1 Samuel 2:21 reads: "And the Lord visited Hannah, so that she conceived and bore three sons and two daughters."

After she gave Samuel to the Lord, Hannah would return to the Tabernacle each year with Elkanah to make their yearly sacrifices. Eli would bless them, and ask God to continue to give them children. God answered Eli's prayer, rewarding and blessing Hannah.

Michael's grandmother, Carol McClure, used to share a story about when she was a young mom. She had four small children back to back, three boys and a girl. On this particular occasion, she dressed them all up in their nicest clothes, and took them to see a play. At the train station, everyone was staring at her and her precious children. She recalled feeling like the richest woman alive. In fact, she used to tell us that she felt like she was wearing huge jewels on her fingers that people were admiring. In her eyes, her children were as precious as jewels!

Grandma Carol's story made a huge impact on me as a young woman and mother. It was the first time I had heard of children described as wealth—as "jewels." When my own children were little, there was a time I remember so vividly. One of my children started crying in the middle of the night. As I walked into the hallway, another child started crying. Suddenly, I realized that every room in the house was filled with children, and this verse came to mind: "Through wisdom a house is built, and by understanding it is established; By knowledge the rooms are filled with all precious and pleasant riches" (Proverbs 24:3-4).

I thought, "Wow! I am so blessed to have such precious treasures filling the rooms of my home. Even as many in the world have sacrificed the blessings of children for expensive cars, modern homes, beautiful jewelry, money in the bank, and extraordinary vacations, I was blessed with children, who would live forever!

I can't tell you how many people who I love and respect, and who are older in their faith, wish they had had more children. One of my friends tells me that she regrets not having more children every day—and, not just one or two more children. She regrets not really trusting God, or blessing Him by having many more children. She wishes she had had a mentor in the church encourage her to have more children, and remind her of the blessing they are. The world is certainly not proclaiming this message.

As a mother of seven, I am not going to tell you that raising seven children is easy or inexpensive—or that I am better than you because of the number of children I have. Honestly, if I had known how much work it was going to be, I don't know if I would have done it. However, I don't regret a single one of our children. I look back and praise God that Michael and I were so full of faith—and so naive that we did not know what we were getting into! Today, Michael and I truly believe that our children make us rich. They are the biggest treasures we could ever have —and they know it!

A few years ago, I was jumping on the trampoline with my kids. This was not a usual thing, but one of my children had dragged me outside. As we jumped, we looked over the fence into our neighbor's backyard, which was huge.   My children dreamed of having that backyard, especially since the neighbor's house was on the market at the time.   I had to explain to my children that we could not afford to move into the neighbor's house. Micah, trying to find a way to purchase the neighbor's house, said, "I know how we can get more money. Have more kids!"

We had been telling our children for years that we were the richest parents because of them. Micah literally thought we were materially wealthy simply because we had a lot of them.   In our world, material wealth is not the number of children you have; but spiritually, Micah was right. Such is the kingdom of heaven!

Children As Arrows
In Psalm 127 children are described as arrows. "Like arrows in the hand of a warrior, so are the children of one's youth" (Psalm 127:4). An arrow is an important weapon; and in the hands of a warrior, it is a source of protection.

In the ancient world, the only way a person could protect themselves was through the might of their family and their family alliances.   The more children a family had, the more family alliances they could create. And, with each new alliance, the family became more protected. Blessed was the man whose quiver was full of children, as they were a source of protection!

Simply having children does not make them into a mighty weapon. It is our intentional training that enables them to become "[l]ike arrows in the hands of a warrior" (Psalm 127:4).   This training is, in a way, a form of art, as we craft our arrows with precision. The crafting includes the careful shaping and guiding our children with skill and strength— before we aim and give direction to them. Spurgeon writes: "We shall see [our children] shot forth into life to our comfort and delight, if we take care from the very beginning that they are directed to the right point."[6]

But, if we do not train our children in the ways of the Lord, watch out!   The English pastor Henry Smith writes, "if [children] be well bred, they shoot at their parents' enemies; and if they be evil bred, they shoot at their parents."[7] I have met many parents who have endured wounds inflicted by their children because they failed to properly shape them. Their children were a sorrow rather than a blessing. With this in mind, Spurgeon writes: "When sons and daughters are arrows, it is well to have a quiver full of them; but if they are only sticks, knotty and useless, the fewer of them the better."[8]

If you have properly shaped and trained your children, then you "shall not be ashamed, but shall speak with [your] enemies in the gate" (Psalm 127:5). In the ancient world, the gate was the chief place of business where justice was administered. It was at the gate that children were the greatest assets. Trained in the ways of the Lord, they would grow up to handle their parents' business affairs within the city. The English minister Alexander MacLaren adds: "in the disputes which might arise with neighbors, and in the intercourse of city life, which would breed enmities enough, the man with his sons about him could hold his own. And such blessing is God's gift."[9]

The wonderful blessing of a "quiver full" of children is that you can increase your blessing throughout your life by the more children you have. Spurgeon states, "Nobody cares to meddle with a man who can gather a clan of brave sons about him."[10]   By properly shaping and training children, parents would have the comfort of children who loved and respected them in their old age.   The more children, the more children to comfort and take care of you in your older years.   Even more, your values would be passed on not only to their grandchildren, but also to the world around you.

You can also increase your influence by launching your "arrows" into a time you may not see.   Our children are not only our future, but God's future ambassadors.   Neil Postman writes, "Children are the living messages we send to a time we will not see."[11]   They are living messengers of the gospel of Jesus Christ!   As we build up our faith and invest it into our children, we can affect the future of the kingdom of God—long after we have gone!   While we are in glory, our children are, in a sense, an extension of ourselves.   As they live their life full of faith, sharing God's love to their children and the world around them, we get the blessing of reaping their rewards eternally, as well!

No matter how many children you have been blessed with, your children are your wealth! As you invest your faith in them, you will reap blessings on this earth, and in the one to come!

Grandchildren

When we invest our faith in our children, we can reap the blessing of our spiritual legacy while we remain on this earth—through grandchildren. Proverbs 17:6 states: "Children's children are the crown of old men, and the glory of children is their father."   Our grandchildren, when they are raised in the ways of the Lord, bring us glory!

However, this blessing is conditional.   We, as parents, must be faithful to keep God's covenant and fulfill His commandments.   Psalm 103:17-18 declares: "But the mercy of the Lord is from everlasting to everlasting on those who fear Him, and His righteousness to children's children, to such as keep His covenant, and to those who remember His commandments to do them." We will only experience the blessing of seeing our spiritual legacy lived out in our grandchildren's lives if we are faithful in the training of our children now.

Years ago, Michael and I spoke with Tim Lahaye, author of the *Left Behind Series*, at a conference we were attending. He had just received a phone call with his granddaughter, who called to tell him that she had received Christ into her heart. He told Michael and me that all the books, awards, and churches he pastored meant nothing compared to the blessing he received from his children, who were raising his grandchildren to know and love God. Nothing could beat a granddaughter receiving Christ as her Savior!

A few years ago, David Green, founder of Hobby Lobby, gave an interview on Fox News. He spoke about his book, *Giving It All Away... and Getting It Back Again: The Way of Living Generously.* In the interview, he stated that true wealth is where your children walk with God and your grandchildren are raised to know and love Him, as well![12] When we are faithful to raise our children according to God's commandments, and honor Him in our home, our children will value what God values.

John Rogers

My legacy of faith begins with the salvation of my mother. On Michael's side of the family, it goes back much further. In fact, his legacy dates back seventeen generations on his father's side to a wonderful saint, John Rogers, the first Christian martyred under Queen Mary of England. What a rich legacy for us to follow!

John Rogers was born in England in 1500, during the Protestant Reformation. He was educated at Cambridge, where he studied to become a priest. While pastoring a church in Belgium, he embraced the teachings of the Reformation, and became aquatinted with William Tyndale. John Rogers began assisting Tyndale in translating the Old Testament into English, in what later became known as the Tyndale Bible.

In 1550, Rogers returned to England to pastor a church in London. When the Catholic Queen Mary took the throne upon her brother Edward's death, she broke her promise not to persecute the Protestant reformers. She had Rogers arrested. After his trial, he was declared a heretic, and condemned to die. In Smithfield, on February 14, 1555, Rogers was burned at the stake, with his wife and ten children watching. He was the first Protestant martyr during Mary's reign, and his death ushered in a more rapid spread of the Reformation across Europe.

John Rogers' life of faith and complete trust in God created a rich legacy—not just for his children, grandchildren, and descendants; but also for Christians throughout history, who desire to live a life of faith for Jesus Christ.

A few years ago, Michael's mom, Jean, gave us a framed copy of a letter Rogers wrote from his prison cell. Knowing his death was near, Rogers penned a letter full of wisdom and advice for the ten children he was leaving behind. What a rich legacy! Today, that letter hangs in the hallway of our home, alongside a picture Michael painted of John Rogers. It is a reminder of the legacy of faith we have been given—and the grave responsibility we have to pass our legacy on to our children.

A Rich Legacy

This past summer, we spent a week in Southern California with Michael's parents. We cleaned out their attic, and explored generations of memories as we went through earthy treasures and pictures. It was a precious time, and we were reminded of the rich legacy that had been passed down through generations of the McClure family. It was also a wonderful reminder of how short this life is.

Michael's dad, Don McClure, has been a pastor for over forty years. In the attic, we found tons of books he has been collecting throughout his ministry. They included Christian classics by Tozer, Spurgeon, Moody, and others. We laid the books out on the dining room table, and Michael and I sorted through them- drooling over such treasures! As we were picking through them, asking which ones he was willing to part with, Mike's Dad started to get a little uncomfortable, as these are his most precious possessions. In fact, he stated, "Jean, it is like the children are picking through all your jewelry, asking if they could have it!"

What a rich legacy we have been given. Many men leave behind their DVD or coin collection, their baseball cards, or some sort of earthy treasure. The legacy we have been given by Michael's parents is wrapped up in the Christian faith, which moth and dust cannot destroy. This legacy will last from generation to generation, and will continue on into eternity!

Uncle Ben's Bible

Our family loves to shop at garage sales. What is even more fun is when we stumble across an estate sale. This past year, we stopped at an estate sale, which was full of earthy treasures. There were old paintings, trunks, tools, dishes, jewelry, and furniture for sale—so much fun! As we looked around, we saw a collection of Bibles.

One Bible had a note tied around it with string. The note read, "Uncle Ben's Bible." Our son, Sam, asked how much the Bible cost, then purchased it for two dollars. On our walk home, I asked Sam, "Why did you purchase that Bible, when we have Bibles lying all around the house at home?" He said, "I couldn't bear the thought of no one wanting Uncle Ben's Bible."

You see, Sam has understood that one's legacy is not wrapped up in their career, money, or possessions; it is their faith! Uncle Ben's Bible is the dearest treasure he could have left behind. What blesses me the most is that I know—if Sam is so concerned about Uncle Ben's legacy—the legacy Michael and I leave behind will be in good hands.

Hannah's Legacy

It does not matter what legacy you have inherited, though. You have the ability to decide what kind of legacy you will leave behind. Your legacy depends on your life of faith. We cannot take our homes, cars, or 401k to heaven, but we can take our children! Our children are worth every sacrifice imaginable. What are you willing to invest into your children's lives today?

In studying Hannah's life, you may have found that you need to make changes in how you are raising your children—and that is okay. It is important that you don't let Hannah's example discourage you; instead, let it inspire you! No matter where you are in your parenting journey, whether your children are toddlers, teenagers, or have families of their own, your faith in God can transform your children's life. Even if your children are not walking with God, or are in complete rebellion, your faith in God, displayed in your life, matters. It can change the course of your children's and grandchildren's lives. The God who created the universe is powerful enough to reach into your children's hearts! Don't get caught up in past mistakes, but, in faith, press on to the future—your legacy is at stake!

Hannah left a legacy that surpassed her life! We are not told about her husband's occupation, or their material wealth, but about her faith and that of her children! We are told, in Luke 7:35: "But wisdom is justified by all her children." Here we are, thousands of years and generations later, studying her life, and the example she set in raising godly children. Hannah was not only wise enough, but willing to make the necessary sacrifices to raise a child that would transform the world for God's glory. We don't know how long Hannah lived; but through her son, Samuel, her nation was delivered from the worship of pagan gods, experienced a spiritual revival, became united under a monarchy, and prepared to build a temple to the living God, a glorious temple designed by Him! Her son left an example of how God uses a man wholly set-apart to do His perfect and pleasing will.

Hannah's legacy of faith was refined through her season of sorrow, proved true through her submission, and demonstrated in her sacrifice of Samuel, as she bound her son to the altar as a "living sacrifice" unto the Lord. Hannah was, truly, one of history's greatest mothers. She leaves behind an amazing legacy of sacrifice that every mom—who desires to leave a legacy of godly children in this world—must follow.

Questions to Consider

1. Are you building your house through the wisdom found in God's Word, or are you building it according to the world's wisdom? In what ways?

2. What is your attitude towards your children? Do you consider them to be a blessing, gift, reward, and an inheritance? How would they say you value them?

3. How are you investing your faith into your children?

4. Are you carefully crafting your children as "arrows", so they might be a blessing to you in your later years?

5. What do you have that you can pass on to your children that "defines" what it important to you? Do these things represent your faith in God?

6. What legacy have you been given? What kind of legacy do you want to leave behind?

7. What changes can you make to better enable you to pass on a greater legacy to your children?

Notes

[1] F.B. Meyer, *Samuel the Prophet* (CrossReach Publications, 2017), 15.

[2] Andrew Carnegie, quoted in David Green, *Giving It All Away...and Getting It Back Again: The Way of Living Generously* (Grand Rapids, Michigan: Zondervan, 2017), 128.

[3] C.H. Spurgeon, *Cheque Book of the Bank of Faith* (Great Britain: Christian Focus Publications, 1996), 116.

[4] Ibid., 236.

[5] Gene Edward Veith, Jr., *Postmodern Times: A Christian Guide to Contemporary Thought and Culture* (Wheaton, Illinois: Good News Publishers, 1994), 75.

[6] C.H. Spurgeon, *The Treasury of David,* Volume VII (New York: Funk & Wagnalls, 1886), 31.

[7] Henry Smith, quoted in C.H. Spurgeon, *The Treasury of David,* 40.

[8] Spurgeon, *The Treasury of David*, 31.

[9] Alexander MacLaren, *The Psalms,* Volume III (New York: A.C. Armstrong and Son, 1902), *325.*

[10] Spurgeon, *The Treasury of David*, 31.

[11] Neil Postman, "Good Reads," accessed July 20, 2019, https://www.goodreads.com/quotes/22675-children-are-the-living-messages-we-send-to-a-time

[12] David Green on "Hobby Lobby founder: I wouldn't cut taxes now," foxbusiness.com, April 25, 2017, accessed August 10, 2019, https://video.foxbusiness.com/v/5410782902001/#sp=show-clips

Recommended Reading

Must Have Books about Raising Children for Christian Parents
Already Gone by Ken Ham and C. Britt Beemer
Baby Wise by Gary Ezzo and Robert Bucknam
Dare to Discipline by James Dobson
How to Bring Your Children to Christ & Keep Them There by Ray Comfort
Parenting By the Book by John Rosemond
Shepherding a Child's Heart by Ted Tripp
The Shaping of a Christian Family by Elisabeth Elliot
What Every Daughter Wants to Know from Her Dad by Michael Harris

Educating Your Children
A Is For Adam by Ken Ham
Christian Heroes: Then & Now by Janet & Geoff Being
Discovering the Lost Tools of Learning by Douglas Wilson
Egermeier's Bible Story Book by Elsie E. Egermeier
Honey for a Child's Heart by Gladys Hunt
Lamplighter Radio Theatre (It's the best)
The Child's Story Bible by Catherine F. Jos
When Children Love to Learn by Elaine Cooper

Discipling Your Teenager
A Young Man/Woman After God's Own Heart by Jim & Elizabeth George
Beautiful Girlhood by Karen Andreola
Disciplines of a Godly Young Man by Kent Hughes
Do Hard Things by Alex & Brett Harris
Lies Girls Believe by Dannah Gresh
Lies Young Women Believe by Nancy Leigh DeMoss
Passport to Purity by Dennis and Barbara Rainy
Raising a Modern-Day Knight by Robert Lewis

Mom's Personal Discipleship
A Women After God's Own Heart by Elizabeth George
Calvary Road by Roy Hessian
Cheque Book of the Bank of Faith by C.H. Spurgeon
Disciplines of a Godly Women by Barbara Hughes
Edges of His Ways by Amy Carmichael
Feminine Appeal by Carolyn Mahaney
Financial Peace by Dave Ramsey
Halley's Bible Handbook by Henry H. Halley
If by Amy Carmichael

Lies Women Believe by Nancy Leigh DeMoss
My Utmost For His Highest by Oswald Chambers
On Being a Servant of God by Warren Weirsbe
Prayer That Works by Jill Briscoe
Spiritual Leadership by Oswald Sanders
Streams In The Desert by Mrs. C.H. Cowman
The Trunk by Jean McClure
The Silver Lining by Nancy Wilson
The Strategy of Satan by Warren Weirsbe
Thou Givest...They Gather by Amy Carmichael
Whispers of His Power by Amy Carmichael

Micah's Chore Chart

Month Of_____

Chore	Day of Week	S	M	T	W	Th	F	S	Total (-.25)
Make Bed	Daily								
Read Bible	Daily								
Brush Teeth	Daily								
Make Sandwiches for Lunches	M-F								
Do Dishes	M/W/F								
Do Laundry	Saturday								
Clean Bathroom (Boys)	Saturday								

McClure Family Chore Chart

Chore	Sunday	Monday	Tuesday	Wednesday	Thursday	Friday	Saturday
Unload Dishwasher (AM)							
Take out Trash (AM & PM)							
Make Sandwiches							
Prepare Lunches							
Make Breakfast							
Pick up Mercy's Bombs							
Set Table							
Clear Table							
Dinner Dishes							
Sweep Floor							
Do Laundry							
Clean & Vacuum Living Room							
Feed Mercy (AM & PM)							
Clean Bathroom